"In vain I tried to tell you"

University of Pennsylvania Publications in
Conduct and Communication
Erving Goffman and Dell Hymes, General Editors

"In vain I tried to tell you"

Essays in Native American Ethnopoetics

DELL HYMES

STUDIES IN NATIVE AMERICAN LITERATURE I

University of Pennsylvania Press
Philadelphia
1981

Library of Congress Cataloging in Publication Data
Hymes, Dell H.
  "In vain I tried to tell you."

  (University of Pennsylvania publications in conduct and
communication)
  Bibliography: p.
  Includes indexes.
    1. Indians of North America—Northwest, Pacific—
Poetry—History and criticism.   2. Indians of North
America—Northwest, Pacific—Legends.   I. Title.
II. Series.
PM483.5.H9   897   81–51138
ISBN 0–8122–7806–2   AACR2
ISBN 0–8122–1117–0 (pbk.)

Printed in the United States of America

Qé:dau gaqíuX iqánuCk Gá:nGadix itq'e:yó:qtikS
"Thus the myth was made by the old people long ago."

Contents

Contents

TABLES

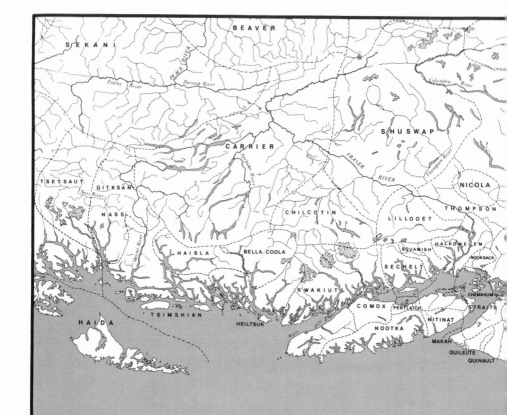

Map labels:
BEAVER

SEKANI

SHUSWAP

CARRIER

TSETSAUT   GITKSAN

NICOLA

NASS

THOMPSON

CHILCOTIN   LILLOOET

HAISLA   BELLA COOLA

SQUAMISH   HALKOMELEM

NOOKSACK

SECHELT

KWAKIUTL

COMOX   PENTLATCH   CHEMAKUM

TSIMSHIAN   HEILTSUK   STRAITS

HAIDA   NITINAT

NOOTKA

MAKAH

QUILEUTE

QUINAULT

Rivers: PEACE RIVER, Finlay River, Parsnip River, FRASER RIVER, Thompson River, Columbia River, Nass River, Skeena River

NORTH

Native Languages of the North Pacific Coast of North America

```
0     50    100   150   200
km  ┕━━┷━━┷━━┷━━┙
```

Base information adapted from USAF Net Navigation Charts JN16-N, JN17-N, JN29-N, and JN44. Language boundaries compiled from maps by M. E. Krauss, C. McClellan, W. Duff, C. Schaeffer, R. L. Benson, A. L. Kroeber, D. E. Walker, O. C. Stewart and other sources. Wayne Suttles, 1978.

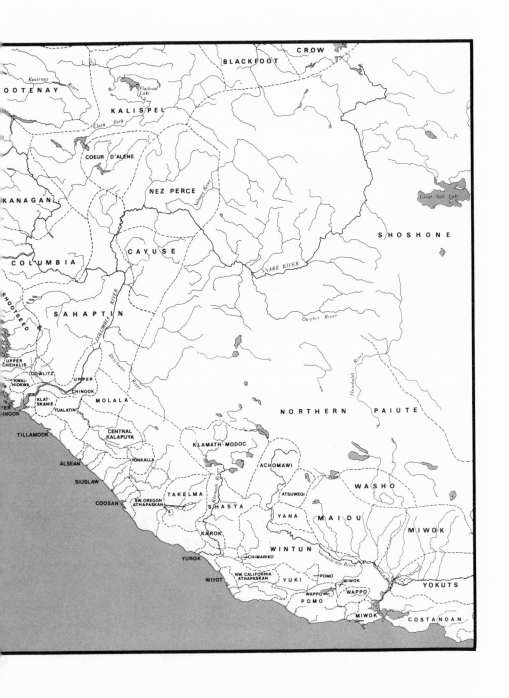

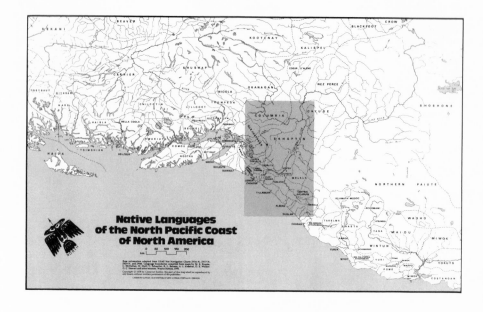

Native Languages
of the North Pacific Coast
of North America

Key to Map:

1 Shoalwater Chinook
2 Clatsop Chinook
3 Kathlamet Chinook
4 Clackamas Chinook
5 Wasco Chinook
6 Wishram Chinook
7 Klikitat Sahaptin
8 Tenino Sahaptin
9 Warm Springs Reservation (agency)

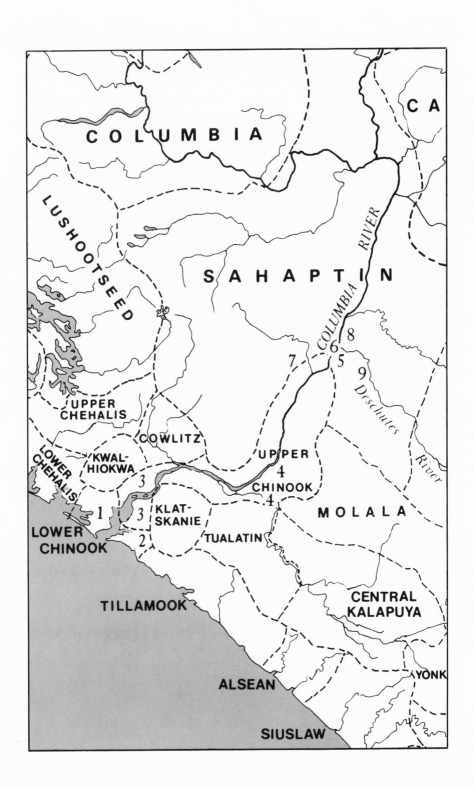

Introduction

This book is the first of a set of four devoted to the first literature of North America, that of the American Indians, or Native Americans. The texts are from the North Pacific Coast, because that is where I am from, and those are the materials I know best. The purpose is general: All traditional American Indian verbal art requires attention of this kind if we are to comprehend what it is and says.

There is linguistics in this book, and that will put some people off. "Too technical," they will say. Perhaps such people would be amused to know that many linguists will not regard the work as linguistics. "Not theoretical," they will say, meaning not part of a certain school of grammar. And many folklorists and anthropologists are likely to say, "too linguistic" and "too literary" both, whereas professors of literature are likely to say, "anthropological" or "folklore," not "literature" at all. But there is no help for it. As with Beowulf and The Tale of Genji, the material requires some understanding of a way of life. Within that way of life, it has in part a role that in English can only be called that of "literature." Within that way of life, and now, I hope, within others, it offers some of the rewards and joys of literature. And if linguistics is the study of language, not grammar alone, then the study of these materials adds to what is known about language.

The joy, the understanding, the language are all of a piece. They come together, because they were put together by the people who made the texts. (I use "made" advisedly; that is how one says it in Chinookan. *Qé:dau gaqíuX iqánuCk Gá:nGadix itq'e:yó:qtikS* "Thus it-was-made the-myth long-ago [by] the-old-people," Louis Simpson told Edward Sapir [Sapir 1909a:48]). Linguistics and linguistic-like analyses are necessary means to the joy and understanding, because words were the means used by the authors of the texts. If we do not deal with the means, we cannot possess the meanings. We remain in the position of the woman in the story discussed in chapters 8 and 9. Her daughter tries to tell her disconcerting information of importance to the future of them both. Intent on maintaining a pre-established norm, the woman refuses to consider and interpret the surprising fact. In the event, her daughter can only remonstrate, "In vain I tried to tell you." If we refuse to consider and interpret the surprising facts of device, design, and performance inherent in the words of the texts, the Indians who made the texts, and those who preserved what they made, will have worked in vain. We will be telling the texts not to speak.

We will mistake, perhaps to our cost, the nature of the power of which they speak.

When things were said or sung within the native culture, explicit analysis —a detailed meta-language for dealing with form—was not needed. Performer and audience shared an implicit knowledge of language and ways of speaking. For us, there is no alternative to explicit analysis. As with the grammar of these languages, so with the verbal art: underlying relationships, taken for granted by their users, must be brought to light by conscious effort. Once brought to light, they can enable us to understand the creativity and cogency of the discourse in which they occur.

It is strange that there has been so little explicit analysis of Native American verbal art. But then it is perhaps also strange that so little of it has been preserved. Native Americans themselves, by and large, had no precedent for maintaining verbal tradition other than through oral learning by successive generations. Conquest, disruption, conversion, schooling, decimation eliminated most such learning. As Louis Simpson told Edward Sapir at the end of the myth, "Coyote's people sing" (discussed in chap. 3), "Thus were the ways (myths). Today none of the children know them. I, Louis, when I was a boy, now then my father, his father, made those myths to me" (my translation from the Wishram in Sapir's field notebook 1, p. 59; Sapir did not publish the passage).

Often non-Indians did not wish to preserve the culture of the Indians. Conviction or guilt persuaded them that it was already gone, or best gone. It is a shameful fact that most of what can be known today about the cultures of the Indians of my state, Oregon, is due to the efforts of men who came across the continent. Franz Boas, a German Jew unable to aspire to scholarly advancement in his native country but versed in the German intellectual tradition that valued individual cultures and their works, recorded Shoalwater and Kathlamet Chinook. His student Sapir recorded Wishram and Takelma; another student, L. J. Frachtenberg, recorded Alsea, Siuslaw, Coos, and Kalapuya. Frachtenberg was followed by a later student with a better ear, Melville Jacobs, who provided superior texts from Coos and Kalapuya, all that has been published so far in Sahaptin, and all that is known, save for one scrap, of Clackamas. To repeat, most of what we can know of the first literature of Oregon is due to representatives of German and Jewish intellectual tradition, who crossed the continent to record it. With regard to that first literature, they are the pioneers. The pioneers of Western song and story and their descendants did little or nothing.

We must count ourselves lucky to have records of the verbal art of even a dozen gifted narrators, a dozen from among the hundreds who must have died unrecorded and are now unremembered. It is not surprising that the attention of the recorders was focused on recording itself, on publication of the texts, on preparation of grammars to help elucidate the texts. What is strange is that no scholarly tradition arose of continuous work with those texts.

Other literatures receive such attention. Somehow the first literature of our country does not. There are no chairs of Native American languages and literatures. Literary scholars have mostly assigned the subject to folklore and anthropology, and American anthropologists and folklorists are not much for knowing or working with languages. Linguistics has focused on methodology and grammar. Indian people have seldom been in a position to pursue such work themselves or to press politically for it. The necessary linguistic materials are themselves in disarray, not integrated and available for use (cf. Hymes 1976b).

Whatever the factors, the texts of Native American tradition have been largely ignored. The translations have been consulted and sometimes analyzed, the originals mostly not. The modern founder of our work, Franz Boas, was clear and insistent about the need to work with the originals. For example, in his general text he stated: "It is obvious that for the understanding of the form of native literature, if we may use this term for their unwritten poetry and tales, a thorough knowledge of the language is indispensable, for without it the elements that appeal to the esthetic sense of the hearer cannot be appreciated" (1938:44). But the obvious has mostly been ignored.

My hope is that this book will make it exceedingly difficult to ignore the obvious. That it will not be possible for scholars to say that they discuss the style of Native American narratives when they are unable to discuss the originals. That it will not be possible to speak of the structure of a narrative without regard to its structure of words. That it will not be possible to publish a major work on the religious tradition of a major Indian culture and say, "In order to make the myths more palatable for the average reader, the translations of certain particles introduced repeatedly by native narrators have been omitted, retaining just enough to give Navajo flavor to the story" (Wyman 1970:xxvii). The reader of this book will realize that the omitted particles were means of shaping the story, means of defining through repetition the structure the narrator intended the text to disclose.

"In vain I tried to tell you" indeed, when editing censors structure. Fortunately, many of the published texts are faithful enough for their character as verse to be discovered. It does prove necessary to consult the original transcription, wherever possible, to control slips and changes (see chap. 4). (One virtue of the approach taken in this book is that it sometimes makes sense of what seemed incoherent.) Mostly what is required is to "listen" to the text in all its details. The work is structural in method, poetic in purpose. The structural method is no more than an application of the elementary principle of structural linguistics: look for covariation in form and meaning. The poetic purpose is to come as close as possible to the intended shape of the text in order to grasp as much as possible of the meanings embodied in this shape. Much will still escape. The gestures, voices, tunes, pauses of the original performances cannot be recovered for most of the materials dealt with here. Still, much of structure persists and can be perceived. Essential real relationships remain. Something of the creative imagination of the source can be seen at work. The significance of the text for its source, and for us, can be considered with a degree of confidence that the text itself is known.

The linguistics and the argumentation, let me stress, are means to that end. I am interested in the linguistic discoveries that result for their own sake, to be sure. When one looks at linguistic elements from the standpoint of their integration into a higher level of discourse in the service of a higher function, new relationships come to light that are contributions to linguistics itself. Poetics requires an evenhanded attention to stylistic and referential function alike, to the benefit of an understanding of language and competence. In chapter 10, for example, a new understanding of the meaning of a noun-prefix is revealed through its role in narrative. And I am interested in the patterns of narrative form, of presentational form, for their own sake. Their discovery is a contribution to the study of culture. Yet often enough one can hear a personal voice as well. It is evident that the text collections for Takelma, Kathlamet, Clackamas, and Wishram constitute a great part of all that can be known about the language and the way of life of the people identified by those names. The texts, as intended by those who recorded them, document both linguistic and cultural content. Indeed, they display ways of speaking, of narrating, that are themselves simultaneously linguistic and cultural, as the verse analyses of the later chapters show. With attentive study one comes to realize as well that the linguistic and cultural ingredients of Takelma, Kathlamet, Clackamas, Wishram, serve as personal expression for Frances Johnson, Charles Cultee, Victoria Howard, Louis Simpson, personal expression that sometimes constitutes enduring knowledge.

A passage from a philosophical work has long stayed in my mind in this regard, a passage copied out years ago and kept with the papers of my work on myth. To consider it will seem a digression, yet I believe it relevant. It helps in the struggle to gain a hearing for works from Native American traditions as genuine "works," aesthetic accomplishments, literature, products of voices. The book is itself an expression of the cultural tradition that informed the pioneering efforts of Boas and his students. The author, Ernst Cassirer, a great German scholar who died in New Haven, a refugee from Nazi Germany, was a pioneer among those in this century who sought an integrated conception of human culture. He called such a vision a "philosophy of symbolic forms," where many today would speak, less richly, I think, of "semiotics." His phenomenological perspective made him a semiotician, an ethnomethodologist, an exponent of hermeneutics, and more, *avant la lettre.* Historical perspective taught him that science, which he championed as one mode of knowledge among others, had reacted against the folk world-view out of which it arose by narrowing its philosophical basis to that of an opposite pole. It felt constrained to accept as a starting point only sense data and the individual, as independent essence, for whom language is externalization of self. In a rich chapter "Perception of things and perception of expression," Cassirer posed an alternative starting point, recognizing that individuals are interdependent in dialogue (1961:107; cf. Voloshinov 1973). In speech and art, he wrote, individuals do not simply share what they already possess; it is only by virtue of the sharing process that they attain what they possess (Cassirer 1961:113), constructing a "shared world" of meaning within the medium of language. Language, art, and each of the other symbolic forms are pathways to the realization of ourselves, are active, productive, specific energies to exercise (Ibid.: 110, 112, 113).

In this context Cassirer spoke of genuine works of art as being perceived as expressions in three respects: physical (e.g., an arrangement of colors), presentational (e.g., a historical scene), personal (the imprint of the maker). His immediate example was a painting, Raphael's *The School of Athens,* showing Plato and Aristotle in conversation. If we take language to be the physical means of existence of a text, a narrative to be the symbolic object it presents, and recognize behind and in the text a performer-author, Cassirer's very words can be adapted:

> But always we discern in a work of art two fundamental factors, which constitute the whole of the work only by means of their union and interpenetration. The [words in a text] have a "presentation-function" only insofar as they suggest an object. Here we do not lose ourselves in sheer observation of the [words]; we do not see them *as* [words]; instead, it is through these [words] that we see what is objective—a definite scene, a conversation between two [actors]. But even what is objective in this sense is not the unique, the true subject matter of the [text]. The [text] is not merely the presentation of [a narrative] scene, a conversation between [Seal and her daughter]. For in reality it is not [Seal and her daughter] who speak to us here but [Victoria Howard her-] self. These three dimensions—the physical thereness [*Dasein*], the object-presentation, and the evidence of a unique personality—are determining and indispensable in anything that is a genuine "work" [*"Werk"*] and not merely a "result" [*"Wirkung"*], and of all that in this sense belongs not only to "nature" but also to "culture." The exclusion of one of these three dimensions, confinement within a single plane of observation, always yields only a surface image of culture, revealing none of its genuine depth (Ibid.:99). [Brackets enclose substitutions]

Such a perspective indicts our status quo. Most interpretation of Native American verbal art fails to include all three of the dimensions identified by Cassirer and thereby fails to comprehend its genuine depth. Interpretation that excludes speech falls short, as would a treatment of painting that excluded paint. Interpretation that seeks only an individual voice, the author's or the interpreter's, falls short as well. Interpretation that attends only to what is culturally defined, excluding both the mode of existence of the work and the personal voice, as is the case with most analyses of myth, yields only a surface image, however much it talks of underlying depth. Abstract relations among categories of plot and content are essential aspects of the understanding of myths, but aspects only. Artistry comes into view only if the text can be seen as a texture within which particular means have been chosen and deployed. Meaning is deepest where that artistry is most evoked. Although it may appear paradoxical, perception of depth depends on perception of detail and of the relationships implicit in its placement.

The essential method, as has been said, is simply persistence in seeking systematic covariation of form and meaning. The spirit of the method is "structural" in the sense of Sapir's linguistics, "emic" and "ethnographic" in the sense of concern for valid description of the individual case. Much of what we understand about Native American languages is due to the stimulus given such work by Boas, who sought grammars "treated as though an intelligent Indian was going to develop the forms of his own thoughts by an analysis of his own form of speech" (Boas 1911:81). We must learn to apply that maxim to texts themselves as forms of speech.

The sequence of chapters in this book somewhat matches the steps of Cassirer's three-part presentation of dimensions. It is only toward the end that personal voice can be grasped, once linguistic and cultural details and relationships have been established. The sequence is chronological within each part as well and, overall, documents the steps toward gradual discovery of the depth of the works in question.

Part One, "Unsuspected devices and designs," deals with devices already known to be such but mistakenly set aside as empty of meaning, as sheer ejaculation or convention. In each case the device is discovered to have a significance. In different ways each unites two elementary functions of language: "stylistic" and "referential" (Hymes 1974b), "expressive" and "cognitive"; "interpersonal" and "ideational" (Halliday 1978); embodying analysis of a context in the enactment of an attitude (cf. Hymes 1979b).

Chapter 1 states the general issue of attending to linguistic form in connection with texts already recognized as poems, the texts of songs. What have often been called "nonsense syllables" are shown in Kwakiutl to be structural abstracts, covarying with the form of stanzas and summing up that form in a pure expression of it through the interplay of two types of syllable that refer to two types of part. These "nonsense syllables" in Kwakiutl can be said to embody a third elementary function of language as well, the "textual" or "cohesive" (Halliday 1978).

Chapter 2 treats a "meaningless" device found intermittently in myth texts and shows it to involve contrast on a semantic dimension. Occurrence or nonoccurrence and choice of form of the device are governed by appropriateness to character and situation. Both devices are seen to share an out-group versus in-group connotation as well. It now seems clear just whom the Takelma mocked in having Coyote speak sometimes with an expletive *s'a!*

Part Two, "Breakthrough to performance," presents the main record of discovery of verse-form, particularly in regard to the Wasco-Wishram branch of Chinookan (Clackamas is taken up in chap. 9). Having shown that the principle of form/meaning covariation can enable me to stand on the shoulders of predecessors (chaps. 1–2; see also chaps. 7–8), I preserve failures of my own in this respect in chapter 3. My presentation of the texts from Philip Kahclamet ("The crier," "Coyote's people sing") publishes significant material but fails to observe that the English garb is cut to a Chinookan pattern. My analysis of the two versions of "The news about Coyote" gets some things right, but in recognizing most of the notes, fails to discern their intrinsic rhythm. The analyses define form too much in terms of categories of content, like many analyses under the headings of structuralism, semiotics, and the like, and not enough in terms of the disposition of words. The shapes of the texts are approximated, but the exact form/meaning covariation is missed. These sections show that one can come close, yet fall short of actual patterning and force through failure to have a precise hypothesis (or "theory") about verbal form. The analyses of chapter 3 help demonstrate by contrast the difference that verse analysis makes. (For the same reason, a sample page of Louis Simpson's "The news about Coyote," as first published, is reproduced.)

My first full recognition of narrative verse patterning is presented in chapter 4, written a few years after chapter 3. The source of the text of "The deserted boy," Louis Simpson, was the source of one of the texts of the news about Coyote imperfectly analyzed in chapter 3. In chapter 5 a text from Hiram Smith, source of the other version of the news about Coyote in chapter 3, is also shown to have patterning as narrative verse. Whereas the text of chapter 4 is used to show the nature of the architecture of verse patterning, the text of chapter 5 is used to demonstrate a format for comparing analyses. The logic of verse analysis and my own fumblings toward it are both laid bare. This chapter will seem forbidding to those interested mainly in literary insight and unacquainted or unsympathetic with the pressure of linguistic training toward explicit statement and explicit consideration of alternative analyses. I do think formats for explicit consideration of alternative analyses will prove necessary, once others conversant with the languages in question join in the work. This chapter, then, is an initial contribution to that anticipated need. It has its origin in the larger study of the figure of Grizzly Woman that will concern the fourth volume of this series.

Chapter 6 returns to the imperfectly analyzed texts of chapter 3. Having independent evidence of the presence of narrative verse in texts of the two men (Louis Simpson, Hiram Smith) in hand (chaps. 4, 5), chapter 6 proceeds to show the nature of the narrative verse in the native language texts of "The news concerning Coyote." The earlier and later analyses of these texts are compared, leading to a consideration of the logic of verse analysis and to a truer sense of the relation of the narratives to a kind of rhetorical form traditional in Western literature. A cognate Clackamas text is added, and the shapes and morals of all three verses are compared within a framework suggested by the work of Kenneth Burke.

Discovery of new structure is not limited to the native language texts of chapter 3. The essentially English language texts from Philip Kahclamet preceding and following "the news concerning Coyote" are found to be rooted in traditional narrative verse patterns as well. The speech, "The crier," and to a less certain extent, a nineteenth-century speech, are set forth in sets of lines. The discovery of the structure of "The crier" leads to a heightened sense of its rhetorical theme and force. Kahclamet's version of "Coyote's people sing" is also found, alongside the bilingual glossing, to be carrying over into English the architecture of Chinookan myth.

Chapter 6 somewhat breaks the frame of the book. It is a conglomerate and reflexive chapter, containing a poem, as well as reanalyses of analyses of my own. The decision to maintain a numerical consistency, that of ten chapters, has worked havoc with consistency of genre. Some readers may find such divagation diverting; it is certainly fashionable today. I think there is a deeper justification. The great linguist Leonard Bloomfield used to tell students that in published work one should not bring the reader into the kitchen. But it is in keeping with the canons of science to let the kitchen sometimes be seen. Always to conceal the turmoil behind the scenes is ultimately to be misleading. The chapter, then, begins with an account of how it came to be a chapter; it comprises a record of debate, last-minute recognition, an earlier objectification of grief, reconsiderations, an exploration of a novel framework for the comparison of myth.

Part Three, "Titles, names and natures," subordinates verse analysis to analysis of genre and meaning. An early discovery about titles is presented in chapter 7. Some comparison to what is known about titles elsewhere in the region helps to indicate the specificity of the Chinookan pattern. The patterning of titles is found to be crucial to the reinterpretation of the text taken up in chapter 8. There discovery of an internal relationship between the order of names in titles and the outcomes of myths supports an interpretation of the text more in keeping with its overt expressive form than the interpretation proposed by its collector. A postscript to the original article reflects on the respect in which the final speech is a "breakthrough into performance" for both the protagonist (Seal's daughter) and the narrator (Victoria Howard), consummating the transformation of perspective from an incident in a story of successful revenge to the experience of a family revenged upon. The same text is taken up in chapter 9 in the light of poetic form. (When first published, chapter 8 presented the text as spruced-up prose.) Understanding of poetic form is itself extended with the discovery of a covarying rhetorical form. The text, one that has become somewhat central to discussions of American Indian literature, is retranslated and some of its features considered more fully.

Chapter 10 rounds out the book by taking up a particular device, as did chapters 1 and 2. At the same time it deepens the consideration of poetic form and personal meaning in the chapters just preceding. The particular device, a noun prefix, is shown to illuminate treatment of Grizzly Woman as a figure embodying threats to maturity. The story of "Seal and her younger brother" itself (chaps. 8, 9) is brought into relation with the stories involving Grizzly Woman, as complementary expressions of the experience of a young woman, the narrator Victoria Howard, growing up on a reservation in the midst of a shattered way of life.

The chapters are republished mostly without change in substance. Still, consistency in format is desirable, and the chapters have been edited to this end. All references are integrated into a single list at the end of the book. Passages on orthography and the location of the Chinookan groups have been consolidated in introductory notes. Footnotes have been revised accordingly in some cases. Details of such editing and of internal revision are given in the first, unnumbered, footnote to each chapter.

Only one chapter has been substantially revised internally. Shortly after the paper that has become chapter 2 was published, I discovered a further example of the "bear talk" it treats. A number of lines had to be recast to accommodate the addition, and in the end the whole thing was redone. In order to preserve the record of discovery over the years of the original articles, new information and reflections relating to the other chapters are added in postscripts.

Chapter 3 elicited a probing review from Dmitri Segal, and a response incorporating some of his points is added as a postscript. To chapter 4 is appended discussion of the response of Mrs. Ruth Estabrook, a Wasco, to the verse analysis contained in the chapter, as well as a comparative discussion that extends to Shakespeare's *The Tempest*. Chapter 7, as first published, dealt only with Chinookan titles; in a postscript the languages around it are examined for analogous phenomena. To chapter 8 is added note of the discussion of the myth by others, and further reflections having to do with the notion of "breakthrough into performance," Bernstein's "elaborated" and "restricted" codes, and "meta-narrative" statements.

In chapter 9 the discussion of final endings is clarified and expanded in response to comments by Dennis Tedlock in the issue of *New Literary History* in which it first appeared. Chapters 5, 6 and 10 lack postscripts, having been completed not long before publication of this volume. Chapter 6, indeed, appears here for the first time.

I should like to thank Cornelius H. Van Schooneveld, John McGuigan and Maurice English for their encouragement to me to undertake this volume. Jerry Ramsey has made a number of helpful suggestions. Mrs. Mary Stevenson prepared the greater part of the manuscript, faster than I could prepare it for her, and Mrs. Rosemary Klumpp plunged in to finish it. Lee Ann Draud has given it a helpful reading. Finally, I should like to dedicate this book to the memory of all the "old people," Indian and non-Indian, those who knew to perform and those who knew to transcribe. Their collaboration, the moments of intersection of their respective traditions made possible the materials the book seeks to illumine. I should like particularly to single out Victoria Howard, who was dead before I was four, yet whom through years with her texts I seem to have come to know. Part of that sense of knowing no doubt is transferred from the women it has been my privilege to know at Warm Springs Reservation, but much, I believe, stems from her own words. She had Seal's daughter say the words that give a title to this book, "In vain I tried to tell you." In her myth those words define a failure to avoid a death. I think it a kind of death for words such as hers to lie unread, even out of print, their form and the meanings dependent on their form, unrecognized. Sometimes I seem to myself to stand in a long line of shushed daughters, beginning perhaps before Boas, warning that without attention to linguistic detail the life of the texts will be lost, but in vain. That analogy puts the reader, perhaps, in the position of choosing to be or not be like Seal. The forces for formal preservation are strong in the academy and general life of the society, but I hope that a few will overcome them. With texts, as sometimes the myths themselves, what is dead can be revived. We cannot bring texts to life by stepping over them five times, but we can by scholarship. There is much to be done and few to do it.

Finally, remembering that myths were told to teach, I take some pleasure in subscribing to this introduction at the Graduate School of Education.

DELL HYMES

University of Pennsylvania
12 March 1980
Mt. Hood National Forest
1 July 1980

Ethnological Note

The songs, narratives, and speeches in this book are from American Indians, or Native Americans, of the far northwest of North America. The traditional homes are in what are now known as the states of Oregon and Washington and as the province of British Columbia.

Most of the texts are from a people who lived along or near the Columbia River, as it flows westward to the Pacific. That course today forms most of the border between Oregon and Washington. In the east the river passes through open plateau country until it approaches the Cascade range with its snow-capped peaks. From there west to the Pacific it passes through green forest, even today, and all the more so, of course, two hundred years ago, before the coming of the whites. The Columbia then knew many deer, elk, bears, and other creatures alongside its course, and sturgeon, even seals, far up river. Most of all it knew great runs of returning salmon, whose coming heralded spring. It was the spring and fall catch of salmon that made survival through the winter possible and life prosperous and good.

For most of its course, from some two hundred or so miles inland to its Pacific mouth, the Columbia was the home of people today called Chinookan. That was not a name they used themselves. The word "Chinook," indeed, is not a Chinookan word, but comes from a neighboring language of southwestern Washington, Chehalis. The Chehalis word referred only to the people and language near the mouth of the Columbia on its northern side. These first people to be called Chinook were of importance among their Indian neighbors as a center of trade and were of importance to the first white traders and explorers. The name applied to them came to be extended to all the related languages and peoples along the river.

To distinguish the original Chinook, then, another name is needed, and I have adopted "Shoalwater" (approximately as used by the ethnologist Leslie Spier [1936]). This name reflects the fact that many of these Chinook lived near the inlet known as Shoalwater Bay that cuts south from the ocean just above the Columbia mouth. (It is now known as Willapa Bay, the name "Willapa" being that of some Athapaskan-speaking Indians once resident in the vicinity.) It is the language of these people that Boas recorded in *Chinook texts* (1894) and analyzed in his grammar of "Chinook" (1911).

At the mouth of the Columbia on the Oregon side were the Clatsop, among whom Lewis and Clark wintered in 1805–1806, in the county that now bears their name. The language of the Clatsop was practically identical with that of the Chinook on the Washington side, and some descendants of people on the Washington side later referred to their lineage as Clatsop generically because of common ancestors (Rolls 1969:13, entries 14–18; 27, statement 14; 30, statement 16; 31, statement 18). The villages on the two sides of the river were politically independent, however, and sometimes hostile; Charles Cultee, the source of Boas's knowledge of Chinook, and later identified as Clatsop by his descendants (Rolls 1969), told Boas a few stories at the expense of Clatsop reputation.

These two groups at the mouth of the Columbia are called the "Lower Chinook" (Melville Jacobs once suggested the name "Coastal Chinook"). They are given a common name by virtue of having a common language, distinct from the related, but mutually unintelligible languages of their kin upriver.

The nearest of these kin spoke a variety of Chinookan known to us as Kathlamet. Sources and maps sometimes show three separate groups, the Wahkiakum on the northern side of the river, the Kathlamet on the southern side, and Skilloot east of the Kathlamet. The language of all three was the same. Collectively, Kathlamet speakers lived from Grays Bay to Oak Point on what is now the Washington side of the river, and from Tongue Point, a little east of Astoria to Oak Point, near present Rainier, on the Oregon side. Their territory included the modern town of Cathlamet, Washington.

The way of life of the Kathlamet was virtually identical with that of the Lower Chinook, and when scholars speak of cultures, they consider the Kathlamet, Clatsop and Shoalwater all Lower Chinook. While sharing a common way of life, however, the Kathlamet differed sufficiently from the others in patterns of pronunciation, grammar, and items of vocabulary to be separate in language. Perhaps the difference between Spanish and Portuguese would be a reasonable analogue.

The language of the Kathlamet is close to the languages of their kin up river in certain respects, and all these are commonly grouped together linguistically as "Upper Chinook" (Melville Jacobs once suggested the name "Columbia Chinook"). Kathlamet stands enough apart, however, for it to be suggested (by Michael Silverstein) that it should be considered a third language, standing between Lower and Upper. I agree with the suggestion. If an analogous locational name were needed, "Middle Chinook" might do.

Charles Cultee, the last fluent speaker of Lower Chinook whom Boas could find when he sought for such in 1890, was also the last fluent speaker to be found of Kathlamet. He had Kathlamet ancestry on his mother's side and had acquired the language while living with her kin on the Oregon side of the river. Cultee spoke several languages—Lower Chinook, Kathlamet, Chehalis (Salish), and Chinook Jargon. Boas shared with him only the trade language, Chinook Jargon, and it was through that medium (and Cultee's remarkable intelligence, as Boas stressed) that a fine set of Kathlamet texts was recorded (Boas 1901). Apart from some vocabulary recorded later by the Edward Curtis expedition (perhaps from Cultee, perhaps from a neighbor, Mrs. Wilson, from whom Boas got two pictures [Ibid.] but no words), Cultee's texts and supplementary explanations are all that survive of the language. My own systematic work with Chinookan began with a grammar and dictionary drawn from the Cultee texts (Hymes 1955).

Despite the absence of a grammar and dictionary of Clackamas itself, Clackamas texts can be interpreted rather readily in the light of knowledge of the dialects spoken still farther east. These dialects—the speech of the Chinookans who lived at the Cascades, Hood River, and near the present-day Dalles—were not identical, but were very much alike. By all accounts, a person knowing one could understand the others easily enough. The differences in vocabulary were not a barrier but a matter for comment and recitation, not unlike the way Americans may point out the different meanings of "bonnet," "caravan," and "knock me up" in British English. The Clackamas at the western end of this chain of dialects and the Wishram and Wasco at the eastern end had a common name for their common speech, Kiksht.

The Kiksht of the people living at the Cascades and at Hood River is not separately documented, apart from a certain number of lexical details. The communities were early victims of settlement and disease. Indeed, many of the people known today as "Wasco" were not ancestrally from the site of the Wasco proper, near the Dalles and the great fishing grounds of Celilo, but from farther down river, as far as Stevenson and Washougal, Washington and Wind Mountain.

The Kiksht preserved in texts, apart from Clackamas, comes from the two communities that survived most intact into the twentieth century. They lived more or less opposite each other at the eastern end of the Chinookan range. When the river was made a political boundary, those on the northern side of the river were moved inland north to the Yakima reservation, and those on the southern side were moved inland south to the Warm Springs Reservation. Had the two not been separated, the larger population might have kept the language alive longer. Only a very few of the oldest people know it today.

Most of the published work with this variety of Kiksht has appeared with a name of the community on the northern, Washington side of the river— "Wishram." Wishram, like Chinook, is not a Chinookan name, but a name that neighbors used. In this case it was Sahaptin-speaking neighbors, who pronounced the name WíSxam. The community bearing the name was a few miles above the Dalles, and it is called "Spearfish" today. (The Wishram on the Oregon side was transferred there by the railroad.)

When Boas sent his great student Edward Sapir to study Upper Chinook, Sapir worked with a man from the community on the Washington side, living then at Yakima. When Sapir sat in an apple orchard to work with Louis Simpson, he, of course, learned that the people at Spearfish called the place

"Nixlúidix" in their own language. Apparently Simpson accepted Wishram as an appellation in English. In any case, Sapir published what Louis Simpson dictated to him as "Wishram texts" (Sapir 1909a).

That "Wishram" did apply to the community on the northern side of the river from early on is indicated by the use of the term in Irving's *Astoria* (1836, chaps. 10, 30) and the use of both terms (Wishram, Nixlúidix) by Curtis in his report (1911); Curtis clearly understood that it was the first-person-singular form of the Chinookan word (I-C-xluit) that Lewis and Clark had transposed into the name they gave the people, "E-che-lute," in 1805. That the Sahaptin term Wishram was ever used to designate more than the community at Nixlúidix, that it was ever the designation of a variety of language or of culture distinct from that of people living opposite on the southern side of the river, I do not believe. Whites and white governments have generally misunderstood the nature of the river. To us it has seemed a boundary. To the Chinookan-speaking peoples, the river was a thoroughfare. The typical pattern of settlement for speakers sharing the same variety of the language was to establish settlements across from each other. Thus, the Chinook proper and the Clatsop were opposite each other at the Pacific mouth of the river; a little inland the Kathlamet proper were opposite the Wahkiakum. This pattern seems to have been followed farther up the Columbia as well. Presumably it was so for the settlements near where the Willamette enters the Columbia and for the Clackamas and Walamt opposite each other on the Willamette near Oregon City. We know it to have been so for the people opposite each other on the Columbia at the Cascades and those at present Hood River (Oregon) and White Salmon (Washington), closer to the Wishram and Wasco (Curtis 1911:180–81).

A village would have a specific name, of course, and a group on one side might distinguish itself by collective name from kin on the other. I cannot help thinking, however, that the literature of anthropology, linguistics, and folklore is deceiving in writing as if there were distinct peoples, Wishrams and Wascos, one on the Washington, the other on the Oregon side. People on either side today trace kin and property often enough to the other, and the surviving speakers of the language use only Wasco, whether at Yakima or at Warm Springs, as its name.

Despite the identity of language, Wishram became established as a separate identity in the scholarly literature. When Sapir published the Wishram texts he had recorded, he also published as a supplement "Wasco myths and tales" (in English), designating thus the narratives that had been obtained in 1885 by the remarkable Jeremiah Curtin. Curtin, a Harvard graduate, world traveler, polyglot, devoted student of folklore, had walked in midwinter (January) through snow and ice from the Columbia to Warm Springs Reservation, where the Wasco had been moved in the mid-nineteenth century. There he recorded vocabularies in Wasco, Warm Springs Sahaptin, and Paiute, the three languages spoken on the reservation. His letters imply that he recorded the stories in the Indian languages as well, not just in English, but his original transcriptions of the stories have never been found.

When in 1930 Sapir sent a student of his own, Walter Dyk, to work with the language, Dyk went to Spearfish and there obtained the aid of a brilliant young man, Philip Kahclamet. Kahclamet helped Dyk obtain information from older people, learned to write the language himself, corresponded with Dyk, and went back with him for a semester to a seminar by Sapir at Yale. Kahclamet ever after called the language Wishram, and his texts are so identified here. Linguistically, they are indistinguishable from Wasco texts.

Dyk wrote a grammar of Wishram for a dissertation at Yale, but the grammar was not published. In his fieldwork he obtained a mass of lexical information, which forms the core of any Wishram-Wasco dictionary. Dyk himself became unable to continue work because of Parkinson's disease. David French, Michael Silverstein, and I have added to the lexical knowledge of the language, but the dictionary remains unfinished. A certain number of texts obtained by Silverstein and myself also remain unpublished. (Some texts and some sections of vocabulary have been prepared by myself for use by people at Warm Springs in programs to teach and maintain the language.)

In summary, then, the Chinookan-speaking peoples flourished two hundred years ago along both sides of the Columbia River, from its mouth at the Pacific to some two hundred or more miles inland. There were two, and perhaps three, distinct Chinookan languages. Since the language boundaries are sharpest to the west, near the mouth of the river, one is led to infer that the oldest homeland of the people is there. The close similarity of language over a much longer stretch of territory in the east indicates more recent settlement, conditions of communication being much the same both east and west. Perhaps the ancient ancestors of the Chinookans had pushed to the coast at the Columbia mouth, thus causing the separation of the Salish (language)-speaking peoples on either side, the Chehalis on the north and the Tillamook on the Oregon coast. If so, that expansion occurred long ago, and probably gradually, through intermarriage and replacive bilingualism, from a base a little upriver, where the Kathlamet were later to be known. This inference as to homeland is made inescapable when one considers that Chinookan has a system of sex gender deeply embedded in its grammar. Such gender (analogous to that of French, Spanish, and German) is rare in American Indian languages in the west, and the only other language family in the vicinity to have it is Salish. The two language families have almost certainly not developed such a rare trait independently and accidentally. The two language families must have been in close communication for a long time, at a time preceding the spread of Chinookan up the Columbia and out of direct contact with Salish speakers. The lower Columbia is the obvious location for that close communication to have occurred, perhaps some two thousand years ago (cf. Silverstein 1974).

What of the culture and history of the Chinookan-speaking groups in recent times? For the Lower Chinook, there is a useful recent book by Ruby and Brown (1976). Something of the culture is directly revealed, of course, in the texts from Cultee (Boas 1894, 1901), especially as to religion and family tradition. A general cultural sketch, stimulated by recollections that may have a Salish ingredient, has been provided by Ray (1938). The early history of Kathlamet territory, sympathetically recalled, is glimpsed in Strong (1905). Beckham (1977) provides an invaluable portrayal of western Oregon as a whole, with many rare illustrations that convey a direct sense of the people and their circumstances; it is the best one book to consult. Something of the Clackamas appears. In addition, there are, of course, the expressions of Clackamas culture in Victoria Howard's texts and in her accounts of recent times in the second of the two volumes (Jacobs 1958, 1959a). There are also Jacobs's interpretations of the cultural concerns behind the texts (1959b, 1960). Curtis (1911), a source too much neglected by scholars, contains a good deal of information on the Wishram and Wasco, as does the ethnographic sketch by Spier and Sapir (1930). French (1961) provides a historically organized account of the people. Forthcoming volumes of the new *Handbook of American Indians*, published by the Smithsonian Institution under the general editorship of William C. Sturtevant, will treat the Chinookans east of Portland airport or thereabouts in the volume on the Plateau and those west of there in the volume on the Northwest.

Some aspects of the oral traditions of the region can be found in Clark (1953). Ramsey (1977) is a comprehensive, superior introduction.

Perhaps the two most useful words to have in mind about the way of life are "salmon" and "cedar." All the Chinookans gathered roots and berries and hunted, but the eminence of their position among their neighbors, and the degree of security and pride they enjoyed, depended on the bounty of annual runs of salmon. Their positions on the river provided sustenance for themselves and importance as middlemen and centers of trade. While implements were made of bone and stone, and ornaments of feather and bead, wood was the essential ingredient of material life. Indeed, the word for cedar could stand for "wood" in general, if qualification were not needed, just as the word for the best of salmon, the Chinook salmon, could stand for "fish" in general.

Do not imagine naked savages in a wilderness. Relatively naked in good weather they often were, but prudish, too, employing euphemisms for body functions and punishing adultery severely. They were no more indifferent to the dangers of the wilderness than you or I. Travel was loved and trade enjoyed, but mainly along waterways in canoes or along well-established trails. Some men would hunt the hinterland, and groups of women would go to plentiful sites for roots and berries, but the forest, even nearby canyons and ridges, was an ambiguous source of both danger and potential acquisition of power. Villages were small, but they were home. One should imagine a center and a periphery, the lodges of a village as a center of security, danger increasing with distance away. In winter, when no fresh food could be gotten, Chinookans lived underground in lodges whose rooms were dug out of the ground and whose roofs slanted down to the ground. In winter the peripheral world of supernatural power and myth came closer, spirit-power was sought and initiations into the control of power held, and myths formally told. Myths, in fact, were not to be told in summer for fear of rattlesnake bite. With spring, Chinookans, like flowers, emerged from underground to a new world. The root for "world, country, land, earth" indeed also has the meaning "year," pointing up the interdependence of recurring time with the recurrences of the seasonal round.

Imagine a very close life, family and kinship all important. And despite the early travelers' reports of poverty and unpleasant living conditions, despite the evident need—expressed in myths—to be concerned about food and to avoid starvation in winter, do not by any means imagine a world thought poor by its inhabitants. Do not expect to find stories of a once-better world, from which there had been a fall, or stories of a better time to come, compensating for present hardship. The Chinookans, like many Indian peoples, thought of their world as the way the world should be. In their myths they imagined an earlier time, to be sure, but an earlier time in which things had been mixed up, not properly known, too dangerous, not yet ready for them. The pervasive point of myth is not a fall, or a salvation to come, but the straightening out of things to prepare for the world as it is now. Clearly material goods are not criteria of mental health. Autonomy of personality and group, the certain knowledge of the usefulness of one's work, evident connection between effort and outcome, a sense of parity and cooperation with other forces of nature: all of these fostered a life that was confident despite hunger, and often proud.

For children, required to listen to myths, the telling was physically very much a part of winter. "You used to have to go to swim in the *ice* water," Lucinda Smith (a Wasco at Warm Springs, who traces her ancestry to a grandfather at Washougal) put it; a number of older people can remember being made to go cut holes in the frozen ice of the river and dip in for falling asleep during myth telling, or simply as part of "sharpening," training for later spirit-power quests.

The telling was very much a part of summer imaginatively. The greater part of the stories—Coyote's travels up the river, the travels and adventures of others—implied that part of the seasonal round when people were out and about. Certainly the stories were entertainment, one element of surviving in close quarters. Again from Lucinda Smith (sister-in-law of Hiram Smith, source of texts in chaps. 3, 5 and 6): "Winter time—that's when they have time to tell stories—nothing to do—old-fashioned one-room house." Part of their attraction must have been the imagination of the seasons when adventures such as theirs could occur. In myth performances relations with two kinds of other time were renewed and maintained—the peripheral time when the world was being set right and the time of good weather, when the fruits of its rightness could be harvested. What children heard came from the one, what they ate from the other; the maintenance of both, the myth-meanings and the people, was interdependent.

And yet, as was said, the stories were entertainment, too. Scholars are sometimes the last to understand that these stories were told and told again, not simply to reflect or express or maintain social structure, interpersonal tensions, or something similar, but because they were great stories, great fun. Cold water would seem worth it. As Mrs. Smith recalled, "Sometimes they'd ask them to tell a story, to an old man like that. He'd tell 'm, 'When I'm finished telling the story, you've got to go jump in cold water.' 'Okay, we'll do it.'" Sometimes no request or exchange would be involved: "Sometimes an old man sitting there restless; he'd say, 'You children, I'm going to tell you a story,' and he'd start telling them stories." And sometimes the exchange would be implicit in hospitality. As Mrs. Smith recalled, "Old man used come down to your house. We'd be sitting round. He eat. Like Daniel Katchia [k' aCáya], he used to come. 'K'aCáya. QanúCkmaX inSlóXwa.' 'Ai.—QanuCk ayamSLoXwa.'" ("Katchia. Make us a myth." "All right. I'll make you a myth.") Even today, for an older person who knew the stories as a child, it is a treat to hear them again, even when the Kiksht is read, and in the imperfect accents of a white.

What has been said about the Chinookan-speaking people would hold in general terms for the Takelma, who figure in chapter 2. Their history and culture are introduced nicely in Beckham (1977) and their fate recounted in Beckham (1971) as part of the fate of other Indians of the region. The Takelma lived inland on the Rogue River in southwestern Oregon. They were not as wealthy as the Chinook, but salmon fishing was of major concern to them as well. As Boas with Cultee and Jacobs with Victoria Howard, so Sapir with Frances Johnson. In 1906 on one of the field trips on which he was sent by Boas, he found her at Grande Ronde Reservation, and she is the sole source of almost all we know about the language and narratives of the Takelma. She is the proximate source as well of a major contribution to linguistics. Sapir's Takelma grammar (1922), written as his dissertation, carries the concern of his mentor Boas for an "analytic" approach that would not impose alien categories still farther. It stands as a full synchronic, structural grammar, complete some years before the posthumous publication of the lectures by de Saussure (*Cours de linguistique generale*, 1916) that are so often and mistakenly cited as the general origin of synchronic structural grammar.

The Haida and Kwakiutl, who figure in chapter 1, are peoples of British Columbia. The Haida live on Queen Charlotte Island off the coast of mainland Canada. The Kwakiutl live somewhat south of them on the northeastern part of Vancouver Island and on the mainland opposite. When one thinks of the Northwest Coast and envisions totem poles and potlatches, it is of people such as the Haida and Kwakiutl that one is thinking. Together with the Tlingit and Tsimshian of southern Alaska and northwestern Canada, they represent what can be called the "high culture" of the Northwest Coast. Like the

Chinookans and the Takelma, they fished, hunted, and gathered, but did so in a realm of such abundance as to permit wealth and craftsmanship unknown to any other nonagricultural people in the world. The inheritance of titles, crests, rights to rituals and myths, became of central importance to rank and status. Social structure was elaborated in complex systems of lineality and corporate identity. Wood, shell, and bone were worked by specialists into great art, whose traditions remain alive today. The languages have been studied by a number of people, beginning most importantly, again, with Boas and his students; the cultures have been written about frequently. Drucker (1965) is a useful introduction.

From the Haida and Kwakiutl, to the Chinookans, the Takelma, and peoples south of them in northern and central California, certain fundamental things hold true: No agriculture or (aboriginally) metal tools; dependence on hunting, gathering, and fishing, with a certain degree of security in subsistence, and elaboration of social structure and art, varying with the abundance available from nature; song, story, speech, put to varying purposes to some extent in accord with variation in way of life. Throughout, however, the same universal human gift, that of shaping speech into imaginative life and satisfying form.

Orthographic Note

The poetics of a language requires citing the words of a language. That is an immediate obstacle to many readers and publishers. American Indian languages often make use of sounds for which the English alphabet makes no provision. For the languages most often cited in this volume—Clackamas Chinook and Wasco Chinook—it is possible to adapt the letters of the English alphabet, avoiding special symbols and diacritics, for almost all sounds. The same is true of the Takelma language, cited in chapter 2, and the Kwakiutl and Haida languages, cited in chapter 1.

In explaining the adaptation, I will necessarily say more than is needed for linguists. Indeed, if only linguists were the intended audience, little explanation would be necessary. There is a standard usage among students of American Indian languages. To be sure, the conventions have changed over time, and some of the materials treated in this book were transcribed according to earlier conventions; but conversion from one system to the other is straightforward. One would mainly need to indicate a few particularities of each of the languages in question.

In saying too much for linguists, I may say too little for those not familiar with phonetic symbols and the range of sounds found in human language. Something must be said, however, and I shall come at the matter in three ways. First, the alphabet used here for the Chinookan materials in chapters 3–10 will be presented, and the letters roughly explained in terms of English equivalents, insofar as possible. Second, the Chinookan symbols and sounds will be presented in a table that brings out their relationships in terms of a system of sounds. Third, the rationale for some of the special features of this alphabet will be given, together with remarks on its relation to other usage.

The particular aspects of Takelma (chap. 2) and of Kwakiutl and Haida (chap. 1) will then be discussed in turn.

The alphabet for the Chinookan languages employed in this book is as follows:

a ä b C C' d (dz) (e) (E) g G h i (j) k k' l L m n (o) p p' q q' s S t t'
tL tL' ts ts' u w x X y

The order is established by placing special symbols (such as C or L) after or at the point of their nearest ordinary equivalent in the English alphabet.

Several of the symbols are rarely used and for that reason are placed in parentheses. The sounds *dz* and *j* occur only in a few borrowed words and onomatopoetic formations. It is rarely necessary to indicate the obscure vowel *E*. The vowels *e* and *o* are not phonemically distinct from *i* and *u*, respectively, and words containing them would be written with *i* and *u* in a dictionary. The performance of a myth, on the other hand, is partly a pattern of sound, and when the phonological units that can be summarized with "i" and "u" are emphasized, they commonly have the phonetic value of *e* and *o*.

Published texts are more attractive, and the grammatical structure of the language more apparent—more perspicuous—if combinations of sounds that function as single units in the structure of the language are spelled with single symbols. It would be preferable to use the Greek lambda with a bar for what is shown here as a combination of *t* and *L* and perhaps to use a single letter, such as *c*, for what is shown here as *ts* (in accord with current Americanist usage). Adaptation to an ordinary English font, however, has preempted "c" and required the combination *tL*.

The letters have the following near equivalents in English:

a	vowel in *a*ll
ä	vowel in *A*l, sh*a*ll
b	initial consonant in *b*ill
C	*ch*ill
C'	glottalized C; see below
d	*d*ill
dz	a*dz*e
e	range of vowels in b*a*le, b*e*ll
E	range of second vowel in butt*e*r, butt*o*n
g	*g*ill
G	farther back than g in *g*oal; see below
h	*h*ill
i	range of vowels in *ee*l, *i*ll
j	*j*ill
k	*k*ill
k'	glottalized k; see below
l	*l*ittle
L	voiceless *l;* like Welsh *ll;* see below
m	*m*ill
n	*n*il
o	range of vowels in g*oa*l, g*aw*d
p	*p*ill
p'	glottalized p; see below
q	farther back than *c* and *k* in *c*oal, *k*ohlrabi; see below
q'	glottalized q; see below
s	*s*ill

S   *sh*ill
t   *t*ill
t'   glottalized t; see below
tL   voiceless lateral affricate (t+L); see below
tL'   glottalized tL; see below
ts   *ts*etse, i*ts*
ts'   glottalized ts; see below
u   range of vowels in f*oo*l, f*u*ll
w   *w*ill
x   similar to *ch* in German I*ch*
X   similar to *ch* in German a*ch*
y   *y*ell
,   glottal stop, similar to catch between the vowels in *oh-oh*
:   lengthening of the preceding vowel
au   semi-vowel, as in *ow*l, f*ou*l
ai   semi-vowel, as in *i*sle, f*i*le

The elements of the alphabet can be displayed in a table that shows something of their phonetic character. Each row contains sounds that are made in a similar manner. Each column contains sounds that are made at about the same place in the mouth by the contact or position of the tongue. In keeping with established convention, the lips are at the left, the throat is at the right.

Much of Table o-1 should be intelligible in terms of English analogues. The righthand columns require comment, as do certain of the rows.

The rightmost column has a familiar symbol, *h*, and an unfamiliar one, '. The latter stands for the glottal stop or for the occurrence of glottalization together with other stops. In English there is a glottal catch between the two

p		t		k	q		voiceless stops
b		d		g	G		voiced stops
p'		t'		k'	q'	'	glottalized stops
	L	s	S	x	X	h	voiceless fricatives
	tL	ts	C				voiceless affricates
		dz	j				voiced affricates
	tL'	ts'	C'				glottalized affricates
m		n					nasal stops
	l						lateral resonant
w			y				semi-vowels
i				u			high vowels
e		E		o			mid vowels
ä		a					low vowels

Table o-1.   Phonetic character of Chinookan alphabet

syllables of "oh-oh"; some dialects have a glottal stop in words such as "bot-tle," replacing the "tt"; but the sound is marginal. In certain areas of the world, such as the Caucasus and the North Pacific Coast, the sound is common. It is made by closure, then release, of the glottis. By itself, between two vowels, as in the Wasco for "crow," *akná'an*, it is a "catch" like that in "oh-oh." Accompanying another stop, it can have a strong crackling force. In Chinookan the glottis is kept closed during the making of the other stop (p, t, k, or the like) and released separately afterwards. Its explosive character was symbolized by Boas and his students earlier in the century with the exclamation mark: p!, t!, k!, and so forth. The modern symbol, employed here, is the sign used in classical Greek for smooth breathing, and sometimes in English for a single close quote.

The next to rightmost column, headed by "Q," contains an order of sounds that is also very common in Indian languages of the Pacific coast. The difference between "k" and "q" is likely to seem to an English speaker a difference between "two kinds of k." The sound symbolized by *k* is made farther forward in the mouth, as in English "king" and "kill," with the tongue touching the palate; the sounds are called "palatals." The sound symbolized by *q* is made farther back in the mouth, the tongue making contact with the velum, and the sounds are called "velars." The closest approximation in English is the initial consonant of words such as "coal" and "caught."

Chinookan and many other Indian languages distinguish several kinds of velar consonant. Among voiced stops, *G* represents the velar, deeper equivalent of *g*. The closest equivalent in English is the initial sound of a word such as *goal*, but the Chinookan *G* is farther back, sometimes sounding almost swallowed. Among glottalized stops, *q'* is, of course, the glottalized velar stop. Among fricatives, consonants in which the tongue impedes but does not stop the outward flow of air, Chinookan again consistently distinguishes two kinds of back sound. The palatal voiceless fricative, similar to the consonant of German *Ich*, is written with *x*, while the velar, similar to the consonant of German *ach*, is written with *X*.

The next to leftmost column contains yet a third kind of sound common in western American Indian languages, the so-called "voiceless l" and affricates based upon it. This sound is found in Welsh, where it is spelled with double "l" and occurs in the native Welsh pronunciation of names we have borrowed into English, such as "Lloyd" and "Floyd." The sound is somewhat similar to that of the sounds spelled "th" and "s" in English "thin" and "sin" but with the friction coming from contact with the side of the tongue. Early settlers and writers were bedeviled by this sound. The *tl*, *cl*, and *thl* in proper names like *Tl*ingit, *Cl*ackamas, *Cl*atsop, Ka*thl*amet come from attempts to interpret it as a voiceless consonant plus an *l*. Close, but not close enough; both these words have a voiceless fricative in the languages from which they come. Capital L was used for the sound earlier in this century but was later replaced by "barred l," *l* with a line through it, thus: *ł*. The capital *L* has been used here to avoid a special symbol not normally available.

The rows of voiceless and voiced stops should be understandable from the English equivalents to *p t k* and *b d g*. Glottalized stops have been explained in connection with the glottal stop, and voiceless fricatives in connection with *x* and *X*. Affricates, such as the initial sound of English "chill," consist of a *t* as onset and a voiceless fricative, such as the initial sound of English "shill," as the rest. In Chinookan affricates are systematic units.

The spelling of consonants is mostly a matter of carrying over English letters, such as *p t k;* adding a necessary symbol, as in the case of *';* and shifting the use of English letters not otherwise needed. Thus *q* and *x* are redundant in English, since *k* could be used for *q*, and *ks* or *z* for *x* (as in "axe," "xylophone," "Xerxes"). Capital letters have been adopted to avoid diacritics not found in ordinary English fonts insofar as possible. Thus we have C instead of the č (c with superposed wedge) usual in Americanist usage; G instead of g (g with subposed dot); L instead of *ł* (l with line through it); S instead of š (s with superposed wedge); and X instead of x̣ (x with subposed dot).

Should one of these capital letters with special phonetic value begin a sentence or proper name, it can be distinguished from capitalization of the ordinary letter by placing H after it. C, G, L, S, X at the beginning of a word would represent capitalization of c, g, l, s, x. CH, GH, LH, SH, XH at the beginning of a word would represent C, G, L, S, X in the special phonetic values assigned them here. These combinations would not otherwise occur in Chinookan.

The spelling of vowels presents different problems than the spelling of consonants if one starts from English and approaches another language. English is indeed famous for the irregularity and inconsistency with which it uses letters to spell vowel sounds. International convention has established the norm of using vowel letters with values "as in Italian." American Indian languages are usually spelled in accordance with the international standard. Thus in Chinookan, *i* and *u* represent vowels made high in the front and back of the mouth, respectively, as in the second syllables of English *latrine* and *rule.* The letters *e* and *o* represent vowels made with the tongue somewhat lower in the front and back of the mouth, respectively, as in *precis* and *prose.* The letter *a* represents a vowel made low and centrally, as in *all* and *enthrall.* (While it is thus possible to find English spellings that match the international conventions, it may require searching out words of foreign origin [*latrine, precis*], and the five sounds just considered are often spelled otherwise, as in *feed, seed, need, eel* or *bead, bean, beak, eat;* as in *chew, yew, ewe* or *choo, ooze,* or *you;* as in *fade, favor, ade,* or *say, way;* as in *savor, waver, wade, ade,* or *say, way,* or *sailor, waiver, aid,* or *sleigh, weigh, eight;* as in *float, oat* or *flown, own;* as in *fraught* or *ought, awed* or *odd.*)

The low front vowel of English *hat* would be spelled commonly with an Old English digraph, *a* joined to the following *e*. The sound occurs in Chinookan, generally for expressive emphasis. It is spelled here with the German *ä* (*a* plus superposed umlaut, which can be made on a typewriter with quotation marks). This symbol was indeed used for the purpose by Boas and Sapir in their recordings of the texts treated here. (In his published Clackamas texts, Melville Jacobs used the Greek epsilon.)

The obscure central vowel, analogous to the vowel of the end syllable of English *button, butter,* and sometimes ranging toward the quality of the first syllable of those words, has no single equivalent in English spelling. (Cf. the second syllables of *fracas, faker, fakir, flavor, focus.*) Modern linguistic usage employs the Hebrew letter schwa, written like an upside down, lower case *e,* to wit, *ə.* Boas and his early students used capital *E,* and that symbol is retained for convenience here. (Sometimes capital *A* was used to distinguish the sound of the first syllable of words like *button, butter.*)

The alphabet adopted for Chinookan for the most part will serve for Takelma (chap. 2). A few explanations are needed, however, since no simple orthography can do justice to all languages. The diversity among languages is such that convenient simple letters, such as *p t k,* cannot have exactly the same values as sounds in each. To be sure, when we write *p t k* for English, Chinookan, and Takelma, it does mean much the same thing, because these voiceless stops are also aspirated—pronounced with a puff of breath—in all three languages. When we write *b d g* for English, Chinookan, and Takelma, however, it does not mean the same thing. English and Chinookan are alike, in that *b d g* are voiced in both languages (although the details of the voicing, that is, vibration of the vocal chords, may differ). In Takelma the sounds so written by Sapir are not voiced. They are stops that are unaspirated, like *b d g* in English but also voiceless, like *p t k* in English.

It would be possible to find a way of indicating the specific character of these sounds. Melville Jacobs does so in presenting texts in Takelma's sister language, Kalapuya, spoken in the Willamette Valley in Oregon. Jacobs makes use of small capital letters for such stops, ʙ ᴅ ɢ. They are more forcefully articulated than ordinary *b d g* yet less forcefully articulated than *p t k* (the former usually voiced, the latter usually aspirated). In chapter 2 I have retained Sapir's way of writing the analogous "intermediate" stops of Takelma. Sapir simply used the available ordinary letters *b d g* and defined their specific value in Takelma: "Voiceless mediae, acoustically intermediate between voiced (sonant) and unvoiced (surd) stops" (1909b:9).

It would be possible to substitute small capital letters, following Jacobs's model for Kalapuya, but that would be to add expense without advantage. It would be possible also to rewrite Takelma with a different use of ordinary English letters. There are three kinds of stops in Takelma: intermediate, voiceless aspirate, and glottalized. Sapir marked the aspiration with the standard symbol, which is also the rough breathing sign of classical Greek and sometimes the beginning single quotation mark in English: '. Where Sapir wrote *b d g, p' t' k',* and *p! t! k!* (1909b, 1922), we can write *p t k, p' t' k'* (or *ph, th, kh*), and *p' t' k'.* The necessary distinctions are maintained, and the basic voicelessness of all Takelma stops is made evident orthographically. But to do so would make it difficult to consult Sapir's texts, grammar, and vocabulary. We would have to remember always to look there under "b" for what was now written "p," and correspondingly for *d* : *t* and *g* : *k*.

The way in which the sources are written, and remain written, thus constrains our choice. Here we differ from Sapir's spelling only in dropping the aspiration mark, since it is automatically present with the voiceless stops and implied by writing *p t k;* and, of course, in substituting ' for *!* as the mark of glottalization. (The exclamation point used at the end of Coyote's expression *s·'a!* is just that, an exclamation point.)

The three sounds written *s, s·* and *c* by Sapir are variants of a single phonological unit, which can be written simply *s*. (*s* has the value of "s" in English "sip," and *c* is equivalent to *S* here, that is, to the value of "sh" in English "ship"; *s·* is intermediate between the two, somewhat like "sy" in "bless you" said hurriedly.) The so-called "Coyote prefix" is often cited as simply *s* in chapter 2. Sometimes, however, the phonetic differences among the variant sounds have expressive and aesthetic force, and so the actual phonetic value found in the original text is often preserved, most often *s·*. (See the discussion of these sounds in section IV of the article.)

The sequence *kw* represents a voiceless *w*, or whispered labialization of the preceding *k*.

Sapir discriminated a large series of vowels in his *Takelma texts.* It seems clear that there are only a few basic vowels, and Sapir's own comments (1909b:8–9) on some of the sounds contribute to this conclusion. As with Kwakiutl and Haida, then, the writing of vowels has been simplified to the set also used for Chinookan; in these languages, unlike Chinookan, the difference between long and short vowels is significant.

Takelma differs from the other languages represented in this book in having an accent that involves contrastive rise and fall of pitch. Sapir distinguished three accents. He used the acute accent mark ´ for falling pitch. He used the grave accent mark ` for the raised accent found on short vowels or long vowels and dipthongs of a single tone (generally in the last syllable of a word). As Sapir himself observed (1909b:11), this raised accent is "best considered as [an] abbreviated form of the rising accent found only on long vowels and dipthongs," and which he marked with the circumflex, ~ .

In short, there are two contrasting pitches, falling and rising. Sapir's use of the grave mark—commonly used for falling accents—to mark the rising accent in Takelma, and conversely, the acute mark—commonly used for rising accents—to mark Takelma's falling accent must strike us as perverse. That was indeed not the choice of Sapir in his later years, nor is it that of contemporary students of Takelma, such as Shipley and Kendall. We use ´ for rising accent, ` for falling accent. (Note that use of the circumflex accent in the texts implies a long vowel, as well as rising accent.)

Note that the hyphen is used by Sapir to separate vowels that are not part of a dipthong. In *wa-iwi* 'girl', both *a* and *i* have full value, rather than coalescing in a single nucleus, as in the pronunciation of the name of the letter "y" in English. In other words, the Takelma word for girl has three syllables, not two.

Finally, the symbol used to represent the voiceless lateral fricative in the *Takelma texts* (1909b), L, was changed to "barred l," *ł*, in the grammar (1922). The L symbol has been used throughout chapter 2, including the initial quotation from the 1922 grammar.

Haida, Kwakiutl. The alphabet adopted for Chinookan will serve for Haida and Kwakiutl for the most part (chap. 1). For Haida, it is necessary to add two symbols, one for a voiced lateral affricate, which Swanton wrote *Ḷ* (capital L with subposed dot), and one for a palatal nasal stop distinct from *n*, which Swanton wrote *ñ*, and identified also as *ng*. These two sounds can be written with *dL* and *ng*, respectively.

For Kwakiutl, it is necessary to recognize a set of palatal consonants, anterior to *k, g, k', x*, which Boas wrote with a raised single dot after each letter, viz., *k·, g·, k·', x·*. The set is written here with a *y* as mark of the palatalization; indeed Boas (1921:47) observed that "g· and k· sound almost like gy and ky (with consonantic y)." We thus have *ky, gy, k'y, xy*. Kwakiutl, like Haida, has the voiced lateral affricate, written here *dL*. Both languages have both palatal and velar voiceless fricatives, written by Swanton and Boas as *x̣* (x with subposed dot) and *x*, respectively, and written here as *x* and *X*. Both languages have a mid-central vowel, written for Haida with capital *A*, for Kwakiutl with capital *E*, and for both here with capital *E*. It is clear from Boas's comments (e.g., 1921:47), and from later interpretation of his work, that Kwakiutl has far fewer phonemically distinct vowels than Boas recorded phonetically. In particular, the difference between what he wrote as *i* and as *e* does not distinguish words, nor does the analogous difference between *u* and *o*. (The same is true of Swanton's recording of Haida.) The difference between short vowel and long vowel *is* distinctive, and the long vowels usually have the qualities of *e:* and *o:*, as is common on the North Pacific Coast. In the song texts I have retained *i, e, o, u* as Boas and Swanton used them in order to preserve more of the original expressive sound quality. It is assumed that these letters, and /a ä E/ are sufficient. Boas's use of a capped *î* (=I) is equated with plain *i;* his capped *ê* (as in English *fell*) is equated with plain *e;* his capped *ô* (as in German *voll*) is equated with *a;* and his capped *â* with *a:*. His umlauted *ë* is equated with *e:*. Swanton's *A* is rewritten *E*.

PART ONE

UNSUSPECTED DEVICES AND DESIGNS

1

Some North Pacific Coast Poems:
A Problem in Anthropological Philology

Introduction

I wish to call attention to materials and problems that represent a neglected past, and, I believe, a neglected future, for American scholarship. The focus of the paper is upon texts from the Indian cultures of the North Pacific Coast, from a classic period of common cause among folklore, linguistics, and ethnology in the service of a general anthropology; but the problems are relevant to materials elsewhere.[1]

On the American scene, the study of the structure of language is joining effectively again with the study of its use, after a period of relative separation. The full gamut of linguistic structures and their functions in social context is coming to be investigated in ways both structurally adequate and functionally interesting. As part of this, one more often finds an interest in linguistic method and an interest in the content of texts joined together—an interest both in texts as documentation for linguistics, and in linguistics as a source of insight into texts. Such joint interest takes various names and stems from several sources, but for anthropology it is most noticeable in the structural study of myth and in a surge of attention to stylistics and poetics. The volume,

Originally published in the *American Anthropologist* 67:316–41 (1965). Only the literary translation of V is revised here. The original has been reprinted in *Stony Brook* 1/2 (1968): 179–204, and two of the new translations ("Workingman's song," "Song of chief's daughter") have been used in a booklet of poems and statements by Native Americans of British Columbia today, *Solo flight*, ed. by Maurice Gibbons and James B. Southward (Vancouver, B. C.: Resource Publications, 1971). The Schoolcraft translation of the Chippewa song has been reprinted without change in John Bierhorst, *Songs of the Chippewa* (New York: Farrar, Straus and Giroux, 1974).

[1] I am indebted to several people for encouragement in the interest that this paper represents. It was first formulated in "Anthropological texts and some humanist concerns" (an unpublished ms. of 1953), written in the stimulating environment of Indiana University, where folklore, linguistics, and anthropology were joined in the interests of David Bidney, Thomas Sebeok, Stith Thompson, and Carl Voegelin, and first expressed in print in a review (Hymes 1956). More recently, Anne Freedgood, John Hollander, Josephine Miles, James Page, and Gary Snyder have encouraged the particular project of translation from which some first results are given here. Let me also thank Helen Codere, William Fenton, Preston Holder, Morton Levine, Ronald Rohner, Wayne Suttles, and Joyce Wike for stimulating discussion of the version of the paper given at the 63rd annual meetings of the American Anthropological Association in Detroit, 30 November 1964. A study fellowship from the American Council of Learned Societies has contributed to historical perspective.

Style in language, and the varied response it has received, are prime examples of the changing American climate in regard to the latter.[2]

This changing climate is one of many changes now serving to bracket much of the American scholarship from somewhat before until somewhat after the Second World War, from perhaps about 1925 to 1950. To generalize oversimplifies unfairly, but, from the standpoint of linguistics and the other disciplines that can constitute an anthropological philology, that period's dominant attitudes and interests and style of work no longer seem unqualified advances, but in many respects the marks of a period now rapidly becoming historical, some of whose steps were forward, some backward or to the side. The period comes increasingly to seem an interregnum, regarding range, integration, and depth.

The change of climate calls for reexamination of past contributions, so as to clarify the base from which we advance. It has taken a French social anthropologist to dramatize the value of our early resources of Amerindian prose narrative, particularly myth, by relating them to our concern with structure, showing the possibility of novel insights and structural relations.[3] Here I wish to deal with the largely neglected heritage of poetry, or, more accurately, of the verbal component of song, and to show ways that it too may yield new knowledge of structure. In particular, I wish to show that poems may have a structural organization, and "nonsense" vocables,[4] or burdens, a structural function, not hitherto perceived. (For novel structural organization, see especially "Comment" to poems II–V. For the structural function of "nonsense" syllables, see "Comment" to II–IV.)

My general thesis is twofold: our heritage of American Indian poetry must be reanalyzed and reevaluated, and from a linguistic basis, if its contribution to American culture and to an anthropological science of culture is to be achieved with anything like the validity expected of responsible disciplines. Such analysis and evaluation should concern several intersecting activities, those of folklorists, anthropologists, linguists, literary scholars, and poets, and each in turn has something to contribute. Hence the analyses of six North Pacific Coast poems are preceded and followed by discussion intended to

[2]Sebeok (1960) and the review of Francis (1961), Malkiel (1962), Messing (1961), Newman (1962), Riffaterre (1961), Uitti (1961–62).

[3]To so single out Lévi-Strauss (1952, 1956, 1958b, 1960) does not minimize the contributions of Paul Radin and Melville Jacobs, publishing and interpreting their own collections with an emphasis on interpretation couched in psychoanalytic terms in part (for an evaluation of Jacobs's Clackamas Chinook work, see Hymes [1965]). Nor should it be overlooked that fieldwork can still enlarge the resources with valuable result, as instanced by the Seneca work of Wallace Chafe and the Haida work of G. L. Bursill-Hall.

[4]I adopt *vocables* as a technical term from Powers (1960:7, 1961:41) and am indebted to W. C. Sturtevant for calling Powers's articles to my attention. I would rephrase Powers's definition, but the phenomena intended are the same.

relate them to the perspectives of the several activities just named. I begin and end with emphasis upon the place of linguistics in an anthropological philology that may serve the interests of all.

Appreciation (I): Anthologies

In a presidential address to the American Folklore Society, MacEdward Leach (1963) has called attention to the importance, to both scholarship and society, of concern with the appreciation, as well as the collection and analysis, of folkloristic materials. He stresses what should be the interdependence of appreciation and scholarship. Let me consider appreciation of Amerindian poetry first in relation to the setting in which it is most generally experienced by scholar and general public alike, that of the anthology. The two major contemporary anthologies in English are Astrov (1946) and Day (1951). The introductions to both are thoughtful, intelligent reflections of the situation of an anthologist, and likewise a reader, in relation to the available materials.

Astrov (1946:17) concludes her introduction with the observation: "In any case, in reading aboriginal prose and poetry, as it is compiled in this anthology, the reader is at the mercy of the translator, not only for bad but also for good." Elsewhere, however, she can only praise the translators whose results seem best, not indicating any basis for evaluating results other than by appreciation. In particular, independent recourse to the original texts is not mentioned. Astrov does state that the dual requirements, re-creation of the spirit and linguistic fidelity to the letter, have been reconciled by Matthews, Cushing, Brinton, Densmore, Sapir, Spinden, Bunzel and Underhill, "to name only a few" (1946:5). Yet it is doubtful if the letter of the originals was even available for consultation in some cases, not having been published with the translations in the sources upon which the anthology draws. It is doubtful if a knowledge of Navaho, Zuni, Nahuatl, Papago, Nootka, Keresan, Takelma, Tewa, etc., was drawn upon, for there were available no adequate grammars or dictionaries of several of these. Perhaps the word-for-word translations were compared with the poetic translations, a useful procedure, but even that could not have been available in every case. One cannot but suspect that the judgment of mutual recreation and fidelity is based solely on the reader's sense of the English and ethnological appropriateness of the translation, and respect for the linguistic ethnographer, each a redoubtable anthropological name.

Day (1951) goes further than Astrov to give Amerindian poetry its place as part of American literature.[5] He treats the Indian poetry both as something

[5]The place was recognized by Mark Van Doren (1928) in the American section of his *Anthology of world poetry* but has generally been neglected by anthologists of American poetry

to be read as a part of American literature (1951:26–27), and as something that can influence, if indirectly, the writing of it (1951:33). Although he recognizes (1951:18) that: "Judgment as to whether an English version is more or less faithful to the letter and spirit of the Indian original is properly a matter for an expert in linguistics," he must continue: "Since all the first-rate translators are specialists in the Indian dialects of the originals, they can presumably be criticized only by their peers in these studies."

In effect, Day, like Astrov, must fall back upon evaluating the translations by appreciation of their literary merit in English (1951:xi, 26–27), supported by the observation that the best translators from a literary point of view (he gives a somewhat different list: Boas, Brinton, Curtis, Densmore, Fletcher, Matthews, Russell, Spinden, Thalbitzer) were professional students of the Indian (and Eskimo). Although Day has recognized the possibility of an independent control of evaluation by recourse to the originals, he limits its status to that of one criterion among several, and one not primary (Ibid.); perforce, he seems to conclude, appreciation must rule alone. Nor is the possibility of other translations of the same poems, and of a living relation, through fresh translation and study of the originals, to modern poetry, envisaged. While noting the possibility of influence on modern poetry, as cited above, Day describes the influence only as coming through familiarity with translations.

Both anthologists think that something of the original stylistic features can be ascertained from the translations at hand. Astrov (1946:11) states: "I have said that from translations one cannot perceive the particular style of a language. This statement, however, ought to be modified, since the ever-recurring patterns of stylistic expression may be recognized even from translations." Day (1951:23) makes a similar, qualified statement: "Aside from repetition, stylistic devices such as contrast, monotony, variation, abbreviated expressions, poetic diction, parallelism, personification, apostrophe, euphony, and onomatopoeia are found which are used as they are used in European poetry. The best translations preserve a number of these effects, as may be seen in the selections in later chapters. Many patterns may be discovered in Indian poetry, even in translation."

From the passages quoted, and the remainder of the discussions in the two books, a certain consensus of the situation seems to emerge. Much of it is not disputable. The part of concern here can be stated as a set of propositions: (a) the ethnologists who collected the material must be relied upon for the validity of the translations, and can be; (b) literary versions are to be

---

since. See, however, the appreciative essay, focused on the publications of the Bureau of American Ethnology—and particularly the work of Frances Densmore—by Kenneth Rexroth (1961b); the interest of the poet and translator Jerome Rothenberg in his "From a shaman's notebook," including American Indian songs; and the weaving of North Pacific Coast material into the fabric of a set of original poems by Gary Snyder (1960).

preferred to literal ones; (c) the style, or structure, of the originals is accessible in significant part through the best translations.

I think it fair to say that these propositions would be widely assented to among those interested in Amerindian poetry (see discussion of attitude in the section after next). It may be unfair, but it is true, that the most preliminary linguistic study of original texts shows these propositions to be misleading enough to be effectively untrue, as will be shown in the two sections on "Translation and Structure." Neither an understanding of the poetry in its own right, nor a use of it in the development of contemporary poetry, can accept these propositions without qualification. Remarkable works of imagination and beauty, to be sure, have been built with a base in similar sand (for its day, Longfellow's *Hiawatha* is an apt case); but anthropologists cannot expect to deserve respect if scholarship is suspended within their own domain and appreciation alone left to judge. The more's the pity that it is so, because, I believe, the joining of scholarship to appreciation better serves the very ends of aesthetic reward and poetic knowledge that may counsel its suspension.

Translation and Structure (I)

As a preliminary example, let me discuss a poem collected and translated by Henry Schoolcraft, the pioneer ethnographer and afficionado of Amerindian verbal art, a man, indeed, moved to lifelong study of the Indians after experience of the verbal art of one group had awakened him to their humanity. The poem in question is cited by Day (1951:27–28) in full, both for its role as a source of a portion of Longfellow's *Song of Hiawatha* and as source of a pattern of presentation still followed: text, literal translation, literary translation. (The example is also used by Greenway [1964], who makes some of the same points.)

Chant to the Fire-Fly

Chippewa (Ojibwa) (Schoolcraft's orthography is preserved):

Wau wau tay see!	Wau wau tay see!
Wau wau tay see!	Wau wau tay see!
E mow e shin	Was sa koon ain je gun.
Tahe bwau ne baun-e wee!	Was sa koon ain je gun.
Be eghaun—be eghaun—ewee!	

Literal translation:

Flitting-white-fire-insect! waving-white-fire-bug! give me light before I go to bed! give me light before I go to sleep. Come, little dancing white-fire-bug! Come, little flitting white-fire-beast! Light me with your bright white-flame-instrument—your little candle.

Literary translation:

Fire-fly, fire-fly! bright little thing,
Light me to bed, and my song I will sing.
Give me your light, as you fly o'er my head,
That I may merrily go to my bed.
Give me your light o'er the grass as you creep,
That I may joyfully go to my sleep.
Come, little fire-fly, come, little beast—
Come! and I'll make you tomorrow a feast.
Come, little candle that flies as I sing,
Bright little fairy-bug—night's little king;
Come, and I'll dance as you guide me along,
Come, and I'll pay you, my bug, with a song.

Thanks to Schoolcraft's scholarship, we can appreciate in depth how bad his translation is. Almost anyone sharing modern standards and taste, first of all, will prefer the *literal* translation as more satisfactorily poetic, both in what it avoids and in what it contains. Not only does the literal translation lack the supervening padding of the literary translation (nine lines to the twelve of the literary version, the latter an expansion not to express the original adequately, but to add a song, an overhead flight, a creep over grass, a feast on the morrow, night's little king, a dance, a payment, and [intervening] merrily and joyfully); but where both translations parallel the original in content, it is the literal version that is the more concrete. Its specificity of image makes it the better version to an audience familiar with the canons and accomplishments of Pound, Williams, and other giants of twentieth-century American verse. (One may recall Sapir's likening of an Algonquian verb to a tiny Imagist poem, and the interest of some Imagists in Amerindian poetry.)

Second, neither translation conveys the structure of the original accurately. The literal translation is far more faithful than the literary version in form, but it too introduces, if not padding, elegant variation where there is none in the Chippewa text. In the original, lines 1, 2, 6, 7 are constant; all are varied in the translation. Lines 8, 9 are constant in the original, but not even parallel in the literal translation. In line 5 there is internal repetition of which there is no indication in the literal translation. (For an extreme example, changing an identity to contrast within a frame, see a song of the Hako rite of the Pawnee cited by Day [1951:25]. After an initial exclamation, the original song consists of a line repeated six times, while the translation expands each line differently.)

Third, as a consequence of the other two points, most of us, despite Schoolcraft's eminence as a pioneer ethnologist, would wish for a specialist in

Algonquian languages, if not in Ojibwa (Chippewa) itself, to analyze the original text. Even better would be to have the text heard by an informant and redictated and retranscribed, a procedure that has been followed in the case of nineteenth-century Delaware (another Algonquian language) by Voegelin, for Kalapuya (a language of Oregon) by Jacobs, and increasingly by contemporary specialists in such cases, where knowledge of the language, but not of certain valued texts, survives. By such a procedure, the defects of earlier materials in form can be remedied. By ascertaining the actual phonological, grammatical and lexical structure of the texts, modern techniques bring out the full value of earlier enterprise in collection, something like the restoration of older paintings.

Merely on the basis of the information provided by Schoolcraft as to the form of the original text—its points of constancy and variation, repetition and contrast, and as to the literal content—one can do much better by way of an English expression for the Ojibwa song. Without consulting linguistic analysis and information (as I have deliberately restricted myself here), one cannot determine certain points, such as, principally, the content of the repetition and partial lack of repetition in lines 3–5. One can, however, suggest the following as a more adequate tribute to the original:

Chant to the Fire-Fly

Flitting insect of white fire!
Flitting insect of white fire!
Come, give me light before I sleep!
Come, give me light before I sleep!
Flitting insect of white fire!
Flitting insect of white fire!
Light me with your bright white instrument of flame.
Light me with your bright white instrument of flame.

[As a contextual note it could be added that "white-flame-instrument" is apparently a descriptive expression for "candle."][6]

One can perhaps smile and dismiss faults so patent to us in a predecessor of a century ago. Unfortunately, the same faults can occur in the translations from a half century ago on which we are accustomed to rely. The faults may be present in lesser degree, but are still the same in kind. When added to the sheer unavailability of the original texts in many cases, the potential presence of these faults means that the three propositions noted toward the

---

[6]I want to thank Robert Fitzgerald for his interest in this example, expressed during a symposium on translation offered by the two of us as part of the Taft Lectures at the University of Cincinnati, 11 April 1978. At one point he said of the two versions words to the effect that "The difference is that one is a poem and the other isn't."

end of the preceding section cannot be relied upon by either the student or the appreciator of Indian poetry. Ethnologists *often* can be relied upon; literary versions *often* may be better than literal counterparts; structure may *often* be accessible in translation—but how is one to tell *when?* The only way to tell is by independent control of the results of translation, through access to the original texts, and, preferably, to the linguistic aids necessary for their analysis.

Some general implications of the latter point will be discussed in the concluding section "Appreciation II." I turn now to documentation of the statement that faults similar to those of Schoolcraft can be found in the more recent translations on which our anthologies, and, indeed, anthropologists, rely. The documentation also will show something of the gain in structural insight that fresh analysis can give.

Translation and Structure (II): Some North Pacific Coast Examples

The term "structure" is used here because of my belief that the true structure of the original poem is essential to knowledge of it, both ethnological and aesthetic. *By structure, I mean here particularly the form of repetition and variation, of constants and contrasts, in verbal organization.* Such structure is manifest in linguistic form. It does not exhaust the structuring of poems, and in particular may not reveal other kinds of structural relations in their content (e.g., two Japanese haiku might be identical to all appearances in the respects in question, yet one have, and one lack, the "internal comparison," which partitions poems meeting the formal requirements into that which is "true" haiku and that which is not for some Japanese.[7] But such structure is the matrix of the meaning and effect of the poem.

One of the particular results of the analyses is to indicate that in Kwakiutl something usually disregarded, the refrain or so-called "nonsense syllables," is in fact of fundamental importance. The refrain is both structural clue and microcosm.

Each poem is presented in the format of the preceding example: text, literal translation, literary translation (1), comment, literary translation (2).

The six poems presented (and their sources) are:[8]

I.   *Cradle Song* (for boys) (Haida, Swanton [1912:27]—not titled in the original text).

II. *Song of Chief's Daughter* (Kwakiutl, Boas [1921:1314]).

---

[7]See Henderson (1958:81–84), discussing the reputation of the famous woman poet Chiyo.
[8]The original orthographic note has been omitted. See the orthographic note at the beginning of this volume.

III. *Workingman's Song of the TL:tLEGi:d of the q'u:mky'ut'Es for his First-Born Son* (Kwakiutl, Boas [1921:1310]).
IV. *Love Song of the Dead, Heard on Shell Island* (Kwakiutl, Boas [1921:1306–7]).
V. *Song of Salmon* (Kwakiutl, Boas [1897:474–75, 709]).
VI. *Cradle Song* (for boys) (Haida, Swanton [1912:8]—not titled in the original text).

Poems I–IV are test cases, in that they have been reprinted in the major anthologies, so that the versions proposed here in the light of analysis can be used to judge the merit of the position I have taken, and the reassessment I propose, so far as the difference made to appreciation of Amerindian poetry is in question. As for the difference made to valid knowledge of the poetry, I think there can be little or no argument.

Poem V, not anthologized to my knowledge, may stand as a type of the additions to anthologizable, and publicly appreciated, material that structural analysis may provide, if, as seems likely, the song has not been reprinted because its presently published form does not reveal its structure and, hence, its effective power.

Poem VI, also not anthologized to my knowledge, may stand as a type of the additions that purely verbal restatement may provide. There are poems, of which this is one, whose published translations show no major departure from the structure of their original, but for which alternative translations suggest themselves. To offer fresh translations of such poems is to depend upon one's own verbal ability. The translation cannot claim to show significant new structure, but only to show new possibilities of verbal choice and rhythm. For the scholarly argument, such poems are not as significant, but for the possibility of a living relation between Amerindian poetry and new American poetry, such poems loom large. Only if it remains possible to accomplish something of value in new translation, even given accurate structure, can a permanently continuing relation thrive.

The absence of the musical portion of the songs may admittedly be a source of error. It is encouraging that the two recent structural analyses of the relations between text and music in North Pacific Coast songs (Yurok, Robins and McLeod 1956, 1957; Haida, Bursill-Hall 1964) have found precise parallelism at the level of the segmentation of musical and textual phrases, and their organization into the whole. Inspection of Tsimshian songs collected by Barbeau (1951) indicates that in some songs the patterning of the tune (often together with repetition of "nonsense syllables," sometimes with portions of text) is far more complex than the text as printed would indicate (cf. n. 10 below). The printed texts, however, seem intended as lexical abstracts, not as verse structures. As this article goes to press, I have not had the opportunity to hear tape recordings promised me of Kwakiutl song performance. The problem does not appear in the printed songs of Kwakiutl and Haida that I have examined (Boas 1896, 1897). In any case, the choice with the present texts is either to analyze them as texts or do nothing, since no music exists. I believe something useful is gained from their analysis as texts, despite the limitation of considering only part of actual performance.

The Indian language text is as follows:

I. Cradle Song (for boys)

dá:gua Gá:gwaiyá Gá:gwaiyá,
dá:gua Gá:gwaiyá Gá:gwaiyá.
dá:gua Gá:gwaiyá Gá:gwaiyá
sq'aos qa:s gu:stE gua
da gagwaiyá gagwaiyá
da gagwaiyá gagwaiyá.

You-? (whence)-have-been-falling, have-been-falling,
you-? (whence)-have-been-falling, have-been-falling.
you-? have-been-falling have-been-falling
Salmon-berry-bushes top-of from?
you have-been-falling have-been-falling
you have-been-falling have-been-falling.

"Whence have you fallen, have you fallen? Whence have you fallen, have you fallen?
"Did you fall, fall, fall, fall, from the top of the salmon-berry bushes?"

Comment:
The text and translations are printed as punctuated by Swanton, except that the hyphen is used uniformly to indicate English words translating a single Haida word. (Swanton published the literal translation in interlinear fashion under the Haida words.) Swanton did not distinguish all the lines in the original text, but ran together lines 1–2, and lines 4–5–6, capitalizing and placing at left margin only the first, third and fourth lines.

Day (1951:57) prints the literary translation given above. But note that Swanton's literary translation (a) omits one of the three repetitions in the first half of the song; (b) translates essentially the same verbal phrase, when it recurs in the second half of the song, by a different repetition, differently placed. The structure of the original simply is not there. Especially since the poem in question is a cradle song, the exact structure of repetition and variation is significant both aesthetically and ethnograpically. Swanton's second half, in literary translation, has a dynamic thrust in its repetition of four monosyllables hard on one another that is inappropriate and not authenticated.

Literary translation (2):
The structure of the original poem can be carried over, as in the following version. In it, the variation as between the repeated phrases in the two stanzas reflects the change in accentuation and word order in Haida. (Note that Haida *gua* marks the interrogative.)

"From where have you been falling, been falling,
From where have you been falling, been falling,
From where have you been falling, been falling?

The top of the salmonberry bushes, is it from there,
You have been falling, have been falling,
You have been falling, have been falling?"

(This version seems effective to my ear, but perhaps because it is associated with a tune I devised that gives its own rhythmic shape to the second stanza.)

II. Song of Chief's Daughter

1. *wädzEL ya Gwa:tLatLatLEq*
       dzo:dzaEyGEme:ts dze:dzEgyime:ts ye:yqEyatse:
     qaEn tsa:'wEnEmts'e:ts
       qadzEn he:'me:dzEn dza:dzEqe:tLe:
     qaEn dze:dzEqe:ye:
       qEn tsa:'wEnEmtsa
     dzo:gwa ada:tsaXdzEn
       wao:ts'a'atse:ky,
     ha ha aya,
       ha ha aya.
2. *wao:ts'a'atsEntsaXdzEn dzaqe:ky*
       qats GEnEmo:ts
     dzo:dzaEygEme:ts dze:dzEGEme:ts ye:yqEyatse:
       ts'aqwadzEn k'watsaye:tso:kw
     Ge:nEmdza ts'e:ts'Eso:
       dzo:gwa dze:dzEGEmts
     qa yayo:tsdza ada:tsats
       yaqEn tsa:'wEnEmtsa,
     ha ha aya,
       ha ha aya.
3. *Qaxts ya'me:ts GwatLdza*
       yipe:dzas a:da
     qaEn wEtse:dzano:tsE
       qEntso: tLa:yoqtse:yaX tLe:lo:qEyi:tLalXdze:tsa:sdza ada:tsats.

yaqEn tsa:'wEnEmtsa
    qu: wa:wadzEtse:s
Ge:nEmtsa he:mao:matso:q a:datsaq
    yaqEn tsa:'wEnEmtsa,
    ha ha aya,
        ha ha aya.

1. Now-go-on be-ready / princes-of chiefs-of-the tribes / for-my future-husbands / for therefore-I ("I" is actually marked in qadzEn) come that-I make-a-chief / my husband with-this my-father-who-I / his-master, / *ha ha aya ha ha aya.*
2. Master-I-shall come / to-be your-wife / princes-of-the chiefs-of-the tribes. / Coppers-my seat many privileges / and (cf. "with this" [#1]) names / for given-by my-father / to-my husband / *ha ha aya ha ha aya.*
3. For now-it-is finished / plated (*sic*)-by my-mother / for-my belt / when-I take-care-of the-future-house-dishes-of-my father / to-my future-husband / when-he-gives-in-the-marriage-feast many kinds-of-food my-father / to-my future-husband / *ha ha aya ha ha aya.*

1. "Be ready, O chiefs' sons of the tribes! to be my husbands; for I come to make my husband a great chief through my father, for I am mistress, ha ha aya ha ha aya!"
2. "I, mistress, come to be your wife, O princes of the chiefs of the tribes! I am seated on coppers, and have many names and privileges that will be given by my father to my future husband, ha ha aya ha ha aya!"
3. "For my belt has been woven by my mother, which I use when I look after the dishes that will be given as a marriage present by my father to him who shall be my husband, when many kinds of food shall be given in the marriage-feast by my father to him who shall be my husband, ha ha aya ha ha aya!"

Comment:

The original text is not printed here as it was by Boas. Boas grouped the text of the song into three block paragraphs (as numbered here), parallel to those of his translation. The song, however, has a finer structure. The two-part repetition of the refrain suggests an organization within the three blocks into paired lines. Further clues to such organization appear at clear junctures in content. Recurrences of forms occurring at such junctures, and parallels and recurrences throughout the text, can be used as hints for provisional segmentation.[9] On the hypothesis of short binary segments, paralleling the organization

---

[9]Such use of parallels and recurrences to delineate the poetic character of material hitherto handled as prose has a history reaching back at least into the eighteenth century, and linking contemporary anthropology with its antecedents in the Romantic movement. Perhaps the first anthropological exemplar is Herder, whose arrangement of Biblical passages as poetry in *Songs of love* and *The spirit of Hebrew poetry* derives, through Michaelis, from Robert Lowth's *Sacra*

of the refrain, it proves possible to organize the poem as a whole. Each segmentation is justified in terms of parallelism within the poem, recurrence of initial segments or types of segment being the chief key, save for one or two segments isolated only by the segmentation and structure of the rest. The result is supported by the consistency with which the whole can be so interpreted and by an analogous binary structure (although different stanzaically) in another song (Boas 1921:1293).

The refrain, as noted, has on the first level a binary structure in keeping with the rest of the stanza. On a second level, the refrain, *ha ha aya,* consists of three elements, grouped two against one *(ha ha: aya).* The number of elements parallels the number of stanzas (three), and it is possible to find respects in which each possible pair of stanzas goes together in contrast to a third.

I: II, III. The latter two stanzas end with "by my Father / to my husband-to-be," whereas stanza I ends *"with* my Father, / I am his master," pairing daughter and father, as against the father-in-law and son-in-law. Also, II and III both contain reference to "many" (a segment-initial element) and "to be gifts" (II, lines e–f, III, line g, and IIg, IIId, f). Also, II and III alone contain mention of feminine roles (wife [II], mother [III], each in the second line); masculine roles are concentrated in I (6 occurrences [6 out of 8 lines], 5 types: sons of the chiefs, husband-to-be, chief, father, master), whereas II has 4 occurrences of 4 types (master, sons of the chiefs, father, husband-to-be) and III has 4 occurrences of but 2 types (father, husband-to-be). Each stanza does indicate 5 types of roles (counting the feminine types in II and III), and the qualitative difference of the presence of feminine types versus their absence, supplemented by the relative concentration of masculine types, seems decisive.

II: I, III. The latter two stanzas show the "I" of the poem in an active role, although contrasting active dominance ("My making a chief") in I to active but subordinate tending ("when I care") in III; stanza II shows the "I" of the poem in a passive or static role ("to *be* your wife," "sit on copper"). (This contrast is qualified by "As master I'll come" in II, but its future reference lessens its active connotation from that of the "I come" in I preceding. There seems to be no future mark with "take care of" in III.) Also, I and III each begin with a reference to a state of readiness ("now be ready," "now it is finished" [i.e., ready]) as opposed to the absence of such in II.

III: I, II. The latter two stanzas agree in indicating sociopolitical roles and non-subsistence property, although contrasting the highest role, that of

---

poesia Hebraorum (1755). Lowth showed that passages of poetry were distinguishable from the rest of the Biblical text by "an accurate recurrence of clauses" (quoted in Emery Neff, *The poetry of history* [New York: Columbia University Press, 1947], p. 60, q.v.). The context of Herder's work is, of course, the first major movement toward an "emic" perspective in anthropology, associated with notions of the individual genius of each language and people, and hence of the form and content, respectively, of each national poetry.

"chief," alone mentioned in I, to mention as well of copper, privileges, and titles (generally shared by men of rank) in II. In III the references are to domestic and more utilitarian or subsistence property, belt, house dishes, food. (Prestige, of course, accrued to the possession and giving of both kinds of property.) Also, I and II alone contain references to the "I" of the poem as "master," and as coming.

Grouping together the ways in which one stanza stands over against the other two, there is an implicit sequence characterizing the girl. In I, she is identified with her father, not as concerned with gifts of wealth and privilege that link father-in-law and son-in-law, but as concerned or identified with power, as associated with the roles of chief, father, and master. In II, she is passive, and, by possible implication of the contrast to I, III, not herself ready (note that "I come" has been modulated to "I shall come"). In III, she is identified with domestic goods and activities; as not associated with mastery; and as stationary. From I to III, masculine roles decline as feminine roles unfold.

There seems further symbolism, or structure, in the occurrence of *aya* as last element of the refrain. On the hypothesis (suggested first by poem IV) that the *ya* element of a refrain signals the "figure," against a ground represented by the *ha* elements, *ha ha aya* suggests a transition *(a-)* to a culminating *-ya*. Within each stanza, there is suggested an emphasis on the final statement, respectively, ". . . with my father, I am mistress (literally: master)," ". . . gifts by my father to my husband-to-be." ". . . many kinds of food (given by) my father to my husband-to-be." The succession of these final statements, and the succession of the three stanzas as wholes, in terms of their points of contrast analyzed above, go together to suggest a culmination in the third. The status and state as to change of identity, which become figure to ground in stanza III, have, in the structure of both the poem and the refrain, the accent of finality.

It is not suggested that the refrain was consciously designed for the purpose, but rather that on an unconscious level, out of awareness, it reflects the structural principle of the whole, and by its position and concision, gives such structural principle expressively compelling statement.

It must be remembered that the song in question is not sung by the girl child, but sung for and to her by adults using a pronunciation ascribed to children. The values are those of adults, not "out of," but "put in" the mouths of babes. (The phonic effect of the substitutions in pronunciation [Boas meticulously obtained and published the corresponding adult pronunciation] is one of much recurrence of substituted syllables with *dz-* plus varied vowels.)

The prose translation given above from Boas is reprinted by Day (1951: 58). The discovered structure (and the translation below to which it gives rise) seems better suited to the context of a song associated with children than do the oratorical periods of the literary translation above. A verse translation following the structure discerned in the original text is as follows:

"Go now, be ready,
   Sons of the chiefs of the tribes,
My husbands-to-be,
   For I come for that,
My making a chief
   My husband-to-be,
And with my father,
   I am his master,
ha ha aya,
   ha ha aya.

As master I'll come,
   To be your wife,
Sons of the chiefs of the tribes.
   On copper I sit,
Many the privileges,
   And with titles,
To be gifts by my father
   To my husband-to-be,
ha ha aya,
   ha ha aya.

For now it is finished,
   Braided by my mother,
To be my belt,
   When I care for the dishes to be gifts by my father
To my husband-to-be,
   When in the wedding-feast he gives
Many kinds of food, my father,
   To my husband-to-be,
ha ha aya,
   ha ha aya."

III. Workingman's Song of the TLi:tLEGi:d of the q'u:mky'utyEs for his First-Born Son.

1.   *hants'e:noqwi'lakwe:ky la:qEn gya:q'e:na'ye:*
     bEgwa:nEmts'e:da dask'wä, ya ha ha ha.

2.   *a:le:winuqwi'lakwe:ky la:qEn gya:q'e:na'ye:*
     bEgwa:nEmts'e:da dask'wä, ya ha ha ha.

3.   *le:q'e:noqwi'lakwe:ky la:qEn gya:g'e:na'ye:*
     bEgwa:nEmtsqe:da dask'wä, ya ha ha ha.

4.   *Lats'ae:noqwi'lakwe:ky la:qEn gyaq'e:na'ye:*
     bEgwa:nEmts'e:da dask'wä, ya ha ha ha.

5.   *e:aqElae:noqwi'tLEky la:qEn gya:q'e:na'ye:*
     bEgwa:nEmts'e:da dask'wä, ya ha ha ha.

6.   *qats ky'eatse:tso:s tsa:yakwe:yatso:s yaqe:s*
     'na:kwatsao:s aqe:qs dEso:tso:s dask'wä,
       ya ha ha ha.

1.   Born-to-be-a-hunter at-my becoming a-man, Father, *ya ha ha ha.*
2.   Born-to-be-a-spearsman at-my becoming a-man, Father, *ya ha ha ha.*
3.   Born-to-be-a-canoe-builder at-my becoming a-man, Father, *ya ha ha ha.*
4.   Born-to-be-a-board-splitter at-my becoming a-man, Father, *ya ha ha ha.*

5.   Will-be-a-worker at-my becoming a-man, Father, *ya ha ha ha.*
6.   That-you you-will-nothing need of all you wanted-by-you, Father, *ya ha ha ha.*

1.   "When I am a man, I shall be a hunter, O father! *ya ha ha ha!*"
2.   "When I am a man, I shall be a harpooneer, O father! *ya ha ha ha!*"
3.   "When I am a man, I shall be a canoe-builder, O father! *ya ha ha ha!*"
4.   "When I am a man, I shall be a board-maker, O father! *ya ha ha ha!*"
5.   "When I am a man, I shall be a workman, O father! *ya ha ha ha!*"
6.   "That there may be nothing of which you will be in want, O father!
       ya ha ha ha!"

(In Boas [1925], the second clause of each unit begins with "then [I shall]
...."; "carpenter" and "artisan" replace "board-maker" and "workman" in 4
and 5; and 6 becomes "That we may not be in want, O father! *ya ha ha ha!*")

Comment:
The literal translation is more concrete and effective in some lexical
respects: "born to be" versus "I shall be" especially; also, "board-splitter"
versus "carpenter," and perhaps "spearsman" versus "harpooneer." The
choice of "artisan" in the literary translation, as revised in 1925, avoids the
culturally inappropriate associations of "worker," but "craftsman," I think,
may be better. The literary translation reverses the order of the first two
clauses, but the order in the literal translation and original text seems more
effective. Following the original order of the two clauses makes possible following the variation in its content in 5, where "born" does not occur; Boas's
choice of order and words does not seem to permit recognizing the change.
The reiteration of "you" in the inflections of words in 6 seems purposive, and
it would be desirable to reflect it in the translation in some way.
      In terms of structure, each unit (1–6) would seem to be a stanza compris-
ing four segments, two invariable throughout ("Father, / *ya ha ha ha*"), one
invariable through the first five of the six stanzas ("when I become a man"),
one variable within a constant frame through the first five of the six stanzas
("[Born] to be a . . ."). The shift in the sixth stanza from the regularities of
the first two segments seems effective, enhancing by direct address the recurring third segment, which, at the same time, together with the fourth, reas-
serts and maintains the structure of the whole.
      This analysis of the structure is plausible in terms of the clear differences
in content of each of the four segments. The analysis is supported by consideration of the refrain, *ya ha ha ha.* It comprises four elements, one different in
part, three identical. In this it is a direct image of the pattern established in
the first five stanzas, in which the first element varies as against the identical
repetition of the remaining three (as between stanzas, of course, not within).
On the hypothesis that in refrains the *ya* element symbolizes the "figure," the

ha elements the "ground," the structure of stanzas 1–5 is confirmation, and the functional significance of line 1 of stanza 6 is highlighted.

Day (1951:9) follows Boas in citing the poem (in its literary translation) as an example of rhythmic repetition with simple variation. Day uses the modified literary translation of Boas (1925:494), which inserts "then" after the first comma in lines 1–5, changes "board-maker" to "carpenter," "workman" to "artisan," and the sixth line to "that we may not be in want, . . ."

In addition to the comments above, two more should be made. (1) Although the literal "spearsman" could only mean a user of the harpoon in the native context, "harpooneer" is perhaps better to convey the contrast of hunting at sea and on land that is involved. (2) "Boatwright" seems better in rhythm than "canoe-builder" and also in specific force. "Wright" seems to have the advantage of "builder" and the converse advantage of "canoe" may be offset if one knows that "boat" meant originally a hollowed tree trunk. "Canoewright" would combine the best of both, if not too saliently a neologism.

Literary translation (2):

"Born to be a hunter,
      when I become a man,
            Father,
                  Ya ha ha ha.

Born to be a harpooneer,
      when I become a man,
            Father,
                  Ya ha ha ha.

Born to be a boatwright,
      when I become a man,
            Father,
                  Ya ha ha ha.

Born to be a board-splitter,
      when I become a man,
            Father,
                  Ya ha ha ha.

To be a craftsman,
      when I become a man,
            Father,
                  Ya ha ha ha.

That you, you will need nothing,
      of all you want,
            Father,
                  Ya ha ha ha."

IV. Love Song of the Dead, Heard on Shell Island

TLams wayade:yahasgyas wayhadayEwahagyo:sahe: hae:
      gyiya'ya ha ha ye ya ha ha.
TLams a:ladiyahasgyas a:lahadayEwahagyo:sahe: hai:
      gyiya'ya ha ha he ya ha ha.
xgyin yayae:X'ale:se:kygyin nahEnky'aGEmle:heso:tLawa hae:
      gyiya'ya ha ha ye ya ha ha.
'ya o:gEXsa:le:he:stLEhahEn q'wats'e:ne:he:tLa qahahas
      gyiya'ya ha ha ye ya ha ha.

'ya babanaXsa:le:hehe:stLahahEn q'wats'e:ne:he:tLa qahahas
gyiya'ya ha ha ye ya ha ha.

You-are hard-hearted-against-me hard-hearted-against-me (the particle *hai:* is not
rendered) my-dear *ha ha ye ya ha ha.*

You-are really-cruel-against-me really-cruel-against-me-my-dear *ha ha ye ya ha ha.*
For-I get-tired of-waiting-for-you-my-dear *ha ha ye ya ha ha.*
Oh differently-I-shall cry [*sic*] for-you my-dear *ha ha ye ya ha ha.*
Oh going-downward-I-shall shall-cry for-you my-dear *ha ha ye ya ha ha.*

"You are hard-hearted against me, you are hard-hearted against me, my dear,
    ha ha ye ya ha ha!
You are cruel against me, you are cruel against me, my dear, *ha ha ye ya ha ha!*
For I am tired of waiting for you to come here, my dear, *ha ha ye ya ha ha!*
Now I shall cry differently on your account, my dear, *ha ha ye ya ha ha!*
Ah, I shall go down to the lower world, there I shall cry for you, my dear, *ha ha
    ye ya ha ha!*"

Comment:
There are several points of difference between the three versions above.
They become significant principally in the light of fresh possibilities of translation suggested by a hypothesis as to the structure. To indicate them: the
identical repetition in the literary translation of lines (stanzas) 1 and 2 above
is not identical in Kwakiutl, where "You are" occurs only initially. "Really"
(-gyas) is omitted from the literary translation of 1 and 2 (and the literal
translation of 1). "To come here" and "to the lower world" are not in the
literal translations of 4 and 5, but seem added as explanation. The literal
translation of the same form in 4 and 5 leaves its character uncertain, but the
-tL in the ending of *q'wats'i:ni:hi:tLa* is presumably a mark of the future in
both occurrences. *'ya* is rendered "oh" in the literal translation, but neither
as that, nor as the same thing, in its two occurrences initially in 4 and 5.

Despite the presentation of the five parts of the poem as each a single
extended line (Boas 1921), each part can be considered a stanza. The justification is a hypothesis as to the structure of the poem, a structure mirrored on
three levels, that of the poem, of the stanza, and of the refrain.

In terms of content and repetition, the *poem* is organized in three parts:
A(1, 2), B(3), C(4, 5), of which the second, or B part, is the pivot. Stanzas
1 and 2, and 4 and 5, are alike in that there is repetition within each, between
the initial portions, as against 3.

As the second literary translation below brings out, each *stanza* also is
organized in three parts: A(lines 1, 2), B(line 3), C(line 4), of which the B part
is again the pivot. Again, also, the A and C parts show repetition internally,
as against B.

Finally, the *refrain* itself is organized in three parts: A (ha ha), B (ye ya), C (ha ha), of which the B part can be considered the pivot. The A and C parts show repetition (here, identity) as against B. If the repetition of initial consonant in B (ye ya) is compared to the nonidentical repetition on the stanza and whole poem levels, it remains the case that the *pattern* of (A, C): (B) is maintained in the refrain by the relative difference of identity: partial repetition. The intensification and compression of the structural pattern within the refrain into a single line and syllables may itself be a matter of functional significance for the poem as a whole.[10]

Literary translation (2):

The first literary translation, given above before the Comment, is reprinted by both Day (1951:54) and Astrov (1946:280).

In the light of the above specific comments and structural analysis, the following translation may be more satisfactory both as a poem and as evidence

[10]An analogous refrain pattern occurs in songs 3 and 4, each a "Doctor dance song," in the excellent paper by R. H. Robins and Norman McLeod (1956). A case can be made that the fourfold pattern of the closing refrain, *hahahaha*, does match the structure analyzed for song 3 (I have noted the details which support such an interpretation in a letter to Dr. Robins (25 Sept. 1964); but no such case can be plausibly made for Song 4. Moreover, as Robins and McLeod point out, similar syllable groups occur in songs of the "Bird" series among the Yuman and Mohave. Yurok music falls within the area of the Yuman style as defined by Herzog. Robins and McLeod suggest that the refrain feature may have traveled independently of music in shaman formulas, citing a Yurok formula from Kroeber (in which the formula occurs at the beginning, not end). The Yurok occurrence of such formulas, then, is limited to shamanistic contexts, possibly borrowed, lacking in internal structure of the sort found with Kwakiutl (with opposed elements in both h- and y-), and almost certainly not related to the internal structure of the song as a whole in one of the two known cases, only possibly so in the other. Having reviewed the evidence for the possibility, Dr. Robins does not think "that any connection can be established between the textual structure of Yurok songs and the sequence of 'nonsense' syllables that occur at the end of the doctor dance songs, of which type of song in Yurok they are characteristic." Calling attention to the use of such syllables at the beginning of a ritual formula, Dr. Robins writes: "This is, I think, the essence of these syllable sequences in Yurok, formulaic in nature, rather than linked in *internal* structure to the composition of the rest of the song" (personal communication, 2 Oct. 1964).

In sum, the structural relationship between final refrain and the rest of a song, shown here for Kwakiutl, is not general. Whether or not it is specific to Kwakiutl remains to be seen.

Two Haida songs analyzed by Bursill-Hall (1964) on the model of the Yurok analyses of Robins and McLeod show diversity and complexity of patterning of vocables. In the first Haida song the vocables occur in somewhat modified forms of the same pattern at the beginning, middle, and end, not, as in the Kwakiutl songs here analyzed, at the end of each part. Bursill-Hall's concern is with the parallelism between text and music, but in personal communication he makes the important point that "the Haida themselves noted intuitively that it (the patterning of vocables) was to give the rhythm and *form* of the song." Bursill-Hall had himself suspected a structural role for the vocables from the music, and remarks that the slight but very important deviations from the pattern imply a formal principle at work. The exact pattern and structural role are not yet clear to either of us but seem certain to differ from the Kwakiutl cases in some respects.

of Kwakiutl poetics. (In point of fact, the translation was completed first, on the basis of hints from the specific details cited, and a desire to achieve something of an appropriate tone. Only sometime after the translation did the principle of examining the refrain for structural clues, added to recognition of the pivotal role of the middle stanza, bring the full hypothesis of structure to light.)

"You are hard-hearted against me,
　　hard-hearted against me,
　　　my dear,
　　　　ha ha ye ya ha ha.

For I get tired,
　　waiting for you,
　　　my dear,
　　　　ha ha ye ya ha ha.

You are really cruel against me,
　　really cruel against me,
　　　my dear,
　　　　ha ha ye ya ha ha.

O differently I'll
　　cry for you, I shall,
　　　my dear,
　　　　ha ha ye ya ha ha.

O going down I'll
　　cry for you, I shall,
　　　my dear,
　　　　ha ha ye ya ha ha."

V. Song of Salmon

1.　*gye:gyáXs'aisEla yu:Xdenó:guas meme:o:xoa:nakyasde:.*
2.　*hálaqas gyágya:Xa:lagyilisi:ilu:tL qáldu:yu:wi:'s lúwa.*
　　haiuxs'aisElagyilitsEmxtEm núguas mimi:u:xua:nakyasdi:.
3.　*hálaqais haiXuanu:magyailutLai hi:itLgyu:tmi: is lúwa.*
　　TLitLaxuya máya:tLas aiXyts'umkyi:yatLi:xdis
　　mimi:u:nakyasdi:.

1.　Many-are-coming-ashore they-with-me salmon-real-past.
2.　For-they come-ashore-to-you post-in-middle-of heaven. Dancing-from-the-outside-to-the-shore-with me the-salmon-real-past.
3.　For-they come-to-dance-to-you at-the-right-side-of-the-face of heaven. Overtowering surpassing outshining the-salmon-real-past.

1.　"Many salmon are coming ashore with me."
2.　"They are coming ashore to you, the post of our heaven."
3.　"They are dancing from the salmon's country to the shore."
4.　"I come to dance before you at the right-hand side of the world, overtowering, outshining, surpassing all; I, the salmon."

Comment:

Although the text is printed in three units, the formal translation in four, an inspection of the text shows that the recurrence of the final segments, "salmon-real-past" and "heaven (world)," organizes the poem into *five* units. In the original text the identification with the "ur-" salmon by the singer is subordinated to the coming and character of the salmon themselves; the "I" come to dance, and "I the salmon," of the literary translation are not apparent in the text. Perhaps Boas supplied them because the song accompanies a dance in which the singer imitates the motion of jumping salmon (Boas [1897:475] describes the context of the song). The order of the descriptive terms in line 5 is altered in the formal translation.

This song symbolizes in many ways the North Pacific Coast as a whole. Its culture, so remarkable and unrivalled among hunting-and-gathering peoples, depended for its richness on the sea, and especially the salmon; and with all its relative wealth and status-consciousness, the culture of the area retained its primitive sense of concreteness and of participant maintenance in relation to nature and gods. (The beliefs reflected in the song are perhaps also those reflected in a song in Chinook Jargon, told me by David French, which can be put in English as: "There is a land of light, / Far away, always light, / And from there the waters shine, / And from there the salmon come.")

Literary translation (2):

The formal translation published by Boas in 1897 did not attempt a poem, but one can be discerned. Parallelism suggests that the first two units form one stanza, the second two another. The first pair of units with "salmon-real-past" and "heaven" are linked in terms of "coming ashore." The second pair of such units are linked in terms of "dancing." The fifth unit, the third occurrence of "salmon-real-past" has an internal pattern of its own. Each of the resulting stanzas has four elements. The result seems more faithful and more effective. It has three parts overall, as did Boas's presentation, but a different three parts.

> "Many are coming ashore, they with me,
> > the true salmon that were.
> For they come ashore to you,
> > to the post at the center of the heavens.

> "Dancing from the far side ashore with me,
> > the true salmon that were,
> For they come to dance to you,
> > at the right side of the face of the heavens.

"Overtowering,
   surpassing,
      outshining,
         the true salmon that were."

VI. Cradle Song (for boys)

hao gí:na GE+n dEng ijagá:jí:was é:ji.
hao gí:na GE+n dEng i:jagá:jí:was é:ji.
NEngkilstLas agEng índatLXagá:GEni.
Skils naGá:ga ku:skíndias é:ji, wEstE Q'akún-gwi ga-iL gagáng
   dEngaL tLju:dal.
Gwa-iskún Xa:idEgaEi XEnhao dEng ná:Ga LkiésiGei gut gut
   guntL'gEndias é:ji.
Hao gí:na GE+n dEng i:jagá:jí:was é:ji.

"This thing for you sitting-as-a-boy are.
This thing for you sitting-as-a-boy are.
NEngkilstLas himself made-a-human-being.
Property in-the-house was, from-it Rose-Spit-towards (lit., "North-Point-towards"-DH) his-flood with tidal-wave-went.
North-Island (lit., "Island-point"-DH) people even your house towards-the-door are-as-many-as-when-waves-meet-each-other-and-are-packed-close-together.
This thing for you sitting-as-a-boy are."

"This is why you are a boy.
This is why you are a boy.
NEngkilstLas has become a human being.
From the property in his house a flood went out toward Rose Spit.
Even from North Island the people are crowded into your house, as when waves meet and are packed together.
That is why you are a boy."

Comment:

Lines 1, 2, 6 are identical in Haida, but the first word becomes "That" in line 6 in the literary translation. The concreteness of the Haida lines (1, 2, 6) is not carried over, but could be. The literary translation of line 3 conceals the sense of reincarnation of a dead ancestor. (The name means literally, "One whose voice is obeyed," or, "the-person-who-accomplished-things-by-his-words, that is, the Creator, Raven," according to Swanton's sketch of Haida grammar [1911:242, 275].) The change in the literary translation of "his flood" (line 4) to "a flood" loses some of the specificity of the metaphor. The end of line 5 paraphrases and explains the Haida verb, for which there is no easy English equivalent; the rhythm at least could be improved.

One point of structure does emerge. The recurrence of the sentence-final verb form *é·ji* indicates a structure of seven lines, rather than the six of Swanton's version, for the same verb form recurs within what Swanton treats as unit 4. Denoting lines ending in *é·ji* with (a), and lines with other endings with (b), the structure of the poem is: a a b a b a a. The sixth line is considerably longer than the others, twice the average syllable length, but shows no apparent internal segmentation, and syntactically parallels (with expansion) line 4. The increasing length of line 5, then of line 6, can be interpreted as a swelling of the pulse of the poem symbolic of the swelling of wealth being described, but brought back within the structural frame by the final line, which repeats what has been established by repetition at the beginning.

The song is part of a sequence, sung at potlatches. In effect, the child is said to be born to give great potlatches, as if the great *NEngkiLsTLas* were reborn. His property is like the flood raised in the time of N., and people must crowd his house like waves. Both images testify to his greatness, and, derivatively, to that of his kin.

Literary translation (2):

> "It is for this you sit a boy.
> It is for this you sit a boy.
> NEngkilsTLas himself is born again.
> In the house was property,
> From it, towards Rose Spit,
> > his flood went a tidal wave.
> From North Island even,
> > people crowd your house to the door,
> > as many converging, compacted waves.
> It is for this you sit a boy."

(An alternative rendering of line 3 of the original, but departing from the original structure by requiring two lines, would translate the proper name, e.g., "One-whose-voice-is-obeyed, himself, / Again is born a human being.")

Appreciation (II): Attitudes and Prospects

In some quarters, appreciation of American Indian poetry has at present a strange, almost schizophrenic, quality. It insists on authenticity, but not on the original texts. It sees and values poetry as expression of Indian cultures, but in material that often is itself poor poetry or not poems at all.

There have been notable exceptions, but ethnologists and poets alike often share an attitude, such that a proper concern for objectivity and authenticity is improperly directed, displaced from the native poets and their native language texts onto the translations and the ethnologists. The qualities that American Indian poetry may have for us are frozen there. Why?

There are three reasons, I think, not all held by all, but mutually reinforcing within the society as a whole. First, the poems tend to be valued as outcroppings of a pristine primitivity, cherished just because responded to as something natural and unaltered. The idea of conscious tampering is abhorred without much regard to what exactly it is proposed to tamper with. One wants to take the poems as found, like natural objects generally, as not having any part of us. Although there have been some serious studies, such are few. One mistrusts poets perhaps, as artificers, but is willing to take ethnologists as impersonal transmitters, or as personally assimilated to that which they transmit.

Second, as a consequence of the first, the poems tend not to be truly perceived as poems. What is asked of poems within our own poetry is not consciously asked of them (although it unconsciously may condition appreciation). It is almost enough that they be Indian, authentic, recognizably representative of Indian themes. Verbally, there is a minimum standard of presentableness to be met, to be sure, and verbal aptness, poetic effect, as judged by contemporary standards for contemporary poems, are valued. But they are not demanded. To be authentically Indian is to be given the benefit of the poetic doubt for the sake of other values ascribed to the text.

Third, and in some ways the necessary condition of the perpetuation of the whole, there is no continuing tradition of philology in most of the languages in which the poems exist. Appreciators, including anthologists, are willy-nilly forced to rely upon and rationalize the uncritical use of whatever English the ethnologists have provided. Even if they would, they cannot usually go behind the English to the original by means of adequate grammatical analyses and dictionaries. True, much can be done merely by scrutiny of literal translations and observation of patent repetitions in the structure of the original texts, as has been illustrated in the preceding section. To raise the question of alternatives to the printed translations, however, is to jeopardize the fabric of appreciation. In the absence of an adequate philology for the languages, nothing like the apprenticeship of translation known to so many poets is possible with the American Indian poetry. The poems being cut off, then, from a living place in contemporary poetry by lack of linguistics, the fabric of appreciation cannot raise linguistic questions. Without linguistics as an active part of philology, the poems themselves disappear behind the veils of primitivity and preconception, which we don to approach them. We approach, indeed, not the poems at all, but the ethnological translations. It is these our museum-like anthologies enshrine. There is little else, for now, they can do.

With regard to the first component of attitude above, we have seen that it is a mark of naïveté, not objectivity, to identify authenticity and pristineness with the ethnological translations. To say so is not to fault the ethnologists. In particular, the comments to the poems in the preceding section are not intended as criticism of Boas. Quite the contrary. It is with Boas's materials, and few others, that it is at present possible to work. His standards of careful checking of texts, of insistence upon collecting material in native text and of publishing it in full, and his ability and effectiveness in publishing linguistic descriptions as well, are at once the essential minimum without which nothing could now be done, and a minimum not many have achieved. In the period in which first Boas established and carried through his standards for philological work, and from which the materials here utilized stem, he had no peer in American anthropology for the quality and responsibility of his work, save his students Sapir and Radin. He has had far too few peers since. Rather, it is that the present period can add one dimension to the tradition he exemplified. To the recording of texts as massive documentation, with linguistics as a means to the ends of ethnography and aesthetic appreciation, we can now add, materials being favorable, the influence of structural linguistics on our ability to perceive poetic structure.

What is objective, in short, is the native text itself, where this has been adequately recorded, a text perhaps subject to multiple interpretations in its own culture. The translation is an act of scholarship of a certain time, place, and person, variable in quality and character, as is all scholarship. As in all philology, new interpretations are possible, especially when new points of view and method emerge. There is no law that the first to examine a text exhausts it. Indeed, as can be argued in principle and supported from experience, a literary text is an open document, susceptible of different interpretation as the audience of interpreters differs, a document not necessarily exhausted by any one interpretation, but quite possibly enriched by many or all. Validity and interpretation have two aspects, the source and the receiver, and the exigencies of translation are such that any one translation is like a spotlight from one angle, highlighting some features, but shadowing others. A plurality of responsible translations can illumine more and in greater depth. All this, indeed, is obvious enough in respect to almost every literature and audience, save perhaps American Indian poetry among some anthropologists and poets.

With regard to the second component of attitude above, the consequence of special standards and of lack of a continuing relationship of translation is that the poems are fixed in the literary garb of the period in which the ethnologist worked, and of the ethnologist himself. In the case of Boas, it is the formal English of a native speaker of German trained in the third quarter of the nineteenth century. The reader who approaches the English versions without preconceived sympathy and suspension of verbal standards shares the lot of the student who is asked to believe, or act as if he believes, that certain Greeks wrote great dramatic poems, although what is before him in class is not a great dramatic poem, but English that he finds odd or distasteful or simply ineffective. The contemporary reader now has modern translations of Greek drama by Lattimore, Fitzgerald, Grene, Arrowsmith, and others that are manifestly poems in a contemporary idiom; but for much Amerindian poetry, he has translations from two poetic generations ago, or more, many of which are not even by intention poems, but careful prose. Some of the early translations do still seem unimprovable, notably those by Washington Matthews of Navaho chants, having become classic in their own rights.[11] I hope to have shown, however, that such is not the case for all.

The third component in the attitude described is the crucial one. For the true values of the original structures and content of the poems to be realized, where now obscured, and for verbally effective translations to be newly made, the perspectives and tools of linguistics are indispensable.

One might think that the fact that aesthetically successful translations are recreations is in conflict with the linguistically motivated emphasis on structural analysis and verbal detail characteristic of the preceding section. There might seem to be conflict with an attitude such as the following:

> . . . the problem, in a sense, is not one of "writing" but one of "visualizing." I have found this to be very true of Chinese poetry translation. I get the verbal meaning into mind as clear as I can, but then make an enormous effort of visualization, to "see" what the poem says, nonlinguistically, like a movie in my mind; and to feel it. If I can do this (and much of the time the poem eludes this effort) then I write the scene down in English. It is not a translation of the words, it is the same poem in a different language, allowing for the peculiar distortions of my own vision —but keeping it straight as possible. If I can do this to a poem the translation is uniformly successful, and is generally well received by scholars and critics. If I can't do this, I can still translate the words, and it may be well received, but it doesn't feel like it should.[12]

The question is in fact one, not of conflict, but of sequence and division of labor. As Snyder points out in the same communication, the recreation of a poem also requires, for knowledge of the verbal meaning of the text, the sort of materials that a linguistically-motivated approach puts in focus. In the present state of Amerindian texts, these materials have two necessary dimen-

---

[11]Goddard (1907:24) already observed shortly after Matthews's death prevented his completion of work for publication in that series, "It is needless to say that the free translations are the unimprovable work of the author (Matthews)."

[12]A personal communication from Gary Snyder, whose translations of the Chinese Han Shan poems have been praised as superior to those of Waley and others. Snyder has himself an intimate knowledge of the North Pacific Coast oral literature, as evidenced in the poems cited in n. 5, and in his Reed College dissertation, *"Dimensions of a myth"* (1951), a study in multiple perspectives on a Haida myth.

sions. Even minimal knowledge of verbal meaning requires the original texts in published form, interlinear translation, and some sort of usable grammar and dictionary, as checks on interlinear translation and on alternative renderings. (Preferably, the text itself would be morphemically analyzed.) Given these materials, a talented and sympathetic translator can do much, and with most Amerindian poetry, the most one can expect in a living tradition of translation is philological recognition of the original, not bilingual control.[13] There is a second dimension as well, as the present paper has shown. For most Amerindian materials, an anthropological philology must provide analysis not only on the linguistic level, but on the level of metrics, or poetics, too. Formal structure of the sort set forth in the preceding section is as necessary as grammar and dictionary to the recognition of the verbal meaning of the original, for it is intrinsic to what in fact happens in the poem, to what there is to be felt in the verbal meaning. In its ritual-like function, a pattern of repetition is a pattern of insistence.[14]

For any body of Amerindian poetry, then, the two approaches to translation just sketched can be complementary, each contributing to the other. What may be lacking, unfortunately, is the contribution on which both must depend, that of anthropological philology. On this score, there has been considerable discontinuity more than cumulative progress since the classic period of Boas, Sapir, Radin, and others. As noted at the outset of this paper, their joint concern with texts and the best available linguistic method, as well as their unanimous insistence that anthropological study of other cultures meet the normal standard of scholarship, linguistic control, have lapsed in many quarters. On the one hand, some of those who concern themselves with the materials of verbal art assert or assume the irrelevance of linguistic control

[13]Cf. Hymes (1956:601–2) (a sample translation to be included there was unfortunately omitted). Rexroth (1961a:19–40) is of interest for the view that philology is a necessary starting point in the study of a language and its literature, but something that must be left behind in most cases for successful translation, sympathy and talent being the requisites. Rexroth goes so far as to argue with examples that the best translations of Chinese poetry are almost wholly mutually exclusive with deep knowledge of Chinese. Cf. also the practice of Rothenberg (1962), whose versions of aboriginal poems are free workings from anthologized French texts and a literal English translation.

[14]With this sort of structure, and the structural significance discovered for refrains in mind, note Rexroth (1961b:57). Having stressed that the texts are mostly extremely simple and in their pure sensibility resemble classical Japanese poetry, Mallarmé, and certain other moderns, Rexroth continues: "It is possible, of course, to say that Miss Densmore greatly simplifies the poem by cutting out repetitions and nonsense vocables. But the Japanese poetry which we think of as so extremely compact on the printed page is similarly sung in extended fashion. Certainly the Indian singer does not feel that he is dulling the poignancy of the transcendental awareness of reality which he is communicating by musical elaboration, but rather the reverse. And, if the song is sung, or the record available, it is immediately apparent that this elaboration is insistence, not diffusion." Cf. also Lévi-Strauss (1955:443; 1963b:229), "The function of repetition is to render the structure of the myth apparent." ("La répétition a une fonction propre, qui est de rendre manifeste la structure du mythe" [1958a:254].)

and analysis to their interpretive interest. Contrary to the experience and standards of scholarship in other fields, the style, content, structure, and functioning of texts seem to be declared "translated" (in the theological sense of the metaphor as well as the linguistic) bodily from their original verbal integument, and available for interpretation without it. Original texts are even declared in a scholarly review in the pages of the *American Anthropologist* to be of concern only to linguists—as if only linguists would mourn the loss of the original texts of Homer or the Bible! On the other hand, those who undertake linguistic description too often pursue it without effective concern for other students of the American Indian, or such fields as comparative poetics, to which American Indian studies should contribute.

The situation is absurd, and it is crippling. No scholarship ignorant of the linguistic foundations of its texts can survive the first breath of rigorous criticism. No American Indian descriptive linguistics that fails to make its material serviceable to general scholarship meets its responsibilities or fairly earns its support. Indeed, a descriptive account that erects *ad hoc* barriers to comprehension vitiates its author's own efforts, for no American Indian grammar today founds a general tradition, or contains such invaluable matter of general interest that a public, linguistic or other, will master all obstacles to gain access. It is not a seller's market, so far as American Indian linguistic accounts are concerned. The price of relevance and audience is clarity, and it is among other students of the American Indian, as much or more than among other linguists, that mutual audience and relevance are to be found.

We must hope that the renewed joining of interests described at the outset of this paper may integrate the study of American Indian languages and the values of American Indian texts more fully, proceeding on the conviction that the study of the languages is too important to be left solely to linguistics (in any narrow sense of the term), the texts too valuable to be interpreted by any who ignore linguistics. We must hope that the Alexandrianism of the one extreme and the shoddy foundations of the other both will be abandoned.

These are hard words, but better hard words within the disciplines concerned than dependence on an infinitely uncritical attitude to forestall criticism from others. In many branches of anthropology today there is an intensified concern with quality of workmanship, partly focused on the use of new tools. The tools of philology are in kind among the oldest the student of human culture knows, but so long as there are texts worth knowing they are indispensable.

Postscript

The project mentioned in note 1 was never completed, although encouraged by an advance from Natural History Press (eventually returned at its request). The parent house, Doubleday, brought out a completed general anthology by Jerome Rothenberg, *Technicians of the sacred* (New York, 1968), and a specific North American anthology, *Shaking the pumpkin* (New York, 1972), by him. New collections and reprints of old appeared almost pell-mell for a few years. Fresh translation was less common, but Rothenberg and Dennis Tedlock gave impetus to an "ethnopoetics" movement by founding the journal *Alcheringa* (now carried on by Tedlock). One part of the original project appeared there, "Masset mourning songs" *Alcheringa* (1972), but preliminary work on Tewa, Eskimo, Mapuche (Araucanian) song texts, and, later, Cherokee chants was not carried through. In 1977/78 I collaborated with Kris Holmes and Charles Bigelow on the translation of short texts (Takelma, and Coos, especially) for an exhibition of Native American verse in calligraphy and especially designed print.

As this book shows, my involvement with verse structure in Native American texts turned, like that of Tedlock, to the apparent "prose" of narrative texts.

Two misunderstandings of the article are perhaps worth noting. First, the manuscript originally was typed in the format of the *Journal of American Folklore* and dedicated to the noted folklorist MacEdward Leach. The then editor of that journal advised omitting mention of Lévi-Strauss (that would only embarrass me, he said) and required a reduction of about 50 percent that would have left the nature of the analysis underlying the results unintelligible. I should not have been surprised, since that editor had stated in a book of his own his low opinion of the literary accomplishments of the first peoples of the New World. One motive for work such as this is to show such prejudice, or misperception, to be wrong.

Second, the author of an article of cross-cultural parallels in the metric of children's verse found these results faulty for not dealing with meter (Burling, 1966:1440, n. 16). It should be clear that "meter" in the conventional sense is not involved, either in these song-texts or in the narratives to follow. The concern is with the recognition and relationships of lines. The very point of the analyses is that the lines are not defined by the kinds of phonological regularity we conventionally think of as "metrical" (see Hymes 1960). Sung or spoken recordings would indeed be invaluable additions to what can be learned from transcriptions of words alone. Without music, pauses, intonations, we do not know the integration of the performance that constituted the real event. We can, however, know the patterning of lines as one autonomous component.

Recently David McAllester has stated with regard to this article (McAllester and McAllester 1980:17):

> I agree with the principle . . . that vocables are by no means mere "nonsense syllables," but are an integral part of American Indian poetic style. Hymes pointed out that in Kwakiutl songs from the Northwest Coast vocabilic introductions prefigured in microcosm the structure of

the poem as a whole. The same thing may be seen in Navajo song texts [citing McAllester 1980].

The Kwakiutl microcosms, of course, *follow* the song text rather than precede it, but the structural relationship between vocables and text remains. McAllester notes that other principles of patterning in Navajo vocables have been analyzed by Frisbie, who has recently contributed an important review of the general problem and literature for North America, as well as Navajo (1980). An upsurge of interest is attested also by Hinton (1980).

Masset children's songs and other songs can be heard now on a record, *Gawa sGalaangaa* (Songs from Massett), produced and partly recorded by J. Enrico, and available from Queen Charlotte Island Museum, Second Beach Skidgate, Queen Charlotte, B.C., Canada. (The capital *G* here substitutes for the lower case *g* with a bar through the tail in Masset orthography.)

2

How to Talk Like a Bear in Takelma

I

In his great Takelma grammar, Edward Sapir made a statement that has been cited a number of times in the half-century since its publication (1922:8, n. 2):

> In the myths, *L* is freely prefixed to any word spoken by the bear. Its uneuphonious character is evidently intended to match the coarseness of the bear, and for this quasi-rhetorical purpose, it was doubtless derisively borrowed from the neighboring Athapascan languages, in which it occurs with great frequency. The prefixed sibilant *s·* serves in a similar way as a sort of sneezing adjunct to indicate the speech of the coyote. *Gwidi* where? says the ordinary mortal; *Lgwidi*, the bear; *s· gwidi*, the coyote.

Sapir also comments twice in the published *Takelma texts* (1909b). In the key to the phonetic system, *L* is listed with the remark: "voiceless palatalized *l*. Common in many Pacific Coast languages, but in Takelma it occurs only in interjections and as inorganic consonant in Grizzly Bear's speech" (1909b:10). And again, as a footnote to an occurrence of *L* in the myth of "Grizzly Bear and Black Bear" (the Takelma version of a widespread myth, known comparatively as "Bear and Deer"): "*L-* is a characteristic, intrinsically meaningless 'grizzly-bear prefix' in the same sense in which *s· -* is a 'coyote prefix'. *L-* does not occur as a normal Takelma sound, though its use as such in the neighboring Athabascan dialects is very frequent" (1909b:118, n. 2).

Sapir himself later referred to the Takelma finding in a discussion of expressive characteristics of Native American oral tradition: "Thus in Takelma we find that Coyote almost regularly begins his sentences or words with a

Originally published in *International Journal of American Linguistics* 45(2):101–6. This chapter is considerably revised from the original publication (Hymes 1979). The changes flow principally from discovery of a use of the *s-* prefix by the Bear brothers in "Eagle and the Grizzly Bears," a use that had been overlooked. The consequent need to revise various statements has provided an opportunity to refine and extend the analysis. In preparing an explanation of the Takelma orthography for this volume (see introductory note), I have noticed the differentiation and progression in the use of the *s-* prefix that is described in IV of this revision. Needless to say, both discoveries reinforce the original argument.

meaningless *s*- or *c*- *(s)*, while Grizzly-Bear uses in parallel fashion an *L* [*ł*],
a sound not otherwise made use of in Takelma" (1910:455–72).[1]
Unfortunately, these statements with regard to Bear, or Grizzly Bear, are
incorrect. A reading of *Takelma texts* shows (1) that the voiceless lateral does
not uniquely distinguish Bear from Coyote; (2) that it does not distinguish all
Bears, or even all Grizzly Bears, and certainly not in parallel fashion to the
"coyote prefix"; and (3) that it is not used "freely."

II

The myth texts show Coyote's speech to begin with the *s*- prefix rather
freely, to be sure. The speech of a Bear actor can begin with *s*- also. In the
myth "Coyote goes courting," the Brown Bear *(Mená)* hears words sung at
a puberty dance which refer to his anus.[2] He comes to the dance, and when
he arrives, utters the apparently threatening refrain associated with Bears, *hau
hau hau hau*, preceding the first *hau* with *s*- (Sapir 1909b:107). Again, in the
myth "Grizzly Bear and Black Bear," Grizzly Bear Woman prefixes the *s*- to
one of her calls, "*S*-come back, *S*- come back" (Ibid.:121). Finally, in the myth
"Eagle and the Grizzly Bears," the ten Grizzly Bear brothers once use *s*- when
they discover Eagle's presence by direct sight: "*S*-didn't I tell you, for that
reason they have not been eating people, I told you? Now they talked to one
another . . ." (Ibid.:137, line 10).
Neither prefix is used by all Bears, or even all Grizzly Bears. In the myth
"Coyote goes courting," the male Grizzly Bear comes to the puberty dance
after Brown Bear. His coming is perceived as a danger. Some girls try to stop
the singing, but to no avail; when he arrives, he jumps among them. (They
all fly up and no one is killed.) This male Grizzly Bear is twice heard to utter
"Hau hau hau hau" but without any prefix. Again, in the fine myth of "Eagle
and the Grizzly Bears" the adult Grizzly Bear Girl—a principal protagonist
—uses *"hau"* six times, when, at the end of the story (Ibid.:141, lines 17–18),
she has become threatening to Eagle; but she does not use an expressive prefix,
then or elsewhere.
Bear actors that use an expressive prefix do not do so freely. The *L*- prefix
is in fact used just twice, so far as I have been able to determine. In "Eagle
and the Grizzly Bears" the parents of Grizzly Bear Girl—Old Man Grizzly
Bear and his wife—are represented as using the *L*- prefix to each other the
first time they speak: "Are not your teeth sharp?", *L*- being prefixed to "your

---

[1]Cf. Sapir (1915, n. 11). This reference and the one to Sapir (1910) can be found on pp.
186 and 466, respectively, in Mandelbaum (1949).
[2]An eastern Canadian trickster myth says that bears eat in seclusion because of self-
consciousness about lack of hair on their rears. (I am indebted to Ron Evans for a chance to hear
the story.) A similar belief may be implicit in this song; perhaps Brown Bear's anus is mentioned
because of its visibility due to lack of hair.

teeth" (Ibid.:127, line 24 = facing Takelma p. 126, line 18). When the remark occurs again (Ibid.:131, line 2 = 128, lines 23–24), and in the other six times that the old Bear people speak (Ibid.: 125, line 26; 131, line 26; 133, line 2; 133, line 15; 135, line 25; 135, lines 34–36 through 137, lines 1–2), no expressive prefix occurs.

In "Grizzly Bear and Black Bear," Grizzly Bear (female) speaks normally at the beginning of the myth, when she talks with her companion, Black Bear (female), about going to pick hazelnuts and about hunting for lice in Black Bear's head. It is after she has killed Black Bear that her words have a prefix, all but once L-. Black Bear's children had been warned by their mother that Grizzly Bear might kill her and had been given instructions about what to do in that event. (Black Bear speaks entirely without prefix.) When the acorn pestle falls at home, as their mother had said it would if she were to be killed, they carry out the instructions. They kill Grizzly Bear's children, rip out and roast their livers, leave them in such a way that Grizzly Bear will find and eat them, and escape through a hidden passage. On her return to the house, Grizzly Bear seeks her own children, then, for revenge, Black Bear's children. Her prefixed utterances are short, exclaimed, and concerned · with the location, fate, and again, location of children: "Where are you?" "Come back," "What is the matter?" "So it is my children," "O my liver!" "Where are the orphans?" In the last incident of the text, when she asks Crane to help her cross the river (making no reference to children), there is no prefix in her speech.

In sum, six kinds of Bear actor are named in the existing Takelma myths. Of these, two—the woman Black Bear *(Nihwíkw)* and Grizzly Bear Girl *(Xamk wa-iwi)*—are never presented as speaking with an expressive prefix. One male Grizzly Bear ("Coyote goes courting") is presented without prefix, while a band of ten Grizzly Bear brothers speak without prefix except once ("Eagle and the Grizzly Bears"), using s-. Brown Bear *(Mená)* is introduced as using the expressive particle *s· 'a!,* also used by Coyote, when he first says, "Where are they talking about my anus?", but there is no expressive feature when he repeats the question a few lines later. When he comes to the puberty dance, his *"hau,"* repeated four times, is prefixed the first time with *s·*. Old Man Grizzly Bear *(Xamk lomt'ì:)* and his wife are represented as speaking with *L-* prefix the first of the eight times old grizzly bear people speak ("Eagle and the Grizzly Bears"). The only Bear actor, besides the old couple, to be shown with *L-* prefix is Grizzly Bear Woman. She also is shown with *s-* prefix.

There are no other uses of expressive prefixation for Bear actors in these texts. From this evidence, one might conclude that the *L-* prefix characterizes just those Grizzly Bear actors who are either mature women or old. It seems more likely that in these texts the *L-* prefix and the *s-* prefix are used with Bear actors in those circumstances that make the prefixes appropriate. It seems likely, in other words, that the prefixes do not just stereotype actors, but have specific expressive meanings as well. It may be that the *L-* prefix is appropriate only for Grizzly Bears, but Grizzly Bears use it only when it is appropriate and may use the *s-* prefix when it is more appropriate.

III

We can infer something of the meaning of the prefixes from their placement and from contrasts in their use within a text by several, or the same, actors (from syntagmatic and paradigmatic considerations, as it were).

Given Sapir's reference of *L-* as a "characteristic, intrinsically meaningless 'grizzly-bear prefix'" in the same sense in which *s.-* is a 'coyote prefix'" (Ibid.:118, n. 2), it would appear that his own account of the expressive effect of the prefixes would have to be entirely in terms of secondary association. Being "meaningless," the prefixes could have no force of their own. Their force would have to derive from their association with Grizzly Bear and Coyote, respectively, and perhaps from the nature of an immediate context. When used, a prefix would serve to intensify locally appropriate characteristics already associated with the actor in question. Two footnoted comments to *Takelma texts* help to suggest this view. The first observes: "Coyote is now greatly excited, hence uses the meaningless but characteristic 'coyote prefix' *s-*" (Ibid.:56, n. 2). Again, Sapir remarks: "Coyote speaks with contemptuous irony, hence the 'coyote prefix' *s-*" (Ibid.:61, n. 2). These are the only textual comments that contain terms alluding to a state of the actor, and presumably, an effect of the use of the prefix. Two later notes simply identify "the familiar 'Coyote prefix'" (Ibid.: 87, n. 4) and comment on the position in the verb of "the meaningless 'Coyote prefix' *s-*" (Ibid.:87, n. 6). A grammatical note toward the end of the text on the origin of death (text 9, pp. 99ff, in *Takelma texts,* analyzed in the grammar [1922:293, n. 41] simply observes that "Words spoken by Coyote often begin with *s-*, which has in itself no grammatical significance." Great excitement, and contemptuous irony, of course, are both in character for Coyote.

Attention to the specific placement of the prefixes indicates that the prefixes can have to do, not only with intensification of characteristics of an actor, but also with the architecture of a story. Consideration of contrasts among actors and within texts indicates that the prefixes are not entirely "meaningless," but have an ingredient of expressive appropriateness, such that one or the other can be chosen to fit a certain actor or a certain moment.

Clearly there is an underlying stereotypic characterization of the sort stated by Sapir. Coyote uses only *s-*, and only Bears use *L-*. We have seen that there is more than stereotypic characterization involved, since *s-* is used by Bears as well as Coyote, not all Bears use *L-*, and neither Coyote nor Bears use a prefix all the time. Stereotypic characterization itself is served by voices as well as prefixes. When the ten Grizzly Bear brothers speak (in "Eagle and the Grizzly Bears"), "Each syllable . . . is pronounced heavily and by itself.

It is evidently desired to convey an idea of the lumbering ungainliness of the grizzly bears" (Sapir 1909b:127, n. 5). Against the background of such characterization by voice, the one use of prefix by the brothers clearly is a moment of intensification. It comes near the end of their turns on stage, with a moment of discovery that culminates one sequence and precipitates a confrontation to follow.

Sometimes the use of s- by Coyote seems to be a moment of culmination as well. In two myths having to do with the origin of permanent death, Coyote uses a prefix only at the end of each in a culminating pronouncement (Ibid.: 99, line 8; 100, line 3).

At other times a single use of prefix (or prefixed particle) appears to be an initial framing. Brown Bear only uses s· 'a! and then s· - the first time he utters the words associated with each. Old Man Grizzly Bear and his wife use L- just the first time they speak.

Pervasive use of a prefix, as of s- by Coyote in the myth "Coyote and pitch" (Ibid.: 87ff), seems to go together with pervasive intensification. Coyote is teased, challenged, insulted, generally provoked from the outset and throughout.

The use of both L- and s- by Grizzly Bear Woman ("Grizzly Bear and Black Bear") seems to combine these considerations. The use of any prefix at all comes at a point of intensification: returning, she seeks her children and discovers and responds to their fate. Within this culminating part of the story, the L- prefix appears as a frame within which the switch to s- is a further intensification (see further discussion below).

In sum, the contrast between presence and absence of expressive prefix reflects choice in use. The characterizing effect of the prefixes is invoked at certain points. The resulting intensification sometimes serves as initial framing, sometimes as culmination, sometimes as pervasive characterization, within which a further moment of intensification can occur by change of prefix. The fact of such switching shows that the prefixes have meanings that are not merely arbitrarily connected with stereotyped actors.

The meaning of the expressive particle s· 'a!, used so often by Coyote and once by Brown Bear, may be linked with the meaning of the prefix s· -, also often used by Coyote and once by Brown Bear. Something of lisping, other than full maturity—indeed of childishness—may be suggested by the prefix. Insofar as the range of diminutive meaning is deprecatory, it appears not to be hostile, but patronizing. The full particle, however, may well have an additional source and force.

When Brown Bear uses the particle, he comes to a girl's puberty dance, very likely in the role of an uninvited visitor from another tribe, but not a dangerous visitor (as is Grizzly Bear, who comes next). It seems likely that his first utterance begins with s· 'a because the particle mimics and mocks a common particle of another Oregon language. In Suislaw and Lower Umpqua, two dialects spoken somewhat to the northwest of the Takelma on the Oregon coast (and, one must remember, dialects whose surviving speakers were thrown together with the Takelma on reservations in the nineteenth century), the third-person particle—he, she, it, that one—was transcribed $s^E a$ by Frachtenberg (1914:116), as s followed by a schwa-like release before the vowel a. It was later discovered to have glottalization (Hymes 1966:332, 336) and to be properly transcribed as $s\,'a$. In other words, the Takelma initial exclamation and the Siuslaw particle are identical. Not only is the Siuslaw form itself common, but it also is the initial element and base of all other third-person independent forms (dual, plural, possessive, dative) and two forms for *thus, in that manner*. It seems likely that anyone who heard Siuslaw or Lower Umpqua would hear that form. Given the widespread tendency to imitate and mock the speech of foreigners, discussed by Sapir himself in a pioneering article (1915), it seems plausible that use of the particle carried for the Takelma the connotation of mocking the speech of certain foreigners.

Recall, of course, Sapir's suggestion that the *L-* prefix was "doubtless derisively borrowed from the neighboring Athapascan languages." Given the exogenous origin of both prefixes, there is still an unexplained contrast between them. The evidence suggests that the Takelma felt less hostile to the Siuslaw of the coast (quite apart, no doubt, from the two languages being ancient Penutian congeners) than to the Athapaskans. Within a context of mocking foreigners, Athapaskan *L-* seems to have expressed greater distance than Siuslaw *s-*.

Three myths allow us to infer something of the specific expressive meaning of the prefixes from internal contrasts.

In "Coyote goes courting," Brown Bear's use of *s-* before his first *"hau"* seems to agree with use of the particle just discussed and to signal that he himself is not really dangerous but can be safely mocked. He comes to the dance, having heard the words of the song making fun of his anus, and does nothing when he comes. Grizzly Bear has not been mocked by the dancers but comes simply because he has heard the singing. He appears to be motivated by malevolence alone, and his coming is anticipated as a danger by some of the girls, a danger, fortunately, which all escape. Brown Bear attends the dance, Grizzly Bear disrupts it. Grizzly Bear is not mocked, and his *"haus"* are not diminished by a prefix.

In "Eagle and the Grizzly Bears," there is a three-way contrast between zero, *s-*, and *L-*. Grizzly Bear Girl uses no expressive prefix. She is central and, in the end, both dangerous and tragic. Unlike the other Bears, she eats camas and manzanita, not people; she accepts and hides Eagle as a husband and joins with him in getting the old Bears to eat venison instead of human beings; when Eagle is discovered, she kills all her kin to save him. She becomes a dangerous being in the end when Eagle's saying "my father" to welcome his parent, Crane, reminds her that she has destroyed her own father, mother, brothers, for him. The presentation separates her in kind and individuality of motive from the rest. Perhaps in her an identification with real-life predicaments of women in a shattered culture is expressed. In any case, the absence of a stereotyping prefix fits a woman whose presentation leaves conventional characterization of Bear actors in myth somewhat behind.

The girl's younger brothers, the Grizzly Bear sons, are represented as speaking with lumbering ungainliness, clumsiness, through heavy separate syllabification (Sapir 1909b:126–27, nn. 5, 6). They are not individualized, but speak the same lines collectively. The recurrence of the first-person pronoun in their shared lines ("I, for my part"; "I thought"; "I said"; "Didn't I tell you") suggests a chattering, slightly vain, cameraderie. Thus, they enter the stage as follows: "Now they came, talking to one another they came, close they came, talking to one another. "I, for my part, did think it was Phoebus Eagle, shining, shining. 'Catch up with him, catch up with him, kinsman!' said the Grizzly Bears of ten houses, talking with each other, as now, having gone out to war, they returned" (Ibid.:127, lines 3–9).[3]

All this suggests a certain patronizing tone toward the brothers and fits the use of the "coyote prefix" s- with them. Its use comes at a peripety. The ten brothers go out each morning to war against human beings and return each evening with children, innards and private parts, soft food, for the toothless old people of their ten houses to eat. After their older sister has brought Eagle home and hidden him, the brothers return, voicing to each other their suspicion that Eagle has been seen shining at a distance, although a chase by the fastest kinsman among them did not find him. They go out and return, voicing the suspicion, four times. Each time Eagle emerges after they are gone, hunts, and brings back venison for the old people. A long time elapses and the returning brothers now infer and confirm that the old people do not eat what they bring, and do not do so because of Eagle. They go again the next day but only nearby. When their sister takes out her husband Eagle, who goes to bathe as is his wont: "Now they discovered him. 'S- didn't I tell you, for that reason they have not been eating people, I told you?' Now they talked to one another; for that reason right there they were assembled together . . .'" (Ibid.:

---

[3]"Phoebus" is my suggestion for a Takelma word that Sapir leaves untranslated, giving the epithet simply as "Eagle sbèxalta" (1909b:127, 129, 131, 133, 135). Sapir comments: "It is not at all clear what is meant by this word. It is evidently some epithet of Eagle, as indicated by the exclusive suffix -ta" (Ibid.:126, n. 3). In the text the word is followed by the doubled participle "shining, shining," and I think that it contains, or is related to, the two Takelma words for heavenly orbs, bé: "sun, day" and bixál: "moon." (Cf. also p'í: "fire, firewood"). There is some suggestion of an old "moveable s" prefix in comparative Penutian, the language family to which Takelma belongs, although such an element cannot be demonstrated to exist within what vocabulary we have from Takelma itself. The "exclusive" suffix specifies the particular one of a set of mutually exclusive possibilities, and the implied contrast sometimes gives an effect like that of a comparative or superlative. Sapir indeed says that the closest rendering in English is generally a dwelling of the voice on the corresponding English word (1922:246). "Phoebus," then, from the Greek phoibos "bright," used as an epithet of the sun god in "Phoebus Apollo," is a way of rendering what I imagine to have been in Takelma something like "Eagle the-bright-one."

137, lines 12–15). They state their plans, but their subsequent speech is without prefix, as has been their preceding speech.

The one use of s- seems a culmination, expressing excitement in discovery and confirmation, Eagle seen directly. A context of solidarity seems clear as well. No individual speaker is identified. Rather, here as in all the brothers' lines, all lines are associated with them all, talking with each other (Ibid.:127, lines 4, 7; 129, lines 19–23; 131, lines 21–22; 133, lines 11–14; 135, lines 2–3; 135, line 20; 137, line 6; 137, line 14). One senses here, perhaps, a momentary sympathy with the brothers, whose older sister is discovered to have betrayed them with a stranger, leading their aged kin to reject food they so devotedly (if cannibalistically, from a human standpoint) provide. The narrator knows that if pressed, she will for his sake kill them all. An underlying tone of amusement at their somewhat self-assertive, ungainly chatter is no doubt present.

The use of the L- prefix by Old Man Grizzly Bear and his wife seems also to signal something amusing, as well as some quality of denseness or pretense. The prefix occurs only with the word for *teeth*, when the old people exhort each other to sharpen their teeth. A little later the old people are said, in fact, to be without teeth. (That fact goes together with their having customarily been fed the soft parts of humans by the young Grizzly Bear men, and with the way Grizzly Bear Girl and her husband Eagle attempt to change their diet.) Not to know that one has no teeth or to pretend vainly that one has, contrary to fact, is perhaps denser or more ludicrous than to be the butt of a song about a private part. The old people continue to express elementary ignorance or pretense, repeating the expression about sharpening teeth a bit later and twice giving short speeches to that effect: "Tomorrow I shall eat it; since I munched their bones the livelong day, therefore I am satiated"; "Well, soon I shall eat it tomorrow, for I have been munching bones. Just soup having made, that did I drink the livelong day" (Ibid.:130 [English on pp. 132–33]). In these subsequent statements, there is no expressive prefix. The prefix in the first statement seems clearly to add a bit of local color and humor, perhaps placed in the first statement as a frame for the rest. If the L- prefix has a diminutive (and deprecatory) reference in this context, it may have to do with the age of the old couple, with the size (nonexistent) of their teeth (the name for which has the prefix attached), or both.

In sum, Grizzly Bear Girl, without prefix, stands somewhat apart. The band of brothers evokes some patronizing amusement, and perhaps, at the moment of culmination marked by prefix, some sympathy. These qualities and the solidarity among the brothers seem to fit the choice of s- as prefix. In contrast, the choice of L- as prefix for the old couple seems to go together with a greater distance in attitude toward them. While the brothers have been suspicious from the outset, and, from Bear point of view, dutiful, the old people are either dense or pretentious (or both). The s- prefix occurs among the brothers at a moment of mutual, if self-assertive, confirmation, while the

L- prefix occurs among the old people, across gender, in mutual admonition, if not criticism and reproach.

In "Grizzly Bear and Black Bear" there is again a contrast between zero, *s-*, and *L-*. (The English translation of this text, preserving the expressive prefix-markers, is reprinted in Ramsey 1977:213–16). Black Bear Woman, the sympathetic mother of the story from the outset, lacks prefix. The three-way contrast is most revealing with a single actor, the main protagonist. In all the Takelma myths preserved, Grizzly Bear Woman is the actor most highly characterized by these prefixes, and the one actor with whom a contrast in the use of both prefixes is found. Despite her role as a murderess and vengeful pursuer, killed at the end of the story, she is also a victim. Indeed, it is her victimization that is graphically portrayed with a version of the motif known classically as Thyestes's feast.[4] Grizzly Bear Woman uses the *s-* prefix at the height of her effort to find her children, whom the reader knows are dead— knows, indeed, that she has unwittingly eaten their livers.

When she first returns from having killed Black Bear, she calls with an *L-* prefix for her children, "Where are you?" and hears childish laughter. (Black Bear's children have set up a shifting image that laughs and leads Grizzly Bear hither and yon.) She enters the house and eats the prepared livers. Hearing daughter, she runs out, calling *"S-* come back, come back." She goes to the water, downriver, upriver, hearing laughter each time and calling *"S-*come back, *S-*come back." After the fourth time (four is the Takelma pattern number), she goes downriver once again, calling "Come back" (without prefix) and upriver once again, where she discovers the deception and keeps shouting, "What *L-* is the matter?"

I think that the *s-* prefix here suggests both the kind of diminutive meaning appropriate in an exchange between a mother and her children and a kind of pitying horror that narrator and audience would find appropriate for a mother—even a monstrous mother—in such a circumstance, rushing about at the beck of laughter she thinks comes from children she thinks are still alive.

With Grizzly Bear Woman's discovery of the deception, the *L-* prefix returns. It pervades her discovery and her subsequent pursuit of Black Bear's children. Going into her own house, she says *"L-* so it is *L-* my children? So that was their livers that I ate?" Going next door (into Black Bear's house), she turns over everything, asks the earth, asks everything, "Where did my children go?" (without prefix). At last discovering the escape route underneath a rock acorn-mortar and the footprints of Black Bear's children, she pursues them, crying, "O *L-*my liver! O *L-*my liver!" She pursues them farther and cries again, "O *L-* my liver! O *L-* my liver!" The children have escaped to the other side of the water with the aid of Crane, who has made a canoe of his leg for them. Meanwhile, Grizzly Bear reaches the house of an old Excrement

[4]See the gripping version of this myth, recorded from Victoria Howard in Clackamas Chinook by Melville Jacobs (1958, text 16), and the discussion of it by Jacobs (1960:102–11).

Woman and asks, "Where are the L-orphans?" The old woman does not answer but repeats self-referring phrases (reminiscent of brief, self-characterizing spirit-power song texts that occur in myths). Grizzly Bear repeats, "Where are the L-orphans? Did you not hear what I said to you?" After awhile, the old woman becomes angry, turns, seizes her awl, and Grizzly Bear jumps out of the house and runs away. When she asks Crane to make a canoe of his leg for her to cross the water, he does so, but throws her into the water, where she drowns. Her call to Crane has no expressive prefix.

When Grizzly Bear Woman speaks to adults in this myth, except when asking about children, she uses no expressive prefix. She does not invariably use such a prefix when she speaks to or about children, but almost always, and her use of the two expressive prefixes is concentrated in the scene which dramatizes her search first for her own children, then for Black Bear's children. It seems, then, that L- and s- form a polar pair in this scene. Something diminutive seems to be required by what is referred to or involved (old age and nonexistent teeth, children) for L- to occur. At the same time, there is a contrast with s- in the kind of attitude and characterization expressed. The s- prefix seems somewhat closer in emotional distance, somewhere in the range of diminutive meanings that have to do with condescension, sympathy, even affection on the part of an audience, and closeness between actors. The L- prefix seems somewhat greater in emotional distance, somewhere in the range of diminutive meanings that have to do with condescension, perhaps, but also deprecation, disdain, for coarseness and stupidity, and with distance between actors. When Grizzly Bear Woman uses the s- prefix, she is a mother seeking her children. When she uses the L- prefix, she is a successful murderess returning home, someone conscious of having been deceived, someone conscious of having eaten parts of her own children, someone bent on murdering again.

These kinds of meanings are not a surprise, and indeed are just the kinds of meanings Sapir himself discussed in his original and illuminating 1915 paper on such devices. But a reading of *Takelma texts* indicates that these meanings, as expressed by these Takelma devices, come into play in specific discourse contexts. They are not used "freely" (in the sense of randomly) and, of course, not mechanically, but selectively, to heighten the effect of the action.

IV

Three further observations can be made. First, Sapir pointed out that the word used by Grizzly Bear Woman when she cries of "my liver" generally refers to a salmon liver, not the liver of a mammal, and in this text has a very unusual type of reduplication. It seems likely that the word is a stereotyped phrase associated specifically with Grizzly Bear Woman in this myth and remembered (and expected) as such. Perhaps it preserved an older form, perhaps one that once had general meaning (although the Takelma form for *"liver"* generally—*p'a:n*— is cognate with the general Chinookan stem *-p'anaqs*). In any case, these expressions indeed characterize Grizzly Bear Woman, but not just as an instance of the *L-* prefix and the type Grizzly Bear, but as this Grizzly Bear Woman in this story. The particular expression "my liver" would have been remembered as what Grizzly Bear Woman said at the high point of this story.

Second, the use of the *s-* prefix itself appears to show expressive variation, or better, differentiation. From the standpoint of distinguishing words of different dictionary meaning, there is but one phonemic unit in Takelma here. Sapir wrote three phonetic variants: *s, s·* and *c*. While *s* has the value of "s" in English "sip," and *c* (our *S*) the value of "sh" in English "ship," *s·* is intermediate between the two (cf. Sapir 1909b:10, 1922:35). Sapir described it as "Perhaps best produced by pressing surface of tongue against alveolar ridge" (1909b:10), and referred to the other two sounds as "really heard variants" of it.

The listing of words in the vocabulary suggests some incidental heard variation to be sure. Some words that begin with *s* plus vowel are listed with the plain *s* and some with *s·*, all in a single alphabetical order. Where consonants are concerned, there is some indication of complementary distribution as well. Only plain *s* is found at the beginning of words before consonants (1922:220–24, 252–54).

The myth texts, however, show what appears to be expressive contrast. Although the vocabulary listings show initial sequences of *sm-* only with plain *s*, Grizzly Woman, seeking her children, calls out "S·-mèyé:p" 'Come back!' (Sapir 1909b:120:2; cf. 120:4, 6, 8, 10). And although the vocabulary listings show initial sequences of *sn-* and *sk-* only with plain *s*, the intermediate sound occurs in interchanges between Coyote and Pitch (Ibid.:86). In fact, this text shows a progression from no expressive prefix to use of the plain *s* as prefix to use of the intermediate *s·*. When Coyote encounters Pitch and his taunting insults, both are transcribed as using no expressive prefix in their first exchange (Ibid.:86:3–4); the plain *s-* in their second exchange (Ibid.: 86:5); and the intermediate *s·-* in subsequent exchanges, beginning with Coyote's use of it in the third exchange (Ibid.:86:6), a use eventually taken up by Pitch (Ibid.:86:14, 15ff). Thus, when Pitch uses the insult rendered by Sapir as "s-cum matre copulans" in the second exchange, he uses plain *s (s-nixayílt)*, and Coyote replies with plain *s-* in "S-what *(s-kài)* are you saying?" The next time Coyote says "What," it is with *s· kài*, and Pitch later says *"s·-níxayílt"* (Ibid.: 86:14, 16).

This progression is one of increasing intensity, in keeping with the progression of the story, in which Pitch enrages Coyote to the point of getting himself completely stuck and temporarily killed, until rescued by his younger brother. (Sapir considered that the "decidedly idiomatic and allusive character of the Indian text proves it beyond doubt to be entirely aboriginal" [Ibid.: 86, n. 1], despite the evident parallel to the Tar Baby story of West Africa and Afro-American tradition.)

Grizzly Woman's use of the s- prefix shows progression also, although not in phonetic choice, but simply in occurrence. When she first calls out "Come back, come back," the expressive prefix occurs on the first, but not the second, of the two verbs. In the thick of her search in the water, downriver and upriver, she calls "Come back, come back" three times, both verbs having the expressive prefix. When she runs downriver again, she says "Come back" only once and without prefix. When she runs the last time, upriver again, she says nothing; "she was plumb tired out" (Ibid.:121). The absence, single, and double use of both expressive prefix and verb intersect to show an arc of increasing intensity, then giving up.

These two progressions strengthen one's conviction that the s- prefix is by no means a rote stereotype, but an expressive device rather subtly integrated into performance. And this conviction leads to a third observation.

The three contrasting forms that Sapir cited (see the quotation that began this chapter) must have come from elicitation. I have not been able to find an instance of a Grizzly Bear actor prefixing L- to gwidi 'where'. The word occurs five times in the speech of Grizzly Bear Woman in the myth just discussed, but never with L-. The L- prefix occurs in four of these utterances, each time on the word following gwidi. (Text occurrences of s- prefix for gwidi in Coyote's speech, however, do appear, e.g., Ibid.:90.) That Sapir could have elicited the neat contrasting series indicates that the s- prefix was overwhelmingly associated with Coyote, the L- prefix with Grizzly Bear actors. The use of s- prefix by Bear actors as well as Coyote and the restricted use of L- prefix by Grizzly Bear actors show that the elicited series misses something of the specific expressive meanings of the two prefixes, meanings that interact with discourse contexts to govern actual occurrence.

Perhaps the Takelma themselves had a stereotyped view of the expressive prefixes, despite the nuances disclosed in actual performance. Perhaps such a Takelma view, articulated by Sapir's source, Frances Johnson, governed his own generalization about the matter. If so, then this study shows in a small way that even genius and native speaker intuition together cannot always substitute for attention to the details of actual texts.

PART TWO

BREAKTHROUGH TO PERFORMANCE

3

Breakthrough into Performance

The notion of performance is central to the study of folklore as communication. Indeed, it is through the study of performance that folklore can integrate its scientific and humanistic aims in a forward-looking way. On the one hand, the notion focuses attention on social interaction and the kinds of communicative competence that enter into interaction. Here folklore research joins hands with a number of interests and approaches in the social and behavioral sciences. On the other hand, folklore makes a distinctive contribution to the study of communicative events, by focusing attention on the stylized content and conduct within them. Here folklore enhances its concern with the aesthetic and evaluative dimensions of life. One might even hope that folklore would take the lead in showing how appreciation and interpretation of performances as unique events can be united with analysis of the underlying rules and regularities which make performances possible and intelligible; in showing how to overcome the divorce between the emergent and the repeatable, between the actual, the realizable, and the systemically possible that has plagued the study of speech.

Several folklorists have made important use of the notion of performance, e.g., Abrahams, Bauman, Ben-Amos, Dundes, Goldstein, Kirshenblatt-Gimblett, Lomax.[1] The term has come to prominence also in linguistics through the work of Noam Chomsky. The relation between these two approaches is

Originally published in *Folklore: Performance and communication*, ed. Dan Ben-Amos and Kenneth S. Goldstein (The Hague: Mouton, 1975), pp. 11–74. The paper was written in the first half of 1971 and appeared first as Working Paper 26–27 of the Centro Internazionale di Semiotica e di Linguistica, Urbino, Italy (1973). The footnotes and references of the original publication have been revised to fit the format of the present book. The orthography of the Chinookan material has been changed from one that used the letter *h* as a diacritic to one that uses capital letters (see the orthographic note and n.10 in this chapter). Chapter 6, "Breakthrough into performance revisited," applies to the texts the method of verse analysis that was not discovered until the year following the writing of the paper. I am indebted to the National Endowment for the Humanities for a Senior Fellowship in 1972–73 that enabled me to continue work in Chinookan mythology and make that discovery, and to Dmitri Segal (1976) for a thoughtful discussion of the original paper. A response to him appears in a postscript to this chapter.

[1]Cf. the earlier discussion between active and passive bearers of tradition (von Sydow 1948) and the influential posing of the question "What is meant by performance? And, what are the degrees of performance?" by Jansen (1957:112). I am indebted to Barbara Kirshenblatt-Gimblett for this and several other points.

discussed in another paper (1971), in which I argue that the analysis of verbal performance offers folklore a special opportunity for progress as a field with a distinctive methodology. Here I should like to develop further one implication of the notion itself.[2]

Some remarks on the relation of performance to behavior are needed as a preliminary. Then I shall present three instances of performance of traditional material by speakers of Wasco, the easternmost variety of Chinookan, now spoken by a few people in Oregon and Washington.[3] The three instances illustrate three types of situation that seem important if we are to understand the subtle relation between traditional material and its contemporary use.

Performance and Behavior

In contemporary transformational generative grammar the term performance treats overt behavior as a realization, quite likely imperfect, of an underlying knowledge on the part of a speaker. In contemporary folklore the term performance has reference to the realization of known traditional material, but

[2]I should like to thank Harold Garfinkel, Erving Goffman, John Gumperz, and William Labov for discussions over the years that have helped shape the perspective of this paper, and Michael Silverstein for a sweeping critique of it.

[3]The term "Wishram" is retained here, insofar as it identifies the material published by Sapir as *Wishram texts,* and because Mr. Kahclamet accepted this identification in his work with Sapir's student, Dyk, and Sapir himself. In the ethnographic and linguistic literature it would appear that there were two aboriginal communities, Wishram on the Washington side of the Columbia River, Wasco on the Oregon side, and that the Chinookan speakers surviving today on the Yakima Reservation, Washington, and the Warm Springs Reservation, Oregon, are, respectively, Wishram and Wasco. In point of fact, the particular villages from which Wishram and Wasco derive were but two prominent villages among a number of others. At the level of language, the native term *kiksht* embraces the slightly varying forms of speech of all of them. In terms of culture, the communities were essentially the same, and in terms of social structure, closely interconnected through intermarriage, trade, common activities, change of residence, and the like. Many Wasco have Wishram ancestors and conversely. The descendants of the aboriginal eastern Chinookan communities are closely interconnected today through ties of marriage, inherited property, visiting, ceremonial trading, and so forth. On both sides of the river they refer to themselves and their language today in English as Wasco. Clear realization of the extent to which a common community links eastern Chinookan descendants in both states is due to the recent fieldwork of Michael Silverstein. On the aboriginal and historically known culture of these people, see French (1961).

Fieldwork with Wasco was begun in 1951 on a grant from the Phillips Fund of the Library of the American Philosophical Society to Professor Carl Voegelin. Fieldwork in 1954 and 1956 was supported by grants from Indiana University Graduate School (Dean Ralph Cleland) and the Laboratory of Social Relations (Professor Samuel Stouffer). Further support from the Phillips Fund to Michael Silverstein and myself has helped shape the present work. Silverstein has valuable instances of the phenomena discussed here from his work at Yakima reservation, Washington, including a case of code-switching that is telling for the interpretation of a version of the myth of Seal and her daughter (Hymes 1968a, p. 323 in 1971b reprinting); see chap. 8 of this book (p. 298).

the emphasis is on the constitution of a social event, quite likely with emergent properties. In each of the cases to be presented below, these two latter considerations will be essential—the performance as situated in a context, the performance as emergent, as unfolding or arising within that context. The concern is with performance, not as something mechanical or inferior, as in some linguistic discussion, but with performance as something creative, realized, achieved, even transcendent of the ordinary course of events (cf. Jacobs 1959b:7; Hymes 1968).

Within this concern, several distinctions seem to be necessary. Performance is not merely behavior, but neither is it the same as all of culture (or conduct or communication). It ought to be possible to compare communities as to the degree to which performance is a characteristic of life, ranging from those in which it is salient and common, as Abrahams (1972) has shown to be the case in parts of the West Indies, to those in which it is subdued and rare. And it ought to be possible to distinguish performance according to the key in which it occurs; some performances are desultory, or perfunctory, or rote, while others are authoritative, authentic.

If some grammarians have confused matters by lumping what does not interest them under "performance" as a residual category, cultural anthropologists and folklorists have not done much to clarify the situation. We have tended to lump what *does* interest us under "performance," simply as an honorific designation.[4]

[4]There has been little or no fruitful integration of work concerned with the methodology of observational description and work concerned with the methodology of cultural description, culture being conceived as a set of recurring standards or arrangements or both. Some observational work has concentrated on painstaking dissection of components of behavior (kinesics, for example) vital to adequate account of folkloristic performance, but no way of making such analysis part of a normal ethnographic tool kit (as phonetic transcription can be) has been provided. The path breaking and invaluable work on sequential observation, behavior settings, and the like, of Roger Barker and his collaborators (see Barker and Wright, 1954, now happily again in print) has been taken up and elaborated with new ideas by Marvin Harris (1964), but one-sidedly. Whereas Barker and Wright did not take local definitions of behavioral standards, as verbally expressed, into account, Harris excludes them on principle and sets behavioral observation and analysis of verbal behavior in opposition (as "etic" vs. "emic"). A significant new approach to behavioral description, emically conceived, by Maner Thorpe was refused acceptance as an anthropological dissertation at Harvard and remains unpublished, apparently because its methodological efforts were thought inappropriate. Probably the best and clearest account of cultural description from a standpoint incorporating language (Goodenough, 1970) finds it necessary to separate cultural description from systematic variation that is central to the Sapirian conception of cultural behavior followed here (see n. 6 below), and apparently also from the character of cultural behavior as situated and emergent that is intrinsic to the Chinookan cases below (Ibid.: 101–3). Generally speaking, the study of behavior and the study of culture go separate ways, and if "cultural behavior" is spoken and written as a phrase, the integrated conception that it bespeaks is not much realized. The situation is deleterious for study of performance, since, as here conceived, performance is by nature simultaneously cultural and behavioral. On the other hand, study of performance may remedy the situation. Finally, there has been no helpful attention by American anthropologists and folklorists, so far as I am aware, to the issues concerning action and

Recently the linguist William Labov has suggested some interesting, rather operational distinctions that have arisen from his research into naturally occurring verbal conduct, both linguistic and folkloristic (Columbia University Seminar on the Use of Language, 1967). Labov has found it useful to distinguish that behavior which persons in a community can interpret (find culturally intelligible) and can report; that which they can interpret but cannot report; and that which they can neither interpret nor report. These distinctions of course imply a fourth behavior: that which persons can report but not interpret (though they may seek an interpretation).

The notion of performance, as developed in this paper, introduces an additional dimension, that which people can do or repeat.

Each of the three dimensions—the INTERPRETABLE, the REPORTABLE, the REPEATABLE—can be regarded as an aspect of the abilities of competent members of a culture or community. Each can also be regarded as an aspect of the circumstances facing the investigator of a culture or community. In either respect, the dimensions would entail the general questions: what behavior is interpretable (cultural?) in this community? for this person? what behavior is reportable in this community? by this person? what behavior is voluntarily doable in this community? by this person? As an aspect of abilities, the questions would lead to a description of the distribution of kinds of competence typical of the community or culture, including the distribution of capacity for performance. As an aspect of investigation, the questions would lead to strategies for discovering the cultural behavior of the community, according as it could be done, or reported, or neither, by whom, where, and when, for whom.

Together the three dimensions imply eight categories of abilities, or circumstances of inquiry. Before illustrating these categories, we must notice that within each of the three dimensions there is a continuum from a minimal to a maximal realization. With regard to the dimension of interpretability in connection with language, for example, Chomskyan transformational grammar postulates and requires of speakers at least a minimal ability to respond to sentences as either interpretable (within the grammatical system under consideration) or not. Speakers may not be usually able to explicate their judgments (Chomsky 1965:21), and such reflections as they may have on interpretability (here, grammatically) are not taken systematically into account. The linguist's grammatical system itself is relied upon to decide difficult cases. The supposed minimal ability itself may not be what it seems, however, for it begins to appear that it involves in important part a rather refined and instructed skill, if it is utilized in isolation from knowledge of other cultural

performance raised in analytic philosophy in recent years. For a useful summary and an original contribution with direct implications for the study of folkloristic performance, see Skinner (1971), especially pp. 4–5 and 15ff., respectively. My own discussion here does not pretend to do more than briefly open up a part of the general subject as it impinges on the process and goal of ethnographic inquiry. Relevant recent articles include Georges (1969), Haring (1972), and papers in Paredes and Bauman (eds.) (1972), and Bauman and Sherzer (1974).

systems. It may be that the more complex judgment of acceptability (subsuming interpretability as a component) must be the true object of investigation.

In any case, the polarity just indicated between *classifying* and *explaining*, on the dimension of INTERPRETABILITY, can be generalized to all of cultural behavior. The dimension would entail specific questions of the type: "Is this an X?" (say, a proverb, or a myth) (classifying), and of the type, "Why?" or "Why not?" (explaining).

Ability to interpret (in the sense given above), of course, is often connected with ability to report. An answer to the question "Is this an X?" may entail an answer to the question, "Is this an X (for any one, for others) in this community?", or to the question, "Was that an X?" and hence draw on a person's ability to report or describe cultural behavior.

The polarity just indicated between *reporting* and *describing*, on the dimension of REPORTABILITY, like the other polarities, manifests considerable underlying complexity. Someone may be unable to report that an act or event has occurred, because to him it was not interpretable; because of the circumstance of not having been present; because in the nature of the phenomenon it is not something he is able to report; because it is not culturally appropriate or permissible for him to report it. The same observations hold, of course, for ability to describe.

If what persons can or will report is less than what they can interpret, what they can or will do is less than what they can report. In a recent class I had thought that a clear instance of something that everyone could interpret (recognize as culturally possible and structured), report (recognize as having occurred), and also do would be to recite the Pledge of Allegiance to the flag. I was mistaken. Eventually the class settled for recitation of the alphabet. Even here one had to take their word for it, and only after an interval was one older member of the class prepared to offer a recitation. And it was clear that under the circumstances performance would have been accompanied by much evincing of what Erving Goffman has termed "role distance" (1967).

There is thus a polarity between voluntarily *doing* and *performing*, on the dimension of REPEATABILITY, taking performing in the sense of truly or seriously performing. There is further the distinction between those ground characteristics of performances that are indeed repeatable, as a musical score or a play is repeatable, and those qualities that emerge in a given interaction or occasion.[5]

Running through the discussion has been a fourth dimension, not hitherto singled out as such, that of the ACCEPTABLE or APPROPRIATE. In one sense, the dimension has to do with the distinguishing of what persons will do in particular contexts from what they can do in principle. In another sense, the relation between the possible and contextually doable is itself specific to a community, and that which the investigator thinks ought to be doable may,

---

[5]On the complexity of what may count as repetition, cf. Lord (1960) and Foster (1971).

if inappropriate, be literally not doable for the person in question. The first Chinookan case below may be an example. An instance of a type fairly familiar to linguists is that of a fieldworker among a group in the American Southwest some years ago. His nickname was "Robin". Dutifully eliciting a possessive paradigm for the noun "wing" he was brought up short by his Indian colleague, who refused to give the first person possessive, although both parties knew what it would be if it could be. Suddenly a pleasant thought occurred. "Only a bird could say that, but you can say that, because your name is 'Robin'." And so that summer it was a standing joke that only one person in the pueblo could say "my wing": the anthropologist.

Abstracting from the dimension of ACCEPTABILITY, the range of possibilities implied by the other three dimensions is tentatively illustrated in Table 3–1.

As has been noted, these distinctions may have some value in reflecting on the general problem of assessing behavioral repertoire, and also for alerting students to the small portion of cultural behavior that persons can be expected to report or describe, when asked, and the much smaller portion that an average person can be expected to manifest by doing on demand. (Some social research seems incredibly to assume that what there is to find out can be found out by asking.) Most important for the present purposes is the showing that *performance*, as cultural behavior for which a person assumes responsibility to an audience, is a quite specific, quite special category. *Performance* is not a wastebasket, but a key to much of the difference in the meaning of life as between communities.

It would not be wise to insist on any one set of terms at this stage of our understanding of performance, and the distinctions just drawn are intended only to open up the subject a little further in linguistics and folklore than has been usually done. (The major contribution in general social analysis is that of Goffman [1959, 1963, 1967].) Analytical categories no doubt will change and improve as a broader base of empirical research is given to them. It does seem clear that at one level there can be agreement on the distinctions with which this section began: there is *behavior*, as simply anything and everything that happens; there is *conduct*, behavior under the aegis of social norms, cultural rules, shared principles of interpretability; there is *performance*, when one or more persons assumes responsibility for presentation. And within performance itself, as the doable or repeatable, there is the pole that can be termed performance in full, authentic or authoritative performance, when the standards intrinsic to the tradition in which the performance occurs are accepted and realized.

In each of the cases to be presented, authentic or authoritative performance occurs only at a certain point or in a certain respect. Other parts or aspects of the performance must be considered illustrative, or reportive, or even as oral *scholia*. Each of the cases raises questions as to the difference between knowing tradition and presenting it; between knowing what and

INTERPRETABLE	REPORTABLE	REPEATABLE	
+	+	+	(1) Recitation of the alphabet.
+	+	−	(2) Recitation of Mark Antony's funeral oration from *Julius Caesar*.
+	−	+	(3) As "report": many skills expected of a linguistic informant, such as paraphrase, phonological contrast; as "describe": tie a shoelace.
+	−	−	(4) Verbally uncoded cultural behavior, such as some maternal behavior according to Bateson's "double-bind" theory of schizophrenia.
−	+	+	(5) As "classify": "Colorless green ideas sleep furiously" as a reportable, repeatable, semantically uninterpretable sentence; as "explain": rote use of an uncomprehended religious language, rote recitation of the Pledge of Allegiance.
−	+	−	(6) Dreams reported to a psychiatrist; visions requiring a specialist; speech in a language recognized but not known.
−	−	+	(7) A reinforceable tic in one's own behavior, elicitable and even conditionable without one's own awareness.
−	−	−	(8) Speech in an unrecognizable language.

Table 3–1. Categories of ability

knowing how; between knowledge, on the one hand, and motivation and identification, on the other, as components of competence in the use of language.[6] In each case it is in certain respects, not all, that to responsibility

[6]On identification as a notion central to the understanding of speech, see Burke (1950), especially Part I. The discussion is wise, prescient, and confirmed by events in its view of issues of science and politics (e.g., pp. 22, 26–31), and is even more pertinent today to the ethnographic study of speech and verbal art.

for knowledge of tradition the speaker joins willingness to assume the identity of tradition's authentic performer. The difference, I believe, is fundamental to interpretation of cultural materials.

Recognition of the difference serves obviously as a caution or warning, less obviously as an opportunity. As a matter of what could now be called "data quality control" (Naroll 1962), concern for authentic performance has long figured in folkloristic research, although not often in published reports; and often enough the personal, situational, and linguistic factors that govern authentic performance in a tradition have not been explicitly investigated or adequately taken into account. Sometimes scholars have even ignored or tried to dismiss such a palpable factor as whether or not the language of presentation was the language of tradition. Perhaps the most obvious influence on what we know of the traditions of nonliterate groups has been the constraint of dictation, and dictation slow enough to be written down; the effect on sentence length and the internal organization of texts has been increasingly revealed by research with tape recorder (cf. Tedlock 1970, 1972a). Less obvious is the dependence on what the speaker thinks the hearer capable of understanding; Boas (1901:6) remarked that Charles Cultee's Kathlamet periods became much more complex as their work progressed. But it is not at all my purpose simply to argue that material failing to meet certain criteria must be rejected or relegated to secondary status. Some material indeed must be rejected or restricted in the use made of it, for some purposes, because of such considerations, although if it is all there is of an aspect of tradition, we should and no doubt will make as much of it as possible. My major purpose is to argue for the systematic study of variation in performance. To think of performance constraints in terms of eliminating inadequacies and obtaining ideal conditions is to perpetuate the same error as the linguist who thinks of performance as something that can be ignored when adequate, something to be noted only when it interferes. On such terms, performance is but a means to an end. But especially in an oral tradition performance is a mode of existence and realization that is partly *constitutive* of what the tradition is. The tradition itself exists partly for the sake of performance; performance is itself partly an end. And while there are cases analogous to the prima donna who cannot go on if any detail is not right, more often the performers of tradition are masters of adaptation to situation. There is no more an *"Ur*-performance" than there is an *"Ur*-text."* Only the systematic study of performances can disclose the true structure.[7]

---

[7]Cf. William Labov's systematic study of variation in phonology (1966) and the theoretical analysis on which it is based, as stated by Weinreich, Labov, and Herzog (1968). As a precursor, see the theoretical perspective staked out by Sapir (1934, 1938). Both are reprinted in Mandelbaum (1949). The perspective is elaborated in Hymes (1967, 1970).

Three Chinookan Cases

The Chinookan cases presented here permit comparative study of performances only to a limited extent, and only with regard to texts of the two
narratives, the speech having no documented parallel. The results are still of
some interest, as to the structure of Chinookan narratives, and as to the
relation between myth and tale. The types of performance represented by all
three cases are, I think, frequent in the world today, and worth being singled
out. The simplest and clearest, a case of breakthrough into authoritative
performance at a certain point within a single text, is presented first. It could
be dubbed a case of simple breakthrough.[8] The second and third cases each
require comparison to another version of the same narrative and consideration
of relations between native genres. Both narratives involve, I think, realization
as essentially a tale of what was once a myth, the retained mythical function
being separated out and bracketed at an initial point. One (the first of the two
to be presented) might be dubbed a case of simple metaphrasis; the other,
because of the introduction of an additional function, as will be explained, can
be dubbed a case of complex metaphrasis, *metaphrasis* being adopted here as
a technical term for interpretive transformation of genre.[9]

The Crier—A Morning Address

The text to follow came about in the course of inquiry about the word
i-ya-giXmniL,[10] literally, 'the one who speaks regularly (repeatedly)', with

[8]The use of the term "breakthrough" here is by analogy to what Paul Friedrich has called
"pronominal breakthrough" in his fine study of usage in Russian novels (1966).

[9]Cf. Sklute (1966: 35): "Thus, old world tales about supernatural beings and occurrences
change in function during the process of transmission from the immigrant generation to the
following generation, if there is such a transmission at all. Among immigrants, such as Berta
Arvidson, the stories exist as memories of strong experiences with the unseen powers in the old
country. Among persons of a subsequent generation, such as August Nelson, they may persist,
but merely as entertaining tales, since the very foundation for such stories, namely the belief in
supernatural beings, is missing." (I am indebted for this reference to Barbara Kirshenblatt-
Gimblett.)

[10]Most of the information of this note is now given in the orthographic note at the
outset of the volume, but it is preserved here as the first publication of certain of the conventions, for a few additional details, and because the alternative way of putting things may
be helpful. In the transcription of Chinookan words, the symbols usual in recent Americanist
work are mostly employed, but several conventions have been adopted for ease of typesetting
or to preserve certain features of performance. As to vowels: the principal phonemic vowels
are /i a u/, "as in Italian," to which must be added /ae/ as in English *hat*, used for stylistic
emphasis and in color terms and a few other words, and a nonphonemic schwa, often carrying primary stress and being sometimes stylistically significant. Schwa, written here (E), varies
across a wide range, including the two nuclei of *button*. The transcription here is not strictly
phonemic, indicating elided grammatical elements within parentheses, on the one hand, and

Philip Kahclamet (d. 1958), who spoke it the night of 25 July 1956 in a booth
in the Rainbow Cafe, just across the Deschutes River from the eastern edge
of the Warm Springs Reservation, Oregon. Mr. Kahclamet had been raised
on the Washington side of the Columbia River, some miles east of The Dalles,
Oregon, at the aboriginal site of the Wishram Chinook. He had a thorough
knowledge of the language and was conversant with much of the traditional
culture. In his youth he had served as interpreter and linguistic informant for
Walter Dyk, a student sent out by Edward Sapir, who had himself studied
Wishram for a short time in the summer of 1905, as a student of Franz Boas.
Mr. Kahclamet had gone to Yale as an informant in Sapir's class for a semester,
but he broke with Dyk and returned, having destroyed, it is reported, his
copies of what he had written for Dyk. In the 1950s at Warm Springs
Reservation, where he had land and was working, he was persuaded to collabo-
rate with David and Katherine French in their studies of traditional Chinookan and Sahaptin culture. (Chinookans from the Oregon side of the Columbia
had been brought to Warm Springs, together with Sahaptins from adjacent
areas, in the mid-nineteenth century.)

When I worked with Mr. Kahclamet in the summer of 1956, he was
forthcoming in matters of lexicon and grammar, but resistant to requests to
dictate connected text or to tell narratives in either Wishram or English. It
was not that he did not know about narratives (as the last case below shows).
I speculated that he still held to a certain faith with traditional conditions of
proper performance, despite disappearance of any overt native context for
such narration at least a generation earlier; that despite the absence of anyone who could judge his narration in native terms, he carried internally a
sense of the critical judgment that an older generation, a reference group
now largely dead, would have made. There is some evidence that older Indians depreciated the lesser Indian language competence of their descendants,
and that Mr. Kahclamet judged creative adaptation of the language to have
ceased when he was young. (Acculturative vocabulary bears this out, ceasing
effectively with the technology of the early part of this century.) Certainly
he now resisted being put in the role of informant as such, having come to

---

certain phonetic realizations on the other. Thus, (o) is phonemically /u/, and (e) is phonemically /i/. Doubled vowels, such as (aa), indicate expressive length. Front and back vowels adjacent to velars are frequently (e) and (o), respectively; long (ee) and (oo) are sometimes used
expressively; primary stress is usually penultimate, secondary stress is usually the second syllable away. As to consonants: ' marks glottalization; for certain consonants normally represented with other diacritics (superposed "hatcheck," subposed dot, bar) capitalization is used
instead. Thus S and C are as in English *ship* and *chip;* L is a voiceless lateral fricative, as in
the *ll* and *fl* of Welsh *Llewelyn* and *Floyd;* whereas q is a voiceless velar stop, somewhat as
in English *kohlrabi,* but with great local friction in its release in Sapir's texts, G is the
voiced velar stop counterpart, the two velars, q and G, being parallel to the palatal pair, k
and g. Whereas x is a palatal voiceless fricative, not quite as far front as that in German *ich,*
X is the velar counterpart, somewhat as in German *ach.* The two fricatives are parallel to
the stop pairs just discussed.

identify with the role of intermediary and, indeed, linguist. In any case, a booth in the Rainbow Cafe as setting, I as audience, at night after work, were suitable to lexicon and grammar, but not to narration. (Nor did other settings prove more suitable.) There were three exceptions. The first (22 June 1956) was a traditional story, told in English, arising out of eth- nobotanical inquiries already under way by David French (the last case below). The last (1 August) was an autobiographical account, also told in English, and corresponding in a way to disclosure of a guardian spirit experi- ence, of the time as a child when he had lost consciousness and breath, and was thought to have died. He recovered and an old woman was able to explain the experience as one of his soul having been turned back at the fork in the road that leads to the afterlife (one road leads beyond, one road leads back to earth and to existence as an evil ghost). After he was twelve, the woman told him that he had been turned back because he had some Sahap- tin ancestry; had he been full-blood Chinook, he would have been dead. "I wouldn't be here now. That's the reason I believe in this longhouse religion [the dominant native religious practice on the reservation]; and I'm going to stay with it." And on the night of 25 July 1956 he told me the text that follows.

The Crier (Philip Kahclamet)

In the morning he steps out. He intones his words.

"This is Sunday morning. You people should know—I don't have to come round this morning to tell you—that you people should put on all your trappings; that you will come to church.

"You know that we were put here by the Great Spirit. We have to worship him. I am getting to my old age; some of you will have to take my place when I'm gone.

"When you hear the drum this morning, it's calling you to worship the Great Spirit. That's where all our ancestors went. If you go by the old religion, you will see them when you leave the earth. You know we are going to have to leave our flesh in the ground; only our souls go; and we'll be sure we'll meet our ancestors.

"You people know that we didn't come here ourselves. He who created us is above. He put us here. We have to be where we are today. Me—I'm not telling you this myself. I'm only giving you the revelations which I've learned from somebody else.

"When you hear these drums, go. We are Nadidanwit here; this is our country. These white people came; they brought Christianity. It's not for us. The Christianity was brought here for the white people only. The white people cheated us out of our country. So don't follow them whatever they teach you. Shushugli was a Jew; he was not Nadidanwit and he was not for the Nadidanwit. SuSugli i-ju i-kiXaX. Yaxdau i-pendikast, i-kathlik, 'Presbyterian,' 'Methodist,' *kwadaw* i-Sik, k'aya amXawiXa. K'aya t'unwit amduXa."[11]

There is reason to believe that formal oratory, such as this, was important to Chinookan communities. The title itself names a role. The end of the fifth paragraph ("I'm only giving you the revelations which I've learned from somebody else") reflects a fundamental criterion of formal speech events, that the speech be repeated; in that lay its formality and often certainty. (Thus, to have claimed to speak on one's own authority alone would have deprived what was said of authority.) I have tried to reconstruct a cultural pattern underlying such formal speaking elsewhere (French 1958; Hymes 1966). Very little is known of actual oratory. There are indications in Sapir's *Wishram texts* (1909a:216, 210, 218, 228–29). This mostly English text is the only other instance, and the longest recorded instance, known to me.

The special interest of the speech here is that it begins as a report, in the third person, in English ("In the morning he steps out . . .") and ends as authentic performance, in the first person, in Wishram. This is the only time at which I knew Philip Kahclamet to assume the role of speaker in Wishram. The setting was late at night, after a good deal of beer drinking that night, after a good part of a summer working together. And even so, the switch into authentic performance, into Wishram, was brief: two sentences, at the end of, or ending, the speech.

Code-switching from one language to another is here, I believe, a sign of "breakthrough" into full performance.[12] This case might be said to develop

[11]*SuSúgli* is from the French *Jesus Christ* (Zezü kri [with Z as in *azure*]). As to consonants, the initial voiced fricative, not found in Chinookan, goes to the voiceless fricative that Chinookan does have (Z → S); while the second consonant might have been adapted in parallel fashion (z → S), Chinookan words tend to have consonantal harmony in this regard, either *S . . . S*, or *s . . . s*, and *S* is the normal form. Moreover, French Canadian /s/ may have been a somewhat palatalized (s·), hence closer to Chinookan /s/. The *r*, not found in Chinookan, goes to the nearest equivalent, *l*. As to vowels, the third vowels match (i : i), and *u* is the nearest Chinookan equivalent to the second French vowel (ü). The first French vowel might have been expected to become *(i)*, giving *SiSúgli*, but it has been assimilated to the following vowel, perhaps somehow in connection with the matching of consonants in the two syllables. The word is known in Chinook jargon. *Nadidánwit* is a formal, collective name for Indians as contrasted to other kinds of people and beings. The final two sentences translate: "Jesus Christ is a Jew. That Pentecostal, Catholic, Presbyterian, Methodist, and that Shaker (church), don't concern yourselves with them. Don't believe in them." See now also Kahclamet and Hymes (1977) for this text, and "For Philip" (Hymes 1975b) for a tribute to Kahclamet.

[12]Three possible aspects of such a switch regarding the white interlocuter (myself) would be (1) to express distance, (2) to soften the impact, (3) to express community, sincerely or by way of flattery ("one of us" by virtue of sharing understanding of our language). A fourth possible aspect would be to prevent other people from knowing what was said. With regard to the content of what is said in *kiksht* (Wasco), note that the indictment of white people occurs in English before the switch, and the identification of *SuSúgli* as a Jew is stated in English before being repeated in *kiksht*. The material in *kiksht* thus begins and ends with repetition of what has been said in English *(SuSúgli)*, exhortation not to believe in Christian denominations); only the intervening specification of denominations, partly quoted English, is novel content. As for other auditors, Mr. Kahclamet and I were in a booth at the end of the row and had been working for

through three stages: *Report: Translation: Full Performance.* The first line is report, concerning a third person. There follows address, quoted in translation. (English performance of such an address is unattested and unlikely, although Mr. Kahclamet very likely had heard such addresses in Sahaptin, a language with which he was familiar.) The last three sentences are full performance, anticipated by the introduction of native terms in the preceding sentence. The dominant speech function is clearly rhetorical in nature, a hortatory focus on the addressee, and a perfect example of enlisting an audience in terms of identification and division (cf. Burke 1950).

The sincerity of the identification with the role of speaker is evidenced by the personal experience, summarized above, which Mr. Kahclamet recounted a week later that summer, directly in English. ("Directly," because in our relationship Wishram was not a medium of communication, but an object of study. I take the breaking into Wishram at the end of the speech to imply not only subjective assumption of the role of the speaker, but also momentary forgetting of the immediate audience.)

The third of Mr. Kahclamet's extended discourses that summer, the traditional story, will be presented later. It is the most complex of the three cases, and can be more readily understood after consideration of a performance in which the realization of a tale-like adventure—only one dimension of Mr. Kahclamet's narrative—is the central concern.

Myth into Tale: "The Story Concerning Coyote"

The performance to be considered here is of one part of the cycle of Coyote stories that constituted the most characteristic, salient feature of the oral literature of Chinookan groups. We have three renderings of the cycle, one collected in 1905 on Yakima reservation (Sapir 1909a), one collected in English a little later at the ancestral home of the Wishram on the Columbia (Curtis 1911), and one obtained by myself in 1954. The "breakthrough" in

---

some time out of contact with other persons in the cafe, as we had many times before. Thus there do not appear to be reasons for concealment from others or softening with regard to myself. Expression of social distance, either distancing or intimacy, cannot be ruled out as a component of the significance of the switch. I think that in a way both were involved: distancing from the immediate scene and myself insofar as I was perceived as part of it, intimacy insofar as I was accepted as audience for oratory. The key, however, in my opinion is the evidence that the switch is prepared for and seems literally a switch into *kiksht* for the sake of *kiksht*. As mentioned in the text below, the full use of *kiksht* is preceded and perhaps precipitated by three uses of individual *kiksht* terms in the prior sentence; as mentioned above, the first sentence in *kiksht* is not new in content, but repeats a content already given in English. Moreover, my remembered impression (the scene returns vividly) is that it was when Mr. Kahclamet realized that he was launched into oratory in *kiksht* that he became self-conscious, aware of surroundings, and stopped. In sum, it does appear that the initial impetus to the switch was not distance, near or far, or concealment, but an impulse to full appropriateness.

the present case thus is not signaled by code-switching, as the story is but one in a sequence of native language dictations. The authoritative assumption of responsibility for presentation manifests itself rather in context and in style.

As to context: in mid-summer of 1954 Mr. Hiram Smith was working at a small farm near Sandy, Oregon. In late afternoon and early evening he would work with me on the language. At first he demurred at the suggestion that he narrate full myths, just as he had the previous summer I had been with him (1951). He had then spoken of the skill at narration of his dead father (from whom he had learned traditional stories)[13] but disclaimed ability to tell them himself, although he took evident pleasure in references to mythological characters in conversation, and when the myth was mentioned in which Coyote transforms two women into stone, he volunteered the location on the Columbia of the particular rocks. After several requests, and then with some seeming reluctance, Mr. Smith did supply two short passages that were missing from the myths collected by Sapir. Both involved mythological characters named but left hanging in *Wishram texts*.[14] In contrast, Mr. Smith related several narratives of late nineteenth-century wars and adventures with relish and assurance. The tales were partly dramatized when Mr. Smith would take both parts of a short dialogue. All the tales were volunteered by him, and enjoyed by his wife and children, who showed no interest in the mythology.

In 1954 I offered to prompt Mr. Smith by getting a copy of *Wishram texts*, as a guarantee of the order in which the stories of the Coyote cycle should go. This seemed to reassure Mr. Smith. I would indicate the stories in turn, and Mr. Smith would narrate without reference to the texts. In the event, Mr. Smith did not rely on *Wishram texts* for order, much less for content. His sequence shares certain fixed reference points at beginning and end with that of Louis Simpson (the narrator of Sapir's *Wishram texts*) and that of the Curtis volume. All agree, for example, on locating the "origin of fish" story near the Pacific and as the first story on Coyote's way up the river. Mr. Smith's sequence, however, goes its own way in between that beginning and the last episodes, for the most part, and consciously so. In *Wishram texts*, for example, the second story on the river is that of "Coyote and the mischievous women"; Mr. Smith told that story sixth in his sequence, and specified the location as "below Hood River" at the time of telling, and at another time as the third episode downriver from below The Dalles. To explain (as the geography of the Columbia is not universally familiar), Mr. Smith, mentally looking back downriver from Wishram and Wasco territory, was locating the story much farther along Coyote's way toward that territory. Again whereas

---

[13]A collection of Wasco stories taken in dictation from Mr. Smith's father perhaps still exists somewhere. Mr. Smith remembers a woman recording stories from his father, perhaps seventy years ago, and particularly that she did not blush at the sexual parts but kept right on writing. She went, he thinks, somewhere in the Southwest. Efforts to identify the person or to locate the material have been unavailing.

[14]See Hymes (1953) on which the account of the 1951 work is based.

in *Wishram texts* the third story on the river, "Coyote as medicine man," must be fairly close to the mouth of the river and Coyote's starting point, Mr. Smith was definite in locating the story precisely at "Spearfish" (a later name for the best known village of the Wishram), well toward the journey's end.

Other indications of Mr. Smith's knowledge of a definite line of tradition, and judgment of his knowledge of that line, are that he would not tell two episodes in *Wishram texts* (about Coyote showing people how to make fish-traps and to spear fish), though he could, of course, have given a paraphrase of the *Wishram texts* versions, and even though his own initial list of communities at which Coyote transformed things included the two communities in question (SkalXalmaX, Namnit). On the other hand, as in the summer of 1951, he supplied incidents lacking in *Wishram texts.*

The existence of alternative lines of tradition was already attested in *Wishram texts,* when Sapir recorded two contrasting outcomes for the story of Coyote and the mischievous women (1909a:9, n. 2):

> Tom Simpson, brother of Louis, took exception to the transformation in the first version, when this was read to him, and denied its correctness. The transformation to water-birds seems more appropriate than that into rocks, however.

Mr. Smith's version agrees with Tom Simpson, and indeed, Mr. Smith entitled the story, "Pillars of Hercules."[15]

In sum, Mr. Smith had knowledge of a definite line of mythological tradition; in his own eyes and the eyes of others, he was an accomplished narrator; but until the intervention of a young ethnographer seeking texts, the knowledge and the skill were disjunct. The stories Mr. Smith spontaneously told, and that family and friends spontaneously enjoyed, were tales, not myths. Myths had not been normally told for at least a generation—in 1967 Mr. Smith and Mr. Urban Bruno could remember from their childhoods the last man they knew to have done so.[16]

[15]The note is interesting for the history of anthropological theory, as well as for the understanding of Chinookan and analogous traditions. In the 1930s Sapir was to begin a famous article on the need for a radically new understanding of culture in relation to personality by citing his shock as a student in reading the ethnographer Mooney's remark in a report on the Omaha, "Two Crows denies this" (Sapir, "Why cultural anthropology needs the psychiatrist"). (The late Clyde Kluckhohn regularly expected Harvard anthropology students to recognize this remark.) Here was an instance from his own predoctoral fieldwork ("Tom Simpson denies this"), but apparently he was not prepared to take theoretical advantage of either the real or encountered instance until a generation later.

[16]Curtis (1911:106) had already anticipated their disappearance nearly a half-century before: "The old men and women possessing knowledge of the stories have largely passed away, and it is likely that no person alive at this time knows all the myths that were current when the tribe was in its prime"; and Sapir described Louis Simpson as "a fair example of the older type of Wishram Indian, now passing away" (1909:ix).

In accepting responsibility for a telling of the Coyote cycle in the summer of 1954, Mr. Smith was influenced perhaps by the special closeness of our relationship at that time amidst family troubles and in separation from the Reservation community. He did enjoy the role of authority for knowledge; and once committed, he carried through and told each story well. I felt, however, that he was being careful and conscientious, more than spontaneous, at the outset. The telling seemed to reach a different level of enjoyment and authority, when, more than halfway through his sequence, I remarked that one story was not at all clear in *Wishram texts*. What I said was quite true; it was also said with the thought of putting *Wishram texts* in its place as a not infallible authority. He responded: "Well, we'll have to fix that up."

Mr. Smith proceeded to tell a clear, well-woven story with pleasure. That the story involved an obscene act on Coyote's part, and his subsequent discomfiture despite his best efforts was, I believe, no accident. For it was not Coyote as transformer, so much as Coyote, the personification of an ethos of a hunting and gathering style of life still persistent despite technological transformations, that the Indian community, including Mr. Smith, remembered, retained, and enjoyed. One member of the community, Tom Brown, was famous to Mr. Smith for tall stories involving the characteristic character of Coyote that he himself invented. The transformations of the pre-cultural world into its proper Indian condition are not all gone from Mr. Smith's cycle, but the principal one to remain is the initial one involving the provision of salmon, to whose fishing he, as some others, remained dedicated. It seems understandable that two episodes found in both Curtis and *Wishram texts*, and missing from Mr. Smith's cycle, involve establishing of a technology now lost at the sites of communities along the river now gone, or that in discharging his responsibility to the myth cycle, Mr. Smith provided a unique "Prologue," in which the mythological import is gathered up and bracketed, as it were, at the outset, before the stories begin. It is just possible that the prologue reflects an aboriginal practice; it is similar in spirit, at least, to the title supplied by Louis Simpson for the cycle (*Wishram texts* 2): "What Coyote did in this land." But Mr. Smith's enumeration does seem to extract and collect what is distributed among individual stories in the Curtis and *Wishram texts* accounts.[17]

So much for context, of the telling, and of the particular narrative. To consider the style of the particular narrative, on which much of the understanding of its performance depends, we must consider Mr. Smith's text not only in itself, but also in contrast to the version of the same story given nearly a half-century earlier by Mr. Simpson. Because reference must be made to characteristics of the original texts, both they and their translations are given,

[17]In translation, the "Prologue" is: "In his travels Coyote was all over. He used to do everything. He would transform things: these creeks and communities. Here are some of their names. Their names: (followed by a list of seven names)."

first Mr. Simpson's, then Mr. Smith's. The texts and translations are arranged here in ways that will be explained in the comparison that follows them. (See Appendix for discussion of the Simpson text philologically).

Mr. Simpson's text

(1) AGa kwapt gayuya.
    (2) Gayuyaa; gayuLait.
(3) AGa kwapt gasiXmk'naukwatsk Isk'ulya.
(4) AGa kwapt Isk'ulya gasiXtuks.
(5) AGa kwapt qedau galiXoX: ewi galiXoX iak'alxixpa,
        ewi galiXoX Ck'ES iaq'aqStaqba.
    (6) Ck'ES gaqiuX.
    (7) Galikim Isk'ulya: "Naq(i) it'uktix
        imSgnoX."
(8) AGa kwapt idwaCa gaCuXabu.
    (9) Naqi tq'eX gaCtoX pu gaqawiqLaxit.
(10) AGa kwapt dak dak gaCiuXix idwaCa.
(11) AGa kwapt kanawee San gaLXlqLaXit qngi
        niGiXatX Isk'ulya.
(12) AGa idwaCa niCuXadwaix.
(13) AGa kwapt dak dak (n)itkSiqi(t)damidaba idwaCa.
(14) AGa kwapt Isk'ulya walu gagiuX.
(15) AGa kwapt niXLuxwait: "AG(a) anXLXÉlma."
(16) AGa kwapt galikta idÉlxamba.
(17) AGa kwapt galugakim: "Iak'amlaix nigiXatX
        Isk'ulya; iak'alxix niSiXatukS."
(18) AGa kwapt wit'a galikta Isk'ulya.
    (19) GaliXLuxwait: "Yaxiba naSqi
        qnÉlqLat; k'aya quSt aGa
        aqnlqLaXida."
    (20) Galikta wit'a dixt itqwLe.
(21) AGa wit'aX uXok'aiawulal: "AGa
        niSiXatukS Isk'ulya", duXikwLilal
        wit'aX idElxam.
(22) AGa kwapt niXLuxwait: "QuSt aGa aqxnÉlqLat."
(23) AGa kwapt gayuya.

The English translation below is that of *Wishram texts,* apparently as polished by Sapir (cf. 1909a:xi). In the original volume text and translation are presented on facing pages, and the even-numbered pages of text are numbered by line (p. 31, lines 5–22, and p. 32, line 1, for the Wishram text; pp. 31, 33 for the English translation; references to *Wt* 32: 1, for example, are thus possible). For the sake of comparison between Mr. Simpson's and Mr. Smith's narrations here, both texts and translations are presented as sequences of numbered sentences. The numbering and the indentation identify the principal units of the "surface structure" of the texts, narrative sentences and narrative segments, respectively. The brackets at the left of the translation, and the spacing between groups of sentences so labeled, identify the principal units of the content structure of the texts, tentatively named here narrative actions and episodes. The plan of the presentation emerged during the comparison and analysis of the two narrations, and the criteria for the several analytical units will be explained in connection with the presentation of the comparison, following the texts and translations.

Translation of Mr. Simpson's text

[ENTRANCE]   (1) And then he went on.
[SITS]   (2) He went and went, [until] he seated himself.
[SUCKS]   (3) And then Coyote looked all around.
                    (4) And then Coyote sucked himself.
                    (5) [And then] thus he did: He turned (up) his penis, he turned down his head.
[DISCOVERED]   (6) Someone pushed him down.
                    (7) Coyote said: "You [plural] have not done me good."
[CLOSES UP NEWS]   (8) And then he locked up the story.
                    (9) He did not wish that people should find out about it.
[NEWS ESCAPES]   (10) And then someone (or something) made the story become loose
                    (11) And then everybody found out what Coyote had done to himself.
                    (12) Thus he had headed the story off.
                    (13) And then they (had) made the story break out (loose).
[GOES AMONG PEOPLE] (14) And then Coyote became hungry.
                    (15) And then he thought: "Now I shall eat."
                    (16) And then he went among the people.
                    (17) And then they said: "Coyote has acted badly; he has sucked his own penis."
[GOES AMONG PEOPLE] (18) And then Coyote went on again.
                    (19) He thought: "Yonder I am not known; truly now they shall not find out about me."

(20) He went on (until he came to) another house.

(21) Now again the people are laughing among themselves: "Now Coyote has sucked his own penis," the people are saying [lit: telling] again to one another.

[CONSEQUENCE]   (22) And then he thought: "Truly now I am found out."

([EXIT])   (23) And then he went on.

Mr. Smith's text

(1) Ikdá:t wít'a Isk'úlya.

   (2) Kwapt aGaLáx galaXóX.

(3) Didmúit.

   (4) Kwapt gayúLait.

(5) ItXÉt.

   (6) Kwapt galiktxúit.

(7) Kwapt gaSíxtukS.

(8) KwaiS náqi qánSipt, Sángi iyaqáqStaqba gaLgiut'íwa.

   (9) GaLgiúlxam: "Ixixia, dan wít'a miúXulal?"

(10) Gasixmk'nágwatsk: K'áya San.

   (11) K'ma gaCLXáCmaq.

   (12) GaliXLúxwait: "IdwáCa aLkdóXwa."

   (13) Kwapt íwi iLyákSn gaCLoX: idlXdímaX galóXwa náwit wímaLba, inádix kwádau gigátka.

(14) K'waS galiXóX: Dala'áx idwáCa aloXaXa.

   (15) K'ma GanGádix ipGólx gaCiup'-íxwaix SáXalba itk'álamat; GánGat aG(a)éwa gadixt'ágwa idwáCa.

(16) QáXba (a)yúya, kwáb(a) itGuímxat náwit aCuXwaCmáGwa idÉlxam.

   (17) Alugagíma: "(A)gha Ci' mSXlCmlit Isk'úlya iSíxtukS?"

(18) QáXba wít'a ayúya, dáukwa wít'a aliXlCmáGwa.

   (19) Kwapt t'Lak gayúya.

98   Breakthrough to Performance

The English translation is that of Mr. Smith, a sentence by sentence rendering of the story in his own English idiom. A few additions based on the Wasco text have been made in brackets; a few English additions by Mr. Smith have been enclosed in parentheses.

Translation of Mr. Smith's text

[ENTRANCE]	(1) He [Coyote] was going along again.
	(2) Then the sun was shining hot.
[SITS]	(3) He was tired.
	(4) Then he sat down.
[SUCKS]	(5) He was sitting.
	(6) Then he got a hard on.
	(7) Then he started sucking [lit: he sucked].
[DISCOVERED]	(8) He just got started [lit: Just not extent-of-time] (and) somebody pushed him down on his head.
	(9) They told him: "Hey, what you doing [again]?"
	(10) He looked [all] around: Nobody.
	(11) [But] he heard them.
[CLOSES UP NEWS]	(12) He thought: "They'll make news."
	(13) Then he done his hands like this [extended arm, elbow bent, palm erect and facing outward, moving left and right in a wide sweep]: (Then) it became rimrock clear to the river from the top of the hill on both sides of the river [lit: straight to the river, on this side and that].
[NEWS ESCAPES]	(14) He got afraid: It might make news.
	(15) [But] already the wind blew the down over the rimrock; already the news got ahead of him.
[GOES AMONG PEOPLE]	(16) Wherever he goes, from house to house, he already hears the people.
	(17) They're saying: "Already you folks know [hear] that the Coyote was sucking off."
[CONSEQUENCES]	(18) Wherever he goes, he hears the same, the same thing again. [lit: Where again he will go, thus he will hear].
	(19) Then he went off and left.

Comparison of texts

The criteria that have been used in presenting the texts and translations
and that enter into the comparison to follow must now be explained.

Narrative sentences.   Although the two texts have been presented line
by line as sequences of numbered sentences, the choice of units to number
has not been based on a priori syntactic or grammatical grounds. One might
conjecture, for example, that there could be said to be as many sentences in
the texts as there are independent verbs. From the standpoint of both linguistic and narrative function, such a criterion proves inadequate. On the one
hand, some Wasco and Wishram sentences have no overt verbs (e.g., the first
and the last two sentences in the original of Mr. Smith's prologue). On the
other hand, many evident narrative units contain more than one verb. In (9)
and (12) of Mr. Smith's text, for example, one clearly does not wish to treat
"They told him" and "He thought" as sentences separate from what follows.
In both texts, indeed, there are instances in which "he did," followed by an
account of a nonverbal act, is parallel to cases with "they said (told)" and "he
thought" ([13] in Mr. Smith's text, [5] in Mr. Simpson's). Repetition and
verbal parallelism within an instance of what is said, thought, or graphically
done also appear to be rhetorical elaborations within a common unit, not
demarcation of a new unit. Cases in Mr. Smith's text are the spatial parallels
of "this side and that" (13), "Wherever . . . , there . . ." (16), and the
spatial-temporal parallel of "Wherever again . . . , same again . . ." (18). In
Mr. Simpson's text there are parallel structures within quotations ("His-badness he-did Coyote, his-penis he-sucked" [17]), and ". . . [negative] someone-
. . . -me-about-know," "[negative] . . . someone- . . . me-about-know-be caused
[='find out']" (19). Compare also the sequences of verbs, up to three in
number, within what are, on other formal grounds as well as intuitively, part
of a single rhetorical sentence in *Wishram texts* (102.2, 102.4, 102.5–6). The
criterion would seem to be that change of verb without change of actor does
not mark a new sentence, at least not from a narrative (or rhetorical) point
of view. (Note that the actor is always pronominally marked in the verb in
Chinookan and need not be marked otherwise.) Change of actor does mark
a new narrative sentence, with one exception, itself statable by a rule: a verb
within an account of something said, thought, experienced, or done, governed
by a verb of saying, thinking, seeing, or the like. (See [9, 12, 13, 17] in Mr.
Smith's text.)

In general, narrative sentences seem to be determined, or delimitable, by
the initial occurrence of a limited number of particles and types of verb. Such
delimitation is especially clear in Mr. Simpson's text, which reflects traditional
myth narration style in the way in which it appears to be "lined out," as it
were, in units defined by the dominant initial particle sequence, *AGa kwapt*
(hereinafter, *AK*). Of the 22 sentences of the text, 14 begin with *AK* (1, 3,

4, 5, 8, 10, 11, 12, 13, 14, 15, 16, 17, 18, 22), one begins with *AGa wit'aX* (21) (cf. *AKW* in [18]), and one with *A* (12). In keeping with the principle that repetition signals structure, occurrences of *AK* have been invariantly translated "And then," although Sapir's translation renders them variously "Now" (14), "Then" (15), "But" (17).

The remaining narrative sentences in Mr. Simpson's text are determined by certain initial verbs. The first type consists of verbs of going, or, more precisely, of traveling, going on. Traveling on is indeed a fundamental premise of the Coyote cycle, both as to his entrances and exits in individual stories, and as to the linking of stories in a cycle. Mr. Simpson uses the standard Coyote myth verb, *gayuya* 'he was going' (*ga-* 'remote past', *y-* 'intransitive male actor', *u-* 'direction [away]', *-ya* 'to move') in the first sentence, and uses it with emphatic vowel length to begin the second. The first sentence thus is doubly marked, consisting indeed solely of a double marking (particle, verb of traveling) of segmentation. A secondary verb of this type is the verb theme *-k-ta*, 'intransitive fast motion', used initially in (20) (and found within [16] and [18]).

The second type of verb has to do with acts of speech. Patently such is *-kim* 'to say' (7). The reflexive verb theme *-X-Luxwa* 'to think' (to wonder with regard to oneself) (19) can be interpreted as denoting inner speech. In the narratives it is treated in a manner parallel to verbs of speaking, being followed, as in quotation, by what is thought (silently said). In (9) the negated verb construction *tq'eX . . . . -X-*, a common Chinookan type, wherein the specific verbal force is marked in the particle and inflectional apparatus (of tense-aspect and persons principally) is attached to the 'factotum' verb system *-X-* which can also be considered an example of this type, even though it would be somewhat artificial in English to place a colon before the conditional particle *pu* and the verb. Cf. (14) in Mr. Smith's text, discussed below.

There remain two cases of sentences delimited by change of actor only (6, 11). Obviously the criteria are overlapping, and, as comment on the first sentence has suggested, cumulation of features capable of marking segmentation may be stylistically significant.

The criteria presented above serve to segment Mr. Simpson's narrative completely and consistently. The two kinds of criteria might be said to be ordered, conjunctive particles first, verbs second. As can be seen, the conjunctives are connectives denoting succession of time or place; the verbs denote change of place (and hence of time) or of actor or communicative act (speech, outer or inner).

The same criteria apply to Mr. Smith's text, but with differences in exemplars and position, and even then, not completely with the same result. The differences are a principal reason for considering Mr. Smith's text as assimilated to the genre of tale.

To consider conjunctive particles first: the *AGa kwapt* of Mr. Simpson's text is paralleled here by simple *Kwapt* (K), but the text does not begin with

K, and whereas *AK* marked more than half the sentences in the other text, *K* marks less than a third in this. Other initial particles here come into play. One is temporal *(KwaiS)*, but with a force within the situation, more than a marking of succession. (There is really here an adverbial phrase in the initial particle position, "Just not extent-of-time.") Mr. Smith twice makes use also of a generic particle of place *(QaXba)*, each time in a somewhat different coordinate construction (*QaXba* . . . , *kwaba; QaXba wit'a* . . . *daukwa wit'a* [16, 18]), reinforced to be sure by a verb of traveling. Most distinctive of all, Mr. Smith twice makes use of a particle marking not succession but co-ordinated contrast, *K'ma* (11, 15). One might think to treat *K'ma* as indicating dependence, and what follows it as part of a preceding sentence. In both cases, however, the preceding sentence is of a type that elsewhere always stands alone, and, bipartite itself, is completed by a second part (which may be taken as a quotation of inner speech?—"nothing" [10], "It might make news" [14]). With (15), one has following *K'ma* a quite complex structure that might itself be candidate for analysis as two sentences. Moreover, as will be seen with regard to narrative segments, the placement of *K'ma* fits into a pattern set by the dominant initial particle of the text, *Kwapt.*

Just as with initial particles, so with initial verbs: Mr. Smith's text contrasts significantly with that of Mr. Simpson. With regard to verbs of traveling, the first sentence begins with one, but not in the remote past tense-aspect *(ga-)* typical of myth, rather in the stative present *(-t)* without apparent initial tense prefix of any kind. In any case, this verb form, used by Mr. Smith initially in other stories of the cycle, has quite a different force. Whereas *ga-y-u-ya* conveys simply the fact of going along, *(-ya)*, in the remote past *(ga-)*, from here to there *(u-) -k-daa-t*, characterizes the figure of Coyote himself, as in a state *(-t)* of traveling fast *(-da)*, indeed *very* fast (lengthened *a*), "on" *(-k-)*, i.e. overland. Mr. Smith begins his stories with a verb that focuses on Coyote himself, not the mythical period, a verb that indeed abstracts from the mythical period; he makes use of *-ya* where it is dramatically appropriate within his text (16, 18). To be sure, Mr. Simpson uses *-k-ta* within his text (16, 18, 20) with dramatic appropriateness (hunger would make Coyote move quickly); but the converse roles of the two verbs of traveling are representative, I think, of differences between the two texts as wholes.

Mr. Smith makes proportionately more use of verbs of overt or inner speech as initial markers, five times out of nineteen narrative sentences as compared to three out of twenty-one, or more than a fourth compared to a seventh of the time. The climax of the story (12–15) indeed is structured partly by them (12, 14) and in a way that fits into the binary structure of "this, then that" pervading the performance. Two instances of verbs of overt speech *(-lxam* [9], *-gim* [17]) and one of inner speech *(X-Luxwa* [12]) correspond to verbs in Mr. Simpson's text. The use of *k'waS* . . . *-X-* (14) with the qualifying 'perhaps' parallels the negated statement of desire with conditional of (9) in Mr. Simpson's text. The fifth instance is parallel to the rest in form; "he-looked-all-around (lit., he caused his two little ones [eyes] to look [?] completely about): no one" (10); and it is quite possibly also to be fitted under the rubric of inner speech. If not, this instance, and perhaps those of fear and desire just discussed, would seem to require extending the criterion to include mental acts generally. But notice that mental states, *wherein the content of the state is not coordinately expressed as well,* as if in inner or indirect speech, do not qualify; and some attested sentences suggest that a verb of inner speech is implicitly understood. Compare the first and second parts of the sentence in *Wt* 64: 6–7: "Afraid she-became-of-them, she thought: 'Now they-have-killed me,' " to (20) in Mr. Simpson's text, and the parallel of (10) and (14), preceding *k'ma* (noted just above with regard to *k'ma*).[18]

There is one initial verb involving simply a change of actor (3) in Mr. Smith's text. And there remains one verb that does not fit any general criterion, the verb that comprises the sentence "he sits" or "he was sitting" (5). There is no change of actor, no act of speech or mental act, no particle. There is simply a verb-sentence which a consistent segmentation of the text, both as to sentences and as to higher units, leaves standing in isolation. The two cases are parallel in an interesting way, in that both are followed by *kwapt*, and both, while ending in the present-participial-like suffix -*t*, have preceding the verb stem a *t-* 'proximal' prefix (phonetically *d-* in [3]) which has a sort of immediate perfective force. The two sequences (3–4) and (5–6) could be rendered, "Having become tired, then he sat down," and "Having been sitting, then 'it-stood-up-on-him' (literal rendering)." Both have the sequence, premise + narrative action. Notice, moreover, that *kwapt* may occur as a second position enclitic in unstressed forms (as in conversational *AK*), and that *kwapt* is the obligatory introductory conjunction of all apodosis clauses of hypothesis, e.g., *SmaniX* ("If") . . . , *kwapt.* (I owe these observations on *kwapt* to Silverstein.) The present sequences may be an analogue. In any case, if (5) is not marked by myth-like formal traits, within a structure that is lined out, it does have a status in a structure that is repeatedly balanced, both locally (the parallelism of [3]–[4] :: [5]–[6]) and throughout, and seems to me indeed a touch of narrative skill.

Narrative segments.   The surface structure of both texts appears to involve organization at a level beyond the sentence. In Mr. Simpson's text, the rule is simply that the occurrence of the particle pair *AK* marks the beginning of a new narrative segment. (1–2) can be seen as elaboration in the introduction of the scene (and indeed in *Wt* 30: 5 Sapir does treat them as all coordinate parts, separated by semi-colons, of a single sentence). (8–9), (10–11), (18–19–20) all clearly involve elaboration of a single point in the narrative, not movement on to a new one. The single exception to the rule

[18]Silverstein points out that the really important criterion would be voice modulations. It is usually the case that quoted speech (thought perception) is consistently kept in the right voice.

is in (6–7). The text itself, however, is obscured here. Sapir does not in fact translate (6), either he or Mr. Simpson or Sapir's assistant Peter McGuff at the point of translation apparently overlooking the change of actor signalled in the verb of (6), *ga-q-i-ux-X*, 'remote past-someone-him-[directive element]-did', perhaps because of the repetition of the verbal particle *Ck'ES* 'to stoop'. The repetition of the particle (if valid—see appendix) is itself a nice touch: 'turn stoop he-did- himself his-head-at; stoop someone-did-to-him'. And the act is clearly required by the story, and expressed in Mr. Smith's text by the verb stem *-t'iwa* 'to push, shove'. One would have thus expected (6) to begin with *AK*, as do all other initiations of action by Coyote and by others in response to him (cf. [17, 21]). Whether a slip in the act of telling or recording (and Sapir himself notes the text to be obscure a few sentences later in this part [*Wt* 31, n. 4]), or a parenthetical narrative touch embedded within the mythical recitation style, the one exception leaves the general rule of this and other texts in that style sufficiently clear. Narrative segments are marked at the beginning by a standard particle sequence. As will have been noticed, sentences within a narrative segment are indented in the graphic presentations above.

In Mr. Smith's text the rule is quite the opposite. Narrative segments are mostly marked at the beginning of the last (second), not the first of their constituent sentences. This is invariably so for segments containing *K:* (1–2), (3–4), (5–6), (12–13), (18–19). The apparent exception (7) is trivially not an exception; being the only sentence in its segment, it is, of course, last as well as first. The exception here proves the rule in a strict sense. Just this sentence states the act without which the story would not exist. Whereas Mr. Simpson calls attention to it by elaboration and dramatic demonstration (5 following 4), Mr. Smith does it, following preparation (2–6), by playing off against a structural rule of his text, so as to highlight, or foreground, the sentence. Notice, too, that this and the two other occurrences of *K* remaining (13, 19) together mark the three crucial acts on Coyote's part in response to what precedes each: suck himself, transform in order to conceal the secret, go away when the secret is irretrievably broadcast. The other sentences involve actions on the part of others, or states, conditions, or responses of Coyote. *K* signals Coyote's definitive acts. It is not, as *AK* in Mr. Simpson's text, a marker of every segment, but a way of foregrounding some.

The use of *K'ma* at the beginning of the second narrative sentence in two other segments (10–11, 14–15) can be seen to fit into the pattern established by *K*. Each case presents a contrast: Coyote sees no one but hears them; he fears what may be, but it has already come to pass. Two other apparent segments remain, and these (8–9, 16–17) can also be seen to be parallel. Each describes first a situation of Coyote (just started, going) and an action of others affecting him (is shoved, hears) (8, 16), then states what those others say (9, 17). (Notice that in [9] the words are addressed to him, but in [17] are simply being said.) In each case the second narrative sentence can be seen as culminating the segment with an explicit saying of its point. These segments thus appear to contain unmarked narrative continuation that is literally "unmarked," i.e., for which there is no connective marker.

In sum, the criteria for narrative segments and the manner of handling them contrast strongly. Whereas Mr. Simpson's narrative is "lined out," by repeated use of initial segment markers, Mr. Smith's narrative really lacks segmentation by initial markers of this sort almost altogether. With the apparent exception of K in (2), all occurrences of K in Mr. Smith's text can be seen to depend for their organizing force directly on the linguistic value of plain K as a connective of logical consistency (or continuity). Mr. Smith's text in fact is organized in relation to three kinds of sequential connection: (a) unmarked, expressed by absence of connective; (b) marked, with continuity, expressed by the connective K; (c) marked, with contrast, expressed by the connective $K'ma$. The pattern of initial segmentation slots, filled predominantly by AK, is just not present. (Notice that surface observation of the presence of K might mislead one in this respect.) The situation becomes clear through recognition of two kinds of pattern, one purely linguistic (the syntactic pattern of the zero, K, and $K'ma$ connectives), and one narrative (as indicated above and in the following section).

It would be a mistake to jump to the conclusion that the difference just described is in and of itself sufficient to demarcate myth performances from performances of tales. In point of fact, Mr. Simpson's narration of a legendary and a personal experience both show the predominant use of AK ("A quarrel of the Wishram," Wt 200 ff., and "A personal narrative of the Paiute War," Wt 204 ff.). Moreover, Silverstein has found that those whom he has asked about the differences between certain texts maintain the clear separation into "myth" $(-qanuCk)$ and "tale" $(-qiXikaLX)$ but present the two in the same way, i.e., in the AK (and ga- remote tense prefix) pattern. The distinction appears to be based on content in this regard. (There are, of course, other stylistic criteria, notably the formal endings specific to myths.)

That myths might be told in Mr. Simpson's time without the pervasive AK pattern is shown by the last two incidents of the Coyote cycle in Sapir's *Wishram texts* ("Coyote at Lapwai, Idaho," and "Coyote and the Sun," Wt 42 ff., and 46 ff., respectively), and by the sharp contrast between Mr. Simpson's abstract of the Raccoon myth, replete with AK (Wt 153) and the full version (Wt 153 ff.). The narratives with infrequent use of AK were recorded by Sapir's assistant, Peter McGuff, perhaps from the same woman, AnEwikus, who dictated one subsequent myth (Wt 164 ff.), and perhaps one or both of the two historical narratives obtained by McGuff (Wt 226 ff., 228 ff.). In any case, all the myth narratives recorded by McGuff agree in an infrequent use of AK as an initial segment. Initial segment markers are used, AK among them, but without the same predominance as a class as in Mr. Simpson's narratives. In some passages K itself takes on a dominant role as initial element (cf. the Raccoon story, Wt 162). Here then would appear to be an alternative manner of myth performance. Is it consistent with tale performance by the same person? Of this we cannot be sure at the moment. It may be possible to determine that AnEwikus, Sophie Klickitat (who narrated the second historical tale, *Wt* 228 ff.), and the unmentioned narrators of the other texts recorded by McGuff are one and the same. In any case, the myth narratives are consistent, but the two historical narratives are strikingly different, so far as *AK* is concerned. It does not appear at all in the one narrative ("A famine at the Cascades," told by "an old woman," *Wt* 226 ff.), and in only one sentence (twice repeated) in the other ("A prophecy of the coming of the Whites," *Wt* 228 ff; cf. 228: 16, 19).

Both of the myth narration styles represented in *Wishram texts* contrast with that of Mr. Smith, whose presentation here has gotten away from reliance on initial segment markers almost altogether. His occasional use of such markers and general style of presentation appear to fall together with that of the two historical narratives just mentioned.

I would conjecture that the presence of initial segment markers, notably *AK*, was a criterion of formal narration; that the degree of use of such markers, notably *AK*, was an indication of the degree of formality; that such formality was a necessary characteristic of formal narration of myth, and for some speakers, of formal narration of legends and tales; that not all speakers (or, not all occasions or contents) required this formality of narration of tales.

In sum, Mr. Smith's text is not in style a formal narration of myth, but one possible manner of performance of tales.

Narrative actions and episodes. Both texts share the same set of essential narrative actions, those indicated by the bracketed labels in the presentation of the translations. The significant differences are in the disposition of attention to each. Associated with these are differences in the overall "shape" of the story and the handling of its close. These differences can best be discussed after the nature of the analysis into actions and episodes is considered and the results for the two texts shown.

Comparison of the two texts would lead almost anyone to identify the same set of narrative actions: Coyote enters; he sits; he sucks himself; he is discovered and pushed down; he closes up the news; the news escapes; he goes among the people and finds them talking about what he has done; he goes away. The overt verbal forms and arrangements in Mr. Simpson's text do not much highlight or signal the junctures and discrete elements of this set. In Mr. Smith's text, however, the narrative develops in such a way as to make the structure of narrative actions manifest in the very form. This is accomplished by the balanced pairing of narrative sentences in relation to the use of *K* and other segment markers. Following the initial entrance and setting of the natural scene with the first *K* (2), (3) and the second *K* (4) give the next action [SITS]; (5) and the third and fourth *K* (6, 7) give the next action [SUCKS]. The next two pairs of narrative sentences (8–11) elaborate Coyote's being [DISCOVERED], then (12) and the fifth K (13) give the action [CLOSES UP NEWS]. The next pair of sentences with $K'ma$ (14–15) give the next action [NEWS ESCAPES]; the next pair (16–17) again give the next action [GOES AMONG PEOPLE]; and the final pair (18–19) give the last [CONSEQUENCES (Reprise and Exit)]. The relation between narrative sentences and actions is not mechanical, as this review has shown, but a relation between pairing and *balancing* of sentences and narrative actions is indeed pervasive. "First this, then that," so to speak, for each narrative action. There is elaboration beyond a pair (5–7) for [SUCKS] and (8–11) for [DISCOVERED] but built upon a base of pairing, or, better perhaps, binary relationships.

I take this difference in integration between overt form ("surface structure") and underlying narrative action to be a telling indication of the difference between reciting a remembered myth in formal style on the one hand, and concentrating on "fixing up" a story, on the other.

The pairs that constitute the narrative actions can be seen themselves as paired to form larger units, tentatively labeled here "episodes": [ENTRANCE] + [SITS]; [SUCKS] + [DISCOVERED]; [CLOSES UP NEWS] + [NEWS ESCAPES]; [GOES AMONG PEOPLE] + [CONSEQUENCES]. Indeed, these larger units can readily be taken as instances of the familiar narrative units,

Exposition, Complication, Climax, and Denouement (Brooks and Warren 1949:312). The units are to be found in both texts, naturally, but, as with the narrative actions, more obviously and clearly in the balanced development given by Mr. Smith. Indeed, his performance could serve as a textbook case of these narrative units, if an Amerindian example were wanted.

Overall shape and style. A great deal has already been shown of the overall shape and the style of the two texts, but relative emphasis, or proportion, and certain features of style need to be considered before conclusion of the analysis.

The relative proportions of attention to the several actions and episodes are indicated in Table 3-2 for each text, showing (from left to right) episodes, actions, narrative sentences, and the total number of narrative sentences for each action and episode.

With regard to the outer episodes (Exposition, Denouement), it can be seen that Mr. Simpson is half as long with the opening as Mr. Smith, if absolute numbers of narrative sentences are considered, and even briefer, perhaps, if proportion relative to total number in each text is considered (2/22 : 4/19) or at most 4/21. Conversely, it is Mr. Smith who is comparatively half as long with the closing (4/19, or 4/21) whereas Mr. Simpson extends it (9/22). With regard to the inner episodes (Complication, Climax), again Mr. Smith gives relatively greater attention to the earlier (7/19 [21] : 5/22 in the Complication, or more than a third as against more than a fifth). With the Climax there is less obviously a difference, with somewhat greater extent for

Mr. Simpson's narrative

Exposition	[ENTRANCE]	(1)	1
	[SITS]	(2)	1———2
Complication	[SUCKS]	(3, 4, 5)	3
	[DISCOVERED]	(6, 7)	2———5
Climax	[CLOSES UP NEWS]	(8, 9, 12)	3
	[NEWS ESCAPES]	(10, 13, 11)	3———6
Denouement	[GOES AMONG PEOPLE]	(14, 15; 16, 17; 18, 19; 20, 21)	8
	[CONSEQUENCES]	(22) ([23])	1 (2)———9 (10)

Mr. Smith's narrative

Exposition	[ENTRANCE]	(1, 2)	2
	[SITS]	(3, 4)	2———4
Complication	[SUCKS]	(5, 6, 7)	3
	[DISCOVERED]	(8, 9, 10, 11)	4———7
Climax	[CLOSES UP NEWS]	(12, 13)	2*
	[NEWS ESCAPES]	(14, 15)	2———4*
Denouement	[GOES AMONG PEOPLE]	(16, 17)	2
	[CONSEQUENCES]	(18, 19)	2———4

*In view of the "then" in Mr. Smith's English version of (13), its second part might also be a sentence (the emphasis being parallel to that in [6, 7]); if so, this number would be 3 and the total 5. (15) also might be considered a separate sentence, in which case, the number for news and escape would be 3, and the total 5 or 6.

Table 3-2. Relative proportions in the two texts

Mr. Simpson, counting the sentences as numbered (6/22 : 4/19 or 27 percent : 21 percent), but almost no difference, if Mr. Smith's Climax is counted as having 5 or 6 sentences (6/22 : 5/20, or 6/21, or 27 percent : 25 percent or 28 percent). The difference is lessened by the fact that in Mr. Simpson's text (11) is almost properly part of the next episode (Denouement). (Silverstein considers the summary prefigurement of [5–9] in [4] and of the rest of the myth in [10–11] as in classic form.)

Such quantitative measures are only a rough indication, of course, but do suggest for Mr. Simpson's version a line steadily rising from beginning to end, culminating with the Denouement, so far as relative attention is concerned, or a rising line with successively higher peaks, in the Complication, then the Climax, then the Denouement. For Mr. Smith's version there is suggested a curve that rises and falls, peaking in the central episodes, the Complication and Climax. Such profiles emerge more clearly from consideration of several other indications of emphasis, or foregrounding: the location of repetition of incident; of rhetorical elaboration within a narrative sentence; of elaboration

	Repetition of incident	Elaboration w/in sentence	Elaboration w/in segment	Gesture
Exposition	(1–2)?	(2)	(1–2)	(?)
Complication	(4–5)	(5)	(5–6–7)	(5)
Climax	(8; 12)		(8–9)	(?)
	(10; 13)			
Denouement	(14–15; 16–17)	(17)	(18–19–20)	(?)
	(18–19; 20–21)	(19)		
		(22)		

Table 3–3.   Emphases in Mr. Simpson's text

within a segment; of dramatizing gesture. Tables 3-3 and 3-4 will help to compare the two narratives.

Further, notice the location of instances of actually quoted speech. There are six in Mr. Simpson's text, of which all but one occur in the Denouement (15, 17, 19, 21, 22); the one exception occurs in the Complication (7). In Mr. Smith's text there are three instances, one in the Complication (9), one in the Climax (12), and one in the Denouement (17). Further, the two instances of reported inner speech occur one in the Complication (10), one in the Climax (14). Since quoted speech appears to have a special saliency in memory for Chinookan narrators, this *concentration of quoted speech* in the one part of Mr. Simpson's text seems an especially strong indication of the location of the emphasis in his performance, i.e., in the Denouement. Insofar as the occurrence of quoted speech in Mr. Smith's text can be said to be concentrated, it is in the Complication and Climax (especially if one considers the two cases of inner speech). (The significance of quoted speech was suggested by Silverstein. It may be an index of what might be called "density of performance," or the "performance load" of a discourse.)

	Repetition of incident	Elaboration w/in sentence	Elaboration w/in segment	Gesture
Exposition	—	—	(1–2)	
			(3–4)	
Complication	?(4–5)	?(8)	(5–6)	
	?(7–8)		(8–9)	
			(9–10)	
			(10–11)	
Climax	(12, 14)	(13)	(12–13)	(13)
		(15)	(14–15)	
Denouement	(16, 18)	(16)	(16–17)	
		(18)	(18–19)	

Table 3–4.   Emphases in Mr. Smith's text

In Mr. Simpson's text, as the chart indicates, there is a rhetorical elaboration within the Exposition (1–2); then all four modes of emphasis, including
the likely instance of gestural dramatization, focused on Coyote's act of sucking (5) in the Complication. The Climax is somewhat elaborated by repetition
of its two events, the closing up and escape of the story; and the Denouement
is elaborated most of all by repetition, with internal elaboration within sentences of segments, of its first event, Coyote's going among the people. The
foci of elaboration successively change: Coyote's act in the Complication, the
related acts of Coyote and of others in the Climax, the thought of Coyote and
the scornful speech of others in the Denouement.

In Mr. Smith's text, there is elaboration in the Climax and Denouement
analogous to that of Mr. Simpson, but repetition of incident is not strictly
parallel in either case. Rather, the repeated part of an incident (14, 18) is
followed by a sentence (15, 19) that advances the story to the conclusion of
the episode in question. The Climax and Denouement are indeed quite parallel in this regard. Elaboration within a sentence is concentrated in the same
two episodes, being used for the resulting actions in the Climax (13, 15) and
for the general state of affairs in the Denouement (16, 18)—in short, not
mechanically, but for the meanings central to each episode. Elaboration
within segments is found simply as the pairing of sentences throughout the
entire text that has already been discussed. The one instance of dramatic
gesture, finally, comes in the Climax, depicting not Coyote's obscene act, but
his display of power.

Almost every indication, I think, points to a view of Mr. Simpson's text
as focused on a moral (in keeping with the pedagogic function of myths
[Hymes 1958, 1959, 1966a]), Mr. Smith's as focused on a character in a
characteristic situation (in keeping with the nature of the continuing interest
in tales). Mr. Simpson provides a somewhat foreshortened "crime" and an
elaborated "consequences"; Mr. Smith provides a rounded tale about Coyote.
A typical trait of Coyote, his expectations contrary to outcome, is present in
both narratives, but woven more into the texture by Mr. Smith. The sucking
is not dramatized by Mr. Smith, but is prepared for step by step (2–6), as if
to give temporal form to a fact of Coyote's essential nature, that of uncon-
strained response to the appetite or opportunity of the moment. Coyote is
given a chance to use his powers by Mr. Smith in dramatized fashion, not by
Mr. Simpson; people speak of Coyote's deed as bad in Mr. Simpson's text (17),
not in Mr. Smith's; Mr. Simpson's story effectively ends with Coyote's admis-
sion, acceptance of the fact that he is found out, whereas in Mr. Smith's story,
confronted with the same situation, Coyote, as in other stories, simply 'takes
off' (t'Lak).

Mr. Simpson's story, in fact, does not strictly end. In *Wishram texts*, and
in Sapir's notebook, the story runs on directly into another. The last cited
sentence, *AK gayuya*, is the beginning of that next story, not the end of the one
now under discussion, which itself begins, as will have been noticed, with just

that sentence. Before the preceding sentence (22), Mr. Simpson had indeed begun with a word frequent in the summing up part of a myth, *qedau* in the Coyote cycle (cf. *Wt* 6: 24, 26; 26: 4, 7, 9; 26: 24, 25; 28: 20, 30: 4, 38: 17, 46: 1, 46: 20); but the word is crossed out. While elaborating the moral of the Denouement of the present story, Mr. Simpson has also introduced a motive, Coyote's hunger, that motivates well not only the immediate action of seeking out people, but also the story he places next in the cycle, that in which Coyote is reduced to accepting an old woman's sores as food.[19] (The flesh turns out to be salmon, but Coyote discovers it only later.) Mr. Smith has the story of the old woman preceding the present one (he elaborates it with an additional episode), but Curtis has only the story of the old lady, not that now being discussed; thus it is not possible to compare the relation between the two stories in the cycle beyond saying that Mr. Smith treats each as a rounded story in its own right, while, as has been said, Mr. Simpson ties them together.

The different status of the present story for the two narrators no doubt is related not only to the roundedness of Mr. Smith's version, but also to the difficulties in the text from Mr. Simpson. As has been brought out, the difficulties are concentrated in the Complication and Climax, not in the Denouement (given the absence of a formal close). It is as if Mr. Simpson was forgetful or impatient regarding what comes before the part that provides both a moral and lead into the next myth. Certainly the text does not contain everything that is known to have been associated with the story. Sapir's footnote 4 (p. 31) makes as much clear:

> The text is obscure. It is said that Coyote requested all things present not to carry off the "story," but forgot about the clouds *(itka)*, just then sailing above the spot. Not bound by a promise, they tore out the "story" from its fastness and conveyed it to the people. Thus was explained [by Louis Simpson's brother, Tom, or Pete McGuff—cf. *Wt* 9, n. 3] how all had heard of Coyote's obscenity, though no one had witnessed it, and though he himself did not tell any one of it. North of the Columbia and opposite Mosier may still be seen a long, high mountain called Idwacha or "Story," in which Coyote attempted to lock up the "story." Its clefts are due to the sudden force with which the "story" broke out.

Most likely a full performance of the myth as known to Mr. Simpson (and/or to Sapir's other sources of information at Yakima) would have included Coyote's request to all things present. Very likely, too, it would have ended with explicit reference to the mountain that owes its name to the myth (cf. the endings of the immediately preceding narratives [*Wt* 26: 25, 30: 2–4]). In point of fact, however, Mr. Simpson's choice of detail and of episodes to

---

[19]The version told in English by Philip Kahclamet begins with Coyote's hunger as motive for his act.

elaborate, while revealing of the character and interest of the particular telling, reflects a right, and indeed a necessary skill, vested in all Chinookan narrators. I cannot be sure how much could be omitted and have the narration still counted as acceptable, but myth narrations do generally leave a good deal implicit. Mr. Smith's text, no more than Mr. Simpson's, does not convey everything that would be needed to make the story entirely clear—notably, just by what and how Coyote's head is pushed down at the outset. Full clarification, and especially explanations and asides, if present, are evidence that the narration is *not* a native performance. (The presence of explanations is often a characteristic of narrations in English, as opposed to narration in Wasco, by one and the same person.) As with many other peoples, a myth was told to an audience many of whom already knew the story. It is difficult now to reconstruct just how full knowledge was transmitted from generation to generation—to what extent by the hearing of details in different narrations of the same story, to what extent by speech outside the narrative event itself. Nevertheless it is clear that in assessing a given narration, one must distinguish between what is missing and what is implicit.

The elements mentioned above—Coyote's request, identification of the named mountain—do seem elements that may have been passed over by Mr. Simpson, the one on the way to the part of the story he elaborates, the other in passing immediately to the second story with which he integrates the present one. Other aspects of the present myth seem clearly to be left largely implicit, and to need such clarification as can be given. The points of particular interest have to do with agents and agency, and lead into an analysis of the status of Mr. Simpson's text, as we have it printed, and a suggestion as to some connotations of the story.

An excursus on agents and agency. An implicit point that is almost certainly common to both texts is that Coyote's head is pushed down by a feather or piece of down. So much is made clear in a version of the story told in English by Philip Kahclamet to David and Katherine French at Warm Springs, Oregon, on 4 September 1955. (I am indebted to the Frenches for providing me with a copy of this version.) Coyote cannot see and does not know what has pushed down his head nor how he has been found out; but after he has been refused by the people in the villages, he defecates his two sisters (feces) and asks them as he commonly does when unable to discover the cause of a frustrating experience. The sisters refuse to tell him what he wants to know, because afterwards he will only say, "I know all about it." Coyote threatens to make it rain (to wash them away) and the two sisters comply: "You was coming along up the river today and you got hungry. And you looked around and nobody was looking. You masturbated. You was eating something. One piece of down flew through the canyon and push you on top of the head and push it down. Your penis piece went up in your throat. 'aagh!' (retching sound). You made that kind of noise. That piece of down went over the cliff ahead of you and told all the news. All the people heard about you."

Mr. Simpson's text contains no reference to down or feathers, but all versions of the story known to me are consistent on this point, i.e., the versions by Mr. Smith and Mr. Kahclamet, and others obtained by Michael Silverstein. It can be taken as implicit in Mr. Simpson's text, and indeed, as pronominally expressed (as will be seen below). The situation as to the force that carries off the down (in the versions by Mr. Smith and Mr. Kahclamet) and as to the force that breaks out in Mr. Simpson's version, however, is not as clear.

Silverstein has commented to me on the role of the feathers, or down, in this regard. It is perfectly obvious, he considers, that down should be airborne at a point on the river, where many trees and birds are around. The moral of the story in fact hinges on something so insignificant as some chance wind-borne feathers having caused Coyote's well laid plans (first looking around to see that no one was watching, later surrounding himself with rimrock) to "gang agley." This is without doubt the moral that Chinookans would put upon the story (if one does something wrong, it will get about). There is a further aspect of the escape of the "news," however, to be explored. This aspect is indicated by the verb with which Mr. Simpson describes the escape. Recall Sapir's n. 4 (*Wt* 31), quoted above, as to the "story" being torn out and breaking out with sudden force. The verb Mr. Simpson uses ([13] of his text) has as its theme *S-. . . . -qi-da-ba*. It is a form of the same theme found three stories earlier in the place name *S-q'l-da-l-p-L* 'It keeps tearing out', with reference to a lake connected with the Columbia River by a narrow creek. The verb theme expresses rapid motion *(-da-)* out of an enclosed space *(q'l-/qi)* with respect to the two sides *(S-/s-)* through which the motion occurs. (The second and third laterals in the place name [*l, L*] are continuative elements; *s-* and *q'-* in the place name are diminutive vis-à-vis *S-* and *q-; qi-* in Mr. Simpson's text is the alternant of the adverbial prefix *ql-* before an underlying directional/tense quantifier *t-* [expressing 'from there to here' in its directional sense].) This verb seems clearly to express, not the wafting of a feather over cliffs, but a bursting through them.

It is not at all apparent that clouds sailing above a spot might break through rimrock below them, and clouds are not otherwise known as an agency in Wasco tradition. Wind, cited by Mr. Smith in his translation, is so known, and is the much more likely agency here. I should like to suggest that "clouds" enter the explanation footnoted by Sapir (*Wt* 31) as a euphemism, and that the down, or feathers, have such an association as well. This suggestion involves the status of *idwaCa* 'news', as well, and is intertwined with explanation of the differences between what Sapir wrote in his field notebooks (to which I have access through the courtesy of the late Walter Dyk) and what he printed in *Wishram texts*.

As has been seen, Mr. Simpson's text mentions no explicit agent or agency. Mr. Smith's text, however, does provide a name for what it is that escapes, *i-pGulXh* 'down', and his English translation names what carries it abroad, the wind. With the aid of these clues, one can clarify in terms of pronominal reference what seemed so obscure to Sapir that he apparently corrected his own transcription (see end of Appendix). That is, when Sapir rewrote *i* in certain words as [u] for printing, it was not, I think, an error in reading his own writing, but a judgment that the pronominal prefix in question must refer, must be in concord with, the nominal prefix of the word for 'story', *id-waCa*. The prefix must then be, not singular, as *i-*, but plural, as *u-* and *id-*. Or so I imagine Sapir to have reasoned. In point of fact, the pronominal reference in Sapir's notebook can be consistently explained, and something added as well to understanding of the symbolism of the story.

Two sets of pronominal reference are of concern, those to the agent of certain actions in the Complication and Climax, and those to the object. (Recall that it is quite acceptable in Chinookan to have an incorporated pronoun in the verb as the only overt nominal reference.) With regard to agents in (7) and (13), it is quite fair to take the plural subject pronouns, *mS-k* 'you' and *tk-* 'they' as in concord with the plural prefix of *it-ka* 'clouds' in the critical sentence. In (6) *q-*, as has been stressed, must be recognized as indefinite agent. There remains *C* 'third person (masculine) singular' in (10); what 'he' or 'it' (for since most nouns must have a pronominal prefix, such a prefix in the verb may refer to other than ordinarily animate beings) could be responsible for loosening the story? Not the plural 'clouds'. I suggest the singular 'wind', which has the appropriate nominal prefix *i-*, whichever of the two main winds, East or West, may be in question (cf. *Wt* 102 for *i-kXalal* 'West Wind', and *i-kaq* 'East Wind'). Just such is the case for the fourth word in (15) of Mr. Smith's text where *C* is the manifestation of what he then gives in English as 'the wind'.[20]

With regard to objects, it is quite fair to take the *-u-* in plural object pronoun, *u-*, in (8), as in concord with the plural prefix of *id-waCa*. But the object pronoun *i-* recorded originally in the verbs of (10), (12), and (13) cannot be in concord with the prefix of *id-waCa*, even though that very word occurs in the same sentence. (There are Chinookan nouns whose plurality is marked by a suffix, so that *i-* could be the prefix, but 'story' or 'news' is not one of them.) I suggest that the object prefix *i-* must be taken as in concord with the noun supplied by Mr. Smith, *i-pGulx* 'down'. There is, so to speak, a suppressed concord here. And I suggest that the word for 'down' shows it

---

[20]The wind is marked in Mr. Smith's Wasco text by the pronominal prefix *C* in the fourth word of (15), parallel to the *C* in (10) of Mr. Simpson's text. Probably the West Wind, blowing east in the direction along the Columbia River Gorge in which Coyote was traveling, and speaking, perhaps, with a touch of coastal Chinookan dialect, is meant. The first word, *ixixia*, unanalyzable in Wasco-Wishram, can be compared to Shoalwater Chinook *xixiau*, emphatic form of the pronoun marking 'nearness to second person, present, visible, masculine' (Boas 1911:618). Cf. also, an analogous Shoalwater form, expressing derision, *ehehiuu* (Ibid.: 635). The rest of the greeting, apart from *wit'a* 'again', is a common expression, *dan miuXulal*, quite literally 'what (are) you doing'?

to be no accident, but motivated by euphemism, amusement, or both. Other, probably etymologically related words, having to do with bird body parts, have a vulgar second meaning in Chinookan: *i-pqulXi* 'feathers' is attested in the Kathlamet dialect as a euphemism for excrement (Boas 1901: 216, l. 4). Mr. Smith cautioned me early in our relationship to be careful of a brother who would teach me the stem *-p'i'* instead of *-piq* for 'wing'; the former is a slang word for a woman's genital organ. While there are words for 'semen' in Wasco, *iLtk'Eptk'Ep-maX* (related possibly to the word for 'white' and to the word for 'salmon milt' [*-tq'in*]), and *iL-Gia-maX*, I suggest that *ipGulX* is here their surrogate. In other words, I suggest, given the indications of bird body-part euphemisms and Coyote's Gargantuan nature, that what gets away from him at this point is suggestive of, if not symbolized by, the product of his act.[21] Hence the involvement of the "clouds" in the explanation reported in *Wt* 31, note 4, which I take to be another euphemistic reference. Hence also the ability of the people round about (presumably upriver) to interpret the evidence of the "story." Sapir put "story" in quotation marks presumably because he did not think it a real story; so might the Wasco have thought as well. Indeed, the pattern of pronominal forms and implicit concord recorded in Sapir's notebook, and discussed above, in (10), (12), and (13), makes *idwaCa* appear to function as if in quotation marks, as surrogate for a noun implicitly meant, and signaled by the object pronoun in the verb whose concord cannot be with *id-waCa*. The sentences appear to read, respectively, as saying to loosen/to head off/to make break loose "news" (i.e., down). And in Mr. Smith's text (15), down and "news" are explicitly equated by parallelism.

Sapir annotated the plural agent prefix of (7) (translated 'You') the following note (*Wt* 30, n. 3):

[You] That is, the "story" of what he did, which would spread among the people and make Coyote their butt. A curious materialization of a narrative or report into an entity independent of the narrator is here exemplified, similarly to the common conception of a name as a thing existing independently of its bearer.

But what has pushed Coyote's head down is singular, not plural, in formal concord. Coyote's use of the plural may be evidence of his being mistaken as

[21]The interpretation assumes that Coyote, having been surprised, continues his activity, once he has surrounded himself with rimrock. This sequence is, in fact, the one found by Silverstein in the versions of the story he has obtained. On this assumption, perhaps, depends the repetition and partial contrast, as between (12) and (14). In (12) Coyote thinks, they will make news, directly, he being exposed, and responds. In (14) he fears *perhaps* there will come to be news (not: they make [tell] news), presumably the escape of what is immediately mentioned, "But already the down. . . ." The "news" then presumably is spread in and by the wind, an adversary of Coyote in another myth (*Wt* 99).

to what has happened to him, as he often enough is in such encounters. (Cf. Mr. Kahclamet's version, quoted above.) There would be humor here in Coyote's supposition that the cause of his discomfiture must be plural, a gang, when it is in fact a single piece of down. If the plural prefix is linguistically accurate on Coyote's part, and the word *id-waCa* (with its plural prefix) is implied, so that Coyote is already anticipating that the down will betray his act, make "news," still he is addressing, not an hypostatized "story," but anthropomorphized feathers. And if the suggestion is accepted that the down is not an arbitrary, but in its whiteness, softness, and smallness, an appropriate means of making known Coyote's act, then there is an additional touch of humor on this interpretation as well. In either case, accurate or inaccurate use of the plural in address on Coyote's part, the quoted statement is intrinsically part of a very humorous situation indeed—Coyote has just been made to choke on his own organ. The point of Coyote's remark is not what the "story" will subsequently do; it is addressed by Coyote in terms of what it has already done. In short, the true interest of the remark is not as an example of materialistic folk belief, but as an aspect of somewhat slapstick, somewhat Pantagruelian folk humor.

Mr. Simpson's text, indeed, has another touch of such humor, invisible to any non-native but the grammarian. In (4) Coyote is said to suck himself with the form *ga-s-i-X-tuks* (*ga-* remote past, *s-* dual object [with implicit concord probably to the noun for testicles, which is inherently dual], *i-X-* 'he with respect to himself' ['reflexive'], *-tuks* 'to suck'). In (17) and (21) the first prefix and the stem of the verbal theme have the form *S-* . . . *-tukS*. The difference employs one of the several patterns of diminutive-augmentative sound symbolism in Wishram and Wasco; what is small in (4) is larger in (17) and (21). (Not as large as it might be; cf. *Wt* 10: 16, 10: 18, 12: 9, 16: 25 for transformations through borrowing and subsequent cutting of Coyote's smaller [normal] *ia-k'alxix* into augmented *ia-galxix* and back.)

Overall shape and style again. The part of the narrative just dealt with is located in its middle, in the second part of the Complication—the discovery —and in the Climax. Here especially the contrast between the two texts in overall shape and style is sharp. As we have seen, Mr. Simpson concentrates attention, so far as specific events are concerned, on the first part of the Complication—Coyote's sucking—and then on the first part of the Denoue-ment—Coyote's going among the people. There is some elaboration by repeti-tion in the Climax, but the repetition (12–13) serves to repeat, rather than to develop, the story, as if further clarification were needed; the sentence preceding the repetition has already anticipated and in a sense given away the point of the coming Denouement; and Coyote's motive for closing up the news (9) is given after the event, rather than as a preparation for the event that would move the story forward. By contrast, Mr. Smith elaborates the second part of the Complication—the discovery—with dramatic depiction, and his Climax is presented in a clear parallel structure that uses Coyote's motives to build the story. Coyote first thinks someone will make it news, then fears (12, 14). The corresponding consequence is first a dramatized depiction of transformational power (13), not a mere report, and second a corresponding concrete depiction of the outcome contrary to his wishes. And as against the linear march of "And then . . . , And then . . . ," notice the heightening here in "But already . . ." (as also in the discovery's "just started").

Mr. Simpson's treatment of this central part of the story is indicated by the absence of *Coyote's proper name*. The action moves forward with *Isk'ulya* as actor in (3, 4, 7) of the Complication, and then again in the elaboration of going among the people (14, 18), but in the Climax he is named only by reference. This "bimodal" distribution of the proper name confirms the other evidence of the twin peaks of Mr. Simpson's attention. And the contrast with Mr. Smith's story, wherein *Isk'ulya* enters by name, but thereafter functions by pronominal prefix, save one case of reference by others (17), is perhaps a further indication of the transformation of myth into tale; in other words, that *Isk'ulya* thereafter does not really function as the myth-age Coyote, but just as an amusing character. (On names, cf. chap. 10.)

The contrast in overall shape of the two stories is further shown by a grammatical point of style. When Mr. Simpson picks up the Denouement, using Coyote's proper name and elaborating his motives in anticipation of an outcome, he does so with successively stated mental states and actions; the story proceeds step by step (and, as noted, leads on into another story). Mr. Smith's Denouement is not only concise, *it is no longer a sequence of narrative action*. The highlighted action of the Complication—especially the discovery —and the Climax is over. The Denouement is presented in the form of balanced generalization, employing not a narrative past tense, but the "future", *a- . . . -a*. This future, there is reason to believe, is perfective; that is, it is used (in isolation without qualifying particles) of outcomes that are certain. An alternative translation of these passages would be: "Wherever he would go, there (at) the camps straightway he would hear the people. They would say: 'Have you already heard Coyote sucked himself?' Wherever again he would go, the same again he would hear. Then he took off (split)." Here is further indication of the rounded shape of Mr. Smith's story, focused on depiction of the character and characteristic acts of Coyote.

The shape and style of the two texts are significantly different with regard to another aspect of elaboration not previously mentioned. With regard to adjacent sentences, to what extent is elaboration *preparatory*, or *subsequent*, to an event? There is little preparatory elaboration in Mr. Simpson's text. The two parts of (2) probably are a case within the event [SITS];[22] (3 : 3) are clearly

---

[22]This interpretation of (2) is supported by the transcription in the field notebook of Sapir, which shows the two verbs going together within a second sentence. Sapir's recording perhaps reflects a fact noted by Silverstein, namely, that either one has three or four repetitions of a continuative verb followed by a closing verb (optionally with *nawit* in motion sequences), or (as is the case here) one has a lengthened vowel with rising intonation, followed by staccato, low-tone monotone finishing verb with stress two syllables down from the lengthened vowel.

a case within the event [SUCKS]. There is none within the [DISCOVERY] or either part of the *Climax*. Preparatory elaboration is concentrated within the *De-nouement*, specifically within the event [GOES AMONG PEOPLE], where (14–15–16 : 17) and (18–19–20 : 21) are elaborated in precisely this way. There is some elaboration of adjacent sentences that is subsequent to the statement of an event: (5 : 4) is such a case, so also (9 : 8); and the second part of (21) may also be noted. At the level of elaboration by repetition of events themselves, the relation between (12–13) : (8–11) and (8–21) : (14–17) is of this same type. Notice that these forms of elaboration are concentrated, first on the event [SUCKS], and secondly, and predominantly, on the conse-quences of the news becoming known. At a broader level, the fact that certain specific points can be seen as *summary* introductions (a point made and stressed by Silverstein)—(4) in relation to (5), (8–10) in relation to (12–13), and (11) in relation to (14–22)—gives the overall structure somewhat the effect of a progression with intersecting loops.

By contrast, Mr. Smith employs preparation for an event throughout his performance. After the [ENTRANCE], preparatory elaboration enters into every event: (2 : 3, 3 : 4), (5 : 6, 6 : 7), (8 : 8), (10 : 10), (10–10 : 11), (12 : 13), (14 : 15), (16 : 17), (18 : 19). At the same time, Mr. Smith's style almost makes a rule of a relation of dependence of a sentence on what has preceded it, so that many narrative sentences face both ways, so to speak (making mechanical categorical analysis difficult, and the well-woven texture of the narration evi-dent). It is striking that cases of subsequent elaboration appear to link sen-tences *across* events: (5 : 4), (8 : 7), (12 : 10–11—note the sequence of Coyote's mental acts, see, hear, think), (16 : 15).

All the considerations of structure and style lead to the same conclusions. Mr. Simpson is partly remembering and/or reporting a myth, in which his greatest interest is the obscene act and the moral consequences of it, first anticipated (7) and then fully acknowledged (22) by Coyote. It is these two disjunct parts of the story, each capped by Coyote's self-recognition, that are elaborated and perhaps one can say, best performed. Mr. Smith is primarily interested in the character of Coyote, a character in which interest had persisted in his generation, and his performance does not point a moral, but treats the situation as another entertaining representation of the kind of character Coyote was. The story is rounded, concentrated in the adjacent Complication and Climax; far fuller of depiction as opposed to abstract report of action; and finely balanced and woven together.

As to genre: neither performance could strictly speaking be a perform-ance of a myth, since none of the Chinookan conditions for such a perform-ance were met (Hymes 1966a). Mr. Simpson's performance has a number of stylistic features of myth recitation, such as the recurrent lining out of the *AK* particles, the use of the remote past tense *(ga-)* pervasively, the use of Coyote's proper name. In these respects Mr. Smith's use of the *K* particle and, in different manner, introduction of Coyote with *ikdaat*, use only of pronomi-nal reference to Coyote in the body of the story, all contrast. There are a number of well-realized accounts in Mr. Simpson's texts, but here, one might say, part of the time at least he is remembering and reporting what he knows within the style of a myth, while Mr. Smith is performing securely within one style of tale, that is, of a Coyote story focused on Coyote and divorced from consideration of moral and cultural consequences for those who had lived along the river, and whose now vanished way of life he had once, they had believed, made feasible.

As a type of breakthrough into performance, Mr. Smith's account of "The story concerning Coyote" might be said to involve a relation between two genres within a narrative cycle. The content, or import, of myth is reported, bracketed, and framed at the outset ("Prologue") to allow increasing ease and assumption of authority, as the telling relationship proceeds in time, and as the tales proceed in mythical space up the Columbia toward sites confidently known.

Myth into Tale with Commentary

Philip Kahclamet once himself made a remark that may be taken to signal the difference between performance and report. In response to the question "Who told you the story?", he replied: "My grandmother, my mother's mother. She was the only one who *told* me stories. I didn't just hear it. She told me the story." [Emphasis as spoken.]

This remark came at the end of a discussion in which Mr. Kahclamet related a story to David French and myself, early in the summer (22 June) of the example of oration given above. The story corresponds to one entitled "Coyote's people sing" in *Wishram texts* (94, 96, 98), and that title is adopted here, although Mr. Kahclamet's presentation could better be identified as "Grizzly Bear and Big Lizard," with a sub-plot about "Rattlesnake and Coon," and a prologue about "Coyote's children sing." The story is presented without editing or rearrangement of comments and supplements, because the actual form of the presentation is itself the point of the discussion to follow.[23]

"Coyote's people sing"

(1) Once upon a time, somewhere about the Wishram people's land— this happened in mythological times. (2) Coyote's sons sing for the first time [i.e., at a winter spirit dance after a successful guardian spirit experience— DH]. (3) One at a time he turned them down—four of them.

[23]I am indebted to David French for the transcript of the story and discussion (which he conducted), and, indeed, for the story itself. Although I was present, the story came in response to his question about a root *(a'Edi)* mentioned in it. The paragraphing is that of Professor French; I have supplied the numbering of sentences. Comments in brackets are those of Professor French, unless initialed DH; comments in parentheses are those of Mr. Kahclamet.

(4) His daughter sing. (5) Her name was *astwawintLX* [this was written (in Sapir's orthography—DH) by PK; he said the *a*-could be omitted]. (6) So, all right. (7) It was all right with him. (8) He went out and collect the people around. (9) His daughter sing. (10) People came; his daughter sing. (11) And after that different people sing, they sang their songs.

(12) Grizzly Bear went over there. (13) He sang. (14) He growled, he growled at the people's feet that were singing. [PK lowered his head in imitation of the Grizzly Bear.] (15) People mumbled his songs. [PK mumbled a song in imitation.]

(16) He told them, "What's the matter with you people? (17) Help me sing. (18) Sing my song. (19) I'm expecting I'm going to eat human head. (20) I'm going to roll it around in front of me and eat it."

(21) There were two little fellows by the door, standing, singing. (22) One of them stepped out. (23) He said to him, "Hey, you Grizzly Bear. (24) This is my people. (25) You're not going to scare them out like that. (26) Not while I'm here." (27) He said to him, "I'm not afraid of you. (28) Why, I could kill you, make you drizzle your excrement out."

(29) Grizzly Bear turned around and looked at him and said, "Oh! *awi* [younger brother], is that you? (30) I didn't know it was you. (31) Why didn't you tell me long time ago. (32) I'd get out of the way. (33) Who are you?"

(34) "I'm *q'aSnan* (Big Lizard)." (35) He quit; he went in. (36) This Lizard he stepped out and said, "Now folks, I'm going to sing." (37) He sing: *"itaama Ciu idaa p'ap'a kwn"* [PK indicated that this was repeated].

(38) People were still afraid of the Grizzly Bear. (39) They mumbled. [PK mumbled.] *hai! hai! haiiii* . . .

(40) (That's when you stopped your song.)

(41) He said, "What's the matter with you people? (42) You still afraid of the Grizzly Bear? (43) I am still here. (44) I am going to kill that Grizzly Bear. (45) I am Lizard, *q'a Snan*, from *wakalaitix*. (46) I am going to kill the Grizzly Bear. (47) You folks going to eat the *p'ap'akwn*, the paws."

(48) Grizzly Bear was sitting over there like this [PK hunched over]. (49) Lizard the same song. (50) That's over with. (51) He quit.

(52) Another *it'uXial* [brave warrior with supernatural power] sing. (53) (I forgot song.) (54) This was a Rattlesnake. (55) He rattled his tail in front of the people. (56) He scare them.

(57) *hai! hai! haiiii* . . .

(58) What's the matter with you people? (59) You scared of me? (60) I'm not going to hurt you. (61) Some of these days I'm going to shoot *Sawalaptn*. (62) (This means the poison is strongest when *walaptn* [cheat grass, *Bromus tectorum* L.] dries up—about the month of August.) (63) Some place I'm going to put my fangs into someone and kill someone. [PK indicated the fangs by curving two fingers downward.] (64) People mumbled. [PK mumbled.] (65) Still afraid of him too.

(66) There were two by the door. (67) Big Lizard had jumped out first

and challenged Grizzly Bear. (68) Now another jumped out and said, "You, Rattlesnake, I know you. (69) These are my people. (70) You are not going to scare them like that. (71) Not while I'm here. (72) Your poison no good on me. (73) I can kill you. (74) Even if you bite me with your poison, I can burn it out with fire." (75) This was Raccoon, Coon. (76) He told them, "I am Coon, q'alalaS."

(77) Rattlesnake, he turn around and look at him. (78) "Ah! awi, I didn't know you was here. (79) You should have told me. (80) I would have got out of your way. (81) I'd have quit." (82) He got out of the way.

(83) The rest of the people sang. (84) These two guys stayed there and watched Grizzly Bear and Rattlesnake. (85) The singing, medicine dance, was disbanded. (86) Everyone went home.

(87) This village was down in the valley. (88) The Lizard lives in the hills, in the rocks. (89) The Grizzly Bear didn't forget this Lizard, what he told him.

(90) Grizzly Bear thought, "I'm going to see this Lizard." (91) He hunt around for him and found him too. (92) The Lizard look around and said, "Here comes this Grizzly Bear."

(93) One day Lizard went out to dig a'Edi [an edible root which may exist only in mythology, possibly only in this story] and eating it. (94) He was the only one that dug that.

(95) He looked around. (96) Here come Grizzly Bear. (97) He sure come with his tremendous weight, size too. (98) He said, "Here he comes now." (99) This happened right by his home, his hole in the rocks. (100) (Lizard live in the rocks.)

(101) He got to him, looked. (102) "Hello Lizard."
(103) "Hello."
(104) "What you doing?"
(105) "I'm digging myself a'Edi. (106) It's my food. (107) I eat it." (108) "Oh. (109) Hm." (110) They held conversation, about spring and so on. (111) Finally, he said to him, "What did you say to me? (112) That time Coyote's daughter was singing in that village down below."
(113) "Oh, I guess I forgot. (114) I don't know what I said." (115) (He excuse to him.)
(116) Finally he got close to him. (117) "Gee, you got little arms." [PK imitated Grizzly Bear by feeling DF's arm.] (118) (Grizzly Bear has got big hands.)
(119) "Oh gee, don't squeeze my arms. (120) I need my arms to dig a'Edi." (121) So finally he got tired of him and said, "I'll tell you what I told you. (122) I told you, 'You Grizzly Bear, I'm not afraid of you.' (123) I can drive my spear right through your belly, with an arrowhead one side broken off from wakalaitix and make you drizzle out excrements."
(124) "O.K. (125) Let's see you do it. (126) Go ahead."
(127) The bear growled. (128) He stood up. (129) Lizard little, Grizzly

Bear big. (130) He got back and jumped on the Lizard and Lizard jumped in his hole in the rocks. (131) Grizzly Bear couldn't find him.

(132) Lizard came out of the hole. (133) He was already painted with grey clay and he had a spear with one point broken off [PK made a drawing of an asymmetrical spear head]. (134) He drove it into him and killed him. (135) Grizzly Bear died. (136) Look at him. (137) Dead. (138) "O.K., he's dead now."

(139) So he come down to the village. (140) "Oh there comes Lizard down. (141) He never comes down here. (142) He never came down here before." (143) They got to the Lizard. (144) "Oh hello Lizard."

(145) "Hello, people."

(146) "Hello."

(147) "Hello. (148) You know what happened last winter—you were scared."

(149) "Yeah, we were scared."

(150) "Well, I come here to tell you people that Grizzly Bear is dead. (151) I killed that Grizzly Bear dead over there in the hills. (152) I promised you p'ap'akwn."

(153) "Oh, oh!" (154) Everybody rejoice. (155) Old people got to Grizzly Bear and got this p'ap'akwn. (156) They cooked it and eat it up.

(157) It was all done; the feast was over with. (158) It was done what i-q'aSnan told them to. (159) (That's the reason I treat the Big Lizard good. (160) I don't throw rocks at him. (161) He got good name today among the Wishram people. (162) We'll cut the story off there [presumably as to Grizzly Bear and Big Lizard, since PK proceeds to pick up the thread of Rattlesnake and Coon—DH].)

(163) One day Coon, sitting in his house, got hungry. (164) He said, "I'm going to get myself some k'astila" [crayfish]. (165) He went to the creek, searching around in the water, eating k'astila.

(166) The Rattlesnake laid out for him in the brush, right in the rose-bushes brush, itC'apamaX. (167) Through the rosebushes he [Coon] felt pain in his foot. (168) He said, "Aduuu! aduuu! aduuu!" [Each in a lower tone than the preceding] (in English that's ouch!). (169) He said, "I got rosebush thorn on my foot." (170) He thought, "Rattlesnake done that to me now." (171) He was expecting that.

(172) So he made fire. (173) He put his foot, palm, over that fire and burned that poison out.

(174) So he went on up. (175) He got another bit [bite]. (176) "Same damn snake again! (177) Oh, hell!" (178) He burned the poison out again with fire again. (179) He went up. (180) He got several bits like that, about three more maybe [which would make the ceremonial number of five—DH], and then it quit.

(181) That's the end of the whole story. (182) Sometimes we'll put them in.

(183) I cut out the different animal songs. (184) Sometimes we'll put them in.

(185) Lot of different songs like Wolf's: *hánaa wi Cai Cai.*

[Q: What did you mean when you said Coyote turned down his sons?]

They were living different places. He sent a messenger to Coyote's house. He told him, "Your sons sing."

Coyote said, "Oh! Which one?"

(I don't know which one but I'll give you this one:) *"Sipa glatsiin."* (The name of Coyote's son.)

"Oh", he said, *"idiaq'úyumat."* (Nobody knows what that means now.) "Tell him, *'aliXasgmgwipGa'* " (to quit and go under the house, maybe).

One or two days (I don't know how long) another one sing. *Sipa q'átkwt-gwaX* [the son's name]. He said the same thing, *"idiaq'uyumat aliXasgm-gwipGa."* He turn two down now.

[PK said that he hoped to get the names of the other two sons.]

[Q: Where is *wakalaitix?*]

It's where flint comes from. This Lizard had that flint. He told the Grizzly Bear, "I can spear with *inatka iyaXanq'witq'wit* [-q'wEtq'wEt]." It means: one side broken off. The Lizard told the Grizzly Bear he had this: "I'll kill you."

My grandmother didn't know whether *wakalaitix* is a real place or not.

[Q: Who told you the story?]

My grandmother, my mother's mother. She was the only one who *told* me stories. I didn't just hear it. She told me the story.

A'Edi is only mentioned in mythology. My grandmother never saw it. The name of Coyote's daughter, *astwáwintLX*, comes from *wawintLX*, which is the skin on the head of a Chinook salmon. The Wishrams eat that.

General comparison

The nature of Mr. Kahclamet's handling of the myth can best be brought out in relation to other handlings of it.

Four Wishram-Wasco versions of a myth of a winter sing are available, none as rich as the original must have been in a full-scale performance. Such a performance could have been a cantata-like inventory of all the natural beings with whom the Chinookans shared possession of powers declared in song and maintenance of their world. The fullest in detail as an account of a winter sing is the version told by Louis Simpson (*Wt* 94, 96, 98) and it is on that version that comparison will be focused. The other versions are an account in English in Curtis (124–26), and a brief sketch told me in Wasco by Mr. Smith. For present purposes, we need not go into as much detail as with the preceding case, and the essential points involving comparison to other versions can be made in terms of an overall outline of the events to be found in any of them. Such an outline requires seven parts:

(A) Coyote's children sing.
(B) Various plants sing.
(C) Grizzly Bear sings and is challenged by Lizard; Rattlesnake sings and is challenged by Coon.
(D) Various others sing (notably animals?).
(E) Crow sings and brings the West Wind.
(F) Grizzly Bear seeks out Lizard; Rattlesnake is encountered by Coon.
(G) Crow encounters Bald Eagle.

The Clackamas Chinook version told by Mrs. Victoria Howard (Jacobs 1958: 67–75), is mainly an elaboration of (A) that comprises all but the last two pages of the printed text. (B) and (D) are briefly alluded to in part of a sentence: "They [Coyote's children] ceased, then those other people there danced," followed immediately by "All done" (Ibid., 73). The challenge of (C) is reduced to Grizzly Bear swallowing a person, war immediately ensuing. The response of (F) has to do with the Mudfish succeeding in finding, deceiving, and slaying Grizzly Bear. An additional section (H) has to do with Coyote claiming the credit; Mudfish denies his claim and is chased. There is nothing about Crow (C, G). The Clackamas version can nonetheless be entered, together with the others, in a comparative table. Each source is identified by initials: LS Louis Simpson, EC Edward Curtis (his narrator being unnamed); PK Philip Kahclamet; HS Hiram Smith; VH Victoria Howard.

Mr. Smith's sketch clearly is limited to the occasion of a winter sing, whose outcome is dispersal of the snow when Crow succeeds in bringing the West Wind. He titled it *Ilxumit,* which he translated 'Singing ceremony'. His English version of his text is:

A long time ago there was a place where the snow was deep on the ground. Then the chief said, "There'll be a singing ceremony. People will sing.

	LS	EC	PK	HS	VH
A	+	(+)	+	–	+
B	+	(?)	(?)	–	(+)
C	+	+	+	–	(+)
D	+	+	+	+	(+)
E	+	+	(–)	+	–
F	–	+	+	–	(+)
G	+	–	–	–	–
H	–	–	–	–	+

Table 3–5. Comparison of five versions (1)

You'll all come. Maybe somebody might make the Chinook wind come and end the snow and cold weather."

The first one that came forth was the mouse. This is her song: "I make eyes in the root bag." Somebody said, "That person with slanting eyes, get out of the way. Let someone else sing." Then she went back into the crowd. (Then Chipmunk, *i'Emt* [a squirrel], *iGwáXCul* [greydigger], and, other animals, getting bigger and bigger, and birds. [These are Mr. Smith's words].) . . .

Then the Crow went forth. She sang. She was singing. Then someone said, "The Chinook wind is blowing now!"

They told Watersnake, "Your house might fall down." He ran out. Watersnake wrapped himself right around his house, tight.

Mr. Smith had remembered in isolation Mouse's song, and further inquiry had led to the text translated above. In sum, we seem to have here recall of the central core of a myth, a winter sing to end the winter, a concern expressed elsewhere in Chinookan myths and tales (cf. *Wt* 131), especially in stylized myth endings, as context for individually remembered moments. Both persons and other beings manifested their spiritual powers through songs at the winter singing (and dancing); a general function of myths was to disclose the character of an actor (cf. *Wt* 44: 13). Here inner nature is disclosed, not through narrative action, but through a caption-like song. The story must have offered special opportunity to some performers, and a series among which children listening might remember individual favorites separately. Pedagogically it would give an idea of what a winter dance was like, what spirits a child might expect to encounter, and so forth. The isolated incident involving Watersnake at the end is apparently an example, and probably belongs earlier on in the story.

The Curtis version has the same general setting as Mr. Smith's sketch, a fact signaled in the title, "The animal people hold a medicine-chant." Like Mr. Smith's sketch, the Curtis version specifies all kinds of bird and animal people as having met at a village in winter to sing their medicine-songs. It incorporates, however, the Grizzly Bear—Lizard and Rattlesnake—Coon confrontations—which all versions but Mr. Smith's share—and gives their sequels in a slightly different version from that of Mr. Kahclamet. Probably the Curtis version had also the initial episodes of Coyote and his children. The episodes are not given, but their implicit presence would explain Curtis's note (p. 124, Note 1): "This [the preceding story] and the following story [of concern here] were related as parts of the transformer myth, but they doubtless should be considered as separate stories of a later period." The clear implication is that the framework of the story involves Coyote. As to yet other singers, the Curtis version has almost nothing. After the pair of confrontations, it is said, "Then Black Bear came out to sing, and he was followed by the other animals, and by all the plant people." It had been specifically said that "Grizzly-bear was the first." The Curtis version thus seems to represent a thread of the tradition, in which the cast of singers begins at the top with the two most dreaded animals (the only two for which the Chinookans had euphemistic respect terms of address) and proceeds down the scale of being through Black Bear to other animals, and then to plants, whereas Mr. Smith begins with the smallest animal (Mouse) and works up (the plants not being mentioned).

After the plant people, the Curtis version proceeds briefly with Crow: "At last it was nearly spring, when Crow started his song. The West Wind began to blow, and the snow to melt, and it was spring when Crow finished." This is used as a step to the sequel to the confrontations: "Lizard went home among the rocks, and one day he sat on the sunny side, making arrows. Grizzly-bear came along. . . ."

In sum, the serious religious and mythological characteristics of the story are reported (or implied, in the case of Coyote's children) but not presented, the attention of the published version being almost entirely on the confrontations and their sequels. One can conjecture that the circumstances were not favorable to performance of the songs, especially since they are spirit-power songs, which people still are reluctant to sing. Curtis did transcribe songs when available, including a Wishram one.

Mr. Simpson's text, recorded by Sapir shortly before the Curtis expedition, shares with Mr. Smith's sketch attention to the series of singers. Whereas Mr. Smith uniquely provides a rationale for the sing linked to its outcome (E), an outline of the animal series, and the incidents of Mouse and Watersnake (D), Mr. Simpson uniquely provides a series of plant singers (B), and a concluding encounter between Crow and Bald Eagle (G) (which explains the coloring of each).

Mr. Simpson also uniquely provides details as to the initial event involving Coyote and his children (A), but here so does Mr. Kahclamet. In Mr. Simpson's version, the incident with Coyote's daughter apparently is given completely—a report that grease flows from her mouth while she sings leads him to predict that she will be a medicine-woman; Coyote, here a medicine-man himself, then smokes. (These details all are indications of serious religious activity.) The incidents with the sons become clear against this background, but are not handled fully. Only one son is mentioned, and none is named. Coyote receives a report that blood flows from his mouth while he sings but Coyote only replies, "He is merely lying." Mr. Kahclamet gives a fuller version with respect to the sons, together with an explicit report of Coyote's rejection of them. (Coyote's four sons, who, with the one daughter, complete the sum of his children at the ceremonial number of five, are named elsewhere by Mr. Simpson [*Wt* 66].) In fact, the two versions reflect different threads of the tradition, both as to order (sons—daughter for Mr. Kahclamet, daughter—sons for Mr. Simpson) and as to the verbal exchanges with Coyote. Mr. Kahclamet indeed, after the nominal end of the story, recalled mythical expressions attested nowhere else. (The contributions of the various versions to a picture of the original tradition show that even fragments may have value, especially when all evidence is partial, and the tradition itself multiform [or, as one might say, extending the metaphor of threads, *filaceous* or *multifiliar*].)

The comparison of the several versions may be summed up in letter formulae that better show perhaps the structure of each:

LS	A	B	C	D	E		G	
EC	(A)		C	D	E	F		
PK	A	(?)	C	D		F		
HS				D	E			
VK	A	(B)	(C)	(D)		(F)		H

Table 3–6. Comparison of five versions (2)

The most significant difference for our present purpose is in what is missing, as between the versions of Mr. Simpson and Mr. Kahclamet. With Mr. Simpson it is what carries the story beyond the setting of the winter sing. With Mr. Kahclamet it is what gives resolution to the situation on which the winter sing is premised. This contrast fits with other differences in what is presented in each version, and with differences in the way it is presented.

Detailed comparison of the Simpson and Kahclamet versions

Regarding what is presented: Mr. Simpson's details of Coyote and his children (A) give the initial scene a religious character in keeping with a winter sing, a character missing from Mr. Kahclamet's version, apart from the fact of the sing. Mr. Simpson presents a series of plant singers, whereas Mr. Kahclamet simply reports that different people sing (11 in his text). (See further comment on songs below.) Both present the initial encounters between Grizzly Bear and Lizard, Rattlesnake and Raccoon. Both merely report that others sing: they all sing (*Wt* 96: 26, 98: 1), the rest sing (*PK* 83), and neither specifies the animals noted by Mr. Smith and the Curtis version. Whereas at this point, Mr. Simpson introduces Crow and the thought of warm weather, Mr. Kahclamet does not. The contrast is all the sharper, because it is the coming of the wind that leads to the next episode in Mr. Simpson's telling, whereas in Mr. Kahclamet's version, the singing, the medicine dance, simply is disbanded (85–86). Whereas Mr. Simpson now continues on with a further episode involving Crow (G), Mr. Kahclamet continues with the second round, as it were, between Grizzly Bear and Lizard, Rattlesnake and Raccoon, and ends the story without any introduction of Crow.

In sum, Mr. Simpson's version has unity of place within the sing and goes beyond that setting only with regard to a denouement for the actor who is central to success. The confrontations are left resolved within the winter sing setting. In Mr. Kahclamet's version the winter sing is an initial setting, indeed background, for a story whose resolution comes later in two different settings. In Mr. Simpson's version there are salient features associated with the religious character and particular magicoreligious purpose of the sing. In Mr. Kahclamet's version such features are missing or subordinate to an adventure in which a resourceful little guy bests a big bully.

Regarding how the presentation occurs: the nature of the performances, especially Mr. Kahclamet's, can be brought out by considering certain genre features (songs, opening, closing) and two kinds of switching, of code and of style.

Songs.   Songs occur in myths as manifestations of identity and particular power. Mr. Simpson gives several songs of plants, and the songs of Grizzly Bear and Rattlesnake, and describes by report the singing of Coyote's daughter and son. Mr. Kahclamet's account of the last does not describe, and the songs presented are entirely within the pair of confrontations. Here he imitates Grizzly Bear's mumbled song (cf. *Wt* 96; n. 1, where the song is said to be in a loud whisper), but also gives Big Lizard's song; Rattlesnake's song had been forgotten (53), but probably would have been given if remembered. (From what is later said of Big Lizard [159–61], I suspect that Mr. Kahclamet remembered this song [nowhere else attested] because of some identification with the figure.) (Note that the songs of plants and animals reflect genuine spirit-powers, while those of Coyote and his children do not; the songs of the latter would be humorous perhaps, but the songs of the former would be the ones valuable to know and convey.)

From the standpoint of the aboriginal culture, the spirit singing and dancing, representing the chief public manifestation of personal religious experience and power, and, like the telling of myths, restricted to the "sacred" season of winter, would have been of major interest. Mr. Simpson makes some effort to supply some of it, and Mr. Smith remembers an incidental song. Mr. Kahclamet remembers some incidental songs, as his epilogue indicates, but in his performance of the story as such, songs enter only to dramatize the confrontation which is the main continuing focus of interest as an adventure. The sequence of songs, which would have been the most distinctive feature of a performance as myth, is missing.

Openings.   Traditional myths have characteristic openings and closings (Hymes 1958). Mr. Kahclamet's narrative begins with the English fairy tale opening. "Once upon a time" locates the action explicitly in Wishram territory and states that the events occurred in mythological times. To take up these three traits in reverse order:

(a) Myths do not need to say that they are myths. They begin directly by identifying actors and a situation, either as going along or as at a type of place. Mr. Simpson's text begins: "And thus again they sang in winter"; the Curtis version begins: "All kinds of people met at a village in the winter to sing their medicine songs"; Mr. Smith begins: "A long time ago there was a place where the snow was deep on the ground."

(b) Location is not specified at the outset of a story in terms of a named place. The one exception is Mr. Simpson's version of Coyote at Sk'in, which seems an abstract almost, and a mistake in this respect. Mr. Smith's version, like all other versions of Coyote myths involving a specific known place, identifies the place by name at the end. The only case in which a myth begins with reference to Wishram territory is when it is said that "The five East-Wind brothers were dwelling *far away* in a certain land" (*Wt* 120: 10).

(c) Behind "once upon a time" might be glimpsed *(G)anGádix* "long ago," with which Mr. Smith's sketch in fact begins. In *Wishram texts* this particle is generally associated with narratives of historical or quasi-historical, legendary character, often cautionary, and with accounts of remembered times before the whites, or even times of one's own youth (*Wt* 183.4, 183.13, 188.8, 226.6, 228.11). It is so used also by Mr. Smith. The particle begins one quasi-historical legend assimilated to the myth genre by its formal ending ("The deserted boy" [*Wt* 138: 13]), but the story is otherwise a tale of abandonment and revenge with only anonymous human actors. (Mr. George Forman recently told Silverstein categorically that this story was *giXikaLXh*, i.e., 'tale,' not myth.) Mr. Smith's setting of a place enveloped in snow has also a quasi-legendary flavor (given legends of just that sort). In sum, either "Once upon a time" is a flat borrowing without analogy in Chinookan myths, or it is a borrowing suggested by a particle associated primarily not with myths but with tales.

Closing. Mr. Kahclamet's narrative does not in fact close. He continues directly with commentary (183 ff.). Partial equivalents to formal closings do occur (162, 181), but both have a metalinguistic element. The first is explicit in reference to the performance situation (rather than the story); not, "Thus the story" (cf. *Wt* 102: 18), but "We'll cut the story off there" (apparently an inclusive "we"). The second also makes reference to the form of the particular presentation: "That's the end of the *whole* story," and does not truly close it, being followed immediately by an explanation of the contrasting outcomes of the two parts that would not have occurred with a native audience.

The handling of opening and closing is understandable in terms of Mr. Kahclamet's relation to his audience, not Wishram children gathered for the express purpose of hearing myths, and offering gifts to the teller beforehand, but two ethnographers. The omission of songs may reflect the cessation of guardian spirit experiences, sings and traditional performances of myths, and consequent forgetting, but also quite likely repression of the material, which is both too serious in traditional life and too scorned outside it to be manifested except under conditions of assured confidence of psychic release. Confrontations of the sort between Grizzly Bear and Big Lizard continued to be remembered and occasionally told, through interest in the characters themselves as expressions of a surviving ethos. The names (and songs) of Coyote's sons are something some older person might remember, if asked, Mr. Kahclamet implied. Big Lizard is still someone not to throw stones at.[24]

Code-switching and style-switching. The fact that the language of telling is not the language of the tradition, but of interpretation, is in itself a major reason for not considering the performance an authentic performance of a myth. Wishram utterances, however, occur. Sometimes they are associated with interpretive role, as when the name of Coyote's daughter is written out (5), the Wishram name of Big Lizard glossed in English (34), or conversely (45). (See also [47, 60, 76, 164, 166, 168], and the comments afterward on the names and utterances of Coyote's sons and Coyote.) Taken all together, the occurrences of Wishram words are not at all random, but fall into two categories. Some are names of native foods and plants, a fact that seems to me a consequence of Mr. Kahclamet's already established role of collaborator with Professor French in the study of Wishram ethno-botany (which, it will be recalled, led to the telling of the story in the first place). As with the character of the opening, this feature of the performance is shaped by its audience. The other Wishram words all have to do with *identities*, by name or by expression. There are the proper names of Coyote's daughter, Big Lizard, Coon, and Big Lizard's home *(wakalaitix);* the names of the role of brave warrior (52) and of younger brother (in interaction, a polite form of address); and there are the expressions of identity in the songs, here that of Big Lizard and, in the epilogue, Wolf. The possible exception within the main narrative is Coon's expression of pain (168), an expression certainly in keeping with and expressive of his character, as not a true hero. A possible exception within the epilogue is in what Coyote says in response to news that his son is singing. Here again, the now untranslatable words, quite likely unique to mythology and this one situation, seem to be expressive of character-

---

[24]In point of fact, a woman still living (1971), Dorothy Spedis, does know the names and songs, and another (Michael Silverstein, personal communication) has said that she is "scared stiff" of Big Lizard. Cf. the importance of Lizard in the Central Sierra Miwok myths told by Thomas Williams (Gifford 1917). Lizard discovers fire for the people (p. 284), saves Deer's children from Bear (pp. 290–91) in a cognate of the Takelma and Clackamas myths of Grizzly Woman and Black Bear, and is the refuge of Chipmunk's wife when she escapes from the Giants, whom, like Grizzly Woman, he also kills (pp. 300–302).

istic identity. The remaining instance within the epilogue is Big Lizard's description of his broken spear. The fact that Mr. Kahclamet made a drawing of the spear head (133) suggests that it is emblematic of Big Lizard in his role as hero of the story.

These spontaneous incursions of Wishram into a story told in English seem to reflect the public function after which the myth genre was named in Wishram, that of displaying the identity (character, nature) of other than human beings (and of human motives, as isolated and embodied in such beings). As the other type of incursion shows, they are myth elements in what is not itself a myth. Code-switching reflects the genre of origin of the story. Style-switching reflects the situation of its telling.

There is genuine performance in the narration, notably in the handling of dialogue. There is also something not usually found (or at least not usually reported), metalinguistic intervention. A Wishram word is written and an alternative form of it noted (5). A mentioned object is drawn (131). Information that a native audience would already have is supplied (40, 62, 100, probably 115, 118) and, as noted, glosses are given.

Two styles of performance thus are interwoven, that of the narrator and that of the interpreter. The latter reflects Mr. Kahclamet's identification with the role of bilingual collaborator, a role which involves both some distancing, intermittently at least, of the role of narrator (native informant) per se, and some validation of the second strand of the more complex role. In the course of the story there is conversation that is convincingly in native style, but the full performance, the performance for which Mr. Kahclamet would have claimed authority, begins with an explanation of setting and ends with an instance of an ability of which Mr. Kahclamet had become a master, linguistic and ethnographic glossing of words.[25]

In Mr. Kahclamet's account there is a good deal more information than in the account in *Wishram texts,* as to the confrontations involving Grizzly Bear and Rattlesnake; there is much that clarifies and amplifies both that version and the version in Curtis, although those two versions were recorded almost a half-century earlier. Mr. Kahclamet's version is clearly in the line of tradition represented by the source of the Curtis version, and provides invaluable confirmation as to how the winter sing myth may have served as a complex frame, not only for the depiction of beings through their songs, but also for the linking of individual stories with explanatory import. (The one encounter explains why Grizzly Bear fears a certain kind of lizard, a deadly food causing dysentery [Curtis 1911:126, n. 1], the only creature he fears besides the eagle, which sometimes carries off his cubs; the second encounter explains why [it is believed] a rattlesnake bite does not kill a raccoon [Curtis 1911: 126, n. 2])

---

[25]For a valuable analysis of a complex case of metalinguistic intervention, see Barbara Kirshenblatt-Gimblett (forthcoming). Such interventions have become a traditional feature of immigrant Yiddish style, so much so that pseudo-glosses may be used in parody.

One can imagine the opportunity provided a skillful performer by such a flexible frame. And in Mr. Kahclamet's account, as noted, there is unique information about uninterpretable words in the dialogue with Coyote. Again, even fragments are valuable for filling out and clarifying the content and form of a tradition that can be seen to have been multifiliar, differentially known and enjoyed. Every indication, indeed, is that knowledge of myths and tales, like other cultural knowledge, had a genealogy for each individual. One or a few particular individuals, who told and probably often told certain stories, were crucial here, his mother's mother for Mr. Kahclamet, his father for Mr. Smith.

The tradition, however, was not only multifiliar, but also "context-sensitive" (to use a linguistic term), "performance-sensitive," differentially realized according to performer, audience, and setting. Clearly the narratives were not necessarily memorized and recited from memory, but rather, as with Yugoslav epics, the performer worked with a knowledge of the structure of the whole and of appropriate incident and style. There is a straightforward case within *Wishram texts* itself, the relation between the short sketch of the Raccoon story recorded in the field from Louis Simpson by Sapir and the full version later written down and forwarded by Sapir's interpreter, Pete McGuff (*Wt* 153 ff.). And in Mr. Kahclamet's account there is not a genuine performance of a myth. There is grist for the mill of the student of mythical plots and motifs, to whom presence or absence is pertinent, but not necessarily status as to indigenous genre or style of performance. But as has been seen, here features that would define a narrative as a Wishram myth are largely omitted, or simply reported, rather than shown; and to the narrative are added features that stem, not from the role of performer of a narrative, but from the role of collaborator in inquiry, to whom the narrative is also partly an object. Much shows through of the traditional manner of handling a type of encounter, that between a dangerous being and a challenger, but if Mr. Kahclamet's account is not regarded merely as documentation, but is seen for what it is, an event with intrinsic character of its own, then it is clear that what we have is material that stems from a myth, originally associated with the main culture-hero (Coyote) in the role of shaman, and with the principal socio-religious event of the sacred winter season, presented essentially as an adventure tale with commentary.

Conclusion

The three types of "breakthrough into performance" can be summarized in brief formulae.

The morning address proceeds within the text through three stages:

[Report]—[Translation]—[Authoritative performance (oration)].

The "story concerning Coyote" is fully realized in itself, but within the sequence of the Coyote cycle (which was, indeed, considered a single myth as a whole) as given by Mr. Smith, there are two stages, one, as has been said, a bracketed reference to the character of the original genre at the outset, the rest a growing assumption of full performance:

[Report as to genre (myth)]—[Authoritative performance (as tale)].

Mr. Kahclamet's account of the winter sing begins in a manner parallel to Mr. Smith's beginning of the Coyote cycle, but its second stage is complex:

[Report as to genre (myth)]—[Authoritative performance

$$\left.\begin{array}{c}\text{(tale as story)}\\ \text{(tale as object)}\end{array}\right]$$

The central theme of this paper has been the distinction between knowledge what and knowledge how, or, more fully, between assumption of responsibility for knowledge of tradition and assumption of responsibility for performance. Much that has been published, I think, has neglected or confused this difference, treating tradition as something known independent of its existence as something done. Where structure is equated with plot and content categories, such a perspective may suffice, rather, never discover its limitations. Such a perspective, I suggest, tends to falsify traditions, analyzing them solely for the light they may shed on something of interest to us, the history of tales or of peoples, or even the uniform working of the mind of man. All these things are important, but do not include something essential to the peoples who shaped the traditions, the shaping of the performances in which tradition was made manifest, through which it was communicated and made part of human lives. Consider the virtual absence of serious stylistic analysis of native American Indian traditions and of individual performers, of the literary criticism, as it were, that should be a first concern and a principal justification of the study of such traditions. This shows how much we tend to expropriate the traditions as *objets d'art* or as documents for scholarship, how little we have attended to the persons whose traditions they are. In a rare discussion of the character and beliefs of an "informant" (*Wishram texts,* xi–xii), Sapir still apparently felt an apologetic introduction necessary: "A few words in reference to Louis Simpson and Pete McGuff may not be out of place." Presumably the "scientific" audience was interested strictly in the Wishram as a collective label and referent. Details as to performer, audience, and setting presumably were accidental. The irony is that a more exact science and method make accidental details essential.

It has been clear, I would hope, that knowledge and performance of tradition are interdependent, in the sense that the nature of the performance affects what is known, for the persons in a community as well as for the outside inquirer into tradition. Certainly the latter consideration enters into what has been presented here. A particular set of conditions, I believe, made possible the telling of the Coyote cycle by Mr. Smith—previous accepted role as narrator of stories and as knower of features of myths; some dependence for moral support in the immediate situation; some suggestion of an acceptance of me as a surrogate for the children, especially perhaps the son, then uninterested, if not hostile, to what he might authoritatively tell, as his father had told to him. With Mr. Kahclamet there was, of course, the previous experience as informant, a complex and troubled history, so that there was authoritative performance in two roles at once. There was also in the particular summer of 1956 a suggestive order to the three occasions on which he presented material at length. First (22 June) a tale—a cultural object—prompted by ethnobotanical inquiry, in English in his role as collaborator; second (25 July) a speech, presupposing his personal belief, but beginning as an account of impersonal cultural tradition, an explanation of a word; third (1 August) a direct account of personal experience and belief. In a sense, the first was in a third-person role; the second began in third person, moving into second, and breaking into first; the third was first person throughout.

These kinds of considerations affect the validity and very possibility of performances whose audience is an outsider. The persistence of the tradition disclosed in performances, however, was not a matter merely of memory from a remote past. As with the language—which is noticeably slipping away now with so little occasion for use—so with tradition. Continued performance has been a condition of survival. The myths and the features of myths validating the aboriginal life along the river, the ritual telling of myths on winter nights to children after presentation of gifts, geared to a conception of winter as a sacred season, all this has indeed gone except in memory. What has survived for the telling now has largely been material that has continued to be relevant to the ethos of the community, to its moral and psychological concerns: certain characters, notably Coyote, for example, as foci of tall stories, and stories of sexual exploit and discomfiture of pretenders, for men, and sometimes as foci for cautionary stories for women; certain kinds of experiences, tending to warrant the possession, at least by old people in the former days, of distinctively Indian identities and powers; stories of recent days, showing the unprepossessing Indian to have the advantage of apparently superior white man, often in the white man's own terms (money). (There is an uncollected sub-genre of such stories about the purchase of automobiles by Indians with dirty clothes and hard cash.) Some of the performance style has persisted and can be met today in the telling of personal experiences and even new jokes.

These are stories, anecdotes, and the like, that have continued to interest people, for which there has continued to be some audience, and so, some nourishing of performance, some reward for style.

The interplay of Indian and rural white ways of speaking in the English of the Indians, the form of performance styles in English at the present time, and their likely future, remain to be comprehended. Distinctive ways of speaking, amalgams from a particular period and situation, may persist, despite overlay and undermining by administrative and educational institutions.

It should be clear that analyses of the sort attempted in this study—analyses of the conditions and character of events involving known persons, who accept responsibility not only for knowledge but also for performance—entail a thoroughgoing break with any standpoint which divorces the study of tradition from the incursion of time and the consequences of modern history. Such standpoints condemn the study of tradition to parochial irrelevance and deny those who would help to shape history necessary insights into their situation. By bracketing the traditional, and stopping there, such standpoints conceal the need to breakthrough into performance in our own time. The sort of analysis attempted here suggests in a small way some of the considerations that must enter into a study of tradition and cultural hegemony, a study that can transcend a conception of structure either as simply equivalent to conscious rule or as necessarily unconscious, and that can understand structure as sometimes emergent in action (cf. Banaji 1970). From such a standpoint, the validity of structural analysis radically depends on interpretation of the praxis of those whose structure it is, and on self-awareness of the praxis of those who comprehend that structure (cf. Hymes 1970:308–10). I honor philology, which this essay is in part, but only from such a standpoint can the study of tradition continue to be ethnography as well.

Appendix: "The Story Concerning Coyote"

This text is not identical with that printed in *Wishram texts* but rather a text re-edited from Sapir's field notebook, now in my possession through the kindness of the late Walter Dyk. The general principle of the re-editing has been to take the field transcription recorded in the notebook as a guide if it was susceptible of a coherent interpretation consistent with what else is known of the language, mythology, and culture.

There are two major points at which the text presented here differs from that in *Wt;* these involve (5–6) and (9–13). In the notebook, and in the text as given here and in *Wt,* there are two occurrences of the particle *Ck'ES* 'bent over, stooped down.' The passage is translated by Sapir as follows: ". . . thus he did: he turned up his penis, and bent down his head (so that) he stooped down." A literal translation of the text printed by Sapir would be: ". . . thus he became (made himself): turn he-became (made himself) his-penis-at, turn stoop-down he-became (made himself) his-head-at; stoop-down someone-him-made (actor unspecified)."

There are two difficulties with Sapir's translation and text in this regard. As the literal translation just given shows, Sapir's published translation treats the second occurrence of the particle *Ck'ES* as an elaboration of the first: he bent down his head (so that) he stooped down. Such elaboration is a common enough pattern, but the text here does not support it. The grammatical structure of the last verb has the stooping down caused by someone other than Coyote. (In the verb *ga-q-i-uX*, *q-* marks indefinite or impersonal actor, while *i-*, referring to Coyote, marks object of action.) Moreover, this rendering of the verb is necessary to the coherence, the narrative sense, of the story at this point. The next sentence (7) has Coyote say, "You have not done me good." Coyote's statement makes sense only in response to having had something done to him.

The second difficulty is that the field notebook shows a position for the first occurrence of the particle that is different from the published text: *"eewi galiXoX iak'alxixpa, eewi galiXoX Ck'ES iaq(')Staqpa. Ck'ES gaqiuX"* (adapting the notebook transcription to the orthography used in this paper). A line for transposition running over *galiXoX* and under *Ck'ES* brings the word order to that printed in *Wt.* Now, such a particle usually occurs before a verb based on the stem *-X.* Presumably this is why Sapir changed the order in the notebook to that in *Wt.* Most likely he marked the transposition at the time of original transcription; I think Sapir wrote in the order that he heard and corrected a moment later on the basis of a quick sense of grammatical pattern (cf. *eewi galiXoX* just preceding and *Ck'ES gagiuX* just following). But the transposition separates the second *eewi* from its verb in *-X*, leaving it without one, and so destroying also the parallelism of *eewi galiXoX . . . , eewi galiXoX. . . .* This leads me to think that the transposition does not reflect what Mr. Simpson actually said but what Sapir considered that he did or should say.

Given the awkwardness of the first occurrence of the particle, one might be tempted to consider it a mistake altogether. One might conjecture that either Mr. Simpson in speaking, or Sapir in transcribing, inadvertently anticipated the occurrence two words later of *Ck'ES* with *gaqiuX.* This conjecture would maintain the integrity of *eewi galiXoX . . . , eewi galiXoX . . . ,* resulting in a balanced and indeed consistent sentence. For notice that there is no need for a particle to mark direction of the head, just as there is no word marking the direction of the penis ("up" being supplied in the translation by Sapir). In both its parts the sentence is consistent with indication of the directions of penis and head by gesture. (Cf. such a dramatization in Mr. Smith's text (13); two narratives recently obtained by Silverstein involve acting out the part.)

It seems likely that both occurrences of the particle were heard. The first transcription of the particle in the notebook shows a final *s,* crossed out, before the symbol for *S,* indicating that the word was indeed heard in its first occurrence. And it seems extremely implausible that the second occurrence could be a mistake. Given the two occurrences as recorded in the notebook, it is possible to take both as intended in the order first given. The first occurrence of *Ck'ES* would be as a directional adverb (analogous to *SaXal* 'up' and *gigwal* 'down'). (The transposed order cannot be ruled out absolutely: *eewi* has partly a deictic force, described once by Philip Kahclamet as that of being a "pronoun" for verbs; one could construe the counterpart of the first *galiXoX* as being (or including) the accompanying gesture, verbally expressed, only in the second instance. This interpretation has no attested parallels—a single *eewi* is known only with an immediately accompanying *-X* verb; but it has some modicum of plausibility.) Whatever the position of *Ck'ES*, its first occurrence has an expressive point. It is part of a cumulative sequence: Coyote turns (up—with gesture) his penis; he turns down (with gesture and word) his head; he is pushed down.

The point, as shown by the correct translation of *gaqiuX*, is that Coyote, having lowered his head, is pushed down further on his penis, choking himself on it (this is quite explicit in Philip Kahclamet's version). The two occurrences of *Ck'ES* can be taken as a play on the word, the repetition serving to highlight the contrast between Coyote's voluntary lowering of his head and his being forced involuntarily even lower.

The second, and more complex point, has to do with reordering of sentences, omission of words, and reinterpretation of a few monophonemic morphemes in (9–13). Broadly speaking, the nature of the problem can be seen by comparing the order of sentences printed in *Wt* with that in the field notebook (omitting here differences in sentence detail). Using the numbers assigned above, the two orders are:

Wt	*Field notebook*
(9)	(9)
–	(10)
	(11)
(12)	(12)
(13)	(13)
(11)	
(14)	(14)

Table 3–7. Order of sentences

The details of the notebook recording are as follows: After (9) there is a lined-out false start: *Naqi pu* [velar gamma]-*a*, and a second sentence lined out: *AGa kwapt gaCuXa*. The notebook then proceeds in the order just shown: (9)–(10) (with *dak dak* lined out before *idwaCa*)—(11) (with a brace at the beginning of the first verb, containing *ni-* above the *ga-* tense prefix) —(12)–(13) (with the beginning of a verb form, *nitk'ix* . . . crossed out preceding the verb form beginning *itkSigXi* . . .). In three cases the notebook shows pronominal object prefix *i-* within individual words, where the corresponding forms printed in *Wt* (in 10, 12, 13) show *u-*.

As has been seen, the order adopted in the present analysis is that of the original notebook. Two observations are pertinent here. First, regarding initial tense prefixes of verbs: it is interesting to notice the occurrence of the prefix *ni-*. This prefix apparently is used to indicate events whose pastness is relative to the local context, falling between *i-*, which indicates actions just undertaken and not necessarily completed, and *ga-*, which indicates completed pastness reaching to the age of the story itself. The fact that (13) (corresponding to the sentence in *Wt* 30:12) has a crossed verb beginning, *nitk'ix . . .* , suggests that the full verb found in the sentence might begin with *ni*, rather than *i* (hence the parenthetic [*n*] in the text used here). Recall also that (11) (corresponding to the sentence in *Wt* 30:14) had a *ni-* in a brace above the *ga-* that occurs in *Wt*. The *ni-* might fit the use of *ni-* in the next verb in the sentence and support the place of the sentence within the conclusion of the preceding part, that is, as not initiating a new part of the story. The notebooks seem to show Mr. Simpson hesitating in the use of *ni-*, but more or less clearly dividing the sentences of the Climax (8–13) between a first set that have *ga-* and a succeeding set that have *ni-*, or for which *ni-* is considered (11–12). This subordinates the latter part of the Climax and changes these sentences from being merely repetitions to having the status of a reprise (suggested by use of "had" in the translation). Were the first verb in (11) to be taken with *ni-*, of course, the first statement of discovery would be remarkably subordinated, being expressed not as the next action but in retrospect (And then everyone *had* found out . . .). The present allocation—the last three verbs of the climax (11b, 12, 13)—is probably correct.

The second observation is that what Sapir mostly did was to take certain prefixes as being in concord with the plural prefix *id-* of *id-waCa*, hence necessarily as *u-*, and to rearrange the material of the Climax so as to bring repeated content together; the notebook, on the other hand, shows *i-* to have been heard, and shows the original narrative to handle repeated content by iteration, as a form of emphasis. As to the prefixes: *Wt* 30:12 (corresponding to [10] has *galuxwaX*, but after *ga-* the notebook shows what is almost certainly *C-i-* (Sapir's *"tc-i,"* clearly not *tg-i-*) and a different suffixal ending, *-ix*. (If forced by context and meaning, the writing might perhaps be stretched to be read as *galuuXix*, but such a form would be difficult to interpret grammatically and has no sense in the context; moreover, the preceding lined-out sequence is clearly *A K gaCuXa*.) *Wt* 30:11 (corresponding to [12]) has *nicu . . .* where one would expect the following *X* to be labialized because of the preceding *u*, but the notebook shows clearly dotted *i* instead of *u*. Finally, *Wt* 30:12 (corresponding to [13]) has *itkSu- . . .* , but again the notebook has dotted *i*. The significance of the original recordings of the pronominal prefixes for the interpretation of the myth is taken up in the *Excursus on agents and agency* (pp. 111 ff.). The interpretation of the order (and form) of sentences and verbs in terms of the field notebook informs the preceding analysis of pattern and style throughout.

A few other crossed forms, apparently false starts, and a grammatical slip are found in the Notebook (I, pp. 21–22). None appear to affect the interpretation.

Postscript

A thoughtful review (Segal 1976) has raised questions about the use of the term "performance" and has suggested another term, "demonstration," for some of what is presented in this chapter. The following letter responds to those questions, elaborating conceptual possibilities, from experience at Warm Springs. In this respect the letter is a later analogue to the opening section of the original chapter. It includes a consideration of Philip Kahclamet's text "The crier" that is amplified in VI. [Letter of 7 January 1977 from Dell Hymes to Dr. Dmitri Segal, Comparative Literature and Slavics, Hebrew University, Jerusalem.]

I have just had a chance to read your review of the book edited by Dan Ben-Amos and Kenneth Goldstein, and of my paper in the volume. I want to thank you for your thoughtful and attentive criticism of my paper. I appreciate it very much. You have given the most careful and useful analysis that something I have written has received in some time.

Your introduction of the distinction between performance and demonstration has validity, I think, and I wish I had thought of it. More precisely, I am sorry I did not think to address the issue you raise which leads to the distinction. You are quite right that the special situation of the relation between a narrator and a scholar must be taken into account. I am afraid that my presentation did not address this issue and so left some aspects of the material insufficiently clear.

It is not in fact the case that the native Wasco culture is long forgotten, and that the informants do not know the tradition connected with the texts; or that the tradition was lost already when Boas recorded texts. At least not in the sense in which I am used to the term "tradition." The picture actually is that the informants had experienced some surviving parts of the tradition and had retained them. In particular, they retained fluent command of the native language. They had considerable memory knowledge of the native culture (as extensive inquiry in the course of developing a dictionary of the language showed, inquiry which was not limited to glosses for native words but asked about much more). The real issue for the two men (Kahclamet, Smith) was assumption of the role of performer in the native language. Both were quite comfortable in the role of authority about the native language and culture and quite willing to converse in the native language; neither felt comfortable in assuming the role of performer of the myths. (Mr. Smith always felt comfortable in performing legends and tales, and I recorded a number from him.)

I do believe that Philip Kahclamet moved into speech in his own person (from "he" to "I" in the first text analyzed). I cannot prove this to someone who doubts it. I had worked with him for some time, was pretty much his only close friend at the time, fitted into a complex personal history of his relationships with anthropologists and linguists. He often demonstrated to me or expatiated to me on the senses and uses of terms, in English. This is the only time he ever shifted into the native language. The quality of the moment is something I have never forgotten. My sense of something special happening is reinforced by what he separately told me that summer about his own religious views.

Perhaps you will want to insist that what happened still should be distinguished from "performance," requiring a native audience for performance. There is a sense in which I became audience for him, but there is also a sense in which for the moment my identity as a researcher was not so much transformed as forgotten. My best sense is that when that was remembered, he stopped.

Whether one considers what happened demonstration or performance, it involved for a moment unique assumption of a role never otherwise assumed by him. It was a "breakthrough" and a "breaking out" in some sense.

Perhaps it would be correct to consider the whole text under the heading you propose "demonstration" (and you are quite right to address analysis of the whole text—I failed to make clear, no doubt, that my sense of "performance" focused on the very last bit as such, not on the whole). It would make sense to me to say that Mr. Kahclamet embarked on a demonstration, and that at the very end, with the shift into the native language, a moment of performance entered as well. (My sense of such a shift as special is reinforced by a number of other experiences, in which shift into the native language is like crossing a boundary of identity or identification.)

Your sense of Kahclamet as oriented toward "demonstration" fits very well the character of the third example in the paper, also from him. Your notion helps clarify what was going on there. One might say that he was willing to take on the role of "performer" at length only inasmuch as he could combine it with, or subsume it under, the role of "demonstrator."

I would agree with your point about tales from myths with regard to the second example, so far as the status of that example is concerned. But I wouldn't want to make a general theory out of it. My experience with materials in Northwest Coast cultures leads me to see the process as one that can go both ways.

With Mr. Smith, I do think that I served the role of audience. Not a normal traditional audience, to be sure. The circumstances of that summer in his personal life were such that our relationship became especially close. There was to me a clear difference in his attitude toward that story and what had preceded. The series began on a note that might be called "demonstration," although once into a story there was no hesitation. Certainly with this story the relish and flair with which it was told fitted the presence of the same elements in certain other stories about Coyote of a similar "obscene" nature which he also told me. Several times Mr. Smith volunteered the stories he told me, within the general premise that I was interested in stories. He told ones he liked and felt authoritative in telling. He consistently refused to tell in any way stories he did not think he knew accurately. The beginning of the cycle was somewhat in between. He knew it but did not feel authoritative. By the time we got to the story analyzed in my paper, or perhaps also, with particular regard to that story, he had no hesitation, quite the reverse.

Again, you might want to reserve the term "performance," but there is a qualitative distinction, an emergence of a quality, here that needs recognition.

What I say about these stories goes together with the experience I have had, and Michael Silverstein, who has worked independently with speakers of the language, has had. The presence or absence of the tradition, of the sense of immediacy, of being face to face with the native tradition, is not all or nothing, but sort of "now you see it, now you don't!" Certain circumstances, topics, occasions, may bring it forward. It seems to be essential that one knows or is assumed to know the native language. Not that every such moment involves recourse to the native language. But somehow sharing the language can be more a bond than racial/ethnic lineage. There is something of an analogy with the French view that sharing French civilization transcends racial/ethnic origin (Cesaire, Senghor as major French writers). More generally, it is a question of how much one knows or is assumed to know. (Knowledge of kinship ties and relationships can be a major factor.)

If one reflects on the total range of ways in which Indian culture is conveyed to others in the modern situation at Warm Springs (and no doubt elsewhere), perhaps four points can be distinguished. Some people have developed patterns of what might be called *"presentation."* They are gifted and effective in speaking to audiences of whites (school children, whatever), explaining and telling stories, customs, and the like. The degree to which they enter into full performance may be questionable, but some of its features are present (direct quotation, at least bits of dramatization).

Some people still know and admire the historically once-important role of *interpreter.* Here the emphasis is upon full knowledge of the languages on each side. The man who narrated six hours of Coyote cycle to my wife (in Sahaptin), once it was done, showed little interest in explication of the original Sahaptin. (Another person had to be consulted for that.) He did show great interest in the adequacy of the English translation (obtained from the other person), correcting points as a demonstration of his equal knowledge of both. (Some locally famous names are still remembered because of this role.) All this fits into the status accruing to a person of knowledge, sought out by others for such knowledge. (There may be an element of this in Kahclamet's role in the third example in the paper.)

Some people have become familiar with the role of collaborator with a linguist/anthropologist/folklorist. Perhaps the notion of "demonstration" might fit here. These relationships can become close, intense friendships, creating a close world between the parties that is special to them. It is not the same as presentation or interpretation, because it involves explication, and reflection, emergence of a self-conscious reflection that "interpretation" and "presentation" do not require (one can go between languages without worrying about the analysis of either; one presents to people who cannot ask analytic questions).

A fair number of people are able to perform narrative and the like in English and some in the Indian languages (mostly Sahaptin). But appropriate circumstances for performance in the Indian languages are increasingly rare. Formal occasions do exist (in Sahaptin)—certain rituals, as memorial dinners, etc.). Informal occasions are unscheduled and depend on the circumstances of those present and whatever may stimulate telling. Mr. Smith has always found a tape recorder inhibiting (but not a pencil and notebook) if the material were like that in the story analyzed in the paper; so also the presence of a woman. But he will hold forth about his grandmother's powers as a shaman without such inhibitions, if he trusts the sympathy of those present. Some kinds of performance are commonly public—what one might call "boasting." It has a short three-part structure that I find now also in myths and tales, and I have heard Mr. Smith do it in the midst of relative strangers.

I will have to reflect more on these distinctions, get my wife to do so as well, and have them in mind when we are back at Warm Springs this March for a week, and this summer. (We go back every summer now.) Perhaps they will need further revision. But I am grateful to you for forcing me to think these things out further.

In the fall I wrote a paper for the journal *New Literary History,* which has more to say about Wasco performance and tradition than I knew when I wrote the article in the book you reviewed. A good part of it is also in the article "Louis Simpson's 'The deserted boy,' " in the issue of *Poetics* that Dan Ben-Amos arranged [see chap. 4]. The Louis Simpson text was told only to Edward Sapir, so in that respect would be under the heading of "demonstration" in the terms of your review. But I hope that it may seem to you convincing as evidence that performance can occur in such a condition. Of course Simpson was thoroughly rooted in the traditional culture before it had been too much affected by white contact, and lived at a time when there were still true native audiences for myth as well.

4

Louis Simpson's "The Deserted Boy"

This paper is part of a longer study of a narrative recited by Louis Simpson to Edward Sapir at Yakima Reservation, Washington, in 1905.[1] The narrative was recorded by Sapir in his field notebook III, on pp. 94–97. The four field notebooks are in my possession, through the courtesy of the late Walter Dyk. The importance of the original recording to the analysis will become apparent.

Sapir published the text and a translation in the volume *Wishram texts* (Sapir 1909a:139–45). In that volume the original text occupies 93 lines. It is presented in 9 paragraphs as prose. The principal purpose of this paper is to show that the text represents some 168 traditional narrative lines, organized in some 56 verses.[2]

Before proceeding to the text and the analysis, let me briefly comment on comparative perspective and on the form of title chosen for the paper.

1.

The general plot of the narrative is widely known among Indian communities of the Northwest Coast. A number of versions of the story were brought together by Boas in his landmark monograph, *Tsimshian mythology* (1916), under the heading "The Prince who is deserted." The main version is no. 32 (Ibid:225ff.) among the Tsimshian narratives presented in full. The comparative study of it and other versions summarizes many more

This chapter is reprinted from the article of the same title in *Poetics* 5:119–55 (1976). The major changes are the updating of a few references and the addition of notes 3, 9, and most of 8; and the additional comments in the appendix; and the omission of information about orthography and ethnological situation, now to be found in the notes at the beginning of this volume.

[1] I want to thank Dan Ben-Amos for inviting me to participate in the symposium of the American Folklore Society in Nashville, Tennessee, at which the initial analysis of this narrative was presented, and for his great kindness and patience in awaiting a text from me for this issue. The analysis presented here is in effect a part of the task of translation, and I should like to dedicate it to a linguist who has dedicated his life to the problems of translation, Eugene Nida. In the field of Native American texts we are only now facing up to issues of accuracy and faithfulness that have long been faced by those who translate the Testaments, Old and New.

[2] The relation of this analysis to the work of Dennis Tedlock with Zuni narratives is discussed in the full study. (See now the end of chap. 9 of this book.)

(Ibid.:784ff.). Let me mention here that the abbreviations and conventions that make the table of versions from various tribes (Ibid.:785) ultimately intelligible are to be found on p. 556. One must be prepared to learn that "Ts*b* 5.300" refers to a version in "Boas 4" (so cited because the work is fourth on a list of books most frequently quoted (Ibid., 566); that "Boas 4" is on the bibliography on pp. 39ff.; and that the specifics of the entry in the bibliography are to be discovered in Appendix V, Index to References, when one reaches pp. 10177ff. (There is no index or guide to the Index.)

Boas mentions the "Wishram" version, recorded by Sapir from Louis Simpson, and also the "Wasco" version collected by Jeremiah Curtin from an unknown source at Warm Springs Reservation, Oregon, in January 1885. Both versions, however, are described quite wrongly with the phrase "Deserted child as introduction to a story" (1916:784, n. 1; 950 [under "32"]); 1016 (with reference to Sapir 1909a:139, 260). The story of the deserted child is in fact the entire story in both versions.

The "Wishram" and "Wasco" versions barely make contact with the details enumerated by Boas in his analysis of variants (1916:784–85). They do agree with the broadest of the outlines given by Boas, and signaled by Roman numerals, but only if the numerals are somewhat realigned, and the associated descriptive headings suitably generalized. Such revision would yield:

I,   A child gives offense and is deserted (= Boas I).
II, The deserted boy is helped (rephrasing Boas II). To the eight points of detail subjoined by Boas, however, there needs to be added a ninth, "Relatives leave food behind." This incident is attested in some of the versions treated by Boas, but is omitted from the summary table. It is vital to the Chinookan versions. Moreover, the details ought to be subdivided to distinguish those in which the boy is helped to survive from those in which he is rewarded with far more. Notice that in Boas's versions the aid given the boy is usually reciprocity for some previous favor on his part to animals or supernaturals, whereas in the Chinookan versions the reward is earned as if through a guardian-spirit quest.
III, The discovery of the good fortune of the deserted child (joining Boas III to Boas IV, whose description is retained). (Boas singled out "A bird carried food to the deserted child's relatives" as III, but the point of the incident is that it leads to discovery.)
IV, The return of the people (= Boas V).

2.

The point of the quotation marks around "Wishram" and "Wasco" is that the two names do not constitute the proper focus for comparative study or for analysis of specific versions. The two communities are not distinct, linguistically or culturally, as wholes. The proper poles for comparative analysis are, on the one hand, the full network of intermarrying and intercommunicating, Chinookan-speaking groups, and, on the other, quite specific, even individual, lines of transmission of tradition. The principal locus of tradition was essentially the family (a point established by some of the fieldwork of Michael Silverstein). Even within a family, members might persistently disagree. A couple married for many years, but from different places within the larger network, may disagree as to the right words for certain things. One brother may insist that another has the ending of a story wrong (cf. Sapir 1909a:8–11). In the latter case, Sapir finds Louis Simpson's ending to a part of the Coyote cycle the more appropriate (p. 9, n. 3), but his brother Tom's ending is quite authentic. It was told me a half-century later by Hiram Smith, of Warm Springs Reservation, Oregon, and the spot on the Columbia at which the transformation in Tom Simpson's ending took place pointed out. For Mr. Smith, indeed, the story takes a title from that spot ("The Pillars of Hercules").

With regard to "The deserted boy," Louis Simpson's text agrees in the main lines of action with that collected by Curtin, specifically enough to indicate a common tradition; but the details and the stated outcome differ enough to indicate distinctive interpretations of the story's moral (cf. Jacobs 1960:312). Furthermore, the integration of selected incident with form of presentation makes clear, as will be seen, that the "Wishram" version, as we have it, is the composed work of the man who recited it.

That is the reason that the title of the paper is not "A Wishram text of 'The deserted boy'," "The deserted boy: A Wishram narrative," or the like. I have myself used such titles in the past, as have others. To do so is to perpetuate an image of Native America as divided into neatly compartmentalized, named "cultures," for whom individual narrators are but representative "culture-bearers." Barre Toelken (1969) has set a precedent in writing of the "pretty languages" of Yellowman, and I am glad to follow it. This text *is* the work of Louis Simpson, a man whose talk is still recalled by people living today in Oregon and Washington.

The Northwest states have done little for Native American literature. If they are ever to be recognized as homes of authors of world reputation, it will be in large part because of what we can know of the art of Louis Simpson, of Victoria Howard (a Clackamas), of Charles Cultee (a Kathlamet and Shoalwater Chinook), and others like them.

3.

Here is the text of the narrative, as freshly translated and analyzed.

[I. The people and the boy.]

i/A (1) Now thén they told a boy,
             "Now let us go for reeds."
                 Long ago the boy was mean.
       (2) Now thén they said,
             "Now you will take him for reeds."
       (3) Now thén they told them,
             "You shall abandon him there."

/B   (4) Now thén the people all went across the river,
            they went on,
            they came to the reeds.
     (5) Now thén they cut them off.
     (6) Now thén they said,
            "If the boy should say,
              'Are you there?',
            you shall answer,
              'uuuuu'."

/C   (7) Now thén they ran off,
            straight home they ran,
            straight across they went;
                not a person on this side,
                all on that side.
     (8) Now thén that boy, too, said,
            "Now let's go home."
              "uuuuu,"
            answered the reeds.
                In *vain* he searched about:
                no person.
     (9) Now thén he too started home,
            he too followed behind them;
              he arrived running:
              now, no people.

[II. The boy, deserted.]

ii/D (10) Now thén the boy wept.
       (11) Now thén he heard:
              "tL' tL' tL'."

(12) Now thén he turned his eyes,
    he looked,
       he dried his tears.

/E (13) Now thén he saw a *very* little bit of flame in a shell.
(14) Now thén he took that very same flame.
(15) Now thén he built up a fire.

/F (16) Now agáin he saw fibre,
    again a little bit of it,
       straightway he took it.
(17) Now agáin he went to the cache,
    he saw five wild potatoes.
(18) Now thén he thought:
    "My poor father's mother saved me potatoes,
       and fire was saved for me by my father's mother,
       and my mother's mother saved me fibre."

iii/G(19) Now thén the boy made a small fish-line,
    and snares he made with string;
       he set a trap for magpies.*
(20) Now thén he caught them.
    Then he made a small cloak with magpie's skin.
       He (could) just put it nicely round himself;
       again (when) he lay down to sleep,
       again he just wrapped himself nicely in it.

/H (21) Now thén did he fish with hook and line;
    he caught one sucker,
       half he ate,
         half did he save;
           again, morning, he ate half.
(22) Now agáin did he go to fish,
    he caught two,
       one he ate,
         one he saved,
           again, morning, he ate one.
(23) Now agáin in the morning did he go to fish,
    he caught three suckers,
       he ate one and a half,
         again, morning, he ate one and a half.

*See 4.2 below.

(24) Now agáin he went to fish,
    he caught four suckers,
      two he ate,
        two he saved,
          morning, he ate now all two.
(25) Now agáin did he go to fish for the fifth time;
    now five times the boy had fished;
    now he had become a grown man.

iv/I (26) Now thén he examined his fish-line.
(27) Indeed! *ats'Epts'Ep* fills to the brim a cooking-trough.
(28) Now thén the boy sang.

/J (29) Now thén all the people watched him.
(30) Now thén they said:
    "What has he become?"
(31) Indeed! he became glad,
    he had caught *ats'Epts'Ep.* [3]

/K (32) Thus he sang:
(33) *"Atséee, atséee,*
    Ah, it waves freely over me,
      Ah, my feathered cloak."
  "Atséee, atséee,
    Ah, it waves freely over me,
      Ah, my feathered cloak."
  "Atséee, atséee,
    Ah, it waves freely over me,
      Ah, my feathered cloak."
(34) Indeed! IC'íxian's virgin daughter had given him food.

/L (35) Now thén the boy had camped over four times;
    he camped over a fifth time.
(36) Now thén he awoke,
    a woman was sleeping with him,
      a very beautiful woman:
    her hair was long,
    and bracelets right up to here on her arms,

[3]Hiram Smith and Mrs. Viola Kalama have spoken to me of the deliciousness of *ats'Epts'Ep.* In combining huckleberries and Chinook salmon, it combined the principal foods obtained by men and women, as fishers and gatherers, respectively. These foods were a focus of both practical and ceremonial attention and a preferred source of sustenance during the winter when no fresh food could be obtained. A little was filling.

and her fingers were full of rings,
and he saw a house all painted inside with designs,
and he saw a mountain-sheep blanket covering him,
                        both him and his wife.
(37) Indeed! *IC'íxian's* very daughter had given him food,
and plenty of Chinook salmon,
and sturgeon,
and blueback salmon,
and eels,
plenty of everything she had brought.

/M (38) Now he married her.
        Now the woman made food.
                Now, morning, it became daylight.
                        Now the two stayed together quietly that day.
                        Now the two stayed together a long time.

[III. The boy and the people.]

v/N (39) Now thén it became spring.
    (40) Now thén the people found out.
    (41) Now thén his father's mother and his mother's mother
                went across straight to his house.

/O (42) Now thén he thought:
            "The two old women are poor.
                My father's mother and my mother's mother
                    took pity on me in this way."
    (43) Now thén he fed them,
            he gave the two old women Chinook salmon,
                and he gave them sturgeon.
    (44) Now thén the two old women started home,
            they went across,
                they were there a long time.

vi/P (45) Now thén it became news,
            they said,
                "Oh! there is much salmon at 'the boy's,
                    and much sturgeon,
                    and eels,
                    and blueback salmon."
    (46) Now thén the people said,
            "Let us go to the boy."

There was no food among the people,
the people went hungry.
Now snow, lightly, lightly.
(47) Now thén agáin first went his father's mother, his mother's mother.
(48) Now thén they were close to the house.
(49) Now thén a great many people started across toward the boy.

/Q (50) Now thén the boy turned,
he looked,
he saw many people coming across in a canoe.
(51) Now thén he thought:
"It was not good the way they abandoned me."
(52) Thén now he raised the east wind
(there became a Walla Walla wind);

the east wind became strong,
and it snowed;

all died in the water,
the people were drowned;

With a bad mind the boy thought:

"This is the way they treated me,
they abandoned me."

/R (53) Now agáin others went across.
(54) Now agáin he treated them this way,
a strong east wind blew,
moreover now there was snow.
(55) Now agáin they died,
twice the people died.
Now only the two old women remained.

[/S] [56] Thus the ways.

4.

Chinookan traditional narratives have an internal organization of presentational segments, segments that in important part are linguistically marked. This was noticed some time ago with regard to myths (Hymes 1958; 1960:575) and found to apply to traditional tales as well. Although myths and tales are distinguished by native terminology and differ in chronological relation to the time of narration (and hence in some correlated features of content), the two together form one system. This is true both of the general structure of normative relationships underlying plot outcomes and evaluations of actors, and of presentational patterns. With regard to the latter, the salient differences appear to be between individuals (and possibly their communities), as between Charles Cultee (Chinook, Kathlamet), Victoria Howard (Clackamas), and Louis Simpson (Wishram), rather than in the disposition of presentational means as between myths and tales for each.

Only a few texts from each collection have been analyzed in full, so that a definitive statement of Chinookan presentational organization is not yet possible, but the indications of its nature given here for Louis Simpson's "The deserted boy" have been found valid in the other texts, representing each of the dialects so attested. The common pattern is the mode of organization. The same kinds of markers of organization recur, but are not used in exactly the same ways.

In general, Chinookan narratives are organized in terms of what can be called "acts," "scenes," "stanzas," "verses," and "lines." The terminology of "act" and "scene" is adopted from the work of Burke (1945), and from the specific precedent in Chinookan work of Jacobs (1959b; 1960). The terminology of "stanza," "verse," and "line" is introduced in this paper.

A variety of features contributes to the organization of the text, and hence to recognizing that organization. Two types of iteration, descriptive cataloguing (as in verses 36, 37) and cumulative repetition of action (as in 21–25), provide evidence of integral units. There are minor forms, or small sub-genres, that are recognizable across texts, such as the idyll (38), the speech of remonstrance (cf. Hymes 1968a: 186), the song as a set piece (stanza K). Within a given verse and stanza there are verbal repetitions that indicate internal cohesion (as in the three-fold occurrence of "No person," "no person," "no people" in verses 7–8–9 [stanza B]). A pattern of grouping into sets of three and of five is an evident, although not automatic, characteristic, as is the consistent placement of a particle such as "Now" (see 4.3 below). Statements of the succession or lapse of time are salient indications of unit in Chinookan materials, together with other indications of change in what Kenneth Burke (1945) calls the "scene-agent" ratio—indications of change of scene, and of change of participants in the action.

The interplay of the various features can be assessed only provisionally as one proceeds to come to grips with a text. The mutual structuring of the several levels of organization is found only through a painstaking process of approximation and testing (some of which will be seen below). In particular, the regularity of the grouping of verses into stanzas, and of stanzas into scenes and acts, in accord with norms of three and five units to a group for the most part, did not come about mechanically. The initial segmentation of the text did not show all of these groupings. Some of them came to light only in late stages of the work—in the course of typing stencils of the text for a presentation to the 1973 meeting of the American Folklore Society, and in the course of typing the full paper for this publication a year later, leading to a retyping of the text.

In short, a satisfactory solution emerges only after several tries. One plunges *in media res*, making a trial segmentation by hand, and reconsiders and adjusts it in the light of the principles of consistent structure and form-meaning covariation. As one gets more deeply into a text, one gains a deeper sense of its inner logic and form, its particular integration of content and expression, and one's sense of inconsistency or arbitrariness of analysis grows finer. Not all Native American texts can be expected to yield such results, given the circumstances of their transcription and differences among narrators and communities, but the impressive fact about the texts narrated to Sapir by Louis Simpson is that they reward the search for consistent structure, while resisting superficial attempts at calibration.

This is not to treat the texts as perfect redactions of a perfect source and to deny the possibility of accident and error. Each text is, in fact, reviewed in the light of available information as to grammar, lexicon, and narrative practice. We fortunately possess the field notebooks in which the texts recorded from Louis Simpson were first transcribed, and it is possible to check the published text against them. It so happens that three points of discrepancy correspond to three difficulties posed by the printed text for a general theory of presentational and semantic structure. Each difficulty is related to an intrusion or change marked in the field notebooks. (Two cases involving presentational form are discussed in this section [4.2, 4.3], and one involving evaluation of actors and outcomes is discussed in section 5.) These cases show the value of the hypothesis of a Chinookan "grammar" of narrative presentation and content: it keeps one searching for all the structure that the evidence permits one to find.

In general, then, the analysis is guided by two principles, taken as interdependent: that there is a consistent structure, and that it is to be found in terms of form-meaning covariation, taking form here to be linguistic form. (Approaches that can recognize only one [form or meaning] are rejected.) These principles entail that one is not free to make ad hoc decisions as to the status of a feature; an apparent exception must be explained in a principled way, or a broader, more adequate hypothesis of structure found.

All levels of organization of the text (line, verse, stanza, scene, act) show relations between content and linguistic form, but the relations vary in directness and consistency. It is the verse that is directly and consistently marked by a single, definable set of linguistic features, namely, sentence-initial particles. Verses in turn provide the frame within which lines are identifiable, and the element whose groupings provide for stanzas, and through stanzas, scenes. In the latter cases there is some direct marking by (or correlation with) linguistic features, but most of the relation to linguistic features derived from, and depends on, the patterning of lower level units, ultimately verses. The highest level, that of acts, depends for its recognition directly on relations of content, although, of course, it shows an indirect relation to linguistic features, through consistency with the boundaries between scenes.

The recurrence and patterning of linguistic features thus is decisive for the organization of the text, directly in the case of verses and lines, and both directly and indirectly in the case of stanzas and scenes.[4]

Let me treat verses first because of their central role (4.1, 4.2, 4.3), then take up patterns into which verses enter, those of stanzas (4.4), scenes (4.5), and acts (4.6). These larger patterns having been considered, the subject of lines (4.7) will bring us back to a question of the nature of the narrative as poetry.

4.1. Initial particles as markers of verses

In Chinookan narratives, for example, sentence-initial particles play a central role in shaping presentational form, but do not do so in exactly the same way in each text. A given initial particle cannot be taken as invariantly demarcative, wherever it occurs, nor can the particles that serve demarcative function be prescribed in advance of study of a given text. There is indeed a limited set of such particles, across texts, and there is regularity in the use

---

[4]To the end of his life, Jacobs refused to countenance "linguistic" insight into such texts; cf. the remark, published posthumously, in Jacobs 1972:15:

> The tenth class treats of linguistic features of style that were peculiar to myth or tale recitals or pre-dawn pedagogic sessions. It is certain that this class was of negligible import, if it was even present, in all Northwest States groups. A well-done structural delineation of all Northwest States classes of style features would exhibit total, or nearly entire, omission of a style class that comprised contrastive linguistic features. Professional linguists seem, today, to be wholly incapable of facing so horrible a fact as a literature style that lacks significant and distinctive linguistic features. They grope for such features like a farmer searching for a diamond in a hay stack.

Jacobs was responsively attentive to accuracy in recorded and published verbal form, but not attentive to verbal form as one side of systems of conventional narrative signs. For that matter, he did not much notice grammatical and lexical aspects of texts in their direct bearing on interpretation (cf. Hymes 1965b), perhaps because of the history of an antagonistic relationship to the dominant trends of the linguistics that developed after his own training and initial linguistic studies (notably, a grammar of Northern Sahaptin). Such linguistics often lost stylistic information in transcription of texts and often neglected, if it did not discourage, interpretation of texts. Jacobs's own invaluable work, seeking out surviving narrators, skillfully and patiently recording their words, seeing the texts through to publication, seeking interpretation of socio-expressive meaning, gained little recognition. What we owe to him will loom larger with the years. We honor his achievement best by recognizing in its fruits, and in cognate materials, all the richness that is there, eschewing if we can the bitterness that disciplinary paradigms leave in their wake. The verbal art of Northwest Native America can thus play its proper part in the life of both communities and scholarship, and so enhance recognition of Jacobs himself as the major figure in this sphere of the mid-twentieth century.

of them within a text; but in each case the role of the particles must be determined in relation to the coherence of the text itself.

This situation becomes apparent in consideration of "The deserted boy." In the record we have of Louis Simpson's performance of it, the initial particle pair 'Now then' (*AGa kwapt*, abbreviated hereafter as AK) demarcates the majority of verses—38 out of 56. (The second figure depends on decisions reached with regard to two textual problems discussed below.) An analogous particle pair, 'Now again' (*AGa wit'a*, abbreviated hereafter as AW), demarcates nine verses in parallel position—the finding of the other items (2nd and 3rd) left the boy by his grandmothers (16, 17); the other times (2nd through 5th) of going fishing, after the first (22–25); the other (2nd) crossing of the people (53–54–55). With the greater part of the text (47 verses) so indicated, one can recognize corresponding features of the remaining verses, and relate the variation in these to expressive purpose.

The first three scenes, and their twenty-five verses, go steadily along with AK, supplemented with AW. As one enters the scene in which the boy discovers his great fortune *(iv)*, an additional pattern appears. The first two stanzas of the scene (I, J) each have two verses set off by AK and a third verse introduced by a single particle, rendered here 'Indeed' (*QuSdiaxa*, abbreviated hereafter as Qu; in its four occurrences Sapir renders it as 'Behold', 'Truly', 'In truth', 'Truly'). The same is true of the fourth stanza of the scene (L). In the third stanza (K) the particle also occurs once, but the stanza has no AK (or AW). It begins with another single particle, 'Thus' (*Qidau*—abbreviated hereafter as Qi). Between Qi and Qu there is a song, repeated many times.

Qu occurs nowhere else in the narrative. Clearly enough, its occurrence once in each of these four stanzas contributes to the demarcation of verses in each, but also contributes expressive force. (See also [II iv] in 4.4 below on Qu.) Qi occurs once again, as the beginning of the concluding statement (verse 56). Its culminating force for the narrative as a whole, suggesting 'Now the nature of the underlying relationships is clear', seems to attach also to its use in this scene of the boy's assumption of power, concerned with the boy's resourcefulness in coping with desertion.

The fifth and final stanza of the scene (M) has lines beginning each with the single particle 'Now' (*AGa*, abbreviated hereafter as A), five such lines. Five is the Chinookan pattern number; the five statements are parallel; and the absence of a second particle is motivated by the nature of the stanza. It is an idyllic moment of union between man and woman, and the absence of 'then' (from the usual AK pair) has the effect of suspending action.[5] There is a parallel scene in the Kathlamet "Sun's Myth."

[5]Milton Singer has pointed out to me an analogous feature in the Radha-Krishna Bhajanas of Madras City (see Singer 1966 [cited from reprinting of 1968:99–100]), and has reminded me of the staying of the sun by Athena during the night that Odysseus and Penelope are reunited. (I am indebted to Michael Silverstein for an opportunity to discuss the analysis of this text at the University of Chicago in early 1974.)

When this scene is considered as a whole, one can see that it constitutes a high point, celebrating the success and reward of the boy. The stanzas are linked by an occurrence of Qu in each of the first four (I–L), followed by an interlude of suspended action in the fifth (M) with its unique five-fold sequence of 'Now . . . Now . . . Now . . . Now . . . Now'. (The last line of the fifth stanza further sets off the scene as a whole by its concluding marker 'long time'.)

The scene comes at the middle of the narrative,[6] and its own middle stanza (K) is the expressively most marked of the entire text. It contains the one song, the boy's song of his acquisition of power (a sacred and personal song); it is the sole verse that is unbounded (there being no fixed limit to repetitions of the song); it is the only stanza without any initial A (except the concluding stanza, verse, and line (S), to whose Qi its own corresponds). In sum, the three verses of this central point of the story are marked uniquely by Qi/Song/Qu.

The last stanza of the five is uniquely, expressively marked also, but, appropriately, by quiet repetition.

Outside this scene, only two putative verses are not set off by AK or AW. In each case the verses are set off by forms drawn from the set of particles already established as demarcative, and the particular choice can be seen to be motivated. First, the three verses of the antepenultimate stanza (Q) show AK/AK, then *KA (Kwapt AGa)*. This third verse, like so many verses that are the third of three in a stanza, gives the culminating action of the stanza, action that here completes the reversal of the relation between the story's principals, the people and the boy: they are drowned by him. This unique reversal of order (*KA* for AK) seems clearly to emphasize this peripety in the plot. Second, the final verse shows Qi, whose summarizing force has been discussed just above with regard to scene *iv* and stanza (K). The first Qi sums up the reversal in the boy's situation in isolation (Act II); the second Qi sums up the reversal in the boy's situation in the story as a whole (I:III).

The triple sequence *AKW* in stanza (P), verse 47, is motivated in meaning (cf. stanza [N], verse 41), but may have expressive force (since AW alone perhaps might have been used).

The pattern of use of initial particles can be summarized as follows:

[6]Approximately the middle: 3 scenes precede it, 2 follow; 8 stanzas precede its 5, and 6 follow; 25 verses precede its 13, and 18 follow. The Janus-like nature of this scene, as culmination of preceding action, and as preparation for what follows, perhaps reflects a Chinookan propensity to interpret experience in terms of polarities, especially between persons. The people desert the boy, and the boy survives; the boy is rewarded, and the people are punished. This scene, or better, Act II as a whole, joins the outcome of one phase of the relationship between people and boy with the condition of the other.

I and scenes ii–iii of II:		AK, AW	(stanzas A–H)
i: AK	(A–C)		
ii: AK	(D–E)		
AW/AW/AK	(F)		
iii: AK	(G)		
AK/AW/AW/AW/AW	(H)		
iv (concluding II):		AK/Qu/AK	(I)
		AK/AK/Qu	(J)
		Qi/Song/Qu	(K)
		AK/AK/Qu	(L)
		A (5 times)	(M)
III:		AK, AW	(N–R)
v: AK	(N–O)		
vi: AK	(P)	(*AKW*)	
AK/AK/AK	(Q)	(KA)	
AW/AW/AW	(R)		
Conclusion:		Qi	(S)

Table 4–1. Patterning of initial particles

4.2. Initial particles: Structural philology (a)

It was said earlier that initial particles are not invariantly demarcative. This statement should now be made more precise. So far as I know, initial *pairs* of particles are invariantly demarcative. It is the status of single particles that must be determined in terms of a given narrative (and the status of other initial forms). The published text of Louis Simpson's "The deserted boy" presents two difficulties in this regard: the single 'Then' (K) in verse 20, and the single 'now' (A) in verse 46 (linked to the triple 'Now then again' [AKW] of line 47). Should a separate verse have been recognized at each of these points?

With regard to 'Then' (K) in verse 20: A consideration of content in relation to form raises a question as to the accuracy, or quality, of performance at this point. The content of the text implies a three-part structure: preparation, catching and use of birds, catching and use of fish. The first two lines of verse (19) would be introductory (the preparation) (cf. [35] in stanza [4]). The third line of verse (19) and verse (20) present the catching and use of the birds. Clearly the form, based on demarcation by AK (verses 19, 20), does not match the content well.

The mismatch of content and form becomes clear especially if one considers the third part, catching and use of fish. It is elaborated symmetrically. There are five verses in all in the stanza devoted to the third part (H). In each of the first four verses (21–24) there are five actions, one in each of five lines. (We shall consider the fifth verse and its artistry later in the paper.) The boy fishes with line, catches fish, eats part, saves part, eats again.

Now in the six lines preceding (H) there is precise parallel in *content.* The boy sets a trap for birds, catches birds, makes a cloak, puts it round him, puts it round him again when he goes to sleep. (The five actions are distributed over six lines, the last action elaborated into a distich.) There is not, however, precise parallel in form, or indeed, any symmetry of form. The first action, setting a trap for birds, has no introductory particle of any kind; the second action, catching birds, is the first in a series to have a demarcative initial particle pair; the remaining actions are grouped together, introduced by the single particle, 'Then' (K). The paired use of 'Again' (W) in the last two lines is part of a single action, the fifth, analogous to the paired use of 'Straight' in the second and third lines of verse (7); 'Again' never by itself sets off a verse in Simpson's narratives; it is here parallel to its use in the last line of each of the first four verses of the next stanza (H).

If the single 'Then' (K), introducing the third of the series of five actions, were recognized as setting off a verse, an overall presentational pattern would be fulfilled. Stanza (G) would have three verses, not just two. Indeed on first analysis, I felt constrained by the common pattern of stanzas of three and five verses to recognize 'Then' as here setting off a third verse. Yet such a role is without parallel within the text, or elsewhere in Louis Simpson's style, so far as known. Nor has the exception any apparent motivation. If a verse is to be marked at this point, there seems no reason for a single 'Then', as opposed to the 'Now then' (AK) (and 'Now again' [AW]) that is normal in this portion of the narrative.

In terms of the overall pattern of the scene, one would indeed expect these actions to have a unified form as a set. Such a form might be parallel to the form of the five-action verses that follow—something like:

*(20). Now then he set a trap for magpies;
    he caught them,
       he made a small cloak with magpie's skin,
         he (could) just put it nicely round himself;
           again (when) he lay down to sleep,
           again he just wrapped himself nicely in it.

So to enclose the lines that we have would still leave the stanza with just two verses, (19) and (20), just differently apportioned.

If the initial pattern of *three* verses per stanza, followed hitherto in the narrative, is sustained, then there are two possibilities. The part having to do with the birds could itself form a stanza of three verses—something like:

*(20). Now then he set a trap for magpies.
*(21). Now then he caught them. [= attested (20), first line]

*(22). Now then he made a small cloak with magpie's skin,
      he (could) just put it nicely round himself;
        again (when) he lay down to sleep,
        again he just wrapped himself nicely in it.

Given the *attested* initial particle pair for *(21) and the presence of one initial particle corresponding to *(22), the conjecture of an intended *(20–21–22), as above, seems reasonable. The result would be that the first of the two main efforts of the boy, concerned with birds, would have three verses in a stanza, the second, and decisive, effort with the fish, would have five. The difficulty is that the first of the three parts of the scene in (19), the preparatory part, would be left a stanza and verse of but two lines, or would have to be conjectured as having been intended to be elaborated into its own three-verse stanza, detailing the making of the line and snare (perhaps with but one line to each verse, as in stanza [E]). The latter is quite conceivable, something like:

*(19a) Now then the boy took that string.
*(19b) Now then he made a small fish-line.
*(19c) Now then he made snares.

There is, however, no indication of such an intention in this text.
    The reconstruction that seems closest to the text (although not perfect to the three-part pattern of the content) would be as follows:

*(19). Now then the boy made a small fish-line,
      and snares he made with string.[7]

*(20). Now then he set a trap for magpies.
*(21). Now then he caught them;
      he made a small cloak with magpie's skin,
        he (could) just put it nicely round himself;
        again (when) he lay down to sleep,
        again he just wrapped himself nicely in it.

This seems as close to the pattern of the content as the text permits. It recognizes three verses within the stanza, as Louis Simpson would have seemed to intend. It departs from the printed text in introducing an initial particle pair at the beginning of the actions involving catching the birds, one line earlier than found in the printed text; and in suppressing the single initial particle ('Then') found in the printed text with the line about making the

[7]Strictly, according to the text:
"Now then the boy made a small fish-line,
    and snares with the string he made."
Cf. stanza (L) for a similar two-line introduction in the first verse of a stanza.

cloak—or, one might say, displacing this particle one line above, and also the preceding particle initial, while reconstructing it as a full initial pair.

What this reconstruction essentially does is to assume that the beginning of the actions involving the birds should have been marked as the beginning of a verse (*20 above), parallel to the marking of the beginning of the actions involving the fish.

Sapir's field notebook III shows that the absence of an initial particle at this point may have an explanation in the circumstances of the original narration. The notebook shows the words in the second line, for literally 'snares string-with he-made-them', as an insertion above the line, between the word for 'and' and the words for 'he set a trap for magpies'. Either the words above the line were initially missed by Sapir, or were retroactively inserted by Louis Simpson. The junction of elements at this point is thus suspect, as an error of recording or oversight of dictation. An on-the-spot retroactive insertion by Louis Simpson seems likely to me. The 'Now then' that would be expected to introduce the setting of the trap for magpies is displaced to the second point in the series (*20 to *21). The overall pattern of three verses to a stanza is maintained, weakly, by the isolated, and otherwise unmotivated, single 'Then' (K), where, according to our last and preferred reconstruction, no verse-initial would have been intended. In sum, the discrepancy of structure at this point in the narrative is taken to reflect, not expressive motivation, but momentary distraction.

The awkwardness of the lines suggests as much. In the first two lines, the preparatory part, the string is mentioned as if an afterthought, with the snares only, leaving the momentary impression that the fish-line might have been made with something else. It is as if the narrator had begun with the pairing of fish-line and snares in mind, and had started to treat them in parallel fashion —"He made a small fish-line and he set a trap for magpies"—only to realize that the parallelism was not quite right. Something had been left out (the *means* of making both line and trap), and one part of the preparation (making the line) had been paired with the wrong subsequent activity (trapping). The preparation for that activity, the making of the snares, had been completely overshot. He backtracks and inserts the preparation, mentioning the string now (perhaps on another occasion he would have mentioned the string with regard to the fish-line as well, or instead [letting its mention with the first of the two instruments be carried over to the second]). In any case, the preparatory use of the fibre left by the grandmothers, the gift of theirs highlighted by being mentioned last in the preceding scene, is now explicit. One is left, however, with a verse whose third line has broached the trapping that belongs to the verse to follow. A new verse is marked where a new verse appropriately should be (after three lines, and after what counts, mostly, as the preparatory part is complete), but, as said, the marker is already within the activity proper to it. The common pattern of three verse-initials to a stanza is in mind; so is the common pattern of five lines to a verse. He adds a third particle, suggestive of a third verse-initial, although not quite such ('Then'), and occurring actually within the sequence already begun as well. This sequence he rounds out as five lines by elaborating the fourth line (in which the fifth and final action has already been reached), utilizing an initial pairing device of a common type. The expressive emphasis on the boy's comfort and protection against death from the winter cold is appropriate enough. Now the part about magpies is behind, the crucial part about fish is in hand; it is elaborated perfectly and ended with a master's touch (of which much will be made in section 5).

4.3. Initial particles: Structural philology (b)

With regard to the status of 'Now' (A) in verse (46): there are two distinct questions. First, does this 'Now' indicate the end of a scene and stanza, so that a new scene and stanza should be taken to begin with verse (47)? This has to do with the patterning of single occurrences of 'Now' in the text as a whole. Second, is this 'Now', its line as a whole, in fact in the proper place? This has to do with a difference between the order of the lines in the field notebook and in the printed text. The answer to the second question will be informed to a great extent by the answer to the first.

(a) Single occurrences of 'Now' in the text fall into three classes. There is the fivefold pattern of stanza (M); this has been taken as clearly demarcative of a verse. There are the three occurrences within quoted speech in Act I, scene *i* (verses 1, 2, 8), in the people's instructions to go for reeds, and the boy's attempted instruction to return home. These seem clearly not demarcative, but to occur securely within verses. Finally, there are the occurrences at the end of verses in (9), (25), (55); these have special interest. Each of the three is at the end of a scene: "Now, no people" (9); "now five times the boy had fished; / now he had become a grown man" (25); "Now only the two old women remained" (55).

Each occurrence of 'Now' (A) at the end of a scene seems to state the result of the scene, to sum up the outcome. The fivefold recurrence of 'Now' in the last verse of scene *iv* fits this use. One can indeed see a discontinuous, rather subtle building up of outcomes of scenes: a single 'Now' with the desertion (I, *i*); a double 'Now' with the boy's accession to maturity (II, *iii*); a quintuple (pattern number) 'Now' with the boy's attainment of power, wealth, and wife (II, *iv*). The single 'Now' at the end of the final scene fits the curve of the narrative as a whole, in that the expressive (though not moral) culmination came in the scene which ends with the fivefold 'Now'.

The one remaining use of 'Now' at the beginning of a line, at the end of verse 46, does not have this summative quality. It is related to the moral culmination of the narrative, but as an anticipatory peaking of its ultimate denouement. That is, the line "Now snow (is falling) lightly, lightly" does not sum up a state of affairs. Perhaps one might think to take the mention of snow to refer to survival of traces of winter, and hardship at the end of winter, and the repeated words can be translated literally as 'little, little'; Sapir renders them, however, 'gently, gently', and they are a way of indicating that snow has begun to fall. This mention of snow in fact initiates a threefold pattern (cf. verses 52, 54) in the last instance of which 'now' is used non-initially in a way *parallel* to its use in 46: 'now snow . . .' : ' . . . now snow . . .'. The line points out a condition of the action to come, a condition which the people ignore in deciding to cross the river, and which becomes a part of the cause of their death. In short, the initial 'Now' (A) in this line is not an instance of the expressive convention underlying the use of 'Now' at the end of the scenes just discussed. It is not, then, an indication that the next verse begins a new scene (and stanza).

A case might still be made that the conjunction of initial 'Now' at the end of verse (46) and the triple particle initial of verse (47) (AKW) together signal a division. The two phenomena do point up the moment of the action, but do not signal stanza structure, even within a scene. Consider that stanza (P) (in which verse 46 occurs) and the following stanza (Q) are parallel to the preceding pair of stanzas (N, O). In the first stanza of each pair, the grand-mothers go across (verses 41, 47) in lines begun, naturally enough, with AK and AKW, respectively. In the second stanza of each pair, there is a consequence: food and a long stay for the grandmothers in the first pair (stanza O), drowning of the people in the second (Q). Now, verses (41, 47) are parallel in their positions within the first stanzas of each pair. Verse (41) is the third verse of a stanza; so is verse (47) the third verse of a stanza already begun, not the beginning of a new stanza. In this regard, notice the parallelism between the individual verses of the two stanzas (N : P):

(39) "Now then it became spring" : (45) "Now then it became news. . . ."
(40) "Now then the people found out" : (46) "Now then the people said
. . . ."
(41) "Now then his father's mother and his mother's mother went across straight to his house" : (47) "Now then again first went his father's mother, his mother's mother."

The verses of the later stanza (P) are each elaborated more than the corresponding verses of the earlier stanza (N). Indeed, to the third verse of (N), namely (41), there correspond not one, but two verses of (P), verse (47), which we have been discussing, and also (48), "Now then they were close to the house."

In effect, the third and fourth verses of the later stanza are a presentational elaboration, corresponding to content that is stated within a single verse of the preceding, three-verse stanza. Only the final, fifth verse of the later stanza is in fact new, and it is of course necessary to state the new element, the crossing of the people. Elaboration of the content of the third verse of the earlier stanza into a third and fourth verse in the later stanza maintains the common pattern of 3 or 5 (but not 4) verses to a stanza.

For these reasons, I conclude that the sequence of initial elements in the last line of verse 46 and the first line of verse 47 ('Now' . . . 'Now then again') constitutes solely a pointing up of the action. The line beginning with 'Now' is especially significant in that the people should have taken the presence of snow as a warning. Having violated social norms by deserting the boy, they now ignore clear empirical signs of danger; their fate is deserved (cf. section 5 below). The initial triplet of verse 47 might by itself be simply the consequence of a formal verse-initial pair, associated with the second occurrence of an action (hence 'again'). The initial 'Now' of the last line of verse 46 is the most significant feature. Perhaps it borrows some of its role here from the end-of-scene use discussed above; perhaps indeed, both roles can be taken to be expressions of a common underlying force, the signaling of significant conditions.

If this is so, then one has in fact exactly five such uses of 'Now' (A) in the narrative, three as part of a culminative series concerned with the boy's desertion and success (I–II), two serving to enclose the fate of the people. The first series goes together with an identification with the boy, with his desperate situation and deserved reward. The second goes together with the retribution that rounds out the story, showing the moral consequences of acting as the people did. (I cannot but hear in the last 'Now' an echo of the peremptory 'Now' in the quoted speech of the people with which the story begins. The first series is in verses 9, 25, 38, and the second series in verses 46, 55.)

(b) The preceding account of 'Now' (A) indicates that it fits neatly into the narrative where it is found, and indeed, may have expressive point just there. The difficulty is that it is found there in the field notebook, but not in the printed text.

The difficulty involves all five lines of verse (46). Let us identify the lines by the letters a, b, c, d, e. The order of lines in the field notebook, and in the text as presented here, is then a–b–c–d–e. The order of lines as printed in *Wishram texts* is e–c–d–a–b. The difference is signaled in the field notebook itself. Two changes are involved: (1) At the end of the sentence concluding verse (46) (the word for 'blueback salmon' [*watsuiha*]), there is a caret mark, beneath parentheses. These parentheses apparently correspond to lines c–d–e, around which parentheses are found. The effect of the caret and parentheses is to signal the transposition of lines c–d–e ahead of lines a–b. (2) At the end of the sentence constituting lines c–d, there is a transposition mark over the period [thus:∿]. This apparently signals transposition of the following line, e ("Now snow, lightly, lightly"), ahead of the sentence (c–d).

The result of the two changes is the order of lines printed in *Wishram texts* (Sapir 1909a: 144, lines 4–6). In terms of the letters adopted here, the order is (e–c–d) (a–b). Let us consider the alternatives in terms of verse analysis.

The printed order of lines might be taken to show a verse and stanza structure as follows, including (ecd) in verse 45, and with (ab) constituting *46, which starts with 'Now then' like all the other verses in the stanza.

vi/P (45) Now then it became news,
            they said,
                   "Oh! there is much salmon at the boy's,
                   and much sturgeon,
                   and eels,
                   and blueback salmon."
          Now snow, lightly, lightly.   (e)
                 There was no food among the people,   (c)
                     the people went hungry.   (d)
    *(46) Now then the people said,   (a)
          "Let us go to the boy."   (b)

This stanza structure would preserve the five-verse pattern. The parallel with stanza (N) would be preserved, as between verses 39 : 45, 40 : *46, 41 : 47, 48. The structure would be aberrant, in that the catalog of kinds of fish is medial in verse (45). Such catalogs always end verses (cf. 36, 37 [and 18]). It is aberrant also in that it has 'Now' (A) medially. As discussed above, line-initial 'Now' occurs medially in a stanza only within quoted speech.

An obvious alternative would be to take verse (45) as ending with the catalog, and to take "Now snow, lightly, lightly" as beginning a new verse. Let us call it (46'). The result would be to add one verse; the original (46) would be replaced by two verses altogether (46', 46"), the second of them being the two lines beginning "Now then the people said." Instead of a stanza (P) with five verses, there would be two stanzas (P', Q'), each with three verses. (P') would contain (45, 46', 46") and (Q') would contain the present verses (47, 48, 49). This alternative would also be aberrant. The parallelism between stanzas (N) and (P) would be lost. The consistency of role for 'Now' in signaling condition in the last *line* of a verse would be lost (and no other ground for motivating its use here is apparent). The use of an isolated, single 'Now' as initial particle, to set off a verse, would indeed be unique to the text; one would expect 'Now then' (AK), as in each of the other verses of this part.

In short, either organization of the order of lines printed in *Wishram texts* mars the structure of presentation otherwise established.

(Notice that there is no reason to separate the two changes, accepting one and not the other. The second by itself [abecd] leaves 'Now' [line e] anomalously in the middle of a verse. The first by itself [cdeab] leaves a five-line verse with no initial. Acceptance of both changes [ecdab], on a conjecture that line [e], beginning with 'Now', belongs at the end of the preceding verse, so as to fit with the verse-final position of other non-quoted 'Now's, is also to leave verse [46] with but four lines [abcd], and one initial.)

It remains that if evidence indicated that the order of lines printed in *Wishram texts* were the order of lines desired by Louis Simpson, one would have no choice but to adopt it, while seeking to puzzle out some reason for the change. But it is not at all apparent that the changes, as between notebook and print, are due to Louis Simpson. First of all, the changes do not appear to involve correction in the course of narration. There is no insertion of a word or phrase, such as might have been forgotten or overshot (compare [a] above). There is no indication of an effort to correct a temporary mismatching of form to content (or content to form); the two fit in the original dictation. The double change, one within the other, appears complex enough to have to be the result of later deliberation.

The later deliberation is not likely to have been that of Louis Simpson. It seems that Sapir did not read the texts back to Louis Simpson for translation, but to his interpreter, Peter McGuff (cf. Silverstein 1974: S53). Moreover, it is known that Sapir was prepared to modify the order, and even the grammatical form, of a dictated text, for the sake of what appeared to be sense, coherence of content. (See the analysis of "The story concerning Coyote" in chapter 3, and the discussion of "Long ago" in the first verse of the present narrative in [5] below.) I infer that McGuff or Sapir thought that the story made better sense in the changed order. Perhaps it was reasoned, first, that the people's statement (a–b) should immediately precede their action (47–49) (hence the first change); and, second, that 'Now' had the character of an initial to a segment of some kind (hence the second change).

Perhaps also, or instead, there was a sense that the parenthetic-like explanation of lines (c–d) is exceptional. Conditions of action are regularly stated before the action (see 4.5 below on this pattern). One would expect the mention of there being no food among the people to occur at the beginning of the verse, if not of the stanza. (Not necessarily at the beginning of the scene as a whole—that the two old women cross in the preceding stanza can be explained by the fact that they are specifically poor (the word in [O:42], as in [F:18], specifically means pitiful because impoverished.) The rest of the people need not have exhausted supplies of food. After the long time of the old women's stay on return to the people, one can understand the supplies of the community as a whole to be exhausted, and fish and berries from the new season to be not yet available (these things can indeed come quite late).

The fact remains that the verse does not as a whole, in any order of the lines, fit the three-part pattern of action just mentioned, by itself. The verse shows conditions (hunger, snow) and a preparation (statement of intention, or collective command), but not setting in motion of action or completion of action and an outcome. Even if the statement is taken as a setting in motion (such statements are not so taken elsewhere in the narrative), the third part of the pervasive pattern is not present in the verse itself. The pattern applies to this verse as part of a *sequence* of verses (and stanzas) (see discussion in 4.5 below). If a sense of the pattern and of the lack of food and hunger and snow as parenthetic-like conditions that should precede the action was involved in the changing of the order of lines in the notebook, it was an imperfect sense, focused too locally. In sum, the statement of the lack of food, hunger, and beginning to snow, is part of the statement of conditions within the stanza.

The elaboration of the statement into a five-line verse, while highlighting the conditions, fits neatly into the form of the stanza as a whole, and particularly into the form of the first two verses of the stanza in relation to the rest.

That the people speak at the outset of this verse (46) (when the lines are taken in the notebook order) is parallel to the fact that they speak in the preceding verse (45). Indeed, the same verb ('they said' [*galugwakim*]) is used in both (45) and (46). And (45), the first verse of the stanza, fits into a parallel of larger scope within the scene. The first statement in (N) is of what becomes, and so is the first statement in (P) (39: spring, 45 'news'). The second statement and line in (N) is an activity of the people (40: they found it); the second line in (P) is an activity of the people (45: they said). The multiple-line verses (45, 56) of (P) can be seen as a picking up and elaboration of a pattern begun in the single-line verses (39, 40) of (N), just as the third and fourth verses (47, 48) of (P) are an elaboration of a point corresponding to the third verse (41) of (N), as brought out earlier in this discussion. The beginning of verse (46), in the order of lines in the notebook, fits the place of the verse in relation to what has preceded, as the end, the beginning to snow, fits dramatically what is to follow.

In other cases of discrepancy between notebook and printed text, a consideration of the structure of content and presentation has shown the original, unchanged order to be satisfactory, indeed, preferable. The same is true here.

In sum, the marking of the notebook for changes in the order of lines appears to be after the event and very likely to have been done apart from consultation with the narrator. There is no indication of an attempt to fit the changed order into the presentational patterns of the narrative. The notebook order is consistent with the use of initial particles for demarcation of verses and expressive point in the narrative as a whole; the changed order is not. The notebook order maintains the parallels in form and content among the stanzas in the scene in a way that the changed order does not. For these reasons, I have retained the order originally spoken by Louis Simpson.

4.4 Stanzas

Linguistic features enter into the recognition of stanzas most of all indirectly, from the fact that they are groupings of verses, themselves directly marked. The grouping of verses into stanzas by three and five is a recurrent characteristic. An overview of the text as a whole in grouping of stanzas is as follows:

Stanza	Number of verses
A	3
B	3
C	3

D	3
E	3
F	3
G	2 (*3? cf. 4.2)
H	5
I	3
J	3
K	3
L	3
M	1 (cf. S below)
N	3
O	3
P	5
Q	3
R	3
S	1

It is indeed striking to find a consistent grouping of stanzas in terms of a numerical pattern, and such a grouping is consistent with other patterns in the text. It remains that there is no overt mark that regularly initiates, or closes, a stanza (unlike the initial particles of verses), and some of the groupings of verses into stanzas could not but appear arbitrary, were it not for features of the stanzas themselves. Stanzas show verbal repetition and parallelism of content, internally and externally—that is, among verses within stanzas, and among stanzas that go together within a scene. Internal repetition (within stanzas) is more prominent in the beginning of the narrative. External repetition (among stanzas) is more prominent at the end of the narrative. I do not yet know the extent to which the kinds of repetition and parallelism found in "The deserted boy" are general to Chinookan narrative; some clearly are.

The features in question can be indicated seriatim.

I:i

(A) they told (1), they said (2), they told (3); the parallel quoted statements that accompany these verbs; the parallel initial particle in each statement: *aGa, aGa, alma* ('now', 'now', 'shall'). (The initial position of 'shall' does not appear in the translation; its use is emphatic, since the verb itself marks the future.)

(B) they went, went on, came to (4), they cut (5), they said (6)—a fivefold series of verbs, the first three grouped in one verse, following a common Chinookan pattern. All three verses maintain a constant actor (as in A).

(C) not a person (7), no person (8), no people (9); repetition of 'home'

in the outer verses (7, 9). (The repetition of 'ran off, ran, running' is an artifact of translation into English; the three original verbs are different constructions).

Notice that the third verse in each stanza (A, B, C) is the culminating, significant verse with regard to the fate of the boy. The last line of each of these third verses begins with an emphatic particle, *alma, alma, aGa* ('shall', 'shall', 'now').

These relationships enter into the grouping of the three stanzas together in one scene, distinct from what follows. The action is continuous across the boundary, but the pattern of verbal repetition changes.

II:ii

(D) he wept (10), he heard (11), he turned, looked, dried (12)—a fivefold series of verbs, the last three grouped in one verse, following a common Chinookan pattern.

(E) he saw (flame) (13), he took (flame) (14), he built-up-fire (15). The three lines move from nouns to a verb: he-saw flame shell-in/ . . . he took flame/ . . . he-built-up-fire. (The "fire" in the third line is signaled in the verb stem.) In the first two lines "he-saw" and "he-took" (both followed by the same word for 'fire, flame') are almost identical rhymes.

(F) fibre (16), potatoes (17), potatoes, fire, fibre (18)—a fivefold series of nouns.

Notice the fivefold series of acts of seeing in the three stanzas as a whole: he turned his eyes (D:12), looked (D:12), saw (E:13), saw (F:16), saw (F:17). In addition to 'he saw', the words for 'a little bit' (E:13, F:16), and 'he took' (E:14, F:16) are repeated between the second and third verses.

Notice that the third verse in each stanza (D, E, F) is the culminating, significant verse with regard to the action and fate of the boy: he dries his tears (a preparation), builds a fire, thinks gratefully of his grandmothers, summarizing as he does what he has with which to survive, and mentioning last (as the last word) the fibre that will be basic to the next scene.

II:iii

(G) See the discussion in (4.2) above as to the likely intention behind the text as we have it.

There is a threefold series of 'he made' (small fish-line [19], snares [19], cloak [20]), all with the same verb construction and root. In each case the smallness of the fish-line (19) and cloak (20) is signaled by diminutive consonantal symbolism, not by a word. The symbolism uses the same consonant in each case, diminutive dual *is-* (instead of *iS-*) for the prefix of the noun, and diminutive dual *s-* (instead of *S-*) for the corresponding pronominal object prefix in the verb. These touches link the two verses of the stanza.

(H) The parallelism of the incremental repetition of words and acts is apparent through four verses (22–24) and the first line of the fifth (25). The sudden shift of perspective, retrospectively, in the last two lines will be made much of in analysis of the interplay between presentation and content. Notice that it leaves unresolved the content of the fifth catch for a new sequence of verses. The last verse in each stanza (G, H) is the culminating, significant verse with regard to the success of the boy.

II:iv

(I, J, K, L, M) There are some features specific to each stanza: (I) he examines (26), he stands it (the trough) (27), he sings (28); (J) the people watch (39), say (30)—but the action, having shifted to the people in this stanza, returns to the boy (31); *(K)* frames and presents the song; (L) the boy had camped, camps (35), awakes, sees, sees (36), but just as (J) shifted to the boy in its last verse, so (L) shifts to the woman (37), associated with two descriptive catalogues (37, 36); (M) 'Now' (five times).

The coherence of these five stanzas is not so much internal to each, as derived from their relationships to each other within the scene as a whole.

The five stanzas can be seen as forming an arc, whose expressive climax is the middle stanza (K). This stanza is most marked in the narrative as a whole by expressive use of initial particles (Qi . . . Qu), and contains the song. This middle stanza is flanked by stanzas (I, L) of the same form in verse-initials: AK/AK/Qu. The middle group of three stanzas (J, K, L) is itself flanked by an introduction (I) and coda (M).

The extraposition into an entire scene of what might have been expected within the last verse of the preceding scene—the outcome of going to fish the fifth time—is introduced by (I), which introduces verse-initial Qu for the first time in its middle verse. After this transition and introduction, Qu is found as initial of the third, final verse of each of the three central stanzas. Notice that in every case (I–L), Qu is associated with food: the discovery that the trough is full of a special food (I:27); gladness because of catching this food (J:31); the first statement that it is the virgin daughter that gives the food (K:34); a catalogue of the kinds of fish she brings as food (L:37). The exclamatory verse-initial is linked to the food fundamental to survival for the community (in normal times as well as in the narrative). This linkage is a principal dimension of the unity of the scene.

Food (its preparation by the woman) is mentioned in (M) as well (its second and third lines, and, by implication, throughout the long time mentioned in the fifth line). The reference to food in each of the five stanzas is one link among them.

Notice that the coda provided by (M), with its sequence of 'Then'-less initial 'Now', is preceded by the culminating elaboration of the reward of the boy, namely, the two catalogues of (L), the handsome attributes of the woman (36), and the munificent supply of food (37), and that once food is mentioned, the three last lines each refer to a unit of time (morning, day, long time).

The stanzas are woven together in additional ways with regard to food. (I, J), (K, L), and (M) form three successive units. In (I, J) the special food is something the boy has found (27, 31), and the name for it is repeated. In (K, L) the woman enters, as source, and the verb, literally 'she-fed (provided as food)-it-to-him' is repeated (34, 37). (The 'it' refers to the special food, through agreement of the pronominal object prefix [a-] with the prefix of the implied noun [a-]). In (M), as noted, the preparation of food is stated.

(I, J) are paired further, and contrasted, in their first verses, the boy examining his fish-net, the people (presumably from hearing singing) watching (examining the situation of) the boy (I:26, J:29).

(I, J, K) are linked as a sequence, culminating the specific outcome of the boy's fifth time of going to fish. (L) takes up the fivefold form on a new point, speaking of the boy having slept four times, and promptly completing the pattern by stating that he now sleeps a fifth time. The preceding four times had not been mentioned, only that the boy wrapped himself in the magpie-skin cloak when he slept. Still, the preceding times are implicit in the account of the fishing in the preceding scene, when each time the boy eats half the catch, saves half, and eats the remaining half the next morning. Now that implication is brought out. In his fifth time of going to fish, the boy had been rewarded with special food; in his fifth time of sleeping, after fishing, he is rewarded with a special wife.

Thus (I, J, K) are linked as the outcome of going to fish five times (food), and (L–M) as the outcome of going to sleep five times (wife). (Though [L–M] include further forms of the first reward, food, and in effect sum up all the reward of all the preceding self-reliance and effort.) But notice that the woman is announced in the last verse of (K). In one sense, this is parallel to the last verse of (I); (I:28) announces what is to be the highpoint of what the boy does in this sequence (he sings), and (K:34) announces the highpoint of what the boy does in the next sequence (he marries the woman). In stating that it is this woman who has provided the food, the middle stanza (K) participates in both sequences.

III:v

(N, O, P, Q, R) There are features specific to each stanza: (N) the people find out, the grandmothers come across (that is, action is focused on the other side); (O) the boy thinks (42), feeds, gives (43)—but the action, having shifted to the boy for these three verbs, returns to the grandmothers for three—they start, go across, are there (on the other side) a long time (44). Each verse in the stanza repeats the term 'two old (women)' (dual prefix iS- plus stem for 'old person')—three times in all.

(P) the people say (45), say (46), the grandmothers cross (47), are close (48), many people start across (49)—five verses focused on the other side. The first, second, and fifth verses each have lines ending with 'boy' plus a locational postposition (boy-at [45], boy-to [46], boy-to [49]), three times in all, and the last line of the stanza ends with the last of these. In the last three verses the particles 'across', 'close', 'across' again, are in origin symbolic alternates of a common stem (augmentative *Gwap*, diminutive *q'wap*, *Gwap* again).

(Q) the boy turns, looks, sees (50), thinks (51), makes an east wind (52) —a fivefold series of verbs and actions on his part. The stanza is particularly complex, however, for it comprises also a fivefold series of verbs pertaining to the people: they abandoned me (51), they die, they drown (go under), they did (thus) to me, they abandoned me (52). (The last verse also includes a threefold sequence of the form 'it [there] became': a Walla Walla wind, a strong wind, snow.)

The last three lines of the last verse, grouped as a "tristich" here, the fifth "stich" of this complex, culminating sequence, seem something of an explicit summing up of the moral of the narrative and of words associated with the moral. The stem for 'bad, mean' recurs (for the first time since the opening verse of the narrative); the key verb-stem 'to desert, abandon' recurs for the third and final time (A:3, Q:51, Q:52); the equally key verb-stem 'to think' recurs for the third and final time in the scene (O:42, Q:51, Q:52), the fourth and final time in the narrative (cf. D:18). (The boy thinks in gratitude twice about the old women, twice in retribution about the people.)

(R) shows no apparent internal repetition in the stanza as a whole, apart from the three initial particles *(A W)*. Each of the verses with three lines shows rhyme or near rhyme of verbs, ending the first and third lines (*gaCLuX* . . . *gaLXuX* [54], *galuxwaLait* . . . *gaLXilait* [55] [with the middle line of (55) containing *galuxwaLait* too]).

The coherence of these five stanzas is not so much internal to each, as derived from their relationships to each other within the scene as a whole. The parallel relationships in content and words of (N):(O) :: (P):(Q) have been discussed above (4.3).

Notice that the five stanzas encompass five crossings of the river (N:41, O:44, P:47, P:49 = Q:50, R:53). A crossing is mentioned in each stanza. (As would not be true, were the line order and verse division not that adopted in [4.3].) The recurrent content is invariably expressed with 'across' (Gwap).

The first three stanzas (N, O, P) are linked by use of the kin terms for the two grandmothers (N:41, O:42, P:47). The last two stanzas (Q, R) are linked by mention three times of the east wind (twice in Q:53, once in R:54) and of dying (once in Q:52, twice in R:55), the first three stanzas have five occurrences of 'people' (N:40, P:46, [3], P:49), the last two stanzas three (Q:50, Q:53, R:55).

The middle stanza (P) links the two groups. It is the last of three to use the kin terms for the grandmothers, and the first of three to refer to snow.

Its last line (P:49) introduces the action that is the focus of the remaining two stanzas (just as the last line of the middle stanza in the preceding scene [K:34] introduces the person who is the focus of the remaining two stanzas).

4.5. Scenes

Many features that enter into the determination of scenes have been considered in the preceding parts of this section. The internal relationships of the stanzas that comprise each of the last two scenes, in particular, have been considered in detail, as an outgrowth of discussion of verse-initials and stanzas. Here we can consider the general question of scenes as units within the narrative as a whole.

The analysis of the narrative into scenes can be summarized as follows:

Act	Scene	Stanzas	(Last lines)
I	i	3 (ABC)	AK-A (C:9)
II	ii	3 (DEF)	AK-and, and (F:18)
	iii	2(*3) (G[*]H)	AKAA (H:25)
	iv	5 (IJKLM)	AAAAA (M : 38)
III	v	5 (NOPQR)	AK-A (R:55)

Table 4-2. Act/scene ratios

The clearest boundary between scenes is between *iv* and *v*. The concluding verse and stanza of *iv* (M) is unique in its pattern of verse-initials, and suspension of onward movement. Moreover, it includes three successive references to units of time (morning, day, long time), ending on the last. The next verse begins with a further reference to time, to lapse of time (it became spring). The boundary at this point is, if anything, hyper-characterized.

The action is continuous from the beginning until this point, across the boundaries recognized as distinguishing scenes *i, ii,* and *iii;* and after this point there is a temporal disjunction. (But notice that *ii* and *iii* each end with a moment of retrospection. There is a temporal pause, if not a disjunction.)

No other division between scenes is manifest in this way. The action is continuous from the beginning until the end of *iv,* quite across the points recognized as distinguishing *i, ii,* and *iii.* Obviously temporal disjuncture has not been found to be a necessary condition of scenes. Again, there is a lapse of time within scene *v,* between stanzas (O) and (P); stanza (O) indeed ends with the same word as scene *iv* ('long time'). Obviously temporal disjuncture has not been found to be a sufficient condition.

This result has been a surprise to me. Marking of time is a significant marker at the beginning of units in some Chinookan narratives. This narrative shows it to be not by itself decisive at the end of units. When multiply marked, as at the end of *iv,* it is undoubtedly significant. Yet the marking coincides with the end of a unit that is dependent on what seem to be other, recurrent, consistent, hence fundamental, considerations.

The first of these is a matter of content. *What seems fundamental as a shift in content is not relation to time or place, but relations between participants.* Each of the five scenes coincides with one such relationship: *(i)* the people : the boy; *(ii)* the boy : his grandmothers (retrospectively, but introduced for the first time here); *(iii)* the boy : "nature" (manifest in birds and fish, and the response to his resourcefulness implicit in his magical growth); *(iv)* the boy : the woman; *(v)* the boy : the people.

The second consideration is the internal unity of the scenes, and their unity as wholes vis-à-vis each other, on various grounds, in addition to that just mentioned. On first attempt, some seven scenes were distinguished (summer and fall 1973); then six (1974), and finally, five (1975), through reconsideration of the proportions and relations among the scenes, and a deepening sense of just how the particular narrative works. Finding five scenes to the narrative as a whole, finding the scenes in the proportion of 1 : 3 : 1 to acts, finding stanzas in the proportion of 3 : 3 : *3 : 5 : 5 to scenes—all this seems right. The numbers are fitting, and the stanzas, scenes, and acts hang together well on this analysis. Yet even though such an analysis emerged over a period of two years and was not imposed at the outset, it might be suspect of being arbitrary or subjective.

Two features of the narrative provide empirical warrant beyond a sense of fitness and proportion. Both give warrant to the analysis at the two points at which confidence in it had been incomplete (the end of *ii*, the putative boundary between [O] and [P]).

The first feature is the use of 'Now' as a marker at the end of scenes. This came to light in solving the problem of the division into stanzas of a section involving the word (but not its use as a marker) (see 4.3 above). The use of 'Now' initially in the last line of a scene, summing up the resultant state of affairs, occurs at the end of four of the five scenes and in an arc of expressivity —once, twice, five times, then again once (the boy's success is elaborated as a peak, the fate of the people is signaled starkly). The end of scene *ii* lacks initial 'Now', but the boy's statement does correspond to the kind of meaning associated with this use of 'Now'; he sums up the state of affairs, giving an inventory in gratitude of what his grandmothers have provided as resources with which he can proceed to survive. The putative boundary between (O) and (P) lacks both a use of 'Now' and any other expression summing up the state of affairs.

The second feature is a pattern of action. It was noticed in dealing with the difficulties in stanza (G) (see 4.2 above), but its generality came to light only in the course of writing up an already completed analysis of scenes. Scene *ii* seemed for a time less certain a unit, through lack of 'Now'; its existence seemed mostly dependent on its fit with patterning of the whole. It then appeared that it showed a pattern common to each of the first three groups of stanzas (scenes *i, ii, iii*), and present in elaborated form in the remaining groups (scenes *iv, v*). *The pattern, indeed, recurs at every level of structure in the narrative.*

The pattern has three parts: a *preparatory action,* or condition of action; an *onset, or setting in motion,* of the main action; *completion* of the main action, together with outcome.

Such a pattern is an obvious enough one, in retrospect, but it did not appear at the outset, and it is not a necessary pattern. The crucial point is that not only are these three aspects of action present in a unit in the narrative, but also they *correspond* to structural elements in the unit *in the order in question.* The repertoire of effects in this pattern does not include giving a condition or preparation in the midst of an action or after it (as explanation or highlight); it does not include distributing the three aspects of action variously among units (two steps of preparation, the rest compounded in a third unit, for example); it does not include assigning the aspects of action to a different number of units (four units, for example, a preparation, an onset, a conclusion of action, an outcome).

Let us consider the several scenes in the light of this pattern and other features.

i.   The action is continuous between the last stanza of this scene (C) and the first stanza of the next (D). A major shift in scene-agent ratio occurs at this point, however. In *(i)* there are the people and the boy, and again in *(v),* as principal participants. With stanza (D), scene *ii,* begins the central, crucial action, the response of the boy to the situation of being abandoned. Moreover, there are linguistic indications. As noted above (4.4), the pattern of verbal repetitions changes, linking (C) with (A, B), and (D) with (E, F), even though one might superficially scan right across the boundary. Moreover, 'Now' is used initially in the last line of (C) to sum up the outcome of the scene.

Each of the stanzas of the scene corresponds to a part of the conventional pattern of action: in (A) the people prepare to desert the boy; in (B) they put the plan into action by crossing the river to the reeds; in (C) they complete the desertion, and the outcome—the boy alone—is stated.

ii.   The basis for the initial boundary of this scene has been considered with regard to *i.* The basis for the other boundary is not as clearcut, but the equivalence of the boy's concluding statement to the summarizing statement introduced by initial 'Now' in other scenes has been noted. The grouping into three stanzas fits the general pattern of the narrative, of course; each of the stanzas corresponds to a part of the conventional pattern of action: in (D) the boy stops weeping, and looks, prepared to discover his environment; in (E) he discovers the first element of survival in the oncoming winter in which the story is implicitly set (the gathering of reeds in the late fall in *i,* the subsequent onset of spring in *v*); in (F) he completes discovery of the resources left by his grandmothers, and itemizes them in gratitude.

Notice that individual stanzas repeat the pattern. This is clear in (E): he sees the bit of flame (preparation or condition) (13); he takes it (14); he builds up a fire (15). (D) seems analogous: he is weeping (condition) (10); he hears the sound (onset of action) (11); he turns, looks, and dries his tears (outcome) (12). (F) seems rather to complete the action assigned to the scene, than to show the three-part pattern in itself.

Individual verses repeat the pattern. This is clear in (D:12): ". . . he turned his eyes/ he looked/ he dried his tears"—a preparation, onset, outcome. It is also clear in stanza (E), each of whose three verses (13, 14, 15) is a single line (the pace is rapid at this point).

Scene *ii*, and its stanzas and verses and lines, shows that the conventional pattern of action is not automatically present, not a mold into which every unit is forced. It is rather a constantly available resource for patterning units at any level, pervasive but not omnipresent.

iii.   The slip in relations between form and content in this scene has been discussed in detail (4.2). The first two verses imperfectly present the preparation (making fish-line, and snares) and the onset of action (catching magpies and making a cloak). The concluding stanza (H) presents splendidly the concluding action and outcome. It ends with two lines beginning with 'Now', summarizing the state of affairs, and introducing in the last line a suddenly surprising, retrospective, indication of what had been occurring.

The individual verses of (H) repeat the pattern: he goes to fish (preparation, condition); he catches fish (onset); he eats, saves, and eats again (outcome).

iv.   The five stanzas of this scene are well integrated, as has been discussed in detail, and are well bounded (two 'Now's preceding, five concluding). The three-part pattern of action obtains over the five stanzas: (I, J) are preparation, condition; (K) is onset of action; (L, M) are completion and outcome. One can also see the pattern within each of the two sub-groups of stanzas (see discussion under stanzas), although not so simply matched to form. It is possible to see (I) as condition in relation to the completion of action and outcome in (K), but difficult to see intervening (J) as onset, unless one is to understand that mention of the people constitutes the audience for the performance to follow. (On the significance of audience as constituting formal communicative events in Chinookan culture, see French 1958.) It is also possible to see the last three stanzas according to the pattern of action: announcement of the virgin daughter is condition and preparation (K), for the onset of full reward in (L), and its completion and outcome in (M). In other words, as anticipated in discussion of stanzas earlier, the middle stanza (K) is pivotal.

The individual verses of (I) show the pattern: the boy examines his line, stands the special food on the ground, sings. So do the verses of (L): the boy camps over, wakes to find a beautiful woman, finds that she has brought plenty of everything.

In sum, the pattern of action appears in clear correspondence to form at the level of the scene as a whole, grouping the five stanzas into three sets (2 : 1 : 2), and in some individual stanzas and verses. It appears to inform intermediate relations among stanzas in a more complex, interlocking way.

v.   The five stanzas of this scene have been discussed in detail. The beginning and end are well bounded. What is in question is a possible boundary within the five.

The occurrence of "long time" at the end of stanza (O) suggests that it may mark a boundary between scenes, since the same expression occurs at a scene boundary at the end of (M). We have noticed the cumulation of temporal markers at the end of (M) and beginning of (N), in contrast to the lone occurrence here, and have noticed the absence here both of 'Now' and of any summarizing quality. The close parallelism of structure across the stanzas in question, integrating (N) : (O) :: (P) : (Q), reinforces the conclusion that there is not a scene boundary at the end of (O). In addition, the pattern of action does not point to a boundary there.

Three-part pattern of action obtains, first of all, over the five stanzas of the scene as a whole: (N, O) are preparation, conditions of the action to follow (it is necessary for the two old women to discover the presence of food at the boy's for the rest to be set in motion); (P) sets the denouement in motion; (Q, R) complete the action and give the outcome. Insofar as one can glimpse a subordinate use of the pattern of action, informing subgroups of stanzas, it obtains across the distinction between (O) and (P). In the subgroup of initial stanzas, (N) would be condition, preparation; (O) onset of main action; (P) completion and outcome (the people are led to start across toward the boy).

All these considerations converge on the analysis into scenes that has been given.

As with the preceding scene, it is possible to see the last three stanzas according to the pattern of action: the starting out of the people is condition (P), for the onset of the denouement (Q), and its completion and outcome (R). As anticipated in discussion of stanzas, the middle stanza (P) is pivotal.

The individual verses (each a single line) of (N) show the pattern: it becomes spring (condition), the people find out (onset), the grandmothers cross over (outcome). So do those of (O): the boy thinks gratefully (condition), he feeds them (onset), the women return home (outcome). So also for (P): it becomes news (condition), and the people plan to go (condition also); the grandmothers go first and are close (onset); many people start across (outcome). So perhaps do the verses of (Q): the boy sees the people coming (condition), thinks in retributive fashion (onset?), raises the wind that causes them to drown (completion and outcome). Finally, the verses of (R) fit as well:

others cross (condition), the boy raises the wind (onset), they die, and only the two old women remain (completion and outcome).

Thus the scenes.

4.6. Acts

The basis of division into acts is the same as that of division into scenes: relations between participants. The second, third, and fourth scenes belong together, in that each is a facet of the boy's situation cut off from direct relationship with the people, who desert him in the first act, and whom he punishes in the third.

The relation of acts to scenes and stanzas has been seen in the table at the beginning of the preceding discussion (4.5). Notice that the division into three acts coincides with a pattern of summary use of 'Now': once (I), five times (II), once (III).

The division into three acts was made before recognition of the pattern of action, just discussed with regard to scenes. The division can be seen to fit the pattern: desertion of the boy by the people (condition) (I); coping with desertion on the part of the boy (onset, setting in motion) (II); punishment of the people by the boy (and reward of the grandmothers) (completion and outcome) (III). In chapters 5 and 9, the three parts of the pattern of action will be reformulated as onset, ongoing, outcome. The change seems still to fit the relations in "The deserted boy."

Now that these relationships among acts, scenes, and stanzas have been found, it may seem that one could have proceeded from general patterning of content, insight into that, and have come to the same results. This seems unlikely to me, given the clotted, run-on appearance of the text in notebook and print. The various markers of relationships must have been to Sapir and to others, as they first seemed to me, merely recurrent superficial traits. Segmentation of the text into significant units, and the clear disposition of these units for visual inspection, seems to me to have been necessary. It is difficult to imagine the testing of hypotheses, or the discovery of unsuspected features and relationships, if the text has not been analyzed into its presentational form at the level of verses and lines. The several aspects of the structure of the text are of course interdependent, but one kind of clarity seems prerequisite, heuristically, to the other.

4.7. Lines and measured verse

The identification of lines is not as clear as the identification of larger units. My practice of putting quoted speech on a separate line is a convention to which others might not subscribe. It commonly fits into patterns, but these are perhaps not the only possible patterns. Nevertheless, there is a considerable basis for recognition of lines within the verses.

A first consideration is the presence of a verb. This can be taken as criterion of a line in most cases. Not all Chinookan sentences require a verb (e.g., the second line of [42], the last line of [46], the last line of the whole [57]). Nor are separate verbs found in the separate lines recognized in the song (H:33) and the descriptive catalogues (L:36, 37). In the latter cases the recognition of lines is dependent on repetitions, parallelisms, and in the case of 'and', a convention.

Several patterns of repetition and parallelism are to be found. There is initial parallelism, or repetition, as in the second and third lines of (7) ('straight', 'straight'); the first two lines of (16) ('Now again', 'again'); the last two lines of (18) ('and', 'and'); the last two lines of (20) ('again', 'again'); the third and fourth lines of (22) ('one', 'one'); the third and fourth lines of (24) ('two', 'two'); the last two lines of (25) ('now', 'now'). Such initial couplings suggest that the single use of such elements initiates a line, as in the third line of (16) ('straight[way]').

There is sometimes final parallelism, or repetition, as in the fourth and fifth lines of (7) ('this side', 'that side'); the first two lines of (26) ('fifth', 'fifth'), and (in the original) the first two lines of (9) (literally, 'he-too', 'he-too'). There is sometimes parallelism and repetition within lines, as variously in the five-line verses of (22–25).

Sometimes the first and third lines of a verse end in the same, or nearly the same, form, as in verse (1), whose first and third lines in the original end in the word for 'boy'; verse (4), whose first and third lines end in the postposition -pa; and verse (55), whose first and third lines end in the stems -Lait, -lait.

Sequential patterns of lines play an essential part. Examples of three- and five-line sequences have already been noted in discussion of stanzas. Such sequences sometimes clearly show the three-part pattern of action discussed above. Compare, for example, (D:12) and (Q:50):

"Now then he turned his eyes,
   he looked
      he dried his tears."

"Now then the boy turned,
   he looked,
      he saw many people coming across in a canoe."

One can see the pattern also in verses concerning travel, such as (B:4), (C:7), (O:44):

"Now then the people all went across the river;
   they went on;
      they came to the reeds."

"Now then they ran off;
    straight home they ran,
    straight across they went;
        not a person on this side,
        all on that side."

"Now then the two old women started home;
    they went across;
        they were there a long time."

Parallelism between verses, and parts of verses, is obviously a major factor in recognizing lines.

In sum, no single criterion enables one to identify lines in the material. A variety of intersecting features and patterns contribute to their recognition. The lines are derivative of the patterning of the narrative as a whole, for the most part. Strictly linguistic criteria (presence of a verb, presence of certain elements initially) go far toward a provisional segmentation, but it is the patterning of the whole that gives some confidence in the result.

Further analyses of Chinookan texts, and work with other Native American languages, may provide greater certainty in the identification of lines in such narratives. Even so, it would probably trouble many scholars to take such lines as lines of poetry. Their identification would seem to be on bases far from those that are usually regarded as proper to poetry, that is, to meter. One does not have phonological regulation of lines, nor does one have consistent grammatical parallelism. The fact that one can present lines on a page is a cheap, definitional victory. In and of itself it demonstrates nothing.

Some years ago, stimulated by Austerlitz's study of Ob-Ugric metrics, I proposed the following (Hymes 1960: 576):

The essential feature of verse may be the line (this is implicit in Austerlitz's study). Moreover, for verse in oral tradition, the line may necessarily exhibit some type of (I) numerical regularity, (II) repetition within a frame, or both; the material may be (A) phonic, (B) semiotic [grammatico-semantic], or both; the result may be (a) defining (sufficient to segment the text into lines or other units) or (b) characterizing with regard to some unit. This does not exhaust the features which may identify verse in a culture (e.g., forms which occur only in verse) or which contribute to its effect, and leaves open the place of modern written verse. Space does not permit elaboration, but, summarily, Ob-Ugric folk-poetry is IAb, IIAb, IIBa; Toda poetry is IAa, IIBa; the Japanese Haiku is IAa; the English sonnet is IAa, IIAa.

This scheme may be more usefully presented in an order corresponding to the order of words in an English sentence derived from it, that is, in reverse:

| (a) defining | (A) phonic | (I) numerical regularity |
| (b) characterizing | (B) semantic | (II) repetition within frame |

Verse having a defining phonic numerical regularity (aAI) is typically in view in discussion of "meter" and of what is "metrical" (cf. Crystal ms.). Chinookan oral narrative is at quite the opposite pole: it has a characterizing grammatico-semantic repetition within a frame as its base (bBII). Rather than argue about the proper use of the term "meter," one might simply grant that "meter" should be used for verse that answers to the first pole or that approximates it. One might introduce use of the term "measure" for verse that answers to the second pole or that approximates it. The Shakespearean sonnet is metrical; Louis Simpson's "The deserted boy" is measured.[8]

The two ideal types are, of course, not wholly discrete. Some portions of "The deserted boy" show intermittent numerical regularity in the make-up of lines (as to number of words—all but the first line of verses [1–2–3] [= stanza (a)] have three words). We have noticed some occasional rhyme-like repetition. But such instances of numerical regularity and phonic recurrence enter into a matrix of characterizing, not defining features.

The notion of measured verse allows us to give work such as Louis Simpson's "The deserted boy" a place within the sphere of poetry, while remaining faithful to its specific nature as verbal art.

Postscript

I

The longer study mentioned in the opening sentence involves comparisons of both structure and method. Part of the methodological comparison, that relating to the work of Dennis Tedlock with Zuni, was included in the

---

[8]One can take this use of "measure" as perhaps in keeping with a use once made of the word by Sapir (1917:99): "Incidentally, I could not help feeling impressed by the purely ethnological consideration that rhyme is rarely, if ever, found in the lyrics of primitive people, whereas there is probably not a tribe that does not possess its stock of measured songs" (Sapir also writes of "set rhythm").

I am also heartened in use of the word by words of the poet and theorist of poetry, Cid Corman (1976: no page number, but next to last page in the essay): "Meter as described, along fairly classical Western lines by Chatman, in this book is only one possible way of measuring poetry." Corman is addressing a similar purpose, for he is concerned to account for poetry of many kinds and in different languages (such as Japanese and modern French). I would not go as far as Corman does to consider poetry as a freeing, lifting effect of language apart from any form, but believe that the recognition that Native American narratives, such as Louis Simpson's "The deserted boy," are measured verse is quite in the spirit of Corman's preceding statement:

"Meter is ONE of the options a poet has in the mustering of language toward maximal usage. To use language at its MOST is precisely what 'defines' (if it ever can be defined at all—since individual judgment must be arraigned) poetry" (Ibid.).

article that has become chapter 9 (cf. n. 2 of the present chapter) and has to do with the validity of verse analysis. The other part has to do with frameworks for relating versions of a common story, or part of a story, to each other. The "Deserted boy" is an exemplary case. It was among the first to be singled out by a "catch-word" (Lowie 1908:25), with reference to occurrences in the Plains (as no. 20, "Deserted children"). A connected story, wherein a girl is deserted because she gave birth to pups ("Dog-Husband"), was used by Boas early in his methodological arguments about the historical nature of culture, as exemplified in the development of myths and tales (1891:13, 16). In his major analytic study (1916) Boas treated the deserted boy itself, along with the related aspect of the dog-husband, as no. 32, "The Prince who was deserted" (784–91). This part of the study was taken as representative of Boas's general approach to analysis of culture by his student Leslie Spier in his contribution to a book symbolizing the state of method in the social sciences (Spier 1931). Spier's account, in turn, was noted in textbooks a generation later (Beals and Hoijer 1953: 608–9). The Boas analysis focused on Tsimshian and other versions from the Pacific Northwest, of course. Stith Thompson used a version from the Gros Ventre of the Plains in the important anthology that reflected his own general approach (1929:174–8, 349) and took up the story again in his major book (1946:355–56). Under his direction, students analyzed part or all of the North American material three times: Jackson in 1929, Wycoco in 1951, and myself in 1954. In addition Gladys Reichard's analysis of myths of the Coeur d'Alene of Idaho (one of which has a significant relationship to Louis Simpson's myth) contains comparative notes by Adele Froelich (1947:125–28).

The material has not been focused upon by Lévi-Strauss in his *Mythologiques*, yet the deserted boy and the dog-husband show the transformational relationship he has discovered in Native American myth. Where a boy is deserted, a key to his success is to hunt birds and so obtain a blanket, as in Louis Simpson's narrative (and in versions from the Coeur d'Alene of Idaho and Lillooet of interior British Columbia [Bouchard and Kennedy 1977:30]). Where a girl is deserted (as in a version from the Quileute of Washington [Andrade 1931:137]), a key to her success is discovering that her children are not just dogs, but have dog skins that they take off away from her, and destroying the skins, so that they remain children. The contrast in gender (boy : girl) goes together with a contrast in generation, consistent with the cultures: the deserted boy can succeed in his own right, the deserted girl must succeed through the mediation of her children, a step of a generation down (just as Seal's daughter must try to act through her mother, a generation up). These two contrasts go together with an inverse role for blankets: the boy obtains one, the girl destroys them. There is common purpose: the gained robe symbolizes power, overcoming the stigma that led to the boy's desertion, while the destroyed blankets symbolize the stigma that led to the girl's desertion. In each case the boy or the children obtain a major food. It was discovery of this *systematic* relationship among elements of stories long known to be connected that convinced me of the correctness of Lévi-Strauss's principle of transformation. (I accept the principle without believing that it accounts for all relationships among Native American myths or that it has precisely the status and consequences given it in *Mythologiques*).

Both the deserted children and the dog-husband enter into larger narrative sequences with diverse outcomes. In some cases the kind of structural analysis developed by Dundes (1964) will be helpful. No comparative frame of reference now extant seems wholly adequate, and a thorough study will have to devise a framework partly new. Focus on historical development and structure, indeed, has tended to overlook the ethical content of these stories. That Native American myths had a pedagogical intent and moral basis is well known but not always made part of analysis. The deserted boy is particularly significant in this regard. Small variations in the ending of the story reflect different cultural, or personal, assessments of culpability and ethical good particularly clearly. Depending on the version, the success of the deserted child is followed by forgiveness of those who deserted him, by punishment of one, a few, or all. Certain versions from a Kwakiutl group and the Bella Bella (Boas 1932:79–92) show the essential outcome to be the boy's acquisition of his father's social position and privileges, not food, as in versions from most of the continent. Even here there is variation, such that the father may be ostracized in one version and invited back (to relinquish his status to his son voluntarily) in another. The usual focus on food reflects an implicit concern with the effect of the outcome on the community as a whole, so that different versions have a different internal tenor and final resonance in this regard.[9]

Moral interest and literary form can be investigated precisely through a comparison of the several versions available in native language texts in Chinookan. The controlled comparison can bring out the structural role of titles and the evaluative elements placed second in myth narratives, as well as illuminate a Shoalwater Chinook version which links the deserted boy and "deserted mother," as it might be called, of the Dog Children stories. The existence of native language versions in two closely related dialects, Clackamas and Wishram, will make possible inferences as to personal style. Finally, the

[9]Cf. the general observations of Boas (1935: 173, 181, 182, 183, 184): "The difficulties of obtaining an adequate food supply must have been much more serious among the Tsimshian than among the Kwakiutl, for starvation and the rescue of the tribe by the deeds of a great hunter or by supernatural help are an ever-recurring theme which, among the Kwakiutl, is rather rare. . . ." (173)

"The most typical Kwakiutl stories are those of a man who obtains from supernatural beings coveted power or valued ceremonial. The man is frequently explicitly or implicitly the aggressor." (181) "In contrast to these in by far the greatest number of Tsimshian stories of this class the supernatural beings are the aggressors . . . . The tales which refer to men who are taken by supernaturals are less numerous. They marry supernaturals who appear to them as beautiful women, or . . . ." (182) "The principal motivation in Kwakiutl tales is the unlimited desire to obtain new crests, names, dances and other privileges, either by marriage or by initiation." (184)

verse analysis of the Wishram text can be used to illuminate the English-language text published from Curtin (1909:260–63), as I hope to show at a later time.

II

Ultimate comparative perspective is extended by the realization that Shakespeare's *The Tempest* belongs to the series. The essentials of the deserted boy can be taken to be

(1) A boy who is disruptive ("mean") is abandoned to expected death.
(2) Grandmothers secretly provide some resource for him.
(3) He survives, using the natural resources available and his own skill.
(4) He is rewarded with a beautiful, wealthy wife and assumes a robe.
(5) His well-being is discovered and sought by a comic, disreputable character (Blue Jay).
(6) Those who abandoned him come within reach of his power, have need of something he has, are punished, in the course of which their boat is wrecked.

Compare:

(1) A Duke who has neglected his duty is abandoned (set adrift) to expected death.
(2) An old councillor (Gonzalo) secretly provides some resource for him.
(3) He survives, using the natural resources available and his own skill (plus that available from Ariel and Caliban).
(4) He bestows a beautiful (and rank-endowed) wife and resumes a robe.
(5) His well-being is discovered and designed and sought upon by comic, disreputable characters.
(6) Those who have abandoned him come within reach of his power, have need of something he has, are punished, in the course of which their boat is wrecked.

The differences, of course, are clear. In "The deserted boy" the focus is food; that is what the boy is left without, what the old people who help him provide something of, what those who abandoned him return to seek. Food —getting it, the lack of it, the kind of it—pervades Native American myth. To understand the world of these stories requires entering imaginatively into a world in which having something to eat could be a daily question. In *The Tempest* the focus is power: the Duke neglects one kind for another, Gonzalo provides him with books that enable him to use some of the second kind, the issues between Prospero and those who come to him revolve around who shall have power. The sea journey to Tunis that brings the Milan court within reach is for a marriage of royal alliance; it is Prospero's power (not their own search for food) that brings them to the island; conniving for power goes on within their party, Gonzalo imagines a world without it in its current form, Prospero resigns one kind of it at the end. The food of the island figures as a necessity for initial survival but is not the issue between the one abandoned and those who abandoned him.

Overall, one might say that Louis Simpson's narrative shows a young man maturing, through effort of a kind rewarded by guardian spirit power, a kind of power central to his society and which he properly keeps. Shakespeare's play shows an older man maturing, through effort and a kind of power ultimately relinquished once a new balance has been established. There is an analogy here to the ending of Victoria Howard's version in Clackamas, where the man's power is mediated through the wife, where she later regrets her use of it against the people, and where they separate to become what they will be after the end of the myth age. Still, the validity and centrality of the kind of power is not in question. It is almost as if Prospero declares at last an end to the world of Louis Simpson. One can imagine Prospero having abandoned his soul for a time to that other world, having used the powers of that world to get revenge and to give his daughter what his abandonment had cost her, then abandoning in turn both revenge and that other world's kind of power. It still exists, but Ariel is free and the books drowned. In the end it is the power, not the people, that he drowns. The spirit of myth is subsumed in the spirit of play.

There are other Native American versions of the deserted boy whose endings vary in ways that resemble *The Tempest.* Among the socially more stratified Bella Bella, the Deserted Boy (prince) may forgive the one who deserted him. At the end of some versions (Bella Bella, Clackamas Chinook) the successful power may later be lost. Throughout the Native American versions, however, social and supernatural power are identified. Withdrawal for a time from ordinary social relations to obtain the latter is not an aberration.

The richer social and motivational complexity of *The Tempest* can be suggested by considering the deserted boy of Native American tradition as differentiated in *The Tempest* into Prospero and Ferdinand (who wins the bride), and Prospero-Ferdinand dependent on both Caliban and Ariel, contrasting agencies of natural survival and spiritual agency.

III

On 12 August 1974 my wife and I visited Mrs. Ruth Estabrook on Warm Springs Reservation. I gave her a copy of a short Wasco dictionary, we reviewed a few items, Mrs. Estabrook handed the dictionary to a girl with her with the words, "Here—learn Wasco." She mentioned that her husband, Joe, was down at the haystack, getting up hay that had fallen where the horses could get at it, and that he was not well yet. After I came back from helping with the hay, I read Mrs. Estabrook the first part of this analysis (in Wasco) and got only to the word translated "You shall abandon him" at the end of the first stanza, when she spoke up: "It's a story; it means 'left him,' 'deserted him'." She cited the verb in the remote ("mythical") past tense, not the future tense quoted at this point in the text. That response supported the belief that the key to the story is the abandonment, and that the Wasco title would have been like the Clackamas, "They deserted the mean boy."

At the point in the story at which the boy discovered what had been left for him, Mrs. Estabrook intervened:

"He'd hear voice—he'd look and see lots of berries and food.

"qá damt a mú ya wi k'ás kas/
"————gi gát ns La wlx tix."

The syllables are separated to reflect the deliberate syllable-by-syllable rendition of the song. Each stressed syllable was with notably higher pitch. The dashes show where the name of a food would be put. Mrs. Estabrook did not name a food the first time, but went on to say:

"Anything you would put in there as long as it's food—*qia* (strawberries). That's the way he lived then. That's the way the story they used to tell us. I think it's kind of cute. I used to like to hear it. He grew up to be a fine man."

The song can be translated:

"Where are you going, little boy?
"(Strawberries) here we are piled up."

The *w-* on the word for boy is optional; it indicates respect and perhaps that the boy is to be perceived as entering an active, rather than passive, state (cf. chap. 10 on *w-* in Clackamas).

Asked "Did his grandmother help him," Mrs. Estabrook replied, *"No, he was all alone"* or "No, they left him" (These notes were written afterwards). Sketching the rest of the story, I mentioned that the daughter who came to the boy was pretty, wealthy, and Mrs. Estabrook intervened, "Yes, he grew up to be a *fine man."*

5

Verse Analysis of a Wasco Text: Hiram Smith's "At'unaqa"

This paper analyzes into verse a Wasco text told me by Hiram Smith in the summer of 1956 at Warm Springs Reservation, Oregon. I became aware of the story's existence when we were reviewing in alphabetical order a list of Wasco noun stems. The word *(a)-t'unaqa* reminded Mr. Smith of a story that his father, Robert Smith, a principal elder and leader among Wasco people and on Warm Springs Reservation, had told.

The present story can be traced to the same source as a story recorded by Melville Jacobs from Mrs. Victoria Howard, the last recorded narrator of Clackamas Chinook, during work with her in 1929–30. Both stories have links to an account given Franz Boas by Charles Cultee of Cultee's great-grandfather's successful quest for the guardian spirit power that the Shoalwater Chinook called *Ut'ónaqan.* The history and implications of these relationships would take many pages to explore. Here I try to do justice to the form of Mr. Smith's text.[1]

The present analysis has interest beyond itself. It is an occasion for sharing a series of conventions that have been found suitable for revealing texts recorded by Boas, Sapir, Jacobs, and myself to have a discourse structure that can appropriately be called "verse." A detailed analysis of the verse structure of a text from each of the four major dialect groups—Shoalwater, Kathlamet, Clackamas, Wasco-Wishram—has already been published or is in press.[2]

This chapter is revised from the article of the same title in the *International Journal of American Linguistics* 46:65–77 (1980). The principal changes are in the orthography, which has been modified from normal Americanist practice to fit the conventions adopted in this book (see chap. 6); an addition of n. 3 and updating of references to other work of mine in the footnotes that follow; and in rewriting the first part of section 7.3.

[1] I have written a longer study of the three texts, originally titled *Guardian, Ogress, Kangaroo: Stages and texts of a Chinookan belief,* and now tentatively titled, *Faces of feminine power,* or *Bears that save and destroy.* It will include a presentation of the Shoalwater text, which is to appear in a festschrift for Charles Hockett, edited by Adam and Valerie Becker Makkai (see Hymes ms.). I should like to dedicate this paper to George Herzog, once one of my teachers at Indiana University. During my first field experience at Warm Springs Reservation, in the summer of 1951, he visited Hiram Smith and myself one day, and on my return, encouraged me to prepare what became my first scholarly publication, "Two Wasco motifs" (1953). Both motifs had been obtained from Hiram Smith, who told the story studied here a few years later.

[2] A Shoalwater Chinook text will appear in the festschrift noted in n. 1. The English form of an analysis of the Kathlamet Sun's myth was published in "Folklore's nature and the Sun's myth" (Hymes 1975c). A revision will appear in a book based on a lecture at the University of

Need to revise an earlier presentation of Mr. Smith's text in public form has led to refinement and codification of conventions used in other analyses, as is shown here in section 6. Discussion of the way in which the final analysis was reached (sections 1–4, 7.1–7.3) may clarify the approach and show the extent to which it is not mechanical, but a series of approximations. Analyses ultimately depend upon understanding of the form-meaning covariation specific to the ethnolinguistic tradition of the texts, a covariation between an underlying narrative analysis of experience, as it were, and various overt linguistic markers and recurrences. The structural comments in section 5 bring out this aspect of the present text.

The implication of the approach is that the basic structure of well-performed Chinookan texts, and in analogous ways, of other Native American texts, is verse. Analysis at this level of discourse beyond the sentence may be helpful to the interpretation of syntactic features. It would seem prerequisite to any interpretation of texts that considers itself "structural." Whatever may be the relation of language to habitual thought and behavior in other spheres and at other levels, here the two are like the two sides of the sheet of paper to which de Saussure once made analogy. Linguistic means and cultural patterns of poetic-rhetorical form are aspects of the same thing, narrative performance.

1. The successive presentations can be better followed in the light of the overall scheme of the text. It can be seen to have five parts, like so many Chinookan texts. A set of five alliterative names can help keep them in mind: (A) DANGER, (B) DESCRIPTION, (C) DESTRUCTION, (D) DENOUEMENT, (E) DISTANCE. A non-alliterative set would also serve: (A) ATTACK, (B) CLOSE-UP, (C) ESCAPE, (D) COST, (E) DISTANCE. There is reason to think that the interests to which these words refer do motivate the successive steps of the story.

2. The English translation provided by Mr. Smith was organized in the form presented below about 1967. The translation was part of a mimeographed set of stories from Mr. Smith that I prepared at that time, and which Susan Urmston Philips and I individually gave to some people at Warm Springs. There was not a noticeable response, no doubt partly due to the rather unattractive appearance of the mimeographing, and perhaps also to the use of an orthography that tried to be simple by using only the keyboard of the standard English typewriter, and may have ended by being unduly complex.

Mr. Smith's translation is not a literal translation. It is accurate, sentence by sentence, but it is not an attempt to analyze or transfer the Wasco text

California at Los Angeles, March 1979, in honor of the late Harry Hoijer. The book is tentatively entitled *Myth as speech* and is to be published as the second volume in the series of which this volume is the first. Clackamas Chinook texts are analyzed in chaps. 6, 9 and 10 of this volume; Wishram texts are analyzed as verse in chaps. 4 and 6; and another Wasco text in chap. 6. Other texts from all the Chinookan dialects have been analyzed by Charles Bigelow and myself for publication in a book whose format and typeface have been designed by Bigelow and Kris Holmes.

word by word. Rather, Mr. Smith retold the Wasco sentences in idiomatic English. For example, a literal word-by-word rendering of sentence (9) below would be "to *try* in vain," "something," "he will do to her"; as a sentence it might be "He will (would) try in vain to do something to her." Mr. Smith catches some of the expressive strength of the intonation he had used with the word for "to try in vain" by rendering "something" as "everything." There is not literally an "every" in the Wasco text, but it catches something of the absolute frustration of effort that is in the Wasco text.

Here is Mr. Smith's English as organized in 1967. (An alphabetic identification of parts is introduced to make comparison easier.)

(A) 1. A long time ago, about fifty years ago, it attacked them. 2. They were staying on the Clackamas River. 3. One fellow climbed up a pine tree. 4. Then she saw him. 5. He pulled his arrows out. 6. He shot her three or four times. 7. Nothing to her—she bled through her mouth.

(B) 8. This thing looked like a coyote on the head; short ears; teeth like a wild hog; long white front claws; long hind legs; short front legs.

(C) 9. He tried to do everything to her. 10. Then he got afraid. 11. He had two arrows left. 12. He took one—I don't know what he put on it—he lit it on this arrow. 13. Then he shot the arrow. 14. Then it started to burn. 15. He did the same with the other arrow. 16. Then this thing went down into a canyon. 17. That's where it burned up. 18. This is what they call At'unaqa.

(D–E) 19. Then it really started to burn, started a forest fire. 20. Then a lot of men ran up there to fight the fire. 21. The state of Oregon put out a lot of money. 22. There's nothing like that on this side of the mountains in our country. 23. Only on the other side was something like that seen. 24. It was a long time ago, about maybe fifty or sixty years ago, that this thing was seen.

3. In the summers of 1975 and 1976 I began to put together a set of poems and translations about Chinookan texts and people. One section was to be "Hiram Smith near Sandy," for it was while he was working at picking berries on a farm near Sandy, Oregon, that I had first recorded texts from him in the summer of 1954. (We went that way together with Charles Bigelow last summer [1978], what is now the old road.) By that time I had come to understand something of the poetic structure of Chinookan texts and began to look for it in this one. It might be thought that one would begin with texts one had collected oneself, but Mr. Smith had disdained any claim to be able to tell myths as his father had. His knowledge of the language was detailed, astoundingly so with regard to identification of birds, plants, and other things, given that he had been sent away to the Chemawa boarding school, where others had lost their language, and that he worked at trades away from the reservation a good part of his youtl.. Narrative was something else, and proba-

bly I focused on what Sapir and Boas had recorded, in the years just before and after Mr. Smith was born, as "classical" Wasco, fearing to find that my own texts lacked the patterning of theirs.

It was poetry and personal expression, then, that turned my attention to the text of At'unaqa. In the summer of 1976 the text appeared to have three major parts: the encounter and description; the successful escape and fire; an epilogue. The two longer parts appeared each in turn to have three parts themselves: a setting of the scene, the attack and first response, the description in the first; the use of the first arrow, then the use of the second arrow, then the outcome in the second.

It was possible to analyze the subordinate parts, apart from the initial frame, as consisting of five or three units (shown by differences in indentation). (Initial frames commonly are a line or two in Chinookan texts.) Here is that analysis, slightly revised in 1978, and made somewhat more literal in relation to the Wasco. The three major parts are identified alphabetically (A, B, C), while the subordinate parts are identified with letters that are not otherwise used, so as to avoid confusion in later comparisons.

(A) *(m)* A long time ago, about fifty years ago, it attacked them.
    They were staying on the Clackamas River.
  (n) One fellow climbed up a pine tree;
    then she saw him.
  He pulled his arrows out,
    he shot her three or four times:
      nothing to her, she bled through her mouth.
  (o) This thing looked like a coyote on the head, short ears;
    teeth like a wild hog;
      long white front claws;
        long hind legs;
          short front legs.
(B) *(p)* He tried (in vain) to do everything to her;
    then he got afraid.
  He had two arrows left,
    he took one.
  I don't know what he put on it, he lit it on this arrow,
    then he shot the arrow.
  Then it started to burn.
  He did the same with the other arrow.
  (q) Then this thing went down into a canyon.
  That's where it burned up.
  This is what they call At'únaqa.

  (r) Then it really started to burn, started a forest fire.
  Then a lot of men ran up there to fight the fire.
  The state of Oregon put out a lot of money.

(C)   There's nothing like that on this side of the mountains in our
          country.
          Only on the other side was something like that seen.
          It was a long time ago, about maybe fifty or sixty years ago,
                    that this thing was seen.

The translation just given was made available, together with its Wasco
text on a facing page, to participants in the Indian Language Workshop held
at Warm Springs Reservation in July 1978, thanks to the initiative of Mr.
Nathan Jim. Hiram Smith approved the use of several of his texts as materials
for the workshop participants. Subsequent to the workshop, I felt dissatisfied
with the analysis represented in this translation. I had indeed read the text
again to Mr. Smith for any corrections, and he had approved the reading,
while making certain comments. But, of course, the visual patterning does not
appear in the voice, and he would listen to my speaking of the text for the
correctness of the words and the meaning. Wasco does not have a vocabulary
or discourse for discussing implicit poetic and rhetorical structure.

Using parallelism as a criterion, I felt that the repetitions of *yaXkadaya
dan* after each of the two sections of action involving the man were significant
and ought to be the markers of new parts. The translation did not bring out
their parallel ("this thing [looked like . . .]," "this is what they call . . . "), and
the structure was not at all parallel. It also seemed wrong that the *wit'a* 'again'
in the text did not begin a part but was in fact untranslated in the last line
of (p) of the version just given. 'Again' is regularly a marker in Wasco.

4. In August I devised a different analysis, having five parts, which met
these objections. In December, reflecting on that analysis, I discovered one
further feature that resolved a remaining awkwardness. The final result is
presented now, both in English and Wasco, followed by a discussion of the
structure and of the rest of the process by which it was discovered.

(A) *(a)*   1 A long time ago,
              2   maybe fifty years ago,
              3   it attacked them.
      (b)   4 They were staying on the Clackamas river;
              5   one fellow climbed a pine tree,
              6   then she saw them.
      (c)   7 He pulled his arrows out,
              8   he shot her maybe three or four times:
              9   nothing to her,
             10   she bled through her mouth.
(B) *(d)* 11 This thing looked like a coyote on the head,
             12   short ears;
             13   teeth like a wild hog's tusks,
             14   long white front claws;

```
         15          long hind legs,
         16          short front legs.
(C)  (e)  17  He tried to do everything to her,
         18    then he got afraid:
         19       only two arrows left.
     (f)  20  Then he took one,
         21    he lit I don't know what,
         22      he put it on this arrow,
         23        then he shot the (arrow),
         24          then it started to burn.
     (g)  25  Again he did the same with one (arrow),
         26    then this (thing) went down into a canyon,
         27      there it burned.
(D)  (h)  28  This thing is what they call At'únaqa.
         29    Then it really started to burn.
         30      Then a lot of white men ran up,
         31        they put it out;
         32          the state of Oregon put out a lot of money.
(E)  (i)  33  There's nothing of that sort to be seen on our side of the mountains.
         34  Only on the other side could things of that sort be seen.
         35  A long time ago,
         36    maybe as much as fifty or sixty years ago,
         37      this thing was seen.
```

```
(A)  (a)   1  GHanGádix,
           2    dála'ax GwnmaLíaL iLÉlx,
           3      galaLgÉlqwam.
     (b)   4  GaLXídlaitix gayaSq'wímlit wímaL;
           5    íxat gayuk'wáLxiwlx iCáqwSba,
           6      kwapt gagigÉlkl.
     (c)   7  XHwL XwL gaCtóX idiaGámaCX,
           8    dala'áx Lun awáCi lakt itGámaq gaCdáloX:
           9      k'áya dan axkába,
          10        iLgawÉlqt iCákwSatbà gaLagÉlba.
(B)  (d)  11  YaXkádaya dan yukStíx dan áLqi isk'úlya iCagÉC,
          12    itkamtL'áXwimaX idatsk'Étsxa;
          13      iLgáqaC aLqi' dán daúya iSiaxínxat igúSu,
          14        itgaxaxwálagwàdit idátLqt idàtgabúmidmaX;
          15          itgáqwit idátLqda qiqmtqíxiámt,
          16            dáuda itgákwSn idatsk'Étsxa.
(C)  (e)  17  Kí:::::nwa qÉngi aCóXwa,
          18    kwapt k'waS galiXóX:
          19      makwStka idiagámaCX.
```

(f)   20 Kwapt aixt gaCagÉlga,
      21   dan Lqon wax gaCiúX,
      22   axka dáwaba aGámaCX,
      23   kwapt gaCulíma,
      24   kwapt gaCilgálGwix.
(g)   25 Wit'a aixt dáukwa gaCóX,
      26   kwapt yaXkádaya galilCúxwix waqáLba,
      27   kwába gaCilgálq.
(D) (h) 28 YaXkádaya dan aLgiupGnáya At'únaqa.
      29   Kwapt yáXda gaCilgálgwix.
      30   Kwapt qánSipt bÉSdn gatgiúXdama,
      31   Cxp Cxp gaLgúXwam;
      32   qanSipt idála ilXáxelaitix gaCiXíma.
(E) (i) 33 K'áya dan qidáuma pu dan aqíGlgláya gígat lXaikáyamt ibúqux.
      34 Yáima iwadíwa ínadix pu qidáumaX dan aqiGlgláya.
      35 GHanGádix,
      36   dala'ax qánSipt gwÉnmaLiáL awáCi tXÉmLiàL iLÉlx,
      37   dáyadan gaqiGÉlkl.

5. This analysis into five stanzas (A–E), nine verses (a–b–c, d, e–f–g, h, i), and thirty-seven lines fits the underlying pattern of rhetorical presentation common to Chinookan texts. The three-part pattern of onset, ongoing, outcome, recurs at each level.

At the level of the five stanzas, this text shows (as does Cultee's) two intersecting three-stanza sequences. The action of danger and escape, focused on the arrows, begins in A and is completed in C. In this sequence, the close-up of the creature in B is an interlude and a heightening of the danger. The burning that begins in C is completed in D, while the distancing that begins in D with the introduction of 'white men' (bÉSdn) and cost to the state is completed in E. To be sure, E is an epilogue that brings the story full circle, picking up and elaborating the information as to time and place given in the first four lines. What links these three stanzas as a set is that they form a sequence of outcomes: for the man (C), for the state (D), for "us" (and history) (E).

Within the stanzas, one has recurrent use of the rhetorical pattern. The three verses of A are frame in time and action (attack) in (a); frame in place and focus of action (b); initial outcome (c). In sum, general attack, specific attack, failure of defense. Within the verses, there is similar logic: general temporal frame, more specific temporal frame, action outcome (1–2–3); general spatial frame, more specific spatial frame, action outcome (4–5–6); onset of defense, ongoing of defense, outcome (7, 8, 9–10).

The lines of B are a descriptive close-up that can be seen to fall into three parts: head, cutting parts (teeth, claws), legs. These parts can be treated as "couplets" or distichs. The pairing of head and ears is obvious enough, having reference to the comparison to a coyote, as is the pairing of front and hind legs. The teeth and the claws are the dangerous parts of the creature. There seems indeed to be a principle in the order of the parts. The point of view would appear to be that of the man in the tree. From that point of view, the head and its ears would be closest; the teeth and then the claws next; and behind them the legs. The overall order of all six parts is not precisely the order of what is closest to the man. Rather, the second part of each pair is the part projecting out toward the man: ears above the head, claws out in front of the teeth, front legs above hind legs. In sum, one is to picture the creature erect, clawed forelegs raised toward the man in the tree (a picture of direct danger, having no mention of digging out and uprooting the tree, as in Mrs. Howard's narrative). Notice that the word for 'tusks', perhaps coined here, has a root meaning of projection (root -nxa), and that 'front' is added in the translation, as if to clarify projection as well. Notice also that the postposition -iamt in line 15 is intrinsically bipolar, from there to here. (Perhaps also there is an implicit pattern of long head, short ears; long teeth, long claws; long legs, short legs. The insistence on length fits the picture of projection. The two short things [ears, legs] are also close.)

The three couplets do not have a sequence in terms of action, but the visual sequence presents first the nearest and least distinctive, least dangerous features (head, ears); then the dangerous features (teeth, claws); then the physical completion of the implicit stance and situation, the hind legs on which she rears, the front legs on which the claws project toward him.

The three verses of C complete the action with regard to the individual man. Verse (e) frames the situation—only two arrows; (f) develops the action, the response that is to be successful; (g) completes the action—the last arrow, the going off of the creature.

Within (e) there is onset (triad), intermediate outcome (afraid), outcome in the sense of crucial definition of situation: two arrows. The verse can be said to be linked by states of perception and orientation on the part of the man: trying, fear, perceiving that only two arrows are left. Within (f) there is straightforward five-part action. The lines appear to group as onset (20), ongoing (21–23), outcome (24); that is, taking the arrow, lighting and shooting the arrow, the creature starting to burn. There is a parallel to (c), in which the man first takes an arrow (7), shoots (8), and observes an outcome (9–10). Here the middle part—the shooting—is elaborated (21–23), being the key to the outcome and escape. Within (g) there is clearcut onset (25), ongoing (26), outcome (27). The steps of taking and shooting the arrow, found in (c) and (f), here are summarized in a line (25) that leads on to further events.

The five lines of (D) parallel stanza (B) in beginning with identification of the creature, there (B) by description, here (D) by name. Insofar as the three-part pattern is present, the identification seems to be the initial frame (28), the "really started to burn" the ongoing element (29), and effort and cost to the whites and the state the outcome (30–32).

The five lines of E are linked by the theme of the creature being *seen:* not on this side, only on the other side, a long time ago. These three elements seem to represent the elements of the pattern in this stanza.

6. The patterning just discussed seems so obvious, once seen, that it is perhaps puzzling that it was not seen at once. The series of versions just presented shows that perception was slow and intermittent. It does not seem to me that the fact invalidates the result. There are many underlying patterns in science and scholarship that are obvious, once displayed, but whose discovery was slow. The false steps and oversights may be instructive as to how the particular process of discovery involved in Chinookan narrative structure proceeds.

Comparison of alternatives requires a common format. The format has two aspects, that of levels and that of conventions. As to levels: hitherto it has not seemed necessary to identify individual lines by a mark or label (cf. Hymes 1976a, 1977). Comparison requires it. The overall format required for analysis of Chinookan narratives thus has seven levels: Part, Act, Scene, Stanza, Verse, Versicle, Line.

6.1. Not all levels need always be distinguished. Only longer narratives have distinct Parts, such as are indicated in Cultee's narrative as ONE and TWO. Many narratives have more than one section that can be usefully called an Act, for example, the narratives by Cultee and Mrs. Howard. Mr. Smith's narrative seems a single act. All authentic narratives have an organization into stanzas, verses, versicles, and lines.

Beyond major Parts, which can be represented with spelled English numerals in capital letters (ONE, TWO), the levels group readily into three pairs. *Acts* and *Scenes* are the larger units. The relationship can be indicated by the use of roman numerals for both, capitalized roman numerals for Acts, lowercase roman numerals for scenes, as is customary in editions of plays. Thus, (I) is an Act, (i) is a scene.

Stanzas and verses are closely related, stanzas being groupings of verses. The relationship can be indicated by the use of English letters for both, capitalized English letters for stanzas, lower-case English letters for verses. Thus, (A) is a stanza, (a) is verse.

The term "versicle" is not in common use. Its primary meaning is simply "a short verse," and it seems appropriate for the recognition of pairings or other groupings of lines that recur as patterned features, yet are not equivalent in the structure of the narrative to the verses of which stanzas are composed. In Mr. Smith's narrative, the two lines (9–10) seem to be a unit as an outcome in verse (c). In stanza B, verse (d), lines (11–12), (13–14), (15–16) seem to be paired as units and the pairs to be the three constituents of the verse and stanza. One can then say that the verse and stanza consist of three versicles.

Both versicles and lines can be indicated by arabic numerals, the versicles within parentheses. Thus, (1) or (1–2) indicates a versicle, 1, 2 indicates lines.

6.2 The principal problem in comparing different analyses is to compare lines. Sometimes it is a question of difference in what is considered a line; sometimes it is a question of the grouping of lines.

The conventions for indicating relationships among lines are as follows:

(a) Separate numbers indicate separate lines in the analysis of reference.

(b) Numbers on the same line refer to a single series within a verse or part of a verse. Thus, (25–26–27) indicates that these three lines are members of the same verse in the analysis in question.

(c) Numbers joined by a plus sign are not separated in the analysis in question, but are separated in the analysis of reference. Thus, (1 + 2 + 3) in the first analysis above indicates that the words are analyzed into three lines in the final version.

(d) Numbers joined by a slash are members of a versicle, as a unit within a verse. Such lines are printed with the same indentation, except when initial in a verse or stanza (as in 11/12). Thus (9/10) constitute a versicle, as do (11/12), (13/14), (15/16).

(e) Numbers joined by a dash are a single series within a verse. Lines after the first are successively indented. Thus, (7–8–9/10) show a terraced effect where joined by a dash, a block effect where joined by a slash.

(f) Numbers joined by a comma are coordinate, whether within a verse or across verses. In a verse of five lines, the comma can be used to show the grouping into rhetorical steps. Thus (28, 29–30–31, 32) would show the relationships that constitute the steps of onset, ongoing, and outcome in verse (h). While all five lines are successively indented in the text as given here, one could choose to have 28, 29, 32 flush left, indenting successively only 30 and 31. In the second analysis above, verse (n) was regarded as having two coordinate units and verse (p) as having five, as shown by the beginning of lines flush left. The coordinate units would be separated by commas, the lines within them by dashes.

(g) Parentheses are used for convenience and clarity to show groupings of whatever kind.

7. These conventions can be used to show abstractly the relationships between the different analyses of Mr. Smith's narrative.

7.1 The first presentation of the text clearly did not recognize verse and line organization at all. Probably I did not analyze Mr. Smith's narratives of the 1950s for some years after discovering such organization because I really did not expect to find it there. During 1972–73, then, I worked on Kathlamet and Wishram texts (during a senior fellowship from the National Endowment for the Humanities). Perhaps I feared not finding evidence of traditional performance in the texts that were my personal link to tradition, texts that came, as well, from a summer in which Mr. Smith and I had been especially

1956, 1967*	1976, July 1978	December 1978
A 1+2+3,	A (m) (1+2+3)–4	A (a) 1–2–3
4,		
5,	(n) 5–6, 7–8–(9+10)	(b) 4–5–6
6,		
7,		(c) 7–8–(9/10)
8,		
9+10		
B 11;	(o)*(11+12)–13–14–	B (d) (11/12)–(13/14)–(15/16)
12;	15–16	
13;		
14;		
15;		
16		
C 17, 18	B (p) 17–18,	C (e) 17–18–19
19,		
20+21+22	19–20,	(f) 20–21–22–23–24
23,	(21+22)–23,	
24,		(g) 25–26–27
25,	24,	
26,	25	
27,		
28	(q) 26, 27, 28	
(D–E)	(r) 29, (30+31), 32	D (h) 28–29–30–31–32
29,		
30+31,		
32,		
33,		
34,	E (s) 33, 34, 35+36+37	E (i) 33–34–35–36–37
35+36+37		

Table 5–1 Successive analyses of At'únaqa

close, a time of family difficulties for him, the beginning of new family relationships for me. He had done me a favor to tell me texts; let them stand as part of a personal relationship.

Nevertheless, the early blocking out of the story into four paragraphs of numbered sentences bears a fairly clear resemblance to the final version. Reconsidered with fivefold patterning in mind, it is easy to see that the last three numbered sentences of the first version should be separated off as an epilogue, as is done in each of the subsequent versions. The paragraphs already distinguish the equivalents of (A) and (B) and approximate the boundary between (C) and (D). The great differences lie, first, in the absence of any internal analysis of the major blocks, and, second, in the bounding and internal relationships of the middle portion, essentially the (C) of the final version.

7.2. In the summer of 1976 I was startled and happy to discover organization in verses and lines. The initial demarcation of this analysis recognized (A) and (E), the outer stanzas. (B) of the final version is distinguished as a verse (see [o]), if not with the status of a coordinate stanza. (D) is virtually recognized (see verse [r]), if also not distinguished as a coordinate stanza. Again, the great differences have to do with the bounding and internal relationships of the intervening portion, the eventual (C).

7.3. Let me review the internal analysis that has led to the final version. The treatment of (1–2–3) and (34–35–36) as comprised of three separate lines each was motivated initially by an aesthetic sense. Balance and clarity of movement at the beginning and end of the text seemed better that way.[3] As far as structure is concerned, the two additional lines at the end of the text make no difference. Stanza (E) remains intact. Either three constituent parts, as before, or five, as now, agree with the general rhetorical pattern. At the beginning of the text, however, the former structure cannot remain exactly the same. The intuition that prompted the change felt (1–2–3) to be a unit, apart from line (4) with which they had been grouped in a verse (m). It is indeed easy enough to reassign (4) as first line of the next verse. It makes sense as the first of a second set of three lines (4–5–6), and the remaining lines of the verse in question (n) fit together well also (7–10). The result is to find three coordinate units (verses a, b, c) where there had been only two before (verses m, n).

The change may appear to be entirely internal to this portion of the text, having no consequence for the rest. However, the proportions of rhetorical

---

[3]Fewness of vowels and richness of inflection give Wasco sentences an inherent tendency toward recurrence of sound, abetted by grammatical concord. Something is added to this by individual choice, no doubt, but the distinction between the language and the user cannot yet be made with confidence. The presentation of texts in lines does bring out the recurrences that contribute to phonic texture. In this text the following can be noted:

line 1: Ga . . . Ga . . .
line 2: dál . . . LíaL iLÉlx, where stressed vowel plus *l* embeds Li . . . iL.
line 3: stressed gÉl perhaps completing dál . . . LÉl.
line 4: 3 stressed *i*.
line 6: stressed GÉl at the end of this verse parallel to the end of the preceding verse.
line 7: double particle; double ending in -X.
line 8: ending in -X.
line 9: all vowels *a;* k'á . . . ká; ending in -ba.
line 10: double ending in -ba.
lines 21, 22: ending in -X.
lines 23, 24: parallel initial kwapt, followed by ga-C-u-l- and ga-C-i-l-.
lines 26, 27: parallel initial kwapt, kwaba.
line 28: -aya, aya, -aqa
lines 29, 30: parallel initial kwapt.
line 31: double particle.
lines 33–37: recurrences of dan, verb theme -Glkl, pu, qidáuma(X); dal- . . LiáL . . LiàL iLÉlx in (36).

pattern are interdependent in a text, and this one change has a domino effect. The three coordinate units, verses (a, b, c), constitute a unit of their own at the next level of organization, that of stanzas. Verse (o) is left isolated. It cannot remain part of stanza A if normal patterning is to be maintained. There has been very little change in scope. Apart from the reassignment of line (4) and realignment of lines (4–5–6), the internal organization of lines (1–16) remains much the same. The scope of verses (m, n, o) in former stanza (A) is the same as the scope of verses (a, b, c) in new stanza (A), together with what had been verse (o). But the place of (o) in the whole must now be reassessed. A new possibility indeed appears. The text as a whole can be seen as having five parts instead of three. The internal change of proportion leads to a change in the proportions of the rest.

The gain to the relationships internal to the opening verses is itself welcome. Subgroupings of the sort represented by the two flush left parts of (n) were awkward. There was poor fit with usual rhetorical order at certain points. For example, an act of perception, "she saw him" (line 6), ought to be final in a unit. The reanalysis brings out (and benefits from) the general rhetorical pattern.

The larger gain is that the structural parallelism of the new stanza (B) to what will now be stanza (D) can be made clear. Both sets of lines begin with the same expression, *YaXkadaya dan*, in statements of the identity of the creature, one by physical description, one by name. In the earlier arrangement, lines (11–16) (B) were uncomfortable at best as a subordinate part of a stanza of action; lines (28–32) are really an outcome with a different interest than that of the escape of the man up the pine tree. These two accounts of identity magnify the creature, one as a physical marvel, the other as a costly one. Action and identity alternate (A : B, C : D), then both are distanced and rounded off with a return, slightly augmented, of the beginning (E).

All this depends, of course, on the status of lines (28–32) as a separate stanza (D), and that status needs further discussion. The matter brings us back to the point, already stated, that the heart of the successive analyses has to do with the middle section. The major reason for grouping (as I now think, wrongly) lines (17–32) as a single middle stanza was the hypothesis that all verses having the stem "to burn" should be in the same unit. Lexical recurrence is indeed a recurrent fact and criterion in Chinookan patterning. But reflection suggests that "burn" is really part of two parallel sequences here. Each begins with "it started to burn," Mr. Smith's way of rendering in English the presence of the evidential suffix *-ix* in lines 24, 29, as against line 27. The first sequence has the creature start to burn, then burn up (24, 27). The second sequence has the forest start to burn, according to Mr. Smith's translation-retelling; though "forest fire" does not occur in the Wasco, Mr. Smith's sequence "started to burn, started a forest fire" is evidently a repetition that expands and makes clear the distinction intended with the line. All this suggests that while it may be helpful to have native authorities translate literally, it is equally, if not more, helpful to have them translate as a retelling. In any case, the second sequence is not about the creature, but about the forest. Its outcome is not a burning up, but an extinguishing. It is this parallelism that is structurally operative.

A less literal attention to words would, in fact, disclose that there are three references to the notion of fire in (C) as it stands in the final version: the man *lit* the arrow, the creature started to *burn*, it *burned* up. (And in Mr. Smith's English retelling, there are three such references in [D] as well: started to burn, started a forest fire, fought the fire.)

The three-part rhetorical pattern could be seen, of course, in the earlier analysis: the man shoots his arrows, the creature burns, the forest burns. But the broad pattern is at the expense of a more attractive organization of the internal parts, one which allows the rhetorical pattern to apply pervasively within verses and parts of verses. Thus in verse (p) of the second analysis one can recognize a five-part sequence that is not convincing as to the rhetorical meaning that ought to covary with the rhetorical form. And within the five parts of the verse there is no opportunity for the rhetorical form/meaning pattern to apply at all.

The key to a more convincing analysis of this middle section has been present in the Wasco all along, but was overlooked or misunderstood. In developing the final version of the analysis in August, I arrived at a version identical with the one presented here, except for verses (e) and (f). In August these verses were thought to have the following structure:

(e) 17–18–(19/20)
(f) (21+22)–23–24

In words,

(e)   He *tried* to do everything to her
          Then he got afraid.
               Only two arrows left,
                    then he took one.

(f)   I don't know what he put on it, he lit it on this arrow,
          then he shot the arrow.
               Then it started to burn.

This analysis seemed to have the advantage that, together with (g), it grouped lines into sets of three verbs, and that together with this grouping was a coupling of two initial particles in the lines after the first in each set of three verses: *kwapt, kwapt; kwapt, kwapt; kwapt, kwaba* (lines 18, 20; 23, 24; 26, 27). But as far as proportions go, the final version had a single 'then', *kwapt,* in the outer verses (e, g) and three in the central verse (f), a total of five.

Still, the analysis was plausible. At the time I thought that what had thrown me off the track in the 1976 analysis was to consider line 19, literally 'two-only his-arrows', a line without a verb, as coordinate with other lines. In the light of the fivefold schema, I had seen in these lines of (e) and (f) a series of three versicles, the second line of each versicle having *kwapt,* followed by a completion of the stanza with a fourth line with *kwapt* and a fifth line with *wit'a,* 'Again'. All very neat, patterned, and comprising all the lines referring to arrows. (See the 1976 analysis above.)

Still, I should have been distressed then not to have 'Again' (line 25) begin a new verse; and after rectifying that mistake in August, I still should have been troubled by treating lines 21 + 22 as a single line. The coupling in a versicle of lines 19–20 could be seen as having a certain parallel with lines 9/10, even if Mr. Smith had used a sentence with a verb in translating 19, while he had not done so in translating 9. But not only had he used two distinct predications in translating and retelling lines 21–22, he had also shown in his Wasco that the two parts were disjunct.

Line 21, *dan Lqon wax gaCiúX,* is literally 'what I-don't-know light he-did-it'. The verb is a two-place, transitive verb, with third person masculine actor 'he' (C-) and third person masculine object 'it' *(i-).* The latter pronoun is in implicit concord with the object word, the particle *dan* 'thing, what', which always takes masculine concord. Now the point is that the succeeding words, *axka dáwabà aGámaCX,* literally, 'it (feminine) this (feminine) -at arrow', show feminine gender concord throughout. If the concord were masculine, the first two words would be *yaxka* and *dauyaba.* The concord is feminine, of course, because the last third, 'arrow', has a feminine gender prefix in the singular, *a-.* Now this clause is syntactically disjunct, an instance of anacolouthon. Had the man done something to the arrow in the preceding verb, it would have had to mark the action, most likely by including an indirect object sequence, with *a-* for the indirect object, followed by a postposition of spatial reference, such as *g-* 'on'. We would, perhaps, have had *gaCiáguX;* but we don't. The two sets of concord relationships, elaborated in the second set (where a simple 'arrow' might have done if there had been a single construction), and the two sentences of the English translation, "I don't know what he put on it—he lit this arrow," suggest that Mr. Smith indeed conceived the action here in two steps. His English interlocks the two steps, linking "lit" with "arrow," and "put on" with "it," whereas the Wasco shows "lit" with "it," and implies "put on" with "arrow." That he intended two linked steps here seems almost certain. Each of the rhetorical moments of the verse is marked by an initial *kwapt* at this, a highpoint of the action. *Kwapt* 'he took an arrow'; he lit something, he put it on the arrow, *kwapt* he shot it; *kwapt* it started to burn. The internal rhetorical patterning of 'he lit, he put it on, he shot' is perfect, too.

In sum, pervasiveness of the meaning dimension of rhetorical patterning asks for such an analysis, the English retelling provides for it, and the concord relationships in the Wasco text seem to require it.

It is this analysis, at least, that is given as the final version here of the sequence of efforts to deal with the middle portion of Mr. Smith's text. One might have moved more quickly to it. Still, in my experience it always takes a fair amount of time to hear what one sees.

6

Breakthrough into Performance Revisited

Part One: The crier

Part Two: The news about coyote

Part Three: Coyote's people sing

The chapter with which this section of the book begins presented a speech and versions of two stories as instances of kinds of performance. Both Philip Kahclamet's illustration of "The crier" and Hiram Smith's telling of the news about Coyote were responses to a fieldworker's concern to clarify, in the one case, a word, and in the other case, a text, both already written down by others. Kahclamet's presentation of "Coyote's people sing" was a fusion of telling and commentary, informed by a definition of the situation as one in which all participants—teller, recorder, hearer—were assumed to share ethnological responsibilities. In each case the event appeared to involve a breakthrough into genuine performance.

Two decades after the events, some years, indeed, after the writing and publication of the article in which the events are discussed, I came to understand enough of the tradition behind the texts to see the lineaments of performance in each. The prospect of republication renewed attention to them, and I found that the earlier belief in the presence of performance now could be given objective shape.

The understanding came first with the texts wholly in the native language, the two versions of "The news about Coyote";[1] Part Two of this chapter, dealing with those texts, was written first (spring 1980). By itself, it was conceived of as an appendix to chapter 3, but the length to which it grew made the status of an appendix, or postscript, awkward. The addition of Mrs. Howard's Clackamas version and a general comparison of all three versions

The history of this chapter is described in its first pages. It is published here for the first time.

1. The title is changed to "The *news* about Coyote," from Sapir's "The story concerning Coyote," because the key word, *id-wáCa*, does in fact mean 'news', report', and the like, as is made clear in Mrs. Howard's version, wherein Coyote hails a boat to learn the news that turns out to be about himself.

made the whole a chapter in its own right. Moreover, by presenting the material as a separate chapter, I could have the total number of chapters in the book be ten, while using only available work. Ten, of course, is a multiple of the Chinookan pattern number five, a multiple that Chinookans themselves use.

It was only after the manuscript was thought complete and the index to translations was being prepared (summer 1980) that I realized, turning the pages, that the text of "The crier" had never been re-examined. A few moments showed it to have structure in terms of the principles underlying narrative, and an evening resulted in discovery of the shape given here.

Where to put the discovery? At first it seemed that it might go as a postscript to chapter 3, where the letter to Segal, already positioned as a postscript, dealt in part with the same text. Yet the new form of the text depended on a standpoint to be arrived at only in subsequent chapters (4, 5 and 9). It would disrupt the development of the section. And to make a separate chapter of the new text, perhaps entitled "Verse analysis of a Wishram speech: Philip Kahclamet's 'The crier,' " would break the pattern number, ten. Hence at last the solution of coupling the new material with the reconsideration of the stories about Coyote, and of titling the whole, "Breakthrough into performance revisited." The solution proved both necessary and prescient, when inclusion of "Coyote's people sing" in the literary index directed attention to it as well. Sure enough, underlying the English and the metalinguistic commentary there was also narrative verse.

The sudden discovery of traditional form in Philip Kahclamet's texts focused thought and feeling on him, and has led me to complete Part One of this chapter with a poem in memory of him (Hymes 1975b). I hope that the intention will excuse the performance.

Part One. The Crier

Philip Kahclamet's text is a rare instance of recorded Chinookan oratory. As has been noted in chapter 3, very little is known of such oratory, so far as the written record is concerned. There is little to turn to for indication of what traditional form may have been. One might expect that the kind of rhetorical patterning discovered in narrative would be found in oratory also, and that indeed appears to be the case. There are some texts of formal speeches in English in Meacham (1875), and one of them is included by Ramsey in his valuable collection of Oregon country Indian literature (1977). As Ramsey has suggested to me, Meacham's texts appear to follow traditional forms to a degree. The passage he has reprinted, indeed, can be seen to be built up of units of three and five. Such units are clear in the middle sections, having to do with the three women itemized, and plausible elsewhere. Here is a presentation in lines of the passage (Meacham 1875:174–75; Ramsey 1977:54).

Chief Mark considers monogamy, Warm Springs Agency, 1871

"My heart is warm like fire,
        but there are cold spots in it;
                I don't know how to talk.

"I want to be a white man.
        My father did not tell me
                it was wrong
                        to have so many wives.
                                I love all my women.

"My old wife is a mother to the others,
        I can't do without her;
                but she is old,
                        she cannot work very much;
                                I can't send her away to die.

"This woman cost me ten horses;
        she is a good woman;
                I can't do without her.

"That woman cost me eight horses;
        she is young;
                she will take care of me when I am old.

"I don't know how to do;
        I want to do right.
                I am not a bad man.
                        I know your new law is good;
                                The old law is bad.

"We must be like the white man.
        I am a man;
                I will put away the old law.

. . . . .

"I want you to tell me
        how to do right.
                I love my women and children.
                        I can't send any of them away;
                                what must I do?"

The reporter of the speech, A. B. Meacham, was superintendent of Indian Affairs in Oregon and was pressing for abolition of polygamy, together with the superintendent at Warm Springs, Captain Smith. A compromise was ultimately reached, prohibiting new polygamous marriages. Even today the tradition of a chief having two wives or more is remembered and employed in jest.

In presenting the speech reported by Meacham, I am, of course, unable to judge the circumstances. I have tried to imagine what Wasco might lie behind some of the sentences and have not thought that the English could be pressed into a line for every predicate. The speech that follows was taken down verbatim as spoken, as part of lexicographical inquiry that suddenly became something more. Confidence in the source and the patterning that emerges has led me to press the English rather far. It is likely, indeed, that in this century speeches like the one presented here were heard in English as well as in the Indian language. Three-part patterning is clear in the speech reported by Meacham, at least in the enumeration of wives.

The general principles that inform Chinookan narratives appear clearly in the speech given by Kahclamet. There are the pattern numbers, three and five, as in the list of five Christian churches at the end. There is repetition of adverbs of time as markers: "morning" recurring three times at the outset, and again at the beginning of the second stanza, parallel to its use at the beginning of the first. Throughout it is possible to distinguish individual lines in terms of distinct predicates and to find that the lines form groups, sometimes as pairs, as also occurs in Chinookan, often as sets of three and five, and the resulting structure discloses a patterning of theme and emphasis; there is form/meaning covariation at the core of the whole. Let me turn to this patterning of theme and emphasis after presenting the reanalysis of the form of the speech.

Philip Kahclamet, "The crier"

A   (a)   In the morning he steps out,
            he intones his words:
      "This is Sunday morning,
          You people should know—
      "I don't have to come round this morning
            to tell you—
            that you people should put on all your trappings;
            that you will come to church.
     (b)   "You know
            that we were put here by the Great Spirit.
         We have to worship him.

(c) "I am getting to my old age.
>   Some of you will have to take my place
>   >   when I'm gone.

B (a) "When you hear the drum this morning,
>   it's calling you
>   >   to worship the Great Spirit.

  (b) "That's
>   where all our ancestors went;
>   >   if you go by the old religion,
>   >   >   you will see them
>   >   >   >   when you leave the earth.

  (c) "You know
>   we are going to have to leave our flesh in the ground;
>   >   only our souls go;
>   >   and we'll be sure
>   >   >   to meet our ancestors.

C (a) "You people know
>   that we didn't come here ourselves.
>   He who created us is above.

  (b) "He put us here.
>   We have to be
>   >   where we are today.

  (c) "Me—I'm not telling you this myself.
>   I'm only giving you the revelations
>   >   which I've learned from somebody else.

D (a) "When you hear these drums,
>   go.

  (b) "We are Nadidánwit here;
>   this is our country.

  (c) "These white people came;
>   they brought Christianity.

  (d) "It's not for us.
>   The Christianity was brought here for the white people only.

  (e) "The white people cheated us out of our country.
>   So don't follow them,
>   >   whatever they teach you.

E (a) "SHuSúgli was a Jew;
>   he was not Nadidánwit,
>   >   and he was not for the Nadidánwit.

  (b) "SHuSúgli i-ju i-kíXaX.

  (c) "Yaxdau i-pendikast,
>   i-käthlik,

> "Presbyterian,"
> "Methodist,"
> kwadaw i-Sik,
> k'aya amXáwiXa,
> k'aya t'únwit amdúXa.''

The treatment of the single line E(b) as an entire verse is awkward but appears unavoidable. The preceding three lines in E(a) go together, and the succeeding lines in E(c) go together, an elaborated nominal catalog ("Those ... [5 churches]") as one unit, followed by two parallel verb phrases. Perhaps the fact that the single line is the first line of the breakthrough into performance in the Indian language, the point of "code-switching," goes together with the structural weight that the line appears to have.

The text is not a translation into English of a Chinookan original. The general principles of Chinookan measured verse are adapted to means provided by English syntax: The relative clauses, the interpolation (or somersault) in A(a), separating "You people should know" from the two following clauses beginning with "that," do not have known Chinookan sources.

The text is not a strict counterpart of Chinookan narrative verse. For one thing, no narrative known to us has a single turn at talk this long. Devices that enter into the organization of action, linked with and often culminating in short turns at talk, are largely missing—the three-step act, for example. The three-step definition, or quasi-syllogism, of E(a), or D(c-e), for example, seems a different minor genre.

That this instance of oratory has a common grounding, yet different figuration, in relation to narrative texts, is understandable in terms of differences inherent in the two genres. There is a parallel to the relation between verse proper and what I take to be a formal style grounded in the same general principles of repetition in ancient Egyptian (Foster 1980). (Foster demonstrates the existence of thoroughgoing verse in narrative and relates verse to other kinds of verse brilliantly. The text he presents in contrast as true prose also shows some internal parallelism and repetition, and can perhaps also be analyzed in accord with the principles of two-part and four-part patterning that he finds in verse, albeit more broadly and without the tightly cadenced conceptual coupling of verse.)

The oratorical text shares one very important principle of patterning with narrative verse, namely, parallelism in the endings of stanzas. Such parallelism is frequent, but not required, in sections of narrative. It is invariant in this speech. There is, however, a significant difference in the implementation of the principle. In a narrative, the action advances, and parallelism of the endings of stanzas reflects such advance. Here the parallelism of the endings is that of a single theme, considered in various aspects.

The theme is the key to the speech. It can be called the theme of continuity of cultural tradition. The first three stanzas each end with one of its facets: in A, younger succeeding older in roles that maintain tradition; in B, the living joining their ancestors when they die; in C, knowledge being something learned from one's old people. In terms of the speech situation, you will follow me (A); we all will follow those who have gone before (B); I follow others who have gone before (C). The last two stanzas turn from internal process to external threat: don't follow them, whatever they teach you (D); don't concern yourselves with them, don't believe in them (E). To follow them, to believe in them, will destroy the continuity. That consequence is stated explicitly in B(b) with regard to joining one's ancestors after death; it is implicit in A with regard to the role of crier being maintained and in C with regard to spiritual knowledge being maintained.

The ending of each of the five stanzas with the theme of continuity of tradition is paralleled by the beginning of three of them with a call: (A[a-c]), "come to church"; (B), drum, calling you; (D), drum, go.

It may be significant that the first three stanzas, ABC, are the three that have "You know," as well as being the three that end on internal continuity of tradition. Except for the absence of a call at the start of C, all are quite parallel: Call; truths about the Great Spirit; appeal to continuity.

We seem to have here something of the Chinookan five-part sequence, such that the middle part—the third—is pivotal, simultaneously serving as outcome of the first three parts and as onset of the last three parts. C clearly concludes the first three parts. It can be seen as introducing or emphasizing themes that underscore the appeal of the remaining stanzas, D and E. That we didn't come here ourselves may imply not only a Creator, but also that the Creator justifies our being in this particular place. The implication seems to be emphasized by what follows in C(b): "We have to be where we are today." The next stanza (D) states the proposition, "This is our country," and the associated proposition, that Christianity is not part of our country but something brought by and for the white people. To alien status is added villainy —the white people cheated us out of where we have to be, our country.

Stanza E particularizes and elaborates the conclusion of D. Christianity is particularized in terms of its eponymous founder, Christ, as a Jew, not of or for the Indians (not even in some sense properly a Christian?), and in terms of specific Christian groups (five of them, including the Indian-founded Shaker Church). The particularization in terms of Christ, as Jew, seems to imply that Christianity is to be understood, not as a world religion, a religion for the world, but as a matter of particular groups—ethnic (the Jews), institutional (the churches), and whites collectively. The Indians (Nadidánwit) are a group on the same footing. Since this is our country, not theirs; since their religion is of and for them, not us; the line of division is clear. The Great Spirit for us, SHuSúgli for them.

Notice that the French-derived name *SHuSúgli* perhaps has a depreciatory connotation to a Chinookan speaker; the stem -*SuSu* in Wishram names and describes a lisping speech defect. (*I-ya-SuSu* names someone who has a lot of *SuSu* in his speech.) In any case, the way in which the opposition is drawn tacitly denies "God" to the Christians. The fundamental power of the world, the creator, is appropriated to the Indian side as the Great Spirit. Christianity is left with a prophet, one among many.

The rhetorical appeal of the speech comes to a head in the fourth stanza (D). Compare the way in which personal pronouns and speech acts are managed in the first three stanzas and in the fourth. In the first three stanzas the three persons are the speaker, the audience, and the Great Spirit, together with the ancestors. When the audience is directly addressed as "you," the speech act is not a command or exhortation or other form of directive. It is a statement, reaffirming what "you" (and "I," the speaker) know. Whenever the speaker designates himself, it is in a way that merges his identity with the continuity of the group: "I don't have . . . to tell you"; "Some of you will have to take my place"; "Me—I'm not telling you this myself." And, of course, there are many uses of inclusive "we."

It is with the fourth stanza that "you" are not reminded or informed, but commanded: "go." The dialectic of pronouns changes at the end of the fourth stanza from merger and inclusion to opposition and exclusion. The inclusive, integrating "we" of the first three stanzas begins retrospectively to seem to have implicitly excluded a third party, now introduced. In the fourth stanza, the pronominal pattern proceeds, verse by verse:

you/you	(2nd/2nd)
we /our	(inclusive/inclusive)
these/they	(3rd/3rd)
it : us / it : the(m)	(3rd : inclusive/ 3rd : 3rd)
the(y) : us, our,	(3rd : inclusive),
(you) : them,	([2nd] : 3rd),
they : you.	(3rd : 2nd).

Table 6–1. Pronominal relationships

The stanza ends with a negative command, the complement and inverse of the command at the start of the stanza.

The fifth stanza contrasts "he" and "Nadidánwit," the latter a noun that has been defined in D(6) as "we," and concludes with a double negative directive, amplifying that of a D(e).

The affirmations of the first three stanzas, then, lead into three verses of command (D[a], D[e], E[c]). The first of the three puts as command what has twice been put as shared knowledge (A[c], B[a]). Pivotal, Janus-faced, it completes the three-part sequence of what one should do on Sunday morning, while at the same time it initiates the three-part sequence of direct exhortation. (The earlier statements have no doubt been implicitly directive, command couched as reminder of shared knowledge, as a picture of the nature of things.) The "deep structure" of the speech act surfaces, as it were, in "go." The two verses that complete the sequence of direct exhortation themselves contain three negative commands, one in English, two in Kiksht.

There is an element of historical irony in the situation that encompasses the speech. Before the coming of the white man, days were not grouped into weeks; before the coming of Christianity, worship of the Great Spirit would not have been allocated to Sunday morning. Such worship, when not personal, would have been embedded in the calendars of the seasons and of human life, the regular recurrences of salmon, roots, berries, and the inevitable changes of identity and crises of health from birth to death. Yet the speech is true in spirit. To adopt another's scheduling may be a way of protecting one's own claim to having a religion, too, a claim that many whites were prone to deny or dismiss as deviltry. If religion must be made a separate category (as it was really not before, so much did what would be considered "religion" permeate life), then the Indian people have their own, revelations from their own ancestors transmitted among themselves, proper to their name as people and to their country.

There is irony that English is the language of most of the speech as well. Yet religion has ultimately not depended upon language. In the first part of this century, Robert Smith (father of Hiram Smith) was renowned for interpreting the English-language Presbyterian service at Warm Springs into Wasco for those in the congregation who knew too little English. We are forever ignorant of what Presbyterian Wasco was like, but a lifetime ago there were Sundays-ful of it. Conversely, many use English, as perhaps did someone whom Philip Kahclamet had heard, to express Indian conviction. Today the language in which Philip broke into performance has almost no one left to speak it, and, contrary to the rejection urged by his speech, many Indian people find a Christian church compatible with Indian observances. Yet as I write (summer 1980) there is a renewed feeling at Warm Springs that Indian observances themselves (the root feast, the berry feast, namings, memorial dinners) should be reserved for Indians alone.

Whatever the ultimate fate of language and religion among the descendants of Chinookan speakers, there exists, thanks to Philip Kahclamet, one clear statement of Indian conviction in traditional rhetorical form. I am grateful to hear at last what Philip tried to tell me. Belated news of his death some years ago elicited the poem that follows:

For Philip

That August, at the Berry Feast,
you stood beside your Cadillac
among the trees, listening to the
voices echo old power-songs,
watching the stick-game gambling—

"Chief Cadillac," some would say,
as you stood apart,
impassive with pride.

That August, you made an appointment,
for the day we started east,
came but parked just above the turn
to either place, ours, rented, yours
like your other property,
inherited, but empty,
now, left to a cat—
ghosts spoke to you there, you said.
So there at the turn we took your picture,
as you asked, you, your rod and gun,
the Cadillac, so yellow in the glare
through the junipers. And you gave me pictures,
one of a boy,
with braided hair.
I guess now you sensed it good-by
for good, this linguist, like others,
had come for ghosts and to leave.

—of men who had told the myths,
in *kiksht*, as you would not,
as if you'd hear them correct you;
—who, mornings, gave "orientation,"
as drunk, one night, explaining,
you broke into doing, stopped;
—who stepping out of the house
and seeing something new,
"they'd have a word for it like that."

Had come to raise memories, and leave:

—of a shirt-sleeved, dark-haired, short, older man,
taking Wishram words apart on a blackboard,
before the very eyes of Philip,
brought east and young to Yale;
—of a man, dark-haired, short, troubled,
young enough to pal with, proud,
who'd come with summer and hired him,
taught him to write in Wishram,
sent him to ask old people words—
who'd written him brought him east,

where they worked the one semester at Yale,
fought, Philip burnt what he'd written,
he later said, went back to Spearfish.

To call himself Moslem once, go about in a turban,
correspond with a Budapest nobleman
wanting Indians for his island in its river.

To go about with his own book,
ask old people to tell him things
for him to write down in Wishram.

To have been the truth of a joke:
the Indian (dirty, drunken in the story)
breathes over the fieldworker's shoulder:
"I just want to see what orthography you use."

To have learned to write Wishram with German script,
yet discourage Old Man Jackson:
"Indians can't write Wishram, I know, I tried—,"

To never hold any book of his language:
the grammar a thesis, never published,
the words still slips, not a dictionary,
while the man who'd brought him east
became famed for another Indian's life,
then withered gradually with disease.

Had come for ghosts, for memories—
those who coaxed you back to work on Wishram
started to take your life-story, stopped,
too disturbing to you, they said (and to them?).

Coaxed back to work on Wishram,
passed on to me, testing me.
"Can you take words apart like Sapir?"

And though not dark-haired, or short, or Jewish,
like the long line of linguists you'd known.
I could—"Bilingual Linguist," you christened
yourself one night in the Rainbow Cafe.

Though after the summer, that August,
this time too, you could sense,

there'd be no book of Wishram
Philip Kahclamet helped to write?

Though how could you sense, creel on the hood,
rod and gun upright beside you,
hands on hips in the sun,
in a year in a fight you'd be hit
by your brother, die—

In a year or two, under his house,
the trunk of which you never told me
use needed space (your brother would say),
the papers inside be moulding anyway
(he said),
be burned—?

Now that we know,
we want to think of the Wishram rule,
give things away after death,
things kept bring back the ghost,
and you have to burn them.

I keep your pictures.
Grief goes forgotten, but not your face.

Part Two. The News About Coyote

This part compares methods of analysis and versions of a story. In the essay, "Breakthrough into performance" (1975a; chap. 3 of this book), the second of the three cases consists of a telling of an episode in the Coyote cycle by Louis Simpson, Sapir's source for *Wishram texts,* and a telling to me some fifty years later by Hiram Smith. The two texts are analyzed intensively and compared to each other. The discussion of "narrative sentences" points out criteria relevant to verses, and the importance of pairs of initial particles is especially clear. Recognition of their importance hovers at the edge of verse analysis without achieving it. In the event, the two narratives are analyzed primarily as structures of content, and it is their form in this regard that is related to traditional rhetorical form.

The essay, published in 1975, was written in the first part of 1971, just before firm discovery of measured verse during a year in Oregon as a Senior Fellow of the National Endowment for the Humanities (1972–73). There is now an opportunity and an obligation to consider the difference verse analysis makes. Such difference was explored in chapter 5, partly in terms of personal history. The technical result was a framework for comparing alternative analyses of lines. In this chapter, the difference is explored in terms of overall shape and style. A principal result is a different, yet more revealing fit with traditional rhetorical design. The verse analysis of each text is given, both in Chinookan and English, and the rationale of the verse analysis discussed in some detail, with comparison to the earlier (1975) analysis. After Mr. Simpson's and Mr. Smith's texts have been considered in turn, a third text, told in Clackamas Chinook by Victoria Howard, is presented and compared to the other two. Some suggestions are made as to a frame of reference adequate to the comparison of American Indian narratives generally.

Louis Simpson's text

Here is Mr. Simpson's text and its translation. Let me mention that the English wording has been changed from the 1975 version in order to make it a bit more idiomatic and exact. In lines 7–8, the base sense of the word *ewi* (phonemically *iwi*) is motion or direction that makes something accessible to the senses. In many contexts it is best translated either "to examine" or "to turn to see." The parallel use of the word in these lines implies that Coyote moves two body parts to make them sensorially accessible to each other. "Put" (up, down) seems a way of rendering this in English that allows the second repetition in the passage, that of *Ck'ES* (lines 8–9), to have some echo, as between "put" and "push."

i

A	(a)	AGa kwápt gayúya,	1
		gayuyáa,	2
		gayúLait.	3
B	(a)	AGa kwapt gasiXmk'naukwatsk Isk'úlya.	4
	(b)	AGa kwapt Isk'úlya gasíXtuks.	5
	(c)	AGa kwapt qédau galíXoX:	6
		éwi galíXoX iak'álxixpa,	7
		éwi galíXoX Ck'ÉS iaq'áqStaqba.	8
	(d)	Ck'ES gaqíuX.	9
	(e)	Galíkim Isk'úlya:	10
		"Naq(i) it'úktix ImSgnóX."	11
C	(a)	AGa kwapt idwaCa gaCuXábu;—	12
		naqi tq'éX gaCtóX pu gaqawiqLáXit.	13
	(b)	AGa kwapt dak dák gaCíuXix IdwáCa.	14
	(c)	AGa kwapt kánawee San gaLXElqLáXit,	15
		qángi nigiXatX Isk'úlya.	16

(d) AGa idwaCa niCiXadwaix.   17
(e) AGa kwapt dak dák (n)itkSiqídamidaba idwáCa.   18

ii

A (a) AGa kwapt Isk'úlya wálu gagíuX.   19
   (b) AGa kwapt niXLúxwait: 20
   (c)   "AGa anXLXÉlma."   21
B (a) AGa kwapt galíkta idÉlxamba.   22
   (b) AGa kwapt galúgakim: 23
   (c)   "Iak'ámlaix nigíXatX Isk'úlya;   24
            "Iak'álxix niSíXatukS."   25
C (a) AGa kwapt wit'a galíkta Isk'úlya.   26
   (b) GaliXLuxwait: 27
          "Yáxiba náSqi qXnÉlqLat;   28
          "K'aya quSt áGa aqnlqLáXida."   29
D (a) Galíkta wít'a díxt ítqwLe.   30
   (b) AGa wit'aX uXok'áiawulal: 31
   (c)   "AGa niSíXatukS Isk'úlya."   32
E (a) DuXikwLílal wít'aX idÉlxam.   33
   (b) AGa kwapt niXLúxwait: 34
   (c)   "QuSt aGa aqxnÉlqLat."   35

Verse translation of Mr. Simpson's text

i

A (a) Now then he went,   1
          he went,   2
          he sat down.   3
   (b) Now then Coyote looked all around.   4
   (c) Now then Coyote sucked himself.   5

B (a) Now then he did thus: 6
          he put up his penis,   7
          he put down his head.   8
   (b) Someone pushed him down.   9
   (c) Coyote said: 10
          "You've done me no good."   11

C (a) Now then he locked up the news:—   12
          he did not want it to be made known.   13
   (b) Now then someone made the news loose.   14

	(c)	Now then everyone came to know	15
		what Coyote did to himself.	16
	(d)	Now he had headed the news off.	17
	(e)	Now then they made the news break loose.	18

ii

A	(a)	Now then Coyote became hungry.	19
	(b)	Now then he thought:	20
	(c)	"Now I shall eat."	21
B	(a)	Now then he ran among the people.	22
	(b)	Now then they said:	23
	(c)	"He did badly to himself, Coyote,	24
		"He sucked his own penis."	25
C	(a)	Now then again Coyote ran.	26
	(b)	He thought:	27
		"Over there I am not known;	28
		"Truly now I will not be made known."	29
D	(a)	He ran again to a house.	30
	(b)	Now again they are laughing:	31
	(c)	"Now Coyote sucked himself."	32
E	(a)	The people again are telling one another.	33
	(b)	Now then he thought:	34
	(c)	"Truly now I am known."	35

Verse analysis of Louis Simpson's text

The verse analysis requires choice among alternatives. Two decisions are most in question. One is whether to regard lines 6–11 as one verse or as three; that is, whether to assign verse status to line 9 and to lines 10–11. The second is whether to regard lines 12–14 as a continuation of stanza B, its fourth and fifth verses, or as the start of a new stanza C, its first and second verses. The four alternatives are displayed as four columns in Table 6-2. The first and third columns show an analysis that treats lines 9, and 10–11, as verses, while the second and fourth columns show an analysis that does not. The first and second columns show an analysis that treats lines 6–11 as constituting all of stanza B, stanza C beginning with line 12. The third and fourth columns show an analysis that treats B as including lines 12–14.

The analysis embodied in the text as given above is shown in column I. The reasons for deciding on that analysis, as well as why decision was required, can be brought out in the context of a comparison of verse analysis as such to the 1975 analysis in terms of "narrative sentences" (see Table 6-3). Where the 1975 analysis grouped some of the narrative sentences together by indentation, such groupings are marked here by parentheses.

	I	II		III	IV	
(A)	a	a		a	a	1
						2
						3
	b	b		b	b	4
	c	c		c	c	5
(B)	a	a		a	a	6
						7
						8
	b			b		9
	c			c		10
						11
(C)	a	a		d	b	12
						13
	b	b		e	c	14
	c	c	(C)	a	a	15
						16
	d	d		b	b	17
	e	e		c	c	18

Table 6–2. Alternative analyses of Louis Simpson's text

In both the earlier and later analyses, a main division into two parts is obvious and the same (between scenes *i* and *ii*). It is the verse analysis, however, that makes division of the narrative into two parts and a consequent doubling of its moral theme not only obvious but inescapable. The doubling emerges formally in the verse analysis because of patterning at the level of stanzas. ABC of scene *i* and ABCDE of *ii* each constitute a grouping by Chinookan norms. Each shows a pattern of action as onset, ongoing, outcome. In *i* the pattern consists of the initial traveling and sucking (A), the discovery (B), and the consequences (C). In *ii* the pattern is: the onset of hunger (A); going among the people a first time, only to be rebuffed (B); going again, hoping that somewhere the news is not known (C). As is common in Chinookan, the third unit (C) is both outcome of an initial series of three units and onset of another. Having premised in C that he is not known over there (parallel to the equally mistaken premise "Now I shall eat" in A), Coyote again goes and is rebuffed (D); since people are telling one another even there (perhaps everywhere), he accepts finally that he is known (E). In the earlier article, it was found that Mr. Simpson focused on the moral consequences of Coyote's act, doing so in two disjunct parts of the story, each capped by self-awareness (1975a:54; p. 117 above). Verse analysis shows that doubling of focus to be built into the verbal architecture of the story.

"Narrative sentences"	Verses	Stanzas	Scene	Lines
(1–2)	a	A	*i*	1–2–3
3	b			4
4	c			5
(5–6–7)	a	B		6–7–8
	b			9
	c			10–11
(8–9)	a	C		12–13
(10-	b			14
-11)	c			15–16
12	d			17
13	e			18
14	a	A	*ii*	19
15	b, c			20, 21
16	a	B		22
17	b, c			23, 24, 25
(18-	a	C		26
-19-	b, c			27, 28, 29
20)	a	D		30
21-	b, c			31, 32
-21	a	E		33
22	b, c			34, 35
23		[Not part of this story]		

Table 6–3. "Narrative sentences" versus verses in Louis Simpson's text

Let us turn to each of the two scenes in themselves.

In scene *i* the grouping of elements in the two analyses is rather similar. In two instances the earlier groups of narrative sentences by indentation correspond to single verses: 1–2 = A(a), 8–9 = C(a). In another instance, a grouping by indentation corresponds to an arc of three verses: 5–6–7 = B(abc).

As we have said, one might treat these lines (6–11) not as three verses (B[abc]), but as one (B[a]). That would correspond less exactly to the grouping of the earlier analysis, perhaps, submerging its recognition of distinct narrative sentences. But why is there an alternative and a decision to be made? Because Chinookan often groups units in sets of three; initial particle pairs typically mark verses in Louis Simpson's texts; and there is only one initial particle pair in these lines. If initial particles are regarded as absolutely determinative of verse status, then, indeed, there can be only one verse in these lines.

In some respects the result would have an attractive symmetry. Each stanza of scene *i* would have three verses, and each verse would begin with *AGa;* all but the retrospective verse (line 17) would begin with *AGa kwapt.* The middle stanza of the scene would appear as follows:

B (a) Now then he did thus: 6
          he put up his penis,   7
          he put down his head.   8
        Someone pushed him down.   9
            Coyote said: 10
         "You've done me no good."   11
    (b) Now then he locked up the news:—   12
          he did not want it to be made known.   13
    (c) Now then someone made the news loose.   14

A reason for not adopting such an analysis is that change of actor, such as occurs in both lines 9 and 10, usually co-occurs with change of verse. The exceptions are conversational exchanges in which two actors speak within a single verse and larger pattern. Here the pushing and Coyote's response might be taken as equivalent to a conversational exchange, but the changes of actor seem significant and need to be singled out. The three elements of action in lines 6–11 seem themselves the accomplishment of a three-verse arc—an onset, ongoing, outcome—that is structurally parallel to the arcs of action that precede and follow.

In any case, all analyses agree in grouping these lines (6–11) together. They differ in their internal organization. The 1975 analysis showed a group of narrative sentences (5–7). The alternative just presented shows a single verse (columns II and IV in table 6–2). The analysis finally adopted in presenting the text shows the lines as an arc of three verses, possibly also a complete stanza, or the first arc of a stanza in which two such arcs intersect (columns I, III in table 6–2).

The most important consideration, I believe, is the sense that the three elements of action in lines 6–11 accomplish a three-verse arc. In deciding a difficult case, there is tension between a view of a text as a finished whole and a sense of it as developing in time. On the one hand, a view of patterning in the whole is essential. Recurrent patterns are evidence of structuring principles that generate the sequence. In this text from Louis Simpson, three-unit patterns, including grouping of verse-marking particles in threes, are pervasive and basic to interpretation. As we shall see, the second scene, the more symmetrical and finely tuned of the two, is a network of triads. The first scene can also be viewed as sets of threes, given the ninefold occurrence of initial particles. Each particle can be taken to mark a verse, and each three particles a stanza (lines 1, 4, 5; 6, 12, 14; 15, 17, 18). That view would require the analysis indicated in column IV in table 6–2. Not only would lines 6–11 be one verse, but lines 12–14 would necessarily belong to stanza B, completing it as its second and third verses. That is an analysis, indeed, that I felt constrained for a time to adopt.

Let us step back from such a view of the pattern of the whole as an object existing as if at an instant of time and consider the text as a sequence of patterns unfolding through time. The three steps of Coyote's entrance (he went, he went on, he sat down) constitute a triad, but there is parallel within Chinookan texts from Louis Simpson for subordinating such a triad within a single verse. To subordinate the steps of action through line 11 within a single verse in order to extend the second stanza through line 14 and have all verses marked by initial particles is less certain. Other considerations, to be taken up in a moment, point the other way. The heart of the matter, I conjecture, is that Louis Simpson did move through the first scene in three sets of three actions, but his dictation, or Sapir's transcription, or both, obscured marking of the middle set by particles, while his concern to emphasize the consequences of Coyote's action (or perhaps to gain a moment before launching into the second scene) led him to extend the ending. I conjecture that he took the essential sequence of acts in the first scene to be: sat, looked, sucked; sucking, someone pushed, said; locked up the news, someone made it loose, everyone came to know. Then, for emphasis and/or pause, I conjecture, he summed up retrospectively (line 17) and completed a rhetorical pattern with a fifth line (18).

Put another way, the key to the patterning of the text is not the boundary between B and C, but the ending of C itself; not the disputed middle, but the later extension, not lines 12–14, but lines 17–18.

Let us step back from this conjecture, which anticipates the conclusion, and review the evidence. The formal question is the boundary between stanzas B and C. One can be sure that there are two scenes; that scene i comprises lines 1–18; that its lines constitute three stanzas; that A is clearly one of these; and yet not be sure whether B ends in line 11 or in line 14.

The considerations in favor of treating lines 6–11 as the whole of B include the fact that stanzas commonly end with quoted speech. Line 11, "You've done me no good," has the feel of an ending point in Chinookan poetics. A further fact is that the resulting stanza C contains all references of "news." Stanzas are often internally coherent in repetition of a significant lexical item. The parallel between the two stanza-ending lines 11 and 18, each containing reference to the third-person-plural antagonist of Coyote ('You've' [mS-]), ('they' [tk-]) is supportive as well. Parallel stanzas often end on parallel elements. (To be sure, the alternative, putting lines 12–14 in B, would provide a parallel as well, in the recurrence of 'be loose', dak dak.)

A sense of the last two lines and verses (17–18) as an extension is supported by the fact that they do not develop the action. Lacking actual incident to extend the scene formally, Mr. Simpson seems in lines 15–16 to have anticipated the knowledge that is dramatized in scene ii with what could have been the end of the stanza and scene i, then offered a summary backward glance (line 17) and recapitulated still further (line 18). Lines 17–18 in effect mirror lines 12–14; together these lines encapsulate the central point of everyone knowing (lines 15–16). The one new note in the recapitulation of line 18 is a verbal heightening. Whereas line 14 has the news made loose with just the general verb that accompanies particles such as *dak dak* (*-X-* 'to do, make, be'), line 18 has *dak dak* followed, quite unusually, by another root of specific verbal force, 'to break out'.

If the symbolic interpretation presented in the 1975 article is accepted, then the sequence here is indeed more than reiteration. The specific pronouns, as well as the verbs, in lines 14 and 18 express different actors and degrees of force. In line 14 the news is made loose by someone or something referred to by the third-person–masculine-gender pronoun *C-*, presumably the wind (see 1975a:49; p. 113 above). In line 18, the news is made loose by breaking out, caused by a third-person plural *tk-* 'they'. The "they" is presumably, and euphemistically, the "clouds."

That the news breaks itself out is explicit in the version told in Clackamas by Mrs. Victoria Howard (see below). That explicit bursting out in Clackamas supports the symbolic interpretation of references to "clouds" and "down" by Mr. Simpson and Mr. Smith, as connotative of the semen produced by Coyote's act. The role of the wind is to carry that evidence to the people. Line 14 has the wind making the news "loose" (not tight, not controlled); line 18 has the force of the news itself tearing out through the rock.

The analysis adopted here is made attractive by the patterning of pronouns and names within the scene. ("Everyone" is capitalized to show that it is an independent phrase. All other pronouns are prefixed to verbs.) Given the analysis of the three stanzas as lines 1–5, 6–11, 12–18, respectively, these indications of actors align as follows:

A   he,
          he,
               he.
      Coyote, he.
      Coyote, he-himself

B   he:
          he-his
          he-his
      someone-him   [indefinite q-]
      Coyote, He;
               "You-me"

C   he-it,
               he-it
      someone-it   ["he"]
      Everyone, they-it
               he, Coyote.
      he-it
      they-it.

Alternatively, if the stanzas align as 1–5, 6–14, 15–18:

```
A        he,
              he,
                    he.
         Coyote, he.
         Coyote, he-himself.


B        he,
              he-his
              he-his
         someone: him
         Coyote, he:
                           "you"-"me"
         he-it
                    he-it
         someone-it


C        Everyone, they-it
                    he, Coyote.
         he-it
         they-it
```

The sequence by which Coyote is gradually displaced by others is perhaps neatly shaped in either case. In both analyses, one begins with all Coyote in A. On the first analysis, one proceeds with all Coyote plus an intervention (B), then has Coyote with interventions coming to dominate (C). The start is like B: first "he," then "someone," but someone is followed, not by Coyote, but by "everyone," with "Coyote" as object of knowledge. "He" returns, but again followed by "they," which is now the end (whereas Coyote had ended the first two stanzas).

On the second analysis, the all-Coyote stanza (A) is followed by a middle stanza in which three references to Coyote are twice followed by reference to "someone": he, he, he, someone; Coyote, he, he, someone. The third stanza encompasses Coyote within references to "they."

The first of these profiles of pronouns and namings, based on the analysis that restricts stanza B to lines 6–11, is still more attractive. It shows each of the three stanzas beginning with a reiteration of "he." It shows the second and third stanzas each following an initial run of "he" by "someone." It shows the second and third stanzas each ending with address, or reference, to a plural "you."

Decision at this point perhaps becomes aesthetic response. One may wish to stay with the markers that one has, and recurrent patterns of those markers. From such a standpoint, the analysis of scene *i* into stanzas, each of which has three verses with initial particle markers, remains attractive (the third, or especially the fourth, column of the four alternatives outlined above). There is security in counting initial markers, including the lone "now" in line 17 (which fits the sense of summation or retrospection of that line—a "then" following the "now" would move the action forward inappropriately). This is so especially in a text with philological difficulties. Still, one may suspect that initial particles have been lost sight of in the original, and that the philological difficulties are an indication of that. Lines 9 and 10 might well have been intended to have them. Were such markers present, one of the three stanzas would necessarily have five verses, not three. The argument from pattern pressure of threefold sets of verses would be less strong. The argument for treating lines 6–11 as a unit would be almost unexceptionable.

Again, the order of lines and the identity of the pronouns have themselves had to become matters of philological interpretation. The fact that the problematic ordering of lines (Appendix, chap. 3) occurs within narrative sentences 9–13, equivalent to lines 13–18, might be taken as evidence that these lines belong together. One might argue that the crime, so to speak, shows the scene of the crime to be a unit. That would confirm the analysis adopted here, since those lines fall within stanza C and count against an analysis that insists on three initial particle markers and treats B as running through line 14.

The key to understanding, I repeat, seems to me to require a reading of the text as unfolding in time. In terms of the underlying rhetorical pattern— of sequences of three and five elements as onset, ongoing, outcome—the text, like other texts, has several overlapping sequences, the presence of which probably contributes to the sense of continuous flow. The end of any one sequence is candidate for the beginning of another. Some such possibilities fail to eventuate in a consistent organization of the text. Others are punctuated by initial markers, reinforced by lexical repetition, quoted speech, and other devices and levels.

These overlapping relationships can be depicted in a chart. Following the chart, all the sequences can be indicated in order.

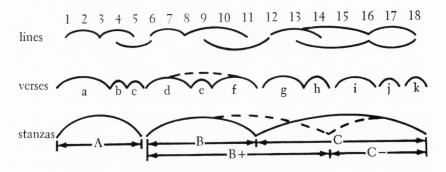

$(1-3) = a$
$(1-3-5) = Aabc$
$(4-6-8) = o$
$(4-8-11) = o$
$(6-8) = Bd$
$(6-8-11) = Bcdef$
$(6-8-11-14) = Bdefgh$
$(8-11) = (B\text{-}def)$
$(9-12) = o$
$(12-14) = Cgh$
$(12-16) = Cghi$
$(12-16-18) = Cghijk$
$(13-18) = o$
$(16-18) = Cijk$

The analysis adopted here and the alternatives remain the same at the level of sequences of lines. They differ at the level of sequences of verses and stanzas but not greatly. Perhaps more than one response to the linear sequence was experienced in a native audience. Perhaps in pursuing resolution of fine points, one is pursuing a refined experience of the text, finer than would have been intended or perceived by most. *I think that the answer lies in the overlapping.* The presence of organized sequences at each of these levels is clear. Certain ostensible possibilities are clearly not realized. The first three lines express the rhetorical pattern (1–3), and a new sequence could be felt to begin with the next line, running through line 8 (4–6–8), with 6 as point of intersection of two three-line arcs. But beyond that point no consistent grouping is possible. One cannot begin with line 9 and get to the end of the scene in terms of the patterns (9–12, 13–18). One could indeed treat A as consisting just of lines 1–3 and say that B begins with line 4, running through line 11, with 6–8 as intersection of two arcs. Such a treatment would require a five-verse stanza C, following the five-verse stanza B. The scene would have three stanzas of one, five, and five verses each, which would get the sucking entirely into one stanza. The two scenes would then be on very different planes indeed. Some of the parallelism discussed above would be lost. I continue to judge that going, going on, sitting, is a subordinate use of the three-part pattern, forming a unit which as a whole is onset to the two initially marked lines that follow. From the standpoint of lines, line 3 is the intersection of two arcs of lines 1–3 and 3–5 within the verse.

The unique occurrence of a *summarizing* AGa 'now' (cf. analysis of Louis Simpson's "The deserted boy" in chapter 4) helps convince me that the main arc of the first scene runs as depicted earlier, completing three sets of three actions by that point (line 16), and extending the form of the scene with a summary and an intensified reiteration in the last two lines (17–18). Such a reading fits all the details and patterns, all the expectations aroused by other narratives from Louis Simpson and other Chinookan speakers.

Let us turn now to scene *ii*. For scene *i* the 1975 analysis and the present one are generally similar. That is not the case with scene *ii*. The earlier and later analyses are quite different. What were single narrative sentences are divided between two verses in each of the five stanzas (sentences 15, 17, 19, 21, 22), and, indeed, among three verses in the case of sentence 21. The differences have a common explanation. Each narrative sentence contains direct speech that is now treated as the end of a verse. Scene *ii* is organized by pairs of lines that introduce a line or two of direct speech.

It took a long time for me to perceive such a simple, regular pattern. I attempted to continue into *ii* the numerical regularity given scene *i* by sets of initial "Now then." But an analysis of scene *ii* on that basis would group lines 19–22 together as a single stanza because of the occurrence three times of "Now then." To do so would contradict the stronger patterning that can be seen in the threefold recurrence of "Coyote ran" and the fivefold recurrence of direct speech. *Once the scene is seen to be built upon five instances of direct speech,* everything falls into place. Coyote's direct speech frames the scene as beginning, middle, and end (A, C, E). The speech of the people intervenes (B, D). The moral of the story is pointed up by the parallel position, and contrast, of the endings of C and E: C(c) has Coyote assert that it is *not* the case that *truly now* he will be made known; E(c) has Coyote admit that *truly now* he is known. And, of course, C is the end of the first of the two arcs in the scene ABC and E the end of the second.

It is unusual to distinguish the framing statements "he thought," "they said," "he thought," "They are laughing," "he thought" as verses distinct from the lines for what is thought or said. I may be in error in making the distinction here. Yet the overall pattern of five instances of direct speech is clear and compelling. Within it the Chinookan "rhetorical arc" of three moments of action—onset, ongoing, outcome—would be expected to color the lines. It is a pattern that turns up in even casual accounts. If I am right in believing it to be active here, then what is thought and said is given additional emphasis for the very fact of something being thought and something being said. Such emphasis would seem to be in accord with Mr. Simpson's moral emphasis. Motion, Coyote's running, is a background device, not even consistently used (he runs three times to two places). In the foreground, consistently emphasized, are the actions of thinking, speaking, and laughing. There is both contrast and development: contrast between what Coyote thinks and the people do; and development, between their saying and laughing (B, D), and between Coyote's expectation and realization (C, D).

Once the scene is seen to be built upon five instances of direct speech, additional details can be observed that reinforce the organization into verses and distinguish direct speech itself as a verse. Each instance of direct speech has a particle or device of the kind that can be used to mark verses. A(c) begins with "Now"; B(c) has a grammatical parallelism in its two lines, literally, "his-badness *ni*-he-did Coyote; his-penis *ni*-he-sucked"; C(c) has an initial particle of location (yaxiba) in its first line and "Truly now" in its second (cf. use of *QuSdiaxa* in "The deserted boy" [chap. 4]), as well as parallelism in the use of forms of the verb construction "someone *(q)*- me *(n)*- knows/causes to be known"; D(c) begins with "Now"; E(c) begins with "Truly now." In addition, the first lines of D and E, although without initial particle, do contain 'again' (*wit'a*[X]) in position parallel to its noninitial use in the first line of C.

From what has been said, it is clear that line 32 (D[c]) should end its verse and that line 33 (E[a]) should begin a new one. There is no punctuation in Sapir's notebook at this point. The preceding word is his usual abbreviation for *Isk'ulya* 'Coyote', namely, *Isk!*. That might have served as punctuation as well in the original recording, even though Sapir did not take it so in later editing for publication. I might add that there are several false starts in the notebook at this point, remarkably many in comparison to adjacent pages. Before present D(a) are crossed-out *naSqi* 'not', the beginning of an uncertain verb, and *k'me* 'but'. Before E(b), *qidau* 'thus' is crossed out. These false starts suggest that Mr. Simpson was tentative about the exact wording of beginnings here.

Still, the only case of a verse *forced* into recognition by the overall pattern but lacking an internal marker is C(b), "He thought." There is a + above the line at this point in Sapir's notebook, but it may well identify a correction of a consonant in a word in the line above. The triple initial particle in the preceding line, "Now then again," and the particle of location, "Truly now," and grammatical parallelism in the quoted speech that follows might together be thought to load the verse with markers enough. It remains that "he thought" as a line in itself is formally bare. The richness of its surroundings, its own parallelism with "Now then he thought" in the same position in a stanza in A and E, and the structure of the scene as a whole point to the place it is given here.

In sum, Mr. Simpson's second scene seems a minor gem of narrative art, weaving interlocking strands around a five-part sequence of direct speech. This result fits the earlier conclusion that the Denouement (=scene *ii*) was his focus for culmination (1975a:43). That conclusion was arrived at by quantitatively comparing Mr. Simpson's treatment of the Denouement and other sections to the version by Mr. Smith. Yet within Mr. Simpson's own narrative, the Denouement, scene *ii*, would not stand out quantitatively. In terms of the unit of the earlier analysis, the preceding sections have thirteen narrative sentences, the Denouement nine. To be sure, the Denouement has more than any other of the four sections distinguished there, the Exposition having two, Complication five, Climax six. That supports the statement of a "line steadily rising from beginning to end, culminating with the Denouement, or a rising line with successively higher peaks, in the Complication, then the Climax, then the Denouement" (Ibid.). But the verse analysis shows the Denouement to be elaborated more than all the preceding sections together. The two scenes of the verse analysis are almost identical in number of lines, 18 : 17, but clearly different in architecture. Scene *i* has three stanzas and eleven verses, whereas scene *ii* has five stanzas and fifteen verses. Such a count confirms the earlier conclusion, yet shows it to be embedded more deeply than could earlier be perceived.

Rhetorical design

The verse analysis, indeed, points to a reconsideration of the relationship between the rhetorical categories of Brooks and Warren (1949:312, 276–80). The verse analysis permits a more "natural" identification of the elements of content to be associated with the traditional categories. The difference in identification can be shown by listing elements of content that summarize each pertinent stanza. Elements used in the earlier analysis are repeated in capital letters. Elements newly singled out are given in italics. To the left is given the relationship with traditional categories that now appears appropriate. Notice that Climax can now be treated as an aspect of Complication, as intended by Brooks and Warren (Ibid.: 278). The three-part rhetorical arc of Chinookan narrative indicates as much. Notice further that the Denouement is no longer a gross summary of the entire final scene, almost half of the lines of the story. Instead, the doubling of the narrative in terms of the theme of moral consequences is shown in the presence of the traditional design, including Denouement, in each of the two scenes. Further again, the articulation of the former Denouement in scene *ii* shows a Chinookan twist. The intersection of two rhetorical arcs (ABC/CDE) is accompanied by a duality, Janus-faced, in the role of the middle unit, stanza C. It is Denouement to the first arc, Exposition to the second. The match of the traditional rhetorical categories to the story is in fact threefold, doubled in the doubling second scene.

i	*Exposition*	SUCKS	A
	Complication		
	(Climax)	DISCOVERED	B
	Denouement	NEWS ESCAPES	C
ii	*Exposition*	*Intends to go among people*	A
	Complication		
	(Climax)	GOES AMONG PEOPLE (1), *they say*	B
	Denouement/		
	Exposition	Intends to go among people (2)	C
	Complication	GOES AMONG PEOPLE (2), *they say* (2)	D
	Denouement	*they say* (3), *admits is known* (=CONSEQUENCE)	E

Table 6–4. Rhetorical design of stanzas (Louis Simpson)

Notice that some of the content categories of the earlier analysis (such as SITS, CLOSES UP NEWS) do not appear in the outline above. To bring them into view, one must go to analysis at the level of verses. Analysis at that level includes all the content categories of the earlier analysis, interspersed among categories of equivalent rank required by the verse analysis. The earlier analysis can be seen to have been structurally incorrect, unbalanced, providing disproportionately more detail in the first scene than in the second. Specific actions that are essential parts of the moral outcome of the story were swallowed up in the general category GOES AMONG THE PEOPLE.

The imbalance between scenes of the earlier analysis also appears in a comparison between narrative sentences and verses (see table 6-3). There is not, in fact, a great difference in number of narrative sentences and number of verses for the first scene: 13 : 11 (abc, abcde, abc). The imbalance is more striking in the second scene. There the earlier analysis has nine narrative sentences (14-22), whereas the verse analysis has fifteen verses (abc, abc, abc, abc, abc).

Perhaps there was ethnocentric bias in finding more to notice in the details of a sexual aberration and a futile attempt to keep it a secret. Certainly for the narrator, Louis Simpson, the moral outcome was not merely a matter of expanding the number of lines for a part that was one of four, but of equivalent articulation for a part that was one of two. And, as noted, the second part is structurally more complex at the level of rhetorical form, having two intersecting arcs of stanzas and of Exposition, Complication, Denouement. The verse analysis forces recognition of this.

Another way of putting the difference between the earlier and later analysis is to say that the earlier analysis confused levels of structure. It promoted to the broader arc of action at the level of stanzas elements that did not belong there and missed elements that did.

Here is the analysis at the level of verses. Again, elements of content given in the earlier analysis are capitalized and elements that were not are italicized. It may be a point in support of the verse analysis that it brings out invariant relationships with the traditional rhetorical categories. *Climax* throughout is associated with Coyote being shamed by others for what he has done: discovered and pushed down (*i* B), talked about (*ii* B, D). *Denouement* throughout is associated with the fact and word "to know": everyone came to know (*i* C), not known there? (*ii* C), known (everywhere) (*ii* E).

Both presentations of content—at the level of stanzas and at the level of verses—bring out the significance, structurally motivated by the verse analysis, of intention and consequence on the part of Coyote and of the community response: "everyone knows" and "they say" (three times). The element of going among the people is recognized as not merely a theme, but as a reiterated element of action. The verse analysis brings out the elements of content that are rhetorically active.

This more natural association of traditional categories (Exposition, Com-

i	Exposition	SITS	A(a)
		looks	(b)
		SUCKS (1)	(c)
	Complication	SUCKS (2)	B(a)
	(Climax)	DISCOVERED *(pushed)*	(b)
		responds	(c)
	Denouement	CLOSES UP NEWS (1)	C(a)
		NEWS ESCAPES (1)	(b)
		everyone knows	(c)
		CLOSES UP NEWS (2)	(d)
		NEWS ESCAPES (2)	(e)
ii	Exposition	*hungry,*	A(a)
		intends to go among people,	(b)
		eat.	(c)
	Complication	GOES AMONG PEOPLE (1)	B(a)
	(Climax)	*they say,*	(b)
		"Coyote sucked"	(c)
	Denouement/		
	Exposition	*goes*	C(a)
		intends to go among people (2)	(b)
		"I am not known."	(c)
	Complication	GOES AMONG PEOPLE (2)	D(a)
		they say (2),	(b)
		"Coyote sucked"	(c)
	Denouement	*They say* (3)	E(a)
		he thinks (=Ab,Cb) (=CONSEQUENCE)	(b)
		"I am known."	(c)

Table 6–5. Rhetorical design of verses (Louis Simpson)

plication [Climax], Denouement) with the form of a Native American narrative is attractive; note well that it is also not arbitrary. The relationships that underlie the association are demonstrable in the text and are supported by recurrence in other texts. It is by no means a matter of pointing to a beginning and an end and calling the rest a middle. The relationships are precise, and they articulate at successive levels. Recall that the narrative as a whole is not considered here an illustration of the traditional categories in the sense of simply having a beginning, a middle, and an end. It is seen, structurally, as a doubling, and, indeed, as a tripling, due to the intersecting arcs in the second scene.

If, indeed, one were to apply the traditional categories just once to the whole narrative, then the way it was done in the earlier analysis would seem necessary. Climax must be separated from Complication; the three stanzas of the first scene must be taken as Exposition, Complication, Climax; and the whole of the second scene must be taken as Denouement. Alternatively, one might take all of scene *i* as Exposition and treat scene *ii* as containing Complication (AB), Climax (CD), and Denouement (E). I do not much like this possibility, because the occurrence of "everyone came to know" within the first scene (Ca) seems to me to state the true Climax of the story. The action of the second scene seems to me an elaboration, a dramatic realization, of the significance of "everyone came to know."

The traditional categories appear to have natural, specific places *within* each of the scenes. To apply them to the whole story, I think, leaves obscure the actual articulation, the dramatic organization, of the second scene, and appears to muddy the relationships among parts and levels of the narrative. I submit that the verse analysis coupled with the traditional categories show two things: (1) the traditional categories can have a valid place within the structural analysis of Native American narrative verse; and (2) the place depends upon, and may vary with, the structural analysis.

Let us turn now to Mr. Smith's narrative.

Hiram Smith's text

A	(a)	Ikdá:t wít'a Isk'úlya,	1
		kwapt aGaLáx galaXóX.	2
	(b)	Didmúit,	3
		kwapt gayuLáit.	4
	(c)	ItXÉt,	5
		kwapt galiktxúit,	6
		kwapt gaSíxtukS.	7
B		KwaiS náqi qánSipt,	8
		Sángi iyaqáqStaqba,	9
		gaLgiut'íwa:	10
		"Ixixia, dan wít'a miúXulal?"	11
C	(a)	Gasixmk'nágwatsk:	12
		k'áya San;	13
	(b)	K'ma gaCLXáCmaq;	14
	(c)	GaliXLúxwait:	15
		"IdwáCa aLkdóXwa."	16
D	(a)	Kwapt íwi iLyákSn gaCLóx:	17
		idlXdímaX galóXwa náwit wiṁaLba,	18
		inádix kwádau gigátka.	19
	(b)	K'waS galiXóX;	20
		dala'áx idwáCa aloXáXa.	21

(c) K'ma GanGádix ipGólx gaCiup'íxwaix SáXalba itk'álamat,   22

GánGat áG(a) éwa gadixt'ágwa idwáCa.   23

E (a) QáXba (a)yúya,   24

kwáb(a) itGuímxat,   25

náwit aCuXwaCmáGwa idÉlxam.   26

(b) Alugagíma,   27

"(A)Ga Ci' mSXlCmĺit,   28

"Isk'úlya iSíxtukS?"   29

(c) QáXba wít'a ayúya,   30

daúkwa wít'a aliXlCmáGwa,   31

kwapt t'Lak gayúya.   32

Verse translation of Mr. Smith's text

A (a) He was running along again,   1

then the sun was shining hot.   2

(b) He was tired,   3

then he sat down.   4

(c) He was sitting,   5

then he got a hard on,   6

then he sucked himself.   7

B   Just got started,   8

somebody pushed down on his head,   9

somebody told him: 10

"Hey, what you doing again?"   11

C (a) He looked all around: 12

nobody;   13

(b) But he heard them;   14

(c) He thought,   15

"They'll make news."   16

D (a) Then he did his hands like this: [sweeping gesture]   17

it was rimrock straightway to the river,   18

this side and that.   19

(b) He got afraid,   20

it might make news;   21

(c) But already it blew the down up over the rocks,   22

already the news got ahead of him.   23

E   (a)   Wherever he goes,   24
              there at a camp,   25
                  straightway he hears the people.   26
   (b)   They're saying,   27
              "You folks hear now,   28
                  "Coyote sucked himself?"   29
   (c)   Wherever he goes again,   30
              he hears the same thing again,   31
                  then he went off and left.   32

I have departed from his own English wording, which was itself a second telling, not a literal translation. In line 7 the revised wording "Then he sucked himself" now parallels Simpson's text in both Indian and English, and the effect of "started" is saved for the next line alone, where it is needed. In that next line (8) there is no "he" in English because there is none in the Wasco. The word *nawit* is translated identically as 'straightway' in both occurrences (lines 18, 26). Lines 24 and 30 would literally be "where he-will-go" and "where again he-will-go," while lines 25 and 31 would literally be "straightway he-will-hear-them people" and "such (thus) again he-will hear."

Verse analysis of Hiram Smith's text

Here are the similarities and differences between the narrative sentences of the earlier analysis and the verse analysis just given. As before, parentheses show sentences grouped as units in the earlier analysis by indentation.

The main break in the narrative, given by the verse analysis, would be in the middle stanza C, facing backward as outcome of ABC and forward as onset of CDE. The earlier analysis could perhaps be said to reflect this, since its middle falls within C. The first four content units end with the first two

"Narrative sentences"	Verses	Stanzas
(1–2)	a	A
(3–4)	b	
(5–6)	c	
7		
(8–9)		B
(10–11)	a, b	C
(12–	c	
(–13)	a	D
(14–15)	b, c	
(16–17)	a, b	E
(18)	c	

Table 6–6. "Narrative sentences" versus verses in Hiram Smith's text

verses of C, and the last four begin with the third verse of C. But it would be more accurate to say that the earlier analysis simply missed what is going on here. The agreement between analyses is good for the first verses, where the pairs (1–2), (3–4), (5–6) correspond both to content elements (Entrance, Sits, Sucks) in the earlier analysis and almost exactly to verses and a stanza in the latter (A [abc]).

However, correspondences break down after that, partly because of a failure to discriminate lines as units within narrative sentences in the earlier analysis. Failure to give weight to direct speech as a local culmination figures as well (narrative sentences 9, 12 are ends of stanzas). Another difficulty was caused by the desire to treat occurrences of 'then' *(Kwapt)* as individually parallel. It now appears that the two occurrences of "then" in lines 6 and 7 go together as a culminating parallelism for the stanza, like the parallelism of 'already' (*GanGat* [*ix*]) at the end of D(c).

Notice that the binary alternations with "then" in the first stanza have an interpretation in terms of the threefold rhetorical pattern of onset, ongoing, outcome. They are interlocking, brought to a conclusion with the second of the double occurrence of "then": going, hot, tired; tired, sat, sitting; sitting, tumescence, sucking. Put in a chart, with numbers referring to lines:

Onset	Ongoing	Outcome
1	2	3
3	4	5
5	6	7.

Table 6–7. Interlocking rhetorical patterns

The alternation of tenses, however, clearly requires the overt pairing given here. Lines 1, 3, 5 each have a verb in the present stative tense with final suffix -*t*; the lines with "then" each have a verb in the remote past tense with initial prefix *ga-*. The final pair of occurrences of "then" with *ga-* (lines 6, 7) stands in immediate apposition to the preceding line 5 and gives a full sequence of the rhetorical pattern. And if the chart above is too subjective, or open to abuse as accommodating anything, then there is no doubt that the three parallel verses of A stand to each other in terms of the rhetorical pattern: onset (a), ongoing (b), outcome (c), with explicit onset, ongoing, outcome within (c).

Stanza C shows the same pattern internally: he looks, he hears, he thinks. So does stanza D: He creates the rimrock, he fears news, already the news is out. Stanza E shows the pattern, but with an internal rondo-like alternation, verse (a) being parallel in onset to verse (c). The dramatic highlight, the direct quotation, is in the center of the stanza. Just so, the other instances of direct quotation are centered, that at the end of B in the first trio or arc of stanzas, ABC, and that at the end of C in the middle of the narrative as a whole. Notice also in E the three-part repetition of "hear," corresponding to, and contrasting with, the three-part repetition at the end of Mr. Simpson's version of "ran." Notice also that Mr. Smith's last stanza, like Mr. Simpson's, has a certain clustering of initial particles for support of lines: "where(ever), there, straightway" in E(a), "Now" within E(b), "where(ever) again," "thus again," "then" in E(c). The centering around the quoted speech of E(b) and the initial parallelism of (a) and (c) appear to require the present analysis and not to point to a treatment of the lines as verses here. So also does the change of tense. These lines are locked together in the future tense, standing apart from the remote past tense of the preceding lines. There is no analysis that could promote the three lines of E(a) to three verses, and correspondingly the three lines of E(c), while maintaining the evident proportion and rhetorical form of the stanza as a unit. Clearly we have three parts in the relationship to each other that is shown. Such dependence on overall pattern for the force of initial elements, as the contrast between the two versions shows, is found elsewhere in Chinookan narrative. Double initial particles are always markers of verses (as is the case with "Where[ever] again" in line 30 here). Single initial particles may or may not be markers of verses. In at least some cases the "promotion" or not of an initial single particle to the status of marking a verse can be seen to be motivated by expressive concerns. That is the case with initial particles not otherwise used as verse initials in the next-to-last act of the Kathlamet Chinook "Sun's myth." Between Mr. Simpson's story and Mr. Smith's, there seems to be pattern pressure of a compact denouement at work in Mr. Smith's text, expansion of a moral at work in Mr. Simpson's.

Rhetorical design

Let us see now how the verse analysis affects the relationship to structural categories based on content alone, as given in the earlier analysis, and to the use made there of the traditional rhetorical categories. At the level of stanzas, the categories of content, and the associated rhetorical categories, are as follows:

Exposition	SUCKS	A
Complication		
(Climax)	DISCOVERED	B
Denouement/		
Exposition		
Complication		
(Climax)	CLOSES UP NEWS, NEWS ESCAPES	D
Denouement	GOES AMONG PEOPLE, CONSEQUENCE	E

Table 6–8. Rhetorical design of stanzas (Hiram Smith)

At the level of verses, the elements and categories appear as follows:

Exposition	*going along*	a	A
	SITS (1)	b	
	SITS (2),	c	
	SUCKS (1)		
Complication			
(Climax)	SUCKS (2),		B
	pushed (=DISCOVERED)		
	told		
Denouement/			
Exposition	*responds*		C
	(looks,	a	
	hears,	b	
	fears news [1])	c	
Complication			
(Climax)	CLOSES UP NEWS	a	D
	fears news (2)	b	
	NEWS ESCAPES	c	
Denouement	GOES AMONG PEOPLE (1)	a	E
	they say	b	
	GOES AMONG PEOPLE (2)	c	

Table 6–9. Rhetorical design of verses (Hiram Smith)

Whereas the mismatch between narrative sentences and verses was greater at the end of Mr. Simpson's story, it is greater at the beginning of Mr. Smith's. Stanzas CDE and their verses match one-to-one with narrative sentences 10–18; there are nine units in each case. Whereas there are nine narrative sentences in the preceding part in the earlier analysis, however, there are but four verses (Aabc, B). The earlier analysis underdifferentiated the end of Mr. Simpson's text and overdifferentiated the beginning of Mr. Smith's. Thus we see that there is no fixed direction of difference, numerically, to be expected in such cases. Thematically, however, both discrepancies have the same character. Finding too little structure at the end, finding too much at the beginning, both yield the same imbalance. Both give more attention to the first part of the story than is correct.

The overall shape and style of the two texts can be compared in terms of verse analysis by examining the summaries at the levels of stanza and verse. The basic contrast shown in the earlier analysis still holds. Indeed, it is all the more evident that there is in Mr. Simpson's version "a line steadily rising from beginning to end, culminating with the Denouement, or a rising line with successively higher peaks, in the Complication, then the Climax, then the Denouement" (Hymes 1975a:43), whereas in Mr. Smith's version there is "a

234 Breakthrough to Performance

curve that rises and falls, peaking in the central episodes, the Complication and Climax" (Ibid.). Verse analysis makes precise what was previously suggested.

While the contrast between the two texts is confirmed and strengthened, the general thesis that, on formal grounds, Mr. Smith's version was no longer myth, but tale, is not. To be sure, if Mr. Smith's version is held to the pattern of use of initial particles found in Louis Simpson's *Wishram texts* and among other Wasco-Wishram narrators consulted by Silverstein (Ibid.: 39), then the general thesis remains valid. If, however, Mr. Smith's style is associated with that of the Clackamas Chinook narrator Victoria Howard, his slight use of initial particles takes on a different complexion. Mrs. Howard does not make much use of them either. And when it is noted that Mr. Smith's family was originally from the Hood River area, near the Cascades along the Columbia and closer to the Clackamas, who lived along the Willamette River south of Portland, one realizes that Mr. Smith's formal style may be just that, a formal style that is different, rather than less formal.

Probably we shall never be able to be sure. There is only one body of Clackamas Chinook narrative, and we cannot tell if Mrs. Howard represented a community norm or a personal style. The architecture and spirit of Mr. Smith's tale remain, as said, that of a story about the character of Coyote, enjoyed for its own sake. There remains a contrast with Mr. Simpson's focus on the pedagogical moral that would have been the public sanction for telling such a story as myth in the traditional culture. In the difference I still sense a movement from pedagogical myth to entertaining tale but can no longer point to a difference in use of initial particles as sure support.

Here, to conclude, is Victoria Howard's narrative. As with the narratives of Louis Simpson and Hiram Smith, it is given in both verse analysis and translation (the latter somewhat revised from Jacobs 1958:95). It is followed by a summary in the fashion of those provided for the other two texts and then by a discussion comparing all three. Notice that in line 10 the verb theme *-Gl-ba-* is literally the root 'to come/go out' *(-ba)* preceded by ' "from" an enclosed place' (-Gl-), whereas in lines 36 and 41 the root of the theme *-Gl-wa-ba* has been glossed in various constructions 'to follow, pursue, chase, drive' *(-wa);* it is preceded again by 'from an enclosed place' (-Gl-) and followed by *-ba-* as a second-position root ('to come/go out'). (Such second-position roots for direction are an integral part of verb structure in the language.) The same verb root *(wa-)* completed by adverbial *-qLq* 'completely' is the word used in chapter 4 for the act of deserting, abandoning the boy. The basic sense appears to be a directionless "actively changed location in relation to someone/something." The rest of the verb construction contributes the direction (from or toward) and degree of force and completeness. In Mrs. Howard's line in effect the news *(t-)* actively changes location *(wa)* itself

(X-) outward *(-ba)* from an enclosed place *(i-Gl);* the final element *-yx* is evidential. I have tried to convey the additional force in English by "rush."

Victoria Howard's text[2]

A	(a)	gayúya,	1
		yú:yt,	2
		aGa niXLúxayt:	3
		"ASnXdúkSa."	4
	(b)	gayúya,	5
		LXÉliwx, gadiXÉlagwa itqÉnakS GwÉnma,	6
		aGa kwabá níXuX.	7
	(c)	gaSíxEtukS,	8
		gaLíXutLq,	9
		níGlbayx.	10
B	(a)	Yú:yt,	11
		gaCáGElkl akÉnim agÉdaCx;	12
		niXLúxayt,	13
		"Níxwa anduGúmCxuga.	14
		"Lúxwan dán idúwaCa."	15
	(b)	gaCugwíluma;	16
		gatgiXCÉmaq,	17
		gatgyúlxam,	18
		" 'á::: dán?"	19
	(c)	gaCdúlxam,	20
		"NéSqi Cí dán idúwaCa?"	21
		"A::w. Mánk gigát mÉti."	22
	(d)	gayúya q'wap wímaL.	23
		"Én:::,"	24
		gatgyúlxam;	25
		"It'álap'as idít.	26
		"AGa diXÉlukt itqÉnakS.	27
		"SiXÉtukS.	28
		"K'watLqí idúwaCa ugáSgiwa."	29
	(e)	NiXLúwayt,	30
		"m̃ mmmm! Lán LGa niLgÉnGitkl?"	31
C	(a)	NixÉdagwa,	32
		qáXba gaSiXÉtukSba;	33

[2]Mrs. Howard's Clackamas text is retranscribed in accordance with the conventions described in the orthographic note.

```
        gaCúGikl,                                                    34
          itqÉnakS C'ÉX ugakíXaX,                                    35
            qáXba idúwaCa gatXiGÉlwabayx.                            36
  (b)  NiXLúxwayt;                                                   37
        aGa níkim:                                                  38
          "A:w,                                                      39
            "qimatXu náyka ála,                                      40
              "idúwaCa itXiGÉlwabayx."                               41
  (c)  "AGa q'wap idÉlxam.                                           42
        "dan aliLXlúXa,                                              43
          "aLXLuxwáyda,                                              44
            "neSqi qánCiX aqnlúXiXida idLáwaCa',                     45
            "tLáX aluXáX."                                           46
```

Verse translation of Mrs. Howard's text

```
A   (a)  He went,                                                    1
          he was going along,                                        2
            now he thought:                                          3
              "I shall suck myself."                                 4
    (b)  He went on,                                                 5
          off the trail, he covered himself with five rocks,         6
            now there he stayed.                                     7
    (c)  He sucked himself,                                          8
          he finished,                                               9
            he came out.                                            10

B   (a)  He was going along,                                        11
          he saw a canoe going downriver;                           12
            he thought,                                             13
              "Let me inquire of them.                              14
              "Perhaps something is news."                          15
    (b)  He hallooed to them;                                       16
          they heard him,                                           17
            they told him,                                          18
              "Ehhh what?"                                          19
    (c)  He told them,                                              20
              "Isn't something news?"                               21
              "Indeed. Come a little this way."                     22
    (d)  He went close to the river.                                23
          "Yesss,"                                                  24
            they told him;                                          25
              "Coyote was coming along,                             26
```

"now he covered himself with rocks.   27
"He sucked himself.   28
"Such is the news that's traveling along."   29
(e) He thought,   30
"Hmmm! Wonder who saw me?"   31

C   (a) He went back,   32
where he sucked himself at;   33
he saw,   34
the rocks are split,   35
where the news had rushed out.   36
(b) He thought: 37
now he said: 38
"Indeed,   39
"even though it was I myself,   40
"the news rushed out."   41
(c) "Now the people are near.   42
"Whatever they may do,   43
"should they suppose,   44
" 'No one will ever make me their news',   45
"out it will come."   46

Rhetorical design

Table 6-10 is a summary in the fashion of those for the texts from Mr. Simpson and Mr. Smith.

It seems no accident that precise analysis brings to the fore instances of speech acts. Authentic performance of American Indian narratives focused much upon voices, their interplay and enactment. Structural analysis can go a long way, a revealing way, by focusing upon the content of myths as sequences of acts of speech.

As can be seen, the overall arc of the story is rather like that of Mr. Smith's, elaborating the middle section. In number of verses the story is short, having eleven (A[abc], B[abcde], C[abc]), but the verses typically are elaborated as sequences of onset, ongoing, outcome patterns. All but one is three or more lines, and there are forty-six lines overall. Mrs. Howard shares Mr. Simpson's dramatic stress on the moral of the story, while making the implications for the future of mankind quite explicit, as he and Mr. Smith do not. She builds Mr. Simpson's elaboration of the escape of the news into a middle stanza, dramatizing Coyote's discomfiture. That resembles Mr. Smith's building Coyote's discomfiture in to the middle of his story (BCD), although with a focus on discovery in the midst of the act and on immediate aftermath. In sum, Mrs. Howard's version is rather like Mr. Simpson's in moral emphasis and like Mr. Smith's in dramatic arc.

At the level of stanzas:

Exposition	SUCKS	A
Complication		
(Climax)	GOES AMONG PEOPLE,	B
	they say	
Denouement	NEWS ESCAPED,	C
	foretells	

At the level of verses:

Exposition	went,	a	A
	was going,		
	intends to suck		
	went,		
	covered self,		
	SITS	b	
	SUCKS,		
	finished,		
	came out	c	
Complication			
(Climax)	was going,	a	B
	saw canoe,		
	intends to ask		
	hailed,	b	
	was heard,		
	was answered		
	Asked,	c	
	was summoned		
	went,	d	
	was told		
	"Coyote sucked"		
	thought (how?)	e	
Denouement	went,	a	C
	saw,		
	NEWS ESCAPED		
	thought,	b	
	said,		
	NEWS ESCAPED		
	"NEWS WILL ESCAPE"	c	

Table 6–10. Rhetorical design (Victoria Howard)

The differences among the three stories are modest in scale. They have to do with emphasis, dramatization, moral resonance and implication. They are not systematic transformations of the sort discovered and studied by Lévi-Strauss, as the mechanism, he believes, underlying thinking in myth and formation of new versions. They are on the scale treated by Melville Jacobs (1959b, chap. 1) in comparing similar versions of the story of Coyote and Skunk from neighboring groups. Such comparison requires a framework somewhat finer than is evident in the pioneering work of Boas (1916), which consisted essentially of grouping and retelling variations (though transformational relationships occasionally were noted). Comparison in terms of established motifs would not be very helpful. Comparison in terms of transformations, motifemes, or other structural categories would miss the control over detail to which verse analysis contributes.

The essential point for a comparative framework, I think, is to capture any and all dimensions that enter into the creative work of the narrator. The dimension that spurs elaboration, synthesis, transformation, recasting may vary from one case to another. Sometimes a particular frame is basic, as here, the journey of Coyote upriver; sometimes a particular actor's character (here again Coyote); sometimes, of course, the plot as a sequence of actions (here somewhat varied); sometimes the theme, or purpose, that informs that narrator's performance (here again somewhat varied); sometimes particular incidents and images (here again somewhat varied). These five dimensions, derived from the pentad developed by Kenneth Burke (1945),[3] have proven helpful in comparing stories more distantly connected than those in this chapter, as will be seen with the Kathlamet "Sun's myth" and the Takelma myth of "The Otter brothers recover their father's heart" in the second volume of this series, and with the Clackamas myth of "Gitskux and his older brother" in the third. Here the dimensions serve a more modest purpose, being introduced partly for their own sake, and partly to round out comparison of the three stories.

Frame. All three stories are part of the same frame, the sequence of Coyote's adventures traveling up the river. For Mr. Simpson and Mr. Smith, it is the same river, the Columbia; for Mrs. Howard, the setting is transposed to the river on which the Clackamas lived, the Willamette, a major tributary of the Columbia. Specific setting and scene within the story do not vary significantly in themselves.

Actors. All three stories embody a relationship between Coyote and the people but do so diversely. The arc of Mrs. Howard's story has Coyote alone on stage in the first and third stanzas (each a distinct setting). In the central stanza it is his own character, his own curiosity, that leads him to people and to the discovery that his news is known. Mr. Simpson opposes Coyote to someone, or "they," in his first scene, to the people only in the second. It is hunger that leads Coyote among the people and to discovery that

[3]Burke's pentad consists of the dimensions of Scene, Agent, Act, Purpose, Agency. See his *A grammar of motives* (1945).

his news is known. In Mr. Smith's story, Coyote enters at first alone, as in the other versions, but soon is confronted with someone, then they, then it (the wind), then the people. Mr. Smith's narrative is altogether more fully populated with alters to Coyote.

Notice the placement of the people in each version: In the center with Mrs. Howard, between stanzas of Coyote alone; in the second half with Mr. Simpson, but twice there, intercalated among verses of Coyote alone; quite at the end with Mr. Smith (E[b]), and also centered. The people speak only in the central verse (E[b]). The people are perceived at the end of the first verse (E[a]) and at the beginning of the third (E[c]), that is, in lines adjacent to the central verse. The stanza begins and ends with Coyote as actor alone. At the end Mrs. Howard does have Coyote perceive and speak with regard to the future people, for whom the lesson he has learned will hold. His discomfiture is turned to general moral principle for all time. For Mr. Simpson, Coyote simply remains hungry, punished by lack of food for the act that has made him news. (He will continue to seek food in the next story in the sequence.) For Mr. Smith, the jig is up, and Coyote takes off, neither pronouncing nor hungry.

Actions. It is in keeping with the nature of this literature to focus upon speech-centered events. Notice the symmetry of Mrs. Howard's narrative in this regard. At the level of stanzas, overall, Coyote thinks fore and aft (A, C), while in the central stanza (B), he thinks fore and aft again, framing interactions: Halloo, responded to by "eh"; News? responded to by directions to come closer; arrival, responded to by the news. This statement of the news is a meta-narrative statement (cf. postscript to chap. 4) and implies remonstrance or fault-finding with the person addressed. Probably it is implied that the people in the boat know full well whom they are bringing closer to tell the news to. Coyote's final speech is meta-narrative, too, restoring the equilibrium with regard to his own status, as he takes on the power of pronouncing for the future.

In Mr. Simpson's narrative, there is almost no speech in scene *i,* a fact that fits its uncertainty of structure. There is only the centered remark by Coyote, "You've done me no good." Scene *ii,* as we have seen, is neatly organized around acts of speech in each of its five stanzas. Coyote's speech (A, C, E) alternates with the meta-narrative statements of the people (B, D). His hearing, or overhearing, of them is implicitly a rebuke to him.

In Mr. Smith's narrative, there is more sensory detail than speaking, but the first arc of three stanzas has the centered remark to Coyote, "Hey, what you doing again?", and the full myth has the centered thought of Coyote, "They'll make news." The meta-narrative statement of the people comes quite at the end (E[b]), in a nicely rounded final stanza, but subordinated to interest in describing what preceded.

Theme. I take each narrative to have a theme, or purpose, for which the narrator's choices in shaping a performance provide evidence. In Mrs. Howard's narrative the theme of Coyote's discomfiture is centered (stanza B) and carefully developed in the action. The theme of the inevitability of news escaping is present in the one discursive speech of that stanza, and doubled by the last stanza C, where the moral is made explicit in a pronouncement for all people in the future: if, even I, Coyote, certainly they. The theme is reinforced by the parallel ending of the verses of the last stanza C(abc).

In Mr. Simpson's narrative the theme of the inevitability of news escaping is doubled and redoubled. It occurs twice at the end of the first scene (C[b, e]), reported, contrary to Coyote's effort to lock it up (C[a], D), and it occurs twice in the second scene, dramatized (B,D). The manner of handling the theme links it with discomfiture of Coyote throughout, whereas Mrs. Howard, as we have seen, balances discomfiture with subsequent exercise of pronouncing power.

In Mr. Smith's narrative the theme of discomfiture is reinforced by the parallel reference to "hears" in each of the three verses of the last stanza but is not as prominent as in the other two narratives. Coyote himself is centrally onstage, first in terms of sensory detail (the sun, tired, sitting, getting a hard on, just getting started, looking, hearing), and then in terms of power. The display of power, dramatized with a sweeping gesture, is not sufficient to keep the news from escaping, to be sure. But notice that the news *does not destroy* what Coyote has made. In Mrs. Howard's story the rocks are split, just as in Mr. Simpson's story they are burst through. Not so in Mr. Smith's story. The wind raises the news above the rocks, which remain as a natural marvel, a shield of rimrock curving to the edge of the view, still to be seen on the Washington side of the Columbia across from the town of Mosier. Both Mr. Smith and Mrs. Howard dramatize Coyote's power, as a balance to his discomfiture, but Mrs. Howard does so at the end in Coyote's role as transformer and benefactor of the people to come. Mr. Smith does it with Coyote being Coyote in the middle of his story.

Incident and imagery. Apart from speech, Mrs. Howard has as a salient ingredient in her story the contrast between *rocks* covering Coyote at the beginning, and being found split apart at the end. The splitting of the rocks serves not as part of the action, to discomfit Coyote, but as evidence after the fact that the news is known. The split rocks are evidence to Coyote of the true nature of such things, so that he may think and then pronounce.

Mr. Simpson makes a good deal of the sensory detail of Coyote's immoral act, describing him as looking around, putting head and penis together, pushing down and being pushed down *(Ck'ES)*. The rocks are alluded to, as what the news broke loose from, but not named or made evident. In the second scene Mr. Simpson makes threefold use of Coyote's characteristic trait of running on, and motivates his running by his hunger.

Mr. Smith is the only one of the three to make Coyote's act seem motivated, a plausible outcome of a set of circumstances. In all three Coyote is going along, and sits. Only in Mr. Smith's detailed account is the sun shining hot, as an apparent consequence of which Coyote is tired, as a consequence of which he sits down, as a consequence of which, perhaps, sitting, he finds himself, so to speak, with a hard on, which only then he sucks. This detailed account motivates the poetic form of the opening stanza with its series of "thens." The shameful act is simply an expression of Coyote's nature in the stories of Mr. Simpson and Mrs. Howard—Coyote arrives and does it. Mr. Smith provides extenuating circumstances. Extenuation goes together with centering of a powerful response, a transformation scene *creating* rock.

In terms of explicit sensory detail and imagery, then, Mrs. Howard's Coyote covers himself with rocks to conceal an immoral act, then learns from seeing the split rocks that such things can never be concealed. Mr. Simpson's Coyote sucks and runs, the one vividly, the other repeatedly and vainly. Mr. Smith's hard-traveling Coyote, finding himself with a hard on, does what comes naturally; discovered, does what comes powerfully; discovered generally, takes off.

These five dimensions covary, and further use of them may disclose more precise formulations and ratios. As it is, they provide a useful frame of reference for final comparison of what these three voices have made of a common story.

Part Three. Coyote's People Sing

Verse patterns may be present in texts composed in English. The two speeches considered in Part One of this chapter have shown as much. If the texts are myths, the same is true. The versions of the myth "Coyote's people sing" (to generalize the title given it by Sapir), considered in the last part of chapter 3, are all in English, yet all show evidence of narrative verse.

The circumstances of each text are somewhat different. It is not surprising that a story first told in the Indian language should preserve traditional patterning when given by the same narrator as a translation. Such is the circumstance of the English version of "Iluxmit," or "Singing ceremony," given by Hiram Smith. Notice that while there are six parts in all, the number of performed parts is the pattern number five.

Mr. Smith's text makes explicit the purpose of winter ritual to bring spring and good weather, as a frame, a purpose that is used as a link in Mr. Simpson's text, and that is probably simply presupposed by Mr. Kahclamet. As to verse pattern, notice that the chief's speech quotes five lines. (The first sentence seems to stand as a preface, since the chief's part proper begins with 'Then', as do the last three parts of the whole.) The scene with Mouse has three lines for her, three for the quoted rejoinder, and a third part for her return. Even the summary of scenes not told has a list of five, and the scenes with Crow and Watersnake each seem to have five lines.

A long time ago there was a place where the snow was deep on the ground.
Then the chief said,
    "There'll be a singing ceremony.
        "People will sing.
            "You'll all come.
                "Maybe somebody might make the Chinook wind come,
                "and end the snow and cold weather."

The first one that come forth was the Mouse.
    This is her song:
        "I make eyes in the root bag."
Somebody said:
    "That person with slanting eyes,
        "get out of the way.
            "Let someone else sing."
Then she went back into the crowd.

(Then Chipmunk
    i'Emt,
        iGwaXCul,
            and, other animals getting bigger and bigger,
            and birds.)

Then the Crow went forth.
    She sang.
        She was singing.
            Then someone said,
            "The Chinook wind is blowing now."

They told Watersnake,
    "Your house might fall down."
        He ran out.
            Watersnake wrapped himself right around his house,
            tight.

The English text that Edward Curtis published under the title, "The animal people hold a medicine-chant" (1911:124–26), may have been told in the Indian language before being interpreted in English. We do not know the circumstances. Most likely the story was told in English, but not in exactly the English that Curtis published. The actual English probably was very close to a Wishram original. Even the edited English of the published text, the only text available, shows something of traditional canons of narrative. It is worthwhile to reconstruct the text as a verse narrative. Such a reconstruction facilitates comparison. It enables us to pinpoint the similarities and differences between this version and that told by Philip Kahclamet.

Before giving the reconstructed version, a few observations: The first sentence appears to stand as a preface to the rest of the text, as with Mr. Smith's text. The version has the same general plan as that from Philip Kahclamet, having five main parts. In both versions the four major parts concern the two pairs of antagonists, Grizzly Bear and Big Lizard, Rattlesnake and Raccoon, who meet twice. Whereas Mr. Kahclamet has the initial frame, involving Coyote, to which Curtis's source alluded only (1911:124, n. 1), for a fifth part, the Curtis text has as fifth part an interlude, summarizing the "roll call" aspect of the story also summarized a half-century later by Hiram Smith, and referring, like Smith, to Crow and good weather. Here the good weather is not an outcome so much as a transition.

The Curtis and Kahclamet versions are clearly from a common tradition. Quite specific details indicate as much. When Grizzly Bear seeks out Lizard, Curtis mentions the crevice, Kahclamet the hole, which Lizard later will use for escape, before it has apparent relevance. Both versions use the three-step depiction of action by a character and use it precisely in the same places, namely, where the two dangerous actors, Grizzly Bear and Rattlesnake, turn and speak to their challengers (Curtis, lines 39–41, 56–58, 99–101, 116–19; Kahclamet 42–44, 106–8, and probably 139–41). The first encounter of Rattlesnake and Raccoon twice notes the people's fear in each.

The Curtis text approximates overall narrative structure rather closely. One could analyze the first encounter of Rattlesnake and Raccoon, such that it had five stanzas (A–E), corresponding to the five segments of action in the Kahclamet text. The Curtis text seems consistent enough to warrant trusting a sense that its organization at this point is rather into three stanzas (A–C), with (A) and (B) each ending on the concern of the people. (The alternative would have identified present B[a] as just B, B[b–c] as C, C[a] as D, and C[bc] as E, corresponding to the taking of turns among Rattlesnake, Raccoon, Rattlesnake, Raccoon, Rattlesnake).

The line structure of the Curtis text is only an approximation. The placement of expressions such as "declared Grizzly-bear" (15), "said the latter" (132), "said Lizard" (135), "persisted Grizzly-bear" (138), after the direct speech is without parallel in texts in Chinookan itself. The lines show arrangements into three, five, and sometimes pairs that are paralleled in Chinookan language texts, but sometimes the number of lines within an evident verse or stanza fits no such pattern. Some uncertainty derives from the fact that English verbs and predicates do not always correspond to such in Chinookan. The extent to which the English falls into patterns of lines is perhaps remarkable in consequence.

What seems strikingly lacking is the marking of verses by initial particles. Hardly any occur at all: "So" (94), "Then" (105), "But just then" (144), "After a while" (156), "Then" (179). These initial elements are scattered and do not together define a sequence. By contrast, Philip Kahclamet presses English "Finally" into service in precisely a Chinookan manner in his part IV, as initial element of the three units of stanza C. "One day" marks the onset of effective action in both IV and V (130, 220). "So" introduces outcomes in IV (160, 189) and V (238, 241).

The great difference between the two versions is in regard to vocalization. I can find only two instances in the Curtis text. Both can be taken to reflect the common Chinookan practice of stating the attitudinal intention of an utterance by framing it with an initial particle, expressively colored. The Curtis text has initial "Oh" (59) and "Why" (102). The Kahclamet text has "oh" (152), "Gee" (156), "oh gee" (158), "oh" (190), "Oh hello" (194), "yeah, well" (200, 201), "oh! oh!" (206), "oh hell" (244). It has also the untranslated and untranslatable expression of Raccoon's pain, *aduu*, three times (232). The greeting "hello" also serves such a function, as do its Wishram equivalents *ai* and *au*. The interchanges with "Hello" serve to express the nonchalance of the hero, the surprise and curiosity of the people (194, 195, 196, 197), or the nonchalance of Lizard as against the menace or deceptiveness of Grizzly Bear (141, 142). Notice finally that in the Curtis text the people say nothing (19) or are very quiet (79) when Grizzly Bear and Rattlesnake sing. In the Kahclamet text, the people mumble (21, 88), twice doing so audibly with "hai" (60, 79).

Closely connected to vocalization is the presence of direct speech. The two texts are alike in having no direct speech in the part that is a summary (Curtis III, Kahclamet I). In the first challenge, the Curtis text has a few more lines of direct speech (34 to 29). In the second challenge, that of Raccoon to Rattlesnake, the two texts have the same number of lines of direct (20 : 20). In the outcome of the relation between Grizzly Bear and Lizard, the Kahclamet text has far more lines absolutely (lines 119–215 in Kahclamet, lines 113–60 in Curtis, or 97 : 48), and far more lines of direct speech (41 : 8). In the outcome of the relation between Rattlesnake and Raccoon, only the Kahclamet text has direct speech, some six lines. Overall, the Kahclamet text has 248 lines of continuous narrative, as against 184 of the Curtis text. A considerable part of the difference, some 64 lines, is accounted for by the difference in lines of direct speech, some 34 (96 as against 62). The difference in proportion is not great: 38.7 percent of the lines in Kahclamet's text are direct speech, 33.7 percent of those in Curtis's text.

The effective difference between the two texts lies in two things. The Kahclamet text is more elaborated, both in number of lines absolutely and in number of lines of direct speech. And the Kahclamet text achieves and extends its preponderance in lines of direct speech in the concluding parts of the story, the return engagements, as it were, between Grizzly Bear and Lizard, Rattlesnake and Raccoon. Insofar as lines of direct speech can serve as an indication, the narrator of the Curtis text focused most performance on the first encounter between Grizzly Bear and Lizard, while Kahclamet clearly focused most performance attention on the second and decisive encounter.

The following table shows the numerical relations. PK = Philip Kahclamet, EC = Edward Curtis, GB = Grizzly Bear, L = Lizard, RS = Rattlesnake, R = Raccoon. The order of parts is I–V for PK, III I II IV V for EC.

Total lines of narrative

	Frame (I/III)	GB:L(1)	RS–R(1)	GB:L(2)	RS–R(2)
PK	16	57	45	97	28
EC	9	65	38	48	24

Lines of direct speech

PK	0	29	20	41	6
EC	0	34	20	8	0

Table 6–11. Direct speech in the Kahclamet and Curtis texts

After the first round of encounters, the Curtis text has only 8 lines of direct speech in all of parts III–IV–V, while the Kahclamet text has 67. That seems a strong indication of increase in performance in the latter as the text proceeds, a decline in the former.

Here now is the Curtis text.

[I. Grizzly Bear and Lizard (1)]

All kinds of bird and animal people met at a village in the winter
to sing their medicine-songs.   1

A (a) Grizzly-bear was the first.
      Everybody was afraid of him.
  He sang
     and danced,   5
  and each time he came near the fire,
     he slapped it,
  and made coals and smoke and wood fly into the air
     and shower down on the others.
  But no one dared say a word.   10
  (b) "If anybody interferes
     with what I am doing,
      I will eat his head,
       bones and all!"
        declared Grizzly-bear,   15

(c)   and to show his bravery
   he again slapped the fire.
    The others lowered their heads
    and said nothing,
     for they were all in fear of such a
      powerful man.   20

B (a) A small person sat there.
    By and by he cried,
     "I am going to stop him!"
 (b) He walked forward quickly
    while Grizzly-bear was singing,   25
    and said:
     "You are going too far, Grizzly-bear!
     "We all know your name.
 (c) "You say
    that if anybody interferes,   30
    you will eat his head.
     You slap the fire
     and burn us.
   "Your name is big enough,
    and you ought not to do this.   35
     I think
      you are not the right kind of man;
      you are a bad fellow."

C   Grizzly-bear turned about
    and glowered at the little person; 40
    then he growled,
     "Who is that interfering?"
   He slapped the fire again,
    and repeated,
     "I want   45
      to know
       who is doing this talking,
       and I will eat him!"

D   "Here I am,"
    said the one who had spoken;   50
     "Look right at me!
      "If you are foolish enough
      to eat me,
       I will make you
        drop everything there is in you!" 55

E   Grizzly-bear looked at the other closely,
                 and, recognizing him as Lizard,
                       he said:
         "Oh, you are my relative,
                 and I do not like to have trouble with you here.   60
         "People all over the country would have the news
                 that we have been fighting.
         "They will have it
                 that Grizzly-bear and his brother were quarreling at the
                                 medicine-singing."
         Grizzly-bear then sat down,   65
                 for he feared Lizard.

[II. Rattlesnake and Raccoon (1)]

A   (a)   Another came forward
                 and sang,
                       making a rattling, buzzing sound.
     (b)   This was Rattlesnake.   70
                 "Let nobody interfere
                     while I sing,"
                       he warned;
                 "If anybody does,
                     I will give him Sawalaptn."   75
     (c)   Rattlesnake began to sing:
                 "I do not know where I shall bite first;
                     "I do not know whom I shall bite first."
         All the people remained very quiet.

B   (a)   About the middle of the song, a person cried out: 80
                 "Stop that
                     "Where I am going to bite,
                     "Whom I am going to bite,
                       you flat-nosed thing!"
                 "Other people here want to sing,   85
                     and you must not take up all the time!"
     (b)   Rattlesnake began to rattle angrily,
                 so that for a time no other sound could be heard.
     (c)   The people were frightened,
                 and urged the one who had spoken: 90
                 "Go out
                     and show yourself;
                       he may bite any of us!"

C   (a)   So Raccoon came out,
            and said: 95
                "I am the one who spoke.
                "If you bite me,
                      I will burn out your eyes!"
  (b)   Rattlesnake turned
            and looked closely;   100
            then he said.
  (c)   "Why, we are relations,
            and I do not wish to have trouble in this gathering."
            So Rattlesnake withdrew.

[*III. Black Bear and others*]

  (a)   Then Black Bear came out to sing,   105
            and he was followed by the other animals,
            and by all the plant people.
  (b)   At last it was nearly spring,
            when Crow started his song.
            The West Wind began to blow,   110
            and the snow to melt,
                and it was Spring when Crow finished.

[*IV. Grizzly Bear and Lizard (2)*]

A   (a)   Lizard went home among the rocks,
            and one day he sat on the sunny side,
                making arrows.   115
  (b)   Grizzly-bear came along
            and looked,
                shading his eyes from the sun,
                and said,
                    "There is the person who interfered with
                      me at the singing."   120
  (c)   He went around
            and approached from the back,
                Lizard knew he was coming,
                but paid no attention.
                He sat in a crevice.   125

B   Something seized him by the hair
            and pulled him back.
      He looked up,
            and saw Grizzly-bear.

     "Do you remember   130
          what you said to me at the singing?"
              said the latter.
     "I do not remember
          saying anything to you,"
              said Lizard.   135
     "Now tell me
          what it was you said to me that time,"
              persisted Grizzly-bear.

C   (a)   He growled fiercely,
          and repeated,   140
              "Tell me!"
                  and raised his paw
                    to slap Lizard.
    (b)   But just then the latter slipped from his grasp,
          darted into the crack,   145
                  and came up a moment later from another crevice
                    armed with bow and arrows,
                        and dressed for a fight.
    (c)   Grizzly-bear leaped toward him again,
          and slapped at him,   150
                  but Lizard dodged into the crack
                  and shot him.
    (d)   In this manner the fight continued,
          Grizzly-bear leaping about
                  and Lizard shooting little arrows into his body.   155
    (e)   After a while Grizzly-bear fell dead,
          and Lizard cut off his claws.
                  Down the breast of Grizzly ran a strip of white fur,
                    which Lizard also cut off
                      to use in his medicine-making.   160

[*V. Rattlesnake and Raccoon (2)*]

    (a)   One day Raccoon was down in the creek, feeling under the stones for little
    suckers and crawfish.
          Rattlesnake saw him,
               and recognizing in him the person
                  who had interrupted his singing,
                    he determined to have revenge.   165
    (b)   He went to the edge of the water
          and waited unseen,

and after a while Raccoon came that way,
    thrust his paw into the crack where Rattlesnake was,
        and got bitten.   170
(c)   He did not notice this,
    and put his paw in again,
    and was bitten five times.
(d)   His paw began to swell,
    and, thinking he must have gotten into some thorns,   175
      he built a fire,
        and held his paw in it
          until the swelling was reduced.
(e)   Then, happening to look around,
    he saw Rattlesnake,   180
      and aware now of the cause of his wounds,
      he picked him up
        and burned his eyes.

The fire is what made his paws so black and slim.

In chapter 3 it was said that "There is genuine performance in the narration, notably in the handling of dialogue." The comparison between the Curtis and Kahclamet texts, especially with regard to direct speech and vocalization, has reinforced this conclusion. By bringing out the architecture of each, the presentation of both texts in the form of narrative verse can make comparison precise in these regards.

The Kahclamet text is direct in another sense, that of idiom. The Curtis wording, "I will make you / drop everything there is in you!" (54–55) is bowdlerized, by Curtis or the informant, in relation to Kahclamet's "make you drizzle your excrement out" (41).

Much of the character of the Kahclamet text derives from two identifications. One is the identification with Big Lizard that is evident both in explicit comment and in narrative elaboration and expressiveness. The other is the identification with the role of colleague, of participant-informant, as it were. The metalinguistic comments, indeed, are incorporated in the patterning of the narration to a considerable extent (IIDc, IIIAa, IVBc, IViia, [132], IViiCa, b [154, 157]). This identification, maintained to an audience of participant-observers, professionals, is itself, indeed, a source of performance. The special qualities of this text stem, I think, from both identifications, both serving as motives. The text reflects performance in a double sense. Perhaps it was performance in the role of consultant, indeed, that made possible performance simultaneously in the role of narrator. Perhaps it is thanks to the assumption of the dual role that others can know now of Big Lizard as both nonchalant hero and friend of the people, qualities uniquely depicted in this other text preserved to us.

Here is Philip Kahclamet's text:

Coyote's people sing

[Preface]

Once upon a time,	1
somewhere about the Wishram people's land—	2
this happened in mythological times.	3

[I. Coyote's children sing]

A	(a)	Coyote's sons sing for the first time.	4
		One at a time he turned them down—	5
		four of them.	6
	(b)	His daughter sing.	7
		Her name was AstwawintLX.	8
		So, all right.	9
		It was all right with him.	10
		He went out and collect the people around.	11
	(c)	His daughter sing.	12
		People came;	13
		his daughter sing.	14
		And after that different people sing,	15
		they sang their songs.	16

[II. Grizzly Bear and Big Lizard (1)]

A	(a)	Grizzly Bear went over there.	17
		He sang.	18
		He growled,	19
		he growled at the people's feet that were singing.	20
		People mumbled his songs.	21
	(b)	He told them,	22
		"What's the matter with you people?	23
		"Help me sing.	24
	(c)	"Sing my song."	25
		"I'm expecting	26
		"I'm going to eat human head.	27
		"I'm going to roll it around in front of me	28
		"and eat it."	29

B (a) There were two little fellows by the door,   30
            standing,   31
              singing.   32
   (b) One of them stepped out.   33
         He said to him,   34
            "Hey, you Grizzly Bear, this is my people.   35
               "You're not going to scare them like that.   36
                  "Not while I'm here."   37
   (c) He said to him,   38
         "I'm not afraid of you.   39
         "Why, I could kill you,   40
            "make you drizzle your excrement out."   41

C (a) Grizzly Bear turned around   42
            and looked at him   43
            and said: 44
   (b) "Oh! áwi, is that you?   45
         "I didn't know it was you.   46
            "Why didn't you tell me long time ago.   47
               "I'd get out of the way.   48
                  "Who are you?"   49
   (c) "I'm Q'áSnan."   50
         He quit;   51
            he went in.   52

D (a) This Lizard he stepped out,   53
            and said,   54
               "Now folks, I'm going to sing."   55
         He sing: 56
               "Itaama Ciu idaa p'ap'a kwn."   57
   (b) People were still afraid of the Grizzly Bear.   58
         They mumbled: 59
            "Hai! hai! haiii. . . . ."   60
   (c) (That's when you stopped your song).   61
         He said,   62
            "What's the matter with you people?   63
               "You still afraid of the Grizzly Bear?   64
         "I am still here.   65
            "I am going to kill that Grizzly Bear.   66
         "I am Lizard, Q'áSnan, from Wakaláitix.   67
            "I am going to kill the Grizzly Bear.   68
         "You folks going to eat the p'ap'akwn, the paws."   69
      Grizzly Bear was sitting over there like this.   70

E   Lizard the same song.   71
            That's over with.   72
            He quit.   73

[*III. Rattlesnake and Raccoon (1)*]

A   (a)   Another it'úXial sing.   74
          (I forget song.)   75
                This was a Rattlesnake.   76
                    He rattled his tail in front of the people.   77
                        He scare them.   78
    (b)   "Hai! hai! haiii. . . . ."   79
    (c)   "What's the matter with you people?   80
                "You scared of me?   81
                    "I'm not going to hurt you.   82
    (d)   "Some of these days I'm going to shoot Sawalaptn.   83
                (This means the poison is strongest   84
                    when walaptn dries up—about the month of August).   85
          "Some place I'm going to put my fangs into someone   86
                and kill someone."   87
    (e)   People mumbled.   88
                Still afraid of him too.   89

B   (a)   There were two by the door.   90
                Big Lizard had jumped out first   91
                    and challenged Grizzly Bear.   92
    (b)   Now another jumped out   93
                and said,   94
                    "You, Rattlesnake, I know you.   95
                "These are my people.   96
                    "You are not going to scare them like that.   97
                        "Not while I'm here.   98
                "Your poison no good on me.   99
                    "I can kill you.   100
                "Even if you bite me with your poison,   101
                    "I can burn it out with fire."   102
    (c)   This was Raccoon, Coon.   103
                He told them,   104
                    "I am Coon, Q'álalaS."   105

C   (a)   Rattlesnake,   106
                he turn around   107
                    and look at him: 108

(b)   "Ah! awi, I didn't know you was here.   109
    "You should have told me.   110
        "I would have got out of your way.   111
            "I'd have quit."   112
                He got out of the way.   113
(c)   The rest of the people sang.   114
    These two guys stayed there   115
        and watched Grizzly Bear and Rattlesnake. 116
    The singing, medicine dance, was disbanded.   117
    Everyone went home.   118

[IV. Grizzly Bear and Big Lizard (2)]

[i]   This village was down in the valley.   119
    The Lizard lives in the hills, in the rocks.   120
The Grizzly Bear didn't forget this Lizard,   121
    what he told him.   122
Grizzly Bear thought,   123
    "I'm going to see this Lizard."   124
He hunt around for him   125
    and found him too.   126
The Lizard look around   127
    and said,   128
        "Here comes this Grizzly Bear."   129

[ii]
A   (a)   One day Lizard went out to dig a'Édi,   130
    and eating it.   131
        He was the only one that dug that.   132
  (b)   He looked around.   133
    Here come Grizzly Bear.   134
        He sure come with his tremendous weight, size too.   135
  (c)   He said,   136
    "Here he comes now."   137
        This happened right by his home, his hole in the rocks.   138

B   (a)   He got to him,   139
    looked.   140
        "Hello Lizard."   141
  "Hello."   142
  (b)   "What you doing?"   143
  "I'm digging myself a'Édi.   144
    "It's my food.   145
        "I eat it."   146

	(c)	"Oh. Hm."	147
		They held conversation, about spring and so on.	148

C	(a)	Finally, he said to him,	149
		"What did you say to me?	150
		"That time Coyote's daughter was singing in	
		that village down below?"	151
		"Oh, I guess I forgot.	152
		"I don't know what I said."	153
		(He excuse to him).	154
	(b)	Finally he got close to him.	155
		"Gee you got little arms."	156
		(Grizzly Bear has got big hands.)	157
		"Oh gee, don't squeeze my arms.	158
		"I need my arms to dig a'Édi."	159
	(c)	So finally he got tired of him	160
		and said,	161
		"I'll tell you	162
		what I told you.	163
		"I told you,	164
		'You Grizzly Bear, I'm not afraid of you.	165
		'I can drive my spear right through your belly,	166
		with an arrowhead one side broken off	
		from Wakaláitix	167
		and make you drizzle out excrements.' "	168
		"O.K.	169
		"Let's see you do it.	170
		"Go ahead."	171

D	(a)	The bear growled.	172
		He stood up.	173
		Lizard little,	174
		Grizzly Bear big.	175
	(b)	He got back	176
		and jumped on the Lizard	177
		and Lizard jumped in his hole in the rocks.	178
	(c)	Grizzly Bear couldn't find him.	179

E	(a)	Lizard came out of the hole.	180
		He was already painted with gray clay	181
		and he had a spear with one point broken off.	182
	(b)	He drove it into him	183
		and killed him.	184
		Grizzly Bear died.	185

(b) He went to the creek,   225
          searching around in the water,   226
               eating k'astila.   227
(c) The Rattlesnake laid out for him in the brush,   228
          right in the rosebushes brush, iC'apamaX.   229
     Through the rosebushes he felt pain in his foot,   230
          he said,   231
               "Aduuu! aduuu! aduuu!"   232
(d) He said,   233
          "I got rosebush thorn on my foot."   234
     He thought,   235
          "Rattlesnake done that to me now."   236
     He was expecting that.   237
(e) So he made fire.   238
          He put his foot, palm, over that fire   239
               and burned that poison out.   240

B   So he went on up.   241
          He got another bit.   242
               "Same damn snake again!"   243
                    "Oh, hell!"   244
                         He burned the poison out again
                              with fire again.   245

C   He went up.   246
          He got several bits like that, about three more maybe,   247
               and then it quit.   248

[Epilog]

That's the end of the whole story.   249
     Sometimes we'll put them in.   250
I cut out the different animal songs.   251
     Sometime we'll put them in.   252
Lot of different songs like Wolf's: 253
     hánaa wi Cai Cai.   254

[Postscript]

A   (a) They were living different places.   255
     (b) He sent a messenger to Coyote's house.   256
               He told him,   257
                    "Your sons sing."   258

(c) Coyote said,   259
         "Oh! Which one?"   260
(d) "Sipa glatsin."   261
(e) "Oh,"   262
         he said,   263
             "idiaq'úyumat.   264
                 "Tell him,   265
                     " 'aliXasgmgwipGna.' "   266

B   One or two days another one sing,   267
             Sipa q'átkwtgwaX.   268
                 He said the same thing,   269
                     "idiaq'uyumat alixasgmgwipGna."   270
                         He turn two down now.   271

TITLES, NAMES, AND NATURES

7

Myth and Tale Titles of the Lower Chinook

Melville Jacobs (1957) has called attention to a neglected aspect of oral literature, the title. His paper has stimulated me to analyze the titles in another body of Chinookan oral literature, that obtained by Franz Boas (1894, 1901) some sixty years ago. I shall consider the provenience of the material briefly, then analyze the titles as to genre, syntactic style, and function, concluding with some comparative remarks and a list.

Provenience. Jacobs has analyzed the titles he recorded in Clackamas Chinook. Although he does not mention the fact, his mentor, Franz Boas, had recorded titles in his collections of texts from Chinookan dialects spoken to the west of the Clackamas, Kathlamet, and Shoalwater,[1] groups known culturally as the "Lower Chinook." The material, indeed, represents two distinct languages, though a common culture. It comprises all we shall know about the myth and tale titles of the Lower Chinook.

Genres. In Jacobs's typology of the titles in Clackamas oral literature, distinctions of genre play no part. Among the Lower Chinook, differences in titles go together with a difference of genre between myths and tales.

This distinction between myths and tales parallels a lexical distinction made by the lower Chinook themselves. Their terms are, for myths, *t-k'anamikS* (Kathlamet), *t-kanam-ukS* (Shoalwater), and, for tales, **t-qixik' aLx* (Kathlamet). (The *t-* is plural prefix to nouns, *-iks* and *-uks* are plural suffixes. The stem for "tales" occurs only in singular possessed form, but this hypothetical unpossessed plural accords with Kathlamet grammar, and, in fact, except for a dialect difference in shape of prefix, is the same as Wishram *it-qixik'aLx.*)

The status of the term for "myths" is clear. As a "title of titles," to use

Originally published in the *Journal of American Folklore* 72:139–45 (1959). References and footnotes have been revised in keeping with the mode of citation in this book but not otherwise changed. Additional data and comments are included in a postscript. For the spelling of Indian words, see the orthographic note. The bulk of information on provenience in the original article has been included in the ethnological note at the beginning of this volume.

[1]I use "Shoalwater," adapting Spier (1936:31), for the dialect of *Chinook texts* in order to avoid the ambiguity of "Chinook"; when used for this dialect or its speakers, the term unfortunately suggests the entire language family.

a phrase of Kenneth Burke's, it denotes the set of myths, whereas particular titles denote members of the set which pertain to particular actors. Future linguistic insight may explain the full import of differences in stem form between the Kathlamet singular -k'ani, the Shoalwater singular -kanam, and the plural -k'anam; the -i and -am are certainly fossilized suffixes. For now, note only that the stem's range of meaning includes not only "story, myth," but also "ways, customs, nature or innate character." (While brought out by Wishram-Wasco data, I believe this range to have been general in Chinookan.)

The status of the term for "tales" is less certain. It does not precede an entire group, as the word for "myths" does in both collections. It is not a part of every tale title recorded in the original dialect, as the word for "myth" is part of all myth titles. So far as the style of individual tale titles is concerned, then, the word has restricted use. So far as native concepts of genre are concerned, we do not know whether the plural of this word would have been used for all or only part of what we call tales. Semantically, the word is general enough; it derives from a verbal theme "to tell a story about," lit., 'to remember an account of.' In my opinion, it would have been used by the Lower Chinook to designate the whole genre. It is so used by the Wishram and Wasco (Upper Chinook).

Syntactic Style. A little can be said about the style of the two titles for genre. Both are inflected by a definite (as opposed to indefinite) plural prefix. The title for the myth genre, like many Chinookan nouns, is hyper-characterized as to plural, having besides a prefix, a collective (as opposed to distributive) plural suffix. This choice of the definite and collective plural affixes points to the conceptualization of the myth genre as a set.

Of individual myth titles, there are seventeen from Kathlamet, eighteen from Shoalwater. With one exception, none fit any of the five types of title which Jacobs has identified in Clackamas Chinook. Rather, Kathlamet and Shoalwater share the same general pattern. In simple form, it comprises the proper name of an actor, plus a possessive inflection of the noun stem for "myth," for example, Kathlamet *Igúnat Iák'ani* 'Salmon His-Myth'. In amplified form, there is added the conjunction *k'a* 'and', plus the proper name of a second actor (in which case the possessive inflection of "myth" is dual), for example, *Amísgaga iSták'ani k'a Alili* 'Robin Their (2)-Myth and Salmonberry'.

The two dialects differ in two respects. First, in Kathlamet the form of the noun stem is -k'ani, while in Shoalwater it is -kanam (see the section on Genre). Second, when two actors are named, the Kathlamet order is Name Their (2)-Myth k'a Name. The Shoalwater order is Name k'a Name Their (2)-Myth. (This is so for five out of six Kathlamet cases, four out of five Shoalwater cases. The exception in each body of myths has the order characteristic of the other; in each case, the exception comes first in a series of myths with amplified titles, the rest of which show the normal order.)

In amplified titles, the order of the names relative to the word for "myth" seems purely stylistic. The Kathlamet style, which associates "myth" more closely with the first name, does not seem correlated with any reduced prominence of the second-named actor. The Shoalwater style, which puts "myth" after both names, does not seem to imply more of a parity in importance for the two actors.

The relative order of the two names themselves, however, does reveal principles of ranking. These principles seem to be those of social status found in Lower Chinook culture quite independently of myths. (The order does not seem to be a function of prominence in the particular myth.) Two of the cases are individual. In the first of these, the name of a chief (highest rank in a Lower Chinook community) precedes the name of the man whose chief he is (K 17). In the second, the name of a being superior in the mythological hierarchy precedes the name of a lower being (Sh 5). (Raven's people, the land birds, comprising eagles, owls, cranes, hawks, are all more important mythologically than the flat-footed water birds who are Gull's people; in the myth war, of course, Raven's people win.)

The remaining cases are based on two principles. Male precedes female (K 11, Sh 15, 15, 16) and elder sibling precedes younger sibling of the same sex (K 12, 13, 14, 16, Sh 13). As a negative confirmation of the principles, note the Kathlamet myth in whose title only the name of Mink appears. The myth itself is about Mink and his elder brother, and the initial element of the myth refers to them, but the name of the elder brother, Panther, does not appear until the myth is well along. Had it appeared in the myth's initial element, it would have had to appear in the title (this is so in all cases), and, as the name of the elder sibling, would have had precedence, just as in "Panther and Lynx" (K 13). The suppression of the name in the first part of the myth correlates with its absence from the title.

This brings out the opportunity for the individual narrator to use a title expressively. If two names appear, there are established rules for giving top billing, rules well rooted in the social structure. By selecting the simple rather than amplified form of title, however, a narrator could favor a character, omitting the name which would have had to precede it. (The pronominal resources of Chinookan verb structure are such that omission of an actor's name is grammatically possible.) In the Mink myth, and perhaps generally, such selection would be in favor of the underdog, such as the younger brother, just as plots tend to favor younger brothers as protagonists. Favoring a character, of course, is not the only reason for which a name might be omitted from the first portion of a myth. The first part of one myth (K 16) does refer only to Owl and his chief, but Panther's name is held back for a dramatic effect at its entrance. Panther's name appears with proper precedence in the title of the myth; Owl is a ridiculous, rather than a rebellious, protagonist, a butt of the audience's laughter, not a figure for their sympathy.

The one myth title fitting a Clackamas type, and thus the one exception to the Lower Chinook pattern, is the Kathlamet "Copper is speared." The close of this narrative shows none of the types of myth-final elements found in myths whose titles are of normal form. On these grounds, it might be judged not a myth at all. On the other hand, the action and actors of its last part are characteristically mythological. In my opinion it is in origin a tale, partly assimilated to the myth canon.

The invariable use of the connective in the Lower Chinook amplified titles contrasts with its limited, perhaps optional, use in Clackamas (Jacobs 1957:171). Texts show this use of the connective between the names of two actors to be the consistent style, although grammatically unnecessary.

Of individual tale titles, there are fifteen from Kathlamet, six from Shoalwater. These show no single style, and, whereas all myth titles are recorded in Chinookan, many of the tale titles are given only in English.

Two Kathlamet tale titles parallel the style of myth titles. These are the two that contain the generic term for "tale." Both are of the form "The so-and-so their-tale," and both concern communities; one as the tale of its progenitor, the other as the tale of retribution by a member's guardian spirit against evil doers from a rival community. The occurrence of this style with two Kathlamet tales concerning names of communities suggests a special genre, or sub genre. The lone Shoalwater tale concerning a single named community has a title simply of the form "The So-and-So," so the two dialects may have differed stylistically in this respect. Lacking enough cases, we can only surmise.

One unique Shoalwater tale title echoes the style of myth titles. It is "Cultee his-grandfather," headed in English "How Cultee's grandfather acquired a guardian spirit." The appropriateness of the style is suggested by the fact that the Lower Chinook were patrilineal, hence his paternal grandfather would stand to Cultee as an individual in a way like that in which its progenitor would stand to a community, or the myth actors to the Chinookans as a whole. Since the guardian spirit was the central religious experience of the individual, and the guardian spirit dance the major religious ceremony of the group, it may be significant that the title is restricted to this one of the three tales Cultee narrated about his grandfather.

When other tales in the two dialects have native titles given, these are of types found also in Clackamas. Fitting Jacobs's first type (displaying only one name) are: (Kathlamet) *TiápixuáSxuaS* (cf. Jacobs 1957:160), *ImuguálakS* and *PíLpiL*. Possibly Shoalwater *The GiLaunaLx*, taking the community collectively as the actor, would fit here. I would add one Kathlamet title given only in English, "The spirit of hunger," because it is equivalent to translation of *wa-lu* 'hunger'. This is conceived as an actor not only mythologically, but also grammatically: Chinookan renders "I am hungry" by *wa-lu g-n-u-X-t* 'hunger (with feminine gender prefix) she-acts-on-me'.

There is one further title given in Kathlamet, which may be said to belong to Jacobs's second type (displaying only a succinct expression of a relatively external or manifest facet of plot): "Winter all-the-year-round."

Three brief titles given only in English are (Kathlamet) "The brothers," (Shoalwater) "The four cousins," and "The elk-hunter." One cannot be sure that these are equivalent to translations. They lack Chinookan equivalents in the tales they head; these refer rather to the youngest brother *(-mxix)* and his elder brothers (-lxt-ikS) (KT 175), to the youngest *(i-xgis'ax)* and his three elder cousins (-xk'un-ikS) (CT 216), and to the boy *(-k'asks)* (CT 235).

The remaining titles given only in English fit Jacobs's third type (one or two names of leading actors, plus an external or manifest facet of plot); these are given in the list in the last section (K4, 5, 11, 12, 13, 14, 15, 16, Sh 5, 6). Quite possibly there were Kathlamet titles of which the English words would be an adequate translation. As in the case of the three titles just mentioned, the parallel to a Clackamas type increases the likelihood of this, but in the absence of the Kathlamet originals, no inferences as to linguistic style can be made.

Finally, note that Jacobs's fourth type, displaying one or two names or references to leading actors, followed by a characterization of their state or condition, does not occur among Lower Chinook titles. Rather, it is a common type of initial element in the formal pattern of the myths and tales themselves.

Function.   In terms of formal pattern, the title of a Lower Chinook myth or tale functions as one in a set of formal units. These units are: Title, Myth Initial, Segment Initial(s), Segment Final(s), Myth Final. I have isolated these classes of units from the continuum of the narratives by a distributional analysis along lines recently developed by Kenneth Pike (1954). I hope to present the analysis of the other formal units, and notes on the method, at a later time.

In terms of content, the title of a myth singles out from the set of supernatural dramatis personae one or two whose ways, innate nature *(-k'ani)*, perhaps ultimate contribution to mankind, are to be defined by being exhibited in the action of the myth. The titled actor need not be the initiator of the myth's action, nor the protagonist. Often enough, the initiator or protagonist is an anonymous human. (One characteristic of the myth genre is that human names do not appear, although human types do.) In the Faustian myth of the Sun, Sun acts only as she is forced to by the hybris of the male protagonist; the point of the myth is to impart the nature of the highest supernatural beings. These are shown as maternally benevolent to man, who may benefit from their power, so long as he does not aspire to possess it. The title of the myth directs attention to the moral, rather than to the action, protagonist, or scene. In general, the telling of myths was an act of pedagogy, of cultural indoctrination, and it is in terms of this goal that the titles were selected.

Jacobs stresses the mnemonic function of Clackamas titles, referring often to the need for unique identification of individual myths. Among the Lower Chinook this seems not to have been an overriding principle. Three separate myths involving Bluejay and his sister have the same title in the Shoalwater collection. Interestingly enough, each of the three has a different initial element, and the differences in initial element correlate with differences in the role each of the two plays in the particular myth. Moreover, it is these initial elements that parallel the types of title found in Clackamas. This suggests that if further identification had been needed, the Lower Chinook might have had recourse to the initial element to differentiate otherwise identically titled myths.

Conclusion. I shall make a few comparative remarks before presenting a list in English of the Lower Chinook titles.

The Lower Chinook material extends the distribution noted by Jacobs (1957: 158–59) for stylization of titles. Being of the same language family as Clackamas, and culturally adjacent, its differences from the Clackamas material are of particular interest. A careful comparison must wait until it can be made in the light of a full analysis of both bodies of narrative, since the titles are functionally related to the other formal units and stylistic patterns.

Points for comparative study brought out by the Lower Chinook material include: 1) the relation of titles to genre; 2) principles of ranking in the relative order of names within titles; 3) expressive choice of simple or amplified form of title; 4) a possible subgenre of tales about the various autonomous Chinookan village communities; 5) the titling of narratives of ancestors; 6) the assignment of the same type of content to different formal units in different stylistic traditions, as when Lower Chinook initial elements show a type of content found in Clackamas titles; and 7) the range and relative importance of the functions served by titles, such as mnemonic, aesthetic, didactic.

The following list gives the titles numbered in the order in which they occur in the published collections. The somewhat literal translation for those recorded in the original dialect is enclosed in quotation marks; other titles are known only in English, and not known to be equivalent to translations of native titles. The supplementary information is restricted to that which documents the principles of ranking presented in the section on syntactic style.

A. Kathlamet Myth Titles. 1) "Aq'asxínasxina her-myth"; 2) "Nik-SiamCáS her-myth"; 3) "Sun her-myth"; 4) "Swan his-myth"; 5) "Copper it-is-speared"; 6) "Coyote his-myth"; 7) "Salmon his-myth"; 8) "Salmon his-myth"; 9) "Elk his-myth"; 10) "Southwest-Wind his-myth"; 11) "Rabbit and Deer their (2)-myth" (Rabbit is son, Deer mother); 12) "Coyote their (2)-myth and Badger" (Coyote is the elder brother); 13) "Panther their (2)-myth and Lynx" (Panther is the elder brother); 14) "Seal their (2)-myth and Crab" (Seal is the elder sister); 15) "Mink his-myth";[2] 16) "Robin their (2)-myth and Salmonberry" (Robin is elder sister); 17) "Panther their (2)-myth and Owl" (Panther is Owl's chief); 18) "Raccoon his-myth." (Nos. 7 and 8 are repetitions of the same myth, so do not count as separate titles.)

B. Shoalwater Myth Titles. 1) "The-SiktLa their (2)-myth"; 2) "Ukulám his-myth"; 3) "AnikCxúlmix her-myth"; 4) "Salmon his-myth"; 5) "Raven and Gull their (2)-myth" (land-birds outrank sea-birds); 6) "Coyote his-myth"; 7) "Crane his-myth"; 8) "Ints'x his-myth"; 9) "Crow her-myth"; 10) "SHáxaL his-myth"; 11) "Stikuá her-myth"; 12) "Skunk her-myth"; 13) "Robin their (2)-myth and Bluejay" (Robin is the elder brother); 14) "Bluejay and Iúi their (2)-myth" (Bluejay and his elder *sister*); 15) "Bluejay and Iúi their (2)-myth" (see 14); 16) "Bluejay and Iúi their (2)-myth" (see 14); 17) "The SkulkulúL their (2)-myth"; 18) "Panther his-myth."

C. Kathlamet Tale Titles. 1) "TiápixuaSxuaS"; 2) "ImuguálakS"; 3) The brothers; 4) The war of the ghosts; 5) The war of the ghosts; 6) "The TkLxiyuguáikS their-tale"; 7) PíLpiL"; 8) "The Nisal their-tale"; 9) "The spirit-of-hunger" (likely translation of *Walú*); 10) "Winter all-the-year-round"; 11) The GiLáunaLx maiden who was carried away by the thunder-bird; 12) The man who was transformed into a snake; 13) How the Clatsop were killed by lightning; 14) War against the Clatsop; 15) Cultee's ancestor conjures the sea lion; 16) Cultee's grandfather visits the ghosts. (Nos. 4 and 5 are repetitions of the same tale, so do not count as separate titles.)

D. Shoalwater Tale Titles. 1) "Cultee his-grandfather" (How Cultee's grandfather acquired a guardian spirit); 2) The four cousins; 3) "The GiLáunaLx"; 4) The elk hunter; 5) War between Quileute and Clatsop; 6) The first ship seen by the Clatsop.

Postscript

Jacobs has discussed Clackamas titles further in his book (1959b:250–65). Since this article was published, I have ascertained, as has also Michael Silverstein, that titles were known among the Wasco-speaking groups east of the Clackamas, although few examples could be recalled by then. Myth titles were not unique to the Chinookans and might well have been general in the area. Just south of the Lower Chinook, the Tillamook are reported as having

[2]Given as literally "Her-Myth"; the slip probably is due to the similarity of *-kusait* 'Mink' and *-kasait* 'Robin', both of which occur anomalously without gender prefix sometimes; Robin is feminine in Kathlamet myths.

had formal titles by Jacobs and Jacobs (1959: ix). They publish only English translations. The unpublished manuscripts in Tillamook of the late May Edel may contain the native language originals. The translations fit Jacobs's discussion of Clackamas titles but do not show the Lower Chinook pattern containing a possessed form of the word for "myth" itself.

Just south of the Tillamook along the Pacific coast, the Alsea had titles. Six are attested in Frachtenberg's collection (1920). Both of Frachtenberg's consultants, Tom Jackson and William Smith, are sources of texts that have titles in Alsea, and both are sources of texts that do not. Not all stories recorded by Frachtenberg in his 1910 fieldwork have Alsea titles; most of the stories recorded by Livingston Farrand in 1900 lack Alsea titles, but one does have one. Such variation across three narrators and two fieldworkers suggests that titles were not a function of any one person but genuinely present in Alsea. The seven titles that we have probably depended on the memory of the individual narrator, especially Frachtenberg's consultants, Jackson and Smith. This is all the more likely in the light of Frachtenberg's work with Coos about the same time (see below); he may have been advised by his sponsor, Boas, to look for titles, and recorded those that were recalled.

Two of the titles recorded by Frachtenberg show the Chinookan pattern. One from William Smith has "Elk story-his-own" (p. 34) and one from Tom Jackson has "Grizzly his-story" (p. 60).

No native language titles are attested in the limited Siuslaw-Lower Umpqua collection (Frachtenberg 1914). The material was, in fact, obtained by Frachtenberg from one of his Alsea consultants, William Smith, who had spoken Lower Umpqua from an early age and was married to the then oldest survivor of the group. While Frachtenberg obtained titles a year before in his Alsea work from the same man, their absence here is presumably not evidence of actual absence in Siuslaw-Lower Umpqua, but lack of knowledge in the language on the part of Smith. (Many of the texts are translated into the language by Smith from Alsea and Coos originals.)

Just south of the Siuslaw, the Hanis and Miluk Coos have titles, recorded some twenty-five years apart by Frachtenberg in 1909 and Jacobs in 1933-34. Frachtenberg published Coos titles for all but three of the nineteen Hanis narratives in his collection of texts (1913). There are no Coos titles, however, for the thirteen stories recorded by Henry Hull St. Clair 2d also included in the volume (pp. 132ff.). None of the St. Clair English titles suggest the Chinookan pattern. One Frachtenberg Coos title does: *"TewítäC hä´Cit!* (Nephew story)." Since the story is given the English title, "The girl and her pet," the Coos title appears to be distinct and authentic. A number of the other Coos titles are given parenthetic literal translations that are distinct from the English title, further indicating their authenticity. None, however, show the Chinookan pattern except this one.

Melville Jacobs published 140 texts of varying kind and length in both Coos languages, Hanis and Miluk. (Frachtenberg's texts are in Hanis.) In the first collection (1939), the ethnologic texts in Hanis (11), Miluk (53), and both (7) concerned with "custom" (*ta:má:Lis* in Miluk) lack Coos titles, as does one narrative obtained in both; the titles are Jacobs's own (1939:5). In contrast, the three semi-myth narratives or tales concerned with relatively recent history (*laGaaiyát'as* in Miluk) in Hanis and all but two of the sixteen narrative texts in Miluk have Coos titles. The titles are mostly descriptive verb phrases; a few are nouns only. One in Miluk has the form "Sea-otter narrative" (1939:48), the second word being the Coos term for tale or historical narrative (Ibid.: 35) (cf. Jacobs 1940:142, n. 8). The preceding text is given an English title of the same form, "Swordfish narrative" (1939:45).

In the second collection (1940) all forty-nine texts have Coos titles, and Jacobs reports (p. 129):

> The myth titles are Mrs. Peterson's, not mine. It seems likely that myth titles were unstable. I suppose that all the natives would have phrased titles somewhat differently, within certain limits which permitted intelligible reference to what was a myth that was perhaps equally familiar to all.

Four of the titles have the Miluk term for myth, *bá:saq'*, in second position: "Fog myth" (p. 139), "Ogress myth" (p. 142), "Dove myth" (p. 143), and "Trickster myth" (p. 224). One has this pattern, followed by an amplifying verb phrase of the sort often used as a title in itself: "Bluejay myth, (his) grandmother tied his head hair with her pubic hair" (p. 181). Another has this pattern in the verbal phrase "Crow myth-will I-tell-you" (p. 170).

There is no doubt of the existence, then, of the pattern " '(Name of Actor)' myth" in Coos. The one instance from Frachtenberg exemplifies the pattern, since the word he translates as "story" in "Nephew story" is the Hanis equivalent of Miluk *bá:saq'* 'myth' (p. 129). The term occurs in two of the eight Hanis myths collected by Jacobs: "Bluejay myth" (p. 230) and "Robin myth" (p. 223) in the form *hé:jit'*. Interestingly enough, the story titled "Ogress myth" in English by Jacobs, with the Miluk title *Nu:sgíli bá:saq'*, from Annie Miner Peterson, his consultant, is the equivalent of a story Frachtenberg obtained in three versions with the constant title "Giant woman," Hanis *No:skíLi: hú:mis* (woman), without the term for myth. But while Mrs. Petersen was not certain that the story was a myth (p. 143, n. 8), Frachtenberg's three versions all end with a formal close that includes the verbalized form of the Hanis term for "myth" (*häCt'e-* [=*héCt'e-*]).

There are no native language titles in the small number of myth texts preserved in Kalapuya, a family of languages spoken beside and south of the Clackamas in the Willamette Valley of Oregon, and directly inland from the Tillamook, Alsea, and Siuslaw-Lower Umpqua, but this lack may be due to the thinness of the early work by Gatschet and Frachtenberg and the lack of involvement with myth repertoire of John B. Hudson, Jacobs's main consultant, a remarkably rich source of ethnological and linguistic information (cf. Jacobs 1945:85). It seems certain that Jacobs would have noted any available during his work with Mr. Hudson in 1930, 1932, 1936, if not at first in 1928 (1945:5) (see Sahaptin below).

Among the Takelma, linguistic kin of the Kalapuya and somewhat south of them in Oregon on the Rogue River, no myth titles are attested (Sapir 1909b, from work in 1906). Since Sapir also did not obtain titles in his work at about the same time (1905) in Wishram Chinook (Sapir 1909a), the absence may have been due to a failure to inquire for them. In his work with the Klikitat Sahaptin language, whose speakers were neighbors of Wishram-Wasco, both aboriginally along the Columbia River and on the Yakima Reservation, Jacobs reported the existence of titles (1934:ix–x). He explained:

> The title at the head of each text was not supplied by an informant. I heard natives apply stereotyped short titles to a few myths; I also heard myths referred to by statements of the usual contents of the first sentences or by rapid plot summaries. Native ways of identifying or referring to stories are of interest and need field observation. I neglected regrettably to inquire concerning myth titles or to note the manner in which myths were referred to in casual conversation. It is impossible for an outsider to invent titles that would satisfy an older native.

Jacobs is commenting on his first fieldwork (1926–30, mainly 1925–27–28 apparently). Perhaps the consistent recording of titles from Victoria Howard in Clackamas in his 1929–30 work with her, and from Annie Miner Petersen in Coos, with whom he worked in 1933–34, is due to this initial experience and regret in Sahaptin. Some Nez Perce titles (in English) are discussed by Stross (1972) in relation to the framework of this study, especially ordering in terms of rank. See also the observations on a few titles (in Nez Perce) by Aoki (1979:7).

In sum, there is evidence for the existence of patterned myth titles over an aboriginal area greater than that of the Chinookan-speaking peoples of the Columbia River. Sparseness of evidence precludes definite conclusions. The seemingly natural and obvious pattern of "Name myth," found in the Shoalwater and Kathlamet texts obtained by Boas from Charles Cultee, appears among two groups of the Penutian family south of them on the Oregon coast, the Alsea and the Coos. In neither is it shown to be more than an infrequent pattern, and in Coos the Chinookan and Alsea possessive marking of the noun for "myth" is absent. The pattern we might most readily expect is, in fact, specific and rare.

It now appears that significant formal relationship is not simply within myth titles, but between them and the myths they mention. This relationship, explained in chapter 8, was not recognized when the present chapter was written. The two kinds of relationship, that of precedence within titles, and that of the relationship of title-precedence to myth outcome, are consistent with each other. The Kathlamet title "Mink his-myth," chosen as against the available "Panther their(2)-myth and Mink," is evidence of this. It is Mink's nature that is to be in focus in the myth. A study in 1967 by Elinor Ochs Keenan under my supervision of all the Clackamas Chinook myths showed a fit between title-precedence and outcome, except in a few cases. Each exception had the conjunction *kwaliwi*, and *kwaliwi* occured only with such exceptions. There is etymological reason to think of *kwaliwi* as having a reversative or inverse force. A full study will show the reasons for its use in detail and indicate the nuances it adds to interpretation.

In Lower Chinook the form of the title, marking the word for "myth, nature" for possession, can be seen as expressing neatly the relation between title and the action whose outcome is the lesson of the myth. In Clackamas the same relationship between title and action holds without possessive marking.

The basic question for interpretation, then, is not whether other Native American groups show a certain form of title as Chinookan, but whether or not they show the same structural relation between title-precedence and myth outcome. Studies of the cases in which authentic titles are attested will show whether this structural relation is something Chinookan alone or part of the place of myth in Native American life more generally.

8

The "Wife" Who "Goes Out" Like a Man: Reinterpretation of a Clackamas Chinook Myth

I shall take up in turn the background of the paper; its methodological significance; a synopsis of the myth in question; the first interpretation of the myth; a reinterpretation of the myth; some further implications of the reinterpretation including application of a mode of analysis developed by Lévi-Strauss; and make a concluding remark.

Background

Melville Jacobs has given us one of the handful of major contributions to our knowledge and understanding of the literatures of the Indians of North America. The quality of the texts he so fortunately rescued a few months before the death of the last capable informant and the quality of the insight and interpretation he has provided for them make his series of monographs of Clackamas Chinook outstanding (Jacobs 1958, 1959a, 1959b, 1960). Perhaps no one can appreciate his contribution more than one who, like myself, also works with Chinookan materials. The field of Chinookan studies has engaged the energies of Franz Boas and Edward Sapir; within it Jacobs's accomplishment is the richest for oral literature, one that redounds to the value of the rest.

In the study of written literatures the work of interpretation is never complete. Major texts are regarded not as closed, but as open to new insight and understanding. The case should be the same for aboriginal literatures. The significance of a body of work such as the Clackamas series will increase as

Originally published in *Social Science Information* 7(3):173–99, and somewhat revised in P. and E. K. Maranda (eds.), *Structural analysis of oral tradition* (1971), pp. 49–80. My translation and analysis of this myth have been reprinted several times. The acknowledgments of the original first footnote to the paper are incorporated into an expanded account of the study and the uses made of it in a postscript to this paper. The postscript notes reprintings and discussions of the paper and adds a discussion of related myths in the region; corrects and amplifies the relation of speech to sensory detail in the original analysis; connects the role of speech in the myth to Basil Bernstein's concept of coding orientations and to the notion of meta-narrative statement (for stimulus to which latter I am indebted to Gerald Prince); and expands on the implications of the story, together with a response to a review. The myth is analyzed in terms of verse, and interpreted further, in chap. 9 of this book. The orthography used has been changed to that described in the orthographic note.

others come to it and keep it vital by building on the basic contribution. Indeed, a secondary literature on Clackamas has already begun (Scharbach 1962). This paper adds to it by reinterpreting a particular Clackamas myth, "Seal and her younger brother dwelt there," published in *Clackamas Chinook texts,* Part II (Jacobs 1959a: 340–41, 37 in the collection), and first interpreted in *People are coming soon* (Jacobs 1960: 238–42).

Jacobs himself has remarked that the Clackamas myths are susceptible of a plurality of interpretations (personal communication). In keeping with that spirit, I wish to avoid appearance of personal criticism that recurrent use of personal names and pronouns can suggest, and so shall generally refer simply to the "first interpretation" and the "second interpretation."

My title calls attention to an actor in the myth, the significance of whose role is a central difference between the two interpretations. The Chinookan idiom on which the title is based is explained in note 2 below; it is adapted to identify her because she is given no name in the myth itself.

Methodological Remarks

The two interpretations are alike in being philological in basis and structural in aim. Since the narrator of the myth and all other participants in Clackamas culture are dead, we cannot collect other variants, interrogate, experiment. Access to the form and meaning of the myth is only through a finite corpus of words; but both Jacobs and I believe it possible to bring to bear a body of knowledge and method that enables one to discern in the words a valid structure.

In practice the two interpretations differ. The first can be said to plunge to the heart of what is taken as the psycho-social core of the myth and to view its structure as unfolding from that vantage point. The second does not discover an import for the myth until a series of lines of evidence as to its structure has been assembled.

The first interpretation might thus be said to practice philology in the spirit of Leo Spitzer's "philological circle" (Spitzer 1948:18–20), but that would not accurately distinguish it from the second. Either approach can hope to find a motivational core from which the whole might be satisfactorily viewed, and both should enjoin what good philological practice always entails: close reading of the verbal action as it develops sentence by sentence in the original text, and interpretation based on using cumulatively all there is to use, as to the significance of details, and as to the situation which implicitly poses the question to which the text is to be regarded as a strategic or stylized answer (Burke 1957:3). The effective difference lies in the greater temptation to the first approach to take a shortcut, to assume that a purportedly universal theory, be it psycho-analytical (as in the present case), dialectical, or whatever, can go straight to the heart of a myth before having considered its place in a genre structurally defined and functionally integrated in ways perhaps particular to the culture in question.

In sum, the second interpretation undertakes philology in the spirit of the structural ethnography developed by Goodenough (1956, 1957), Conklin (1964), Frake (1962), and others (for discussion of other implications of such ethnography, cf. Hymes 1964a, 1964b, 1965a). One is asked to regard the study of a verbal genre as of a kind with the ethnographic study of kinship, residence rules, diagnosis of disease, firewood, or wedding ceremonies. One assumes that there is a native system to be discovered; that what is identified as the same genre, for example, "myth," ethnologically (cross-culturally) may differ significantly in structural characteristics and functional role ethnographically (within individual cultures); that one thus must formulate a theory of the special case, defining a genre in terms of features and relationships valid for the individual culture; and that the meanings and uses of individual texts are to be interpreted in the light of the formal features and relations found for the native genre.

Put otherwise, one assumes that persons growing up in the community in question acquire a grasp of the structures and functions of the genre, such that they are able to judge instances as appropriate or inappropriate, not only in terms of overt formal features ("surface structure"), but also in terms of underlying relations ("deep structure"). One assumes that the structural analysis of a genre, like other structural ethnography, is in principle predictive (cf. Goodenough 1957). That such an approach is correct, that participants in a culture do in fact have the ability to use an implicit knowledge of genre structure, is attested by the assimilation of new materials, either through innovation (I take the Kathlamet Chinook "Myth of the sun" to be a late Chinookan instance) or diffusion (cf. Dundes 1963). The point seems obvious, but it is important to stress it, because the nature of the usual emphasis in folklore research upon the traditional has cost heavily. (I pass by the question as to whether the object of folkloristic study should be defined as traditional material at all; for one aspect of the question see Hymes 1962.)

Folklorists have commonly identified their object of study, traditional material, as a matter of texts, not of underlying rules. The frequent consequence has been that the very material which would decisively test a structural analysis has been disregarded. The occurrence of a reworked European tale in an Indian pueblo (say, *Beowulf*) may evoke amusement, or embarrassment, if one thinks of one's goal as autochthonous texts. If one thinks of one's goal as natively valid rules, such a case may be an invaluable opportunity to verify the principles of the native genre through an instance of their productivity. In one striking case, a collector discovered that some of his tapes represented songs his informant had herself composed to keep him working with her. The songs had seemed perfectly in keeping with all the others obtained from her; only when a later check found them to have no counterparts in other collections from the region was their status suspected. Confronted with the discrepancy, the informant confessed. Because the material (as text) was "non-traditional," the collector destroyed it. What he destroyed was from the standpoint of a structural ethnography the most valuable portion of his work; spontaneous evidence of the productivity of the rules of the genre. (I am indebted for this example to my colleague, Kenneth Goldstein.)

In short, if structural analysis of myth, and of folklore generally, is to keep pace with ethnographic and linguistic theory, it must attempt to achieve what Chomsky (1964:923–25) has recently called "descriptive adequacy"; that is, to give a correct account of the implicit knowledge of the members of the culture competent in the genre and to specify the observed texts in terms of underlying formal regularities.

The highest level of adequacy designated by Chomsky would be that of "explanatory adequacy." Adapted to the study of folklore, the notion would call for a concern with the capacities of persons to acquire a productive, theory-like grasp of genres, and to employ that grasp, that implicit sense of rules and appropriateness in judging performances and instances, in adapting them to social and personal needs, and in handling novel materials. In the sphere of linguistics Chomsky, Lenneberg, and others consider explanatory adequacy to involve innate, species-specific capacities of human beings, which entail quite specific universals of grammatical structure. In the sphere of folklore the capacities are no doubt derived from innate abilities, and the work of Lévi-Strauss would seem to point directly to what some of them might be; such innate abilities, however, are almost certainly not specific to folklore. My concern here is first of all with "descriptive adequacy," that is, with the culturally specific form taken by general capacities with respect to folkloristic genres through participation in a given community. It is at the level of "descriptive adequacy" that the study of folklore can now most profitably join with the recent parallel developments in structural linguistics and structural ethnography. (The concept of descriptive adequacy in linguistics is quite analogous to Goodenough's formulation [1957] of the criterion for adequate ethnographic description; cf. Hymes 1964:10, 16–17, and especially 30–31.)

Synopsis of the Myth

Of the myth Jacobs (1960:238) says aptly: "A remarkable quantity of expressive content is compacted in this short horror drama of an unnamed woman who comes to Seal woman's younger brother."

This myth has a short prologue and three short scenes. The prologue introduces the actors as compresent in one setting. I present the myth in the form of a revised translation which differs from that in Jacobs (1959a:340–41) in its division into segments and in some points of verbal detail. The revised division into segments defines sharply the structure of the content (prologue, first scene, second scene, climax, denouement), but it has not been made in terms of content alone. Rather, considerations of content have been integrated with what are taken to be formal segment markers, that is, recurrent initial and final elements. The segment initial and segment final elements of the prologue and first two scenes have identical or partially identical form: "They lived there," "Don't say that!". The climax and denouement are marked most saliently by final elements of parallel content: "She screamed," "She wept," "She kept saying that," "The girl wept."

Points of verbal detail are revised partly in the light of grammatical and lexical analysis, aided by Wishram data. Such points are supported in footnotes. Other revisions are for the sake of following the Clackamas text as exactly as possible in form.

A later re-reading of the translation (ignoring the footnotes) may integrate the structures and effects analyzed separately in the paper.

Seal (and) her younger brother lived there[1]

They lived there, Seal, her daughter, her younger brother. I do not know when it was, but now a woman got to Seal's younger brother.

They lived there. They would go outside in the evening.[2] The girl would say, she would tell her mother: "Mother! There is something different about my uncle's wife. It sounds like a man when she 'goes out.' "[3] "Don't say that! [She is] your uncle's[4] wife!"

They lived there like that for a long time. They would 'go out'[5] in the evening. And then she would tell her: "Mother! There is something different about my uncle's wife. When she 'goes out,' it sounds like a man." "Don't say that!"

[1]The prefix L- in 'they lived there' already implies more than two present.

[2]Literally so: -y(a) 'to go', tLáxuix 'outside'; xabixix is better 'evening' as contrasted with -pul 'night' later on.

[3]The text and translation require clarification here. Although the first scene is discussed in terms of the sound of the "wife's" urination, the translation contains no reference to a sound. Furthermore, the Clackamas verb in question, -ba-y(a), does not refer to urination but to going out. As to the sound, the text contains an untranslated element tL'a. In Wishram Chinook there is a particle tL'alalala . . . 'the sound of water dripping, or as when it comes out of a hose'. The use of the recursively repeatable element -la for repetition of a sound is attested in Kathlamet Chinook, leaving Wishram and Clackamas tL'a presumably as equivalent in meaning. As to the "going out," the verb in question is attested as an idiom for urination among both the Kathlamet and Wishram (groups to the west and east, respectively, of the Clackamas). The text thus combines a euphemistic verb and an onomatopoeic particle, literally 'a-dripping-sound someman's-like she-"goes out" '. (A corroborative instance from our own society: in families with a boy and girl, mothers in bed can tell which of their children has gotten up during the night precisely from this auditory clue. I owe the observation to Archie Green.)

As adapted from the Chinookan expression, the title of the paper indicates the two features singled out by the first interpretation as crucial to the actor found focus of the myth: questionable sexual identity and the clue disclosing it.

[4]'Uncle' has expanded prefix iwí (instead of wi-), perhaps for emphasis.

[5]With distributive plural suffix -w.

Her uncle and his wife would "lie together" in bed.[6] Some time afterwards the two of them "lay" close to the fire, they "lay" close beside each other.[7] I do not know what time of night it was, but something dripped on her face. She shook her mother. She told her: "Mother! Something dripped on my face." "Hm . . . Don't say that. Your uncle [and his wife] are 'going.' "[8]

Presently then again she heard something dripping down. She told her: "Mother! Something is dripping, I hear something." "Don't say that. Your uncle [and his wife] are 'going.' "

The girl got up, she fixed the fire, she lit pitch, she looked where the two were lying.[9] Oh! Oh! She raised her light to it.[10] In his bed her uncle's neck was cut.[11] He was dead. She screamed.

She told her mother: "I told you something was dripping. You told me: 'Don't say that. They are "going".' I had told you[12] there was something different about my uncle's wife. When she 'goes out,' it sounds like a man when she urinates. You told me: 'Don't say that!' " She wept.

Seal said: "Younger brother! My younger brother! They [his house posts] are valuable standing there.[13] My younger brother!" She kept saying that.[14]

But the girl herself wept. She said: "I tried in vain to tell you. My uncle's wife sounds like a man when she urinates, not like a woman. You told me: 'Don't say that!' Oh! Oh! my uncle!" The girl wept.

Now I remember only that far."[15]

[6]The theme is -x-kwS-it 'to be in bed', used in this construction as a euphemism analogous to English "go to bed." Here -kwS is preceded by ga-, apparently as an intensifier. In Wishram ga- and da- appear before other stem elements marking direction and contribute the sense of "fast motion." 'In bed' as a location is here marked explicitly (wi-lxámit-ba). Hence the choice of 'lie together' in quotation marks as translation.

[7]Same theme as in note 6, but without intensifying ga-. In the second occurrence -S-gm- indicates close beside each other (or beside some implied object with dual prefix S-), not beside 'it' (the fire) as in the first translation. Such a form would have -a-gm, in concord with the prefix of wa-tuL 'fire'.

[8]The form S-x-l-ú-yE-m seems literally to contain -y(a) 'to come, go', and continuative suffix -m, so that in virtue of u- 'direction away', it means 'those two are going together', an apparent analogue to the English sexual idiom "to come." The concrete idiom heightens the scene.

[9]Literally, either 'she saw it (i-)', presumably the bed (wi-lxamit), or 'she saw him (her uncle) where the two were lying down at'.

[10]Perhaps to be translated as 'she looked at it thus' with accompanying gesture to indicate the raising of the light. In Wishram iwi may mean 'thus' and the verb stem -q'wma suggests a diminutive form of -quma 'to look'. (The form -q'wma is not itself attested in Wishram.)

[11]In his (ya-) bed, not merely "the" bed.

[12]A change of tense is signaled by n- . . . t-.

[13]The verb in the reference indicates that long objects stand in a line. The noun is paralleled in Wishram by a form meaning 'a hardwood arrow forepiece, now also one of copper', or 'ornaments of tin, funnel-shaped, tied to belt, saddle'. Presumably the Clackamas expression characterizes the value of the house posts in terms of ornamentation by objects of some such sort.

[14]With intransitive -kim, continuative-repetitive -niL, perfective -Ck.

[15]A similar phrase occurs in a few other places in the collection. Notice the absence of a concluding formula, e.g., k'ani k'ani.

First Interpretation

Most aspects of the myth are noticed in the interpretative discussion (Jacobs 1960:238–42), but the focus of attention can be said to be upon three themes. These are the implications of (1) transvestitism and "the horror reaction to homosexuals" (Ibid.:239); (2) the "wife" and the "society's tense feelings about females" (including the girl) (Ibid.:241); (3) tensions, and norms of conduct, among in-laws. The analysis concludes: "The myth is, in short, a drama whose nightmarish horror theme, murder of one's own kin by a sexually aberrant person who is an in-law, causes profound fear and revulsion as well as deep sympathy. The tension around in-laws is basic to the plot. Several implied moral lessons (one should not marry a wife in such a manner; one should not speak disparagingly of in-laws and others' sexual intimacy; one should heed one's daughter) somewhat relieve the awfulness of conflict with dangerous in-laws" (Ibid.:242).

In terms of narrative action the fabric of the myth is said to be woven about the man and his shocking death (Ibid.:239). The death itself is taken as motivated by the humiliation caused the "wife," who must avenge herself on a family whose daughter has cast aspersions upon her manner of urinating, that is (it is inferred) upon her sexuality (Ibid.:241–42).

Form of the myth

On this view of the basis of the plot one might expect murder to be followed by steps for revenge, as indeed commonly would have been the case in the aboriginal culture and as occurs in some other Clackamas myths (*e.g.*, "Black Bear and Grizzly Woman and their sons"). The absence of any indication of such steps in the final scene is suggested as one reason for thinking the present form of the myth to be truncated.

Significance of actors

Little is said in the myth about any of the four actors (as is typical of Clackamas literature). Their nature and significance, on which the meaning of the myth turns, must be largely inferred from the action that symbolically manifests them in the text, from an understanding of the culture, and from assumptions with which one approaches all these. Having observed (Ibid.:241) that "The drama provides no clear-cut delineations of characters," the first interpretation proceeds to find the significance of the three actors through their identification with social roles: "Seal is nothing more than mother and the older sister of the murdered man. He is only a rich gentleman who marries in a manner which occurred solely in the Myth Age and which symbolizes tensions between in-laws. The daughter is no more than a girl who possesses

insight as to other girls, but she is not mature enough to know when to keep
from saying things that might cause trouble with in-laws" (Ibid.). The expressions "nothing more," "only," "no more" are in keeping with a view that
subordinates all three actors in importance.

Seal's relative insignificance is further indicated in expressions such as
"Seal does little more than . . ." (Ibid.) and "all that Seal does in the myth
as recorded is to . . ." (Ibid.), as well as in the explanation, regarding the myth's
Clackamas title, that "The only reason for naming Seal is to provide a convenient labeling of the myth" (Ibid.:239).

The statement that the fabric of the myth is woven about the husband
and his murder claims little place for him other than as a silent victim.

Seal's daughter receives more attention, but, as the preceding quotation
has shown, essentially as a type labeled "youngest smartest," expressing underlying social tensions. Commenting on the girl as "youngest smartest,"
Jacobs suggests: "Chinooks appear to have thought, in effect, 'Set a young
thief to catch an old thief! Both are feminine!' The society's tense feelings
about females receive nice expression in this plot" (Ibid.: 241). With regard
to her place in the narrative action, the daughter is regarded as having im-
maturely elicited the murder. Her conduct in the last scene is not discussed,
except in the context of the speculation as to the absence of steps for revenge: "The daughter offers only, 'I warned you but you would not listen to
me' " (Ibid.).

The "wife" is interpreted most pointedly in terms of the projection of
tensions and fears found to underlie the myth. The view of her and her
importance is shown in the continuation of the passage about delineation of
characters: "The murderess is both an anxiety-causing in-law and a female who
hates. Such hate is symbolized by the murder. The cause of the hate is pointed
to by the device of having her masquerade so as to appear feminine, while the
sound of her urinating reveals masculinity" (Ibid.). (The sexual identification
intended in the passage is unclear to me: the "wife" is referred to both as a
female and as masquerading so as to appear feminine. Perhaps a hermaphro-
dite is envisaged.)

Clearly the "wife" is found to be the most significant actor. Of the rest,
the girl seems to be most important, judging from the comment about her.
The husband's role as victim might claim the next place for him. Seal is clearly
considered less important than the "wife" and the girl, perhaps least important
of all. This relative order of significance is confirmed by the order in which
the actors are taken up in the passages quoted above; the discussion seems to
proceed from least (Seal) to most significant (the "wife").

The first interpretation of the myth may be summarized as follows. The
myth is in theme based on tensions concerning females and in-laws, expressed
in terms of ambiguous and insulted sexuality. In plot its conflict is based on
relations between in-laws; its climax is caused by the girl's rude speech to an
in-law; and its denouement is incomplete from absence of steps towards

revenge against in-laws. In significance the actors are first of all the "wife," then the girl, the husband, and Seal. Together these strands form a consistent whole; indeed, to a great extent they mutually imply each other.

Second Interpretation

The volume containing the first interpretation is self-sufficient, containing a plot summary with each analysis. Having read it, if one goes back to the Clackamas text, one is somewhat surprised. Each scene is actually a confrontation between Seal and the girl; the "wife" barely appears on stage and has no lines whatever. Interpersonal tension is portrayed, not with regard to an in-law, but between two consanguineal relatives, a mother and daughter.

Such a discrepancy between interpretation and manifest verbal action gives pause. It need not, of course, be decisive. Myths have latent meanings not immediately given in surface structure. It ought to be possible, however, to specify the nature of the connection between the underlying and the manifest dimension of a myth; and it ought to be possible to do this in a way consistent with the nature of such connections in other myths of the same culture. To do this for the first interpretation does not seem possible. Rather, the various lines of evidence available combine to support a different interpretation of the focus of the myth, one for which the discrepancy with manifest structure does not arise, and one which is consistent with a provisional theory of the structuring of much of Chinookan myth as a whole.

Among the lines of evidence are the naming of actors in titles and myths; the structure of myth titles; the relation of myth titles to the body of a myth; the comparative evidence as to the tale type in question; verbal detail, particularly with regard to what is actually presented in Clackamas, over expression of emotion, and a thread of imagery. In the use of the evidence there is a fundamental assumption: that genre embodies a coherent treatment of features and relations, so that the parallels, contrasts, and covariation as between myths can be brought to bear.

In developing the second interpretation it will be best to reverse the order adopted for presenting the first and to begin with questions of structure having to do with the nature of the actors, their roles, and their relative import. Most of the evidence will be introduced in this connection. We shall then be able to reconsider the form of the myth and some new dimensions of its underlying theme.

Titles and named actors

For the first interpretation, titles are to be explained by a need for unmistakable identification of each myth; a particular title is chosen solely with an eye to mnemonic use and convenience of reference (Jacobs

1959b:258, 260; 1960:239). It is suggested that Seal is named in the title of the present myth because she is its only named actor, and because, there being no other myths in which she occurs that bear her name, no confusion could arise.

Such an approach assumes that facts as to names and titles are adventitiously, not structurally, related to myths. One may indeed expect what is found to be important in a myth to be named and represented in its title. Thus Jacobs raises the question as to why the man, who with his murder is found to form the myth's fabric, is not named. If Seal is named and takes pride of place in the title, although an actor of no particular importance, then significance of role, so it would seem, can have nothing to do with the matter. A name is only a convenient peg on which to hang a story, the title only a convenient tag by which to recall it.

In contrast, I maintain that names and titles are structurally motivated, and give evidence of underlying relations implicitly grasped by the makers of the literature. To claim descriptive adequacy, an analysis must formulate a hypothesis that accounts for the facts as to a myth's names and titles. Such facts can disconfirm an interpretation.

The basis for this approach to Chinookan myths was developed first with regard to Kathlamet Chinook. The first insight had to do with the stem -k'ani, which occurs in the formal close of many Clackamas and Kathlamet myths, and which regularly occurs in Kathlamet myth titles together with the name of an actor. The aboriginal range of meaning of -k'ani is variously translated into English as 'myth character; nature; customary traits, habits, ways'. In effect, "the title of a myth singles out from the set of supernatural dramatis personae one or two whose ways, innate nature (-k'ani), perhaps ultimate contribution to mankind, are to be defined by being exhibited in the action of the myth. The titled actor need not be the initiator of the myth's action, nor the protagonist. Often enough, the initiator or protagonist is an anonymous human [. . .]. The title directs attention to the moral rather than to the action, protagonist, or scene. In general, the telling of myths was an act of pedagogy, of cultural indoctrination, and it is in terms of this goal that the titles were selected" (Hymes 1959:143). Generally the first or only named actor of two is the focus of the myth's attention.

If the Clackamas title: "Seal Woman and her younger brother dwelt there" is taken seriously in the way just indicated, the first interpretation is turned on its head. What had seemed the least important figure (Seal) becomes most important. Can such an interpretation actually be sustained? In point of fact, the title can be shown to be motivated in relation to the myth. Such a hypothesis makes coherent sense of the manifest structure of the myth, and of its place in a series of myths, leading to a new understanding of its theme. To show this we must reconsider the evidence as to the nature of the plot.

The plot: The girl's culpability

We have seen that on the first interpretation the conflict central to the plot is one between in-laws, expressed by a climax (murder) caused by the girl's rude speech with regard to the "wife." In point of fact, the girl does not cause the murder.

Notice first that the girl's culpability must be localized in the first scene. In the second scene, the murder is already under way, if not complete. What she says is in response to evidence of the murder (the dripping); it cannot be its cause.

Notice second that the mother's response in both the first and second scenes is of closely parallel form. She replies: *"ák'waSka!"* (Do not say that), followed by a phrase which begins with specification of "your uncle." (In the first scene it is "your-uncle his-wife," in the second "your-uncle those-two-are-copulating-together.") The structural parallels suggest that both scenes make the same point, and that the focus of concern as to propriety in speech is in each case, not the "wife," but the uncle.

With regard to the first scene, the girl's culpability turns on the inference that her statements are heard by the "wife," and so provoke her to murder. If not heard, the statements could hardly provoke. Yet there is no evidence that the statements are heard by anyone ("wife" or uncle) other than the mother to whom they are explicitly addressed. That the audience for the girl's warnings is specifically the mother is indicated further by her remonstrance at the end of the myth: "I tried to tell *you* [my emphasis—D.H.] but in vain [. . .] You said to me . . . ."

The text requires no inference other than that the mother shushes the daughter because one is not supposed to speak in such a way about matters related to one's uncle's private life. As noted, this is in fact what the mother does say: "Don't say that! Your uncle + X!" There is not, for example, a premonitory "Your uncle's wife will hear you," let alone a warning as to consequences of speaking so. In this connection consider the pattern of a myth and a tale in which a younger person is indeed warned not to say something, because bad consequences will befall ("KuSaydi and his older brother," Jacobs 1959a:354–55; "A boy made bad weather," Ibid.:456). The identical shushing word (ák'waSka!) is used as is used by Seal, *and* the bad consequences (which do occur) are stated in the warning. This partial identity and partial contrast indicate that bad consequences are *not* implicit in Seal's response.

Other facts are also at variance with interpretation of the girl as culprit. The motivation of the murder is not expressed in the text. The first interpretation comments that Clackamas would have rationalized the situation by blaming the girl (Jacobs 1960:241). Not only is there no reason to consider that the girl *could* have caused the murder, as we have seen, but also there is no reason to consider that the girl *need* have caused the murder.

First, murders are not necessarily motivated in Clackamas myths. They may be taken as expressions of the intrinsic character of an actor. Jacobs, in fact, observes that the "wife" acts as do dangerous, self-appointed wives who murder in other Clackamas myths (Ibid.).

Second, the "wife" is in origin not a murderous transvestite or homosexual, but a trickster. The only known Northwest Coast parallel to the present myth consists of eight Tlingit, Haida and Tsimshian versions involving the well-known figure of Raven (equivalent to Coyote in the Chinookan area). Boas (1916:692) comments as follows: "This tale occurs in a number of distinct forms. In the Tlingit group it leads up to the tale of how Raven kills the seal and eats it—an incident which is treated independently among the southern tribes." Boas notes that the Haida versions conclude with an account of how the true character of Raven is discovered (e.g., by his tail or gait; cf. Clackamas sound of urination). A Tlingit version concluding with the killing of the husband (Seal) is abstracted as follows (Ibid.:694): "Raven goes to visit the chief of the Seals. He assumes the shape of a woman and transforms a mink into a child. The chief's son marries her [Raven]. The man goes out hunting, and on returning washes himself in the house. One day when he goes out, Raven pinches the child and makes it cry. The man hears it and returns at once. The woman remarks that this is an evil omen. At night she presses Mink on his mouth, and suffocates him; then she cries and wants him buried behind a point of land. She wails at the grave. Another man wants to marry her, and sees her sitting by the body and pecking at it. Then the people catch Raven, smoke him, and make him black." References are given also by Thompson (1929:304, no. 109). Clearly the source of the story is a typical trickster tale in which the trickster assumes woman's form to seduce a victim. (The distribution of a cognate form of the story in the Eastern Woodlands suggests that the tale is an old one; there are possible parallels in Indic and Japanese traditions. I am indebted to Alan Dundes for these observations.)

Whether the "wife" in the Clackamas myth is still essentially a trickster or has been assimilated implicitly to the role of ogre, "she" is entirely capable in Clackamas terms of compassing the death of her husband. No provocation is needed, and none is expressed.

Finally, the assignment of the girl to the "youngest smartest" type is justified precisely because she acts as do her parallels in other Chinookan myths, who sense that someone is a trickster and/or a danger. (Some of Jacobs's comments are to this effect.) It is contradictory and unparalleled to have "youngest smartest" responsible for tragedy in virtue of the very trait for which she is prized. In general, the girl's place in the myth simply is not that of a young person whose conduct has brought on catastrophe. When the Clackamas wish to make such a point in a story, they leave no doubt of it, as in "A boy made bad weather" (cited above) and other "Tales of transitional times" about children in the same collection.

The plot: Seal's culpability

It is not the girl, but Seal, whom the myth treats as culpable. Let us consider the most closely analogous myth in the Clackamas collection, that of "Crawfish and her older sister (Seal)" (Jacobs 1959a:376–79, no. 43). There are a younger and an older woman; the younger woman is troublesome by talking too much about the wrong things: she brings a disaster upon herself and her sister by doing so; she weeps; there is a speech of remonstrance. The differences, however, are instructive. Most important, the speech of remonstrance is made by, rather than to, Seal; and it is quite clear that the actor who receives the speech of remonstrance is taken as being in the wrong. If in the one case it is Crawfish, then in the myth being analyzed, it is Seal.

Recall also the significance of the structure of titles. The myths under consideration are the only two whose titles focus on Seal and a younger woman. The myth whose title is "Crawfish and her older sister" clearly exhibits the consequences of acting as did Crawfish. "Seal and her younger brother dwelt there" must be taken as exhibiting the consequences of acting as did Seal. (Furthermore, the second person identified in each title is one who suffers from the behavior of the named actor.)

The interpretation of the plot along these lines becomes especially clear when we see the situation of "Seal and her younger brother dwelt there" as part of a group of such situations in Clackamas myths. The trio of consanguineal relationships among actors, mother: mother's younger brother: mother's daughter, is in fact not isolated, but one of the recurrent patterns of relationship in Clackamas. It is found in three other myths, or a total of four of the forty-nine known to us. Let us consider the pertinent parts of the three additional myths in turn.

(1) "Grizzly Bear and Black Bear run away with the two girls" (Jacobs 1958:130–41, no. 14). The pertinent part (pp. 132–34) shows the trio and a dangerous spouse as well, this time a male (Grizzly). The wife he has obtained has borne two children, first a girl, then a boy. Four times the mother and her daughter go root-digging. Three times the girl urges her mother to hurry back home, but the mother will not do so; when they do return, the girl strikes her Grizzly brother and is stopped by the mother. The fourth time the girl forces the mother to return earlier, and proves (by forcing a still uneaten toe from the young Grizzly's mouth) that the Grizzlies, the younger one taking the lead, have killed and eaten the mother's four younger brothers, as each came in turn.

The myth as a whole has to do with complex relations between Grizzly nature and human identity, and the portion dealing with the consanguineal trio is not expressed in the title. The situation itself, however, is quite fully parallel to that of the Seal myth. The roles of the consanguineal trio relative to each other are quite the same, and there is no doubt but that the girl is correct in attempting to avert calamity, nor that the mother, by failing to respond, bears a responsibility for the deaths of her younger brothers. Indeed, as a direct parallel, this portion of the Grizzly myth might be said to clinch matters. There is something to be learned, however, by considering other myths as well.

(2) "Cock Robin, his older sister and his sister's daughter" (Jacobs 1959a:301–10, no. 31). The pertinent part (31A) shows only the consanguineal trio. The older sister instructs Cock Robin to bake roots for his niece (her daughter) when she cries; when the girl cries, he misrepeats the instruction to himself and bakes her instead, burning her to death. His sister returns to find him crying. He explains that he had done as told. She explains the actual instructions, and he replies that he had not comprehended.

Here the roles of the consanguineal trio relative to each other are changed. It is the younger brother who does not respond adequately to what is told, the older sister (and mother) who gives the information for dealing with a situation, and the daughter who suffers consequences. Such a change is extremely telling, however, for the structure of the title changes accordingly. The overt order, as between this myth and that of Seal, differs: here, younger brother, older sister, daughter; there, older sister, (daughter), younger brother. (The first sentence of the Seal myth introduces the actors with the daughter between the other two.) The functional order is the same:

Culpable actor: Advising actor: Victim

Thus, the two myths so far considered show one an exact parallel and one an exact covariation in support of the second interpretation of the role of Seal.

A Semantic Field of Myth Situations and Actors

The remaining myth having a situation involving the same consanguineal trio opens up a larger series, one which is in effect a small semantic field, or typology, of Clackamas myth situations and actors.

(3) The myth is "Blue Jay and his older sister" (Jacobs 1959a:366–69, no. 41). Jacobs describes the latter part of the myth (which is a series of similar episodes) as garbled (the myth having been the first dictation taken from his informant), but the initial episode (41A), which is the only one showing the consanguineal trio as a whole, is clear. His elder sister speaks to Blue Jay in jest. He responds as if the statement were an instruction and copulates in the sweathouse with a corpse. The girl (his niece) hears him laughing and tells her mother. (Copulation is associated with laughter among the Indians of the area.) Her mother considers the information, gives it a polite explanation, and cautions the girl not to go to the place ("ák'waSga"). The girl, noticing a foot sticking out from the sweathouse, goes to it anyway, pulls, and when the foot comes off, takes it to her mother. Blue Jay's older sister now runs, discloses the corpse inside the sweathouse, and tells Blue Jay to put it back, which he does.

The roles of the consanguineal trio relative to each other are the same as in the previous myth of Cock Robin, except for one notable fact: no injury is done to any of them (in particular, not to the girl). This myth might thus seem to count against, or be an exception to, the analysis given so far. The fact is that it, together with the other myths just discussed, is not an exception, but takes its place as a part of a larger set.

The existence of such a set was discovered by use of the method described by Lévi-Strauss (1963c: 16):

(1) define the phenomenon under study as a relation between two or more terms, real or supposed;

(2) construct a table of possible permutations between these terms;

(3) take this table as the general object of analysis.

The two terms from which the series is generated must obviously be defined in a way appropriate to the myth of Seal and her younger brother with which we have begun. If we consider the myth from the standpoint of Seal, she is seen to uphold a social norm (as to propriety of speech) at the expense of heeding and making adequate response to her daughter's attempts to inform her. Generalizing, we may say that the opposition is one between maintenance of formal expectations, general social roles, proprieties, on the one hand, and the heeding of or appropriate response to information about a particular empirical situation, on the other. If we summarize the two terms of the relation as the maintenance of two types of conduct and rationality, that of SOCIAL NORM, and that of EMPIRICAL SITUATION, each term can readily be seen as capable of two values. For SOCIAL NORM, the values are (+) *Upheld,* and (—) *Violated.* For EMPIRICAL SITUATION, the values are (+) *Adequate response,* and (—) *Inadequate response.* The possible permutations give rise to a series:

	1	2	3	4
SOCIAL NORM	+	+	—	—
EMPIRICAL SITUATION	+	—	+	—

Table 8–1. Four types of conduct and outcome

Of the myths containing the consanguineal trio in question, the first three (those of Seal, Grizzly, Cock Robin) are all of the type 2 (+—). The case with regard to Seal has just been stated above. In the Grizzly myth the mother persists in her responsibility to provide food (replying to the girl: "Go dig roots!," and: "We will be bringing nothing back" (if we return now) (Jacobs 1953:132, 133). The urging of her daughter and the daughter's strange behavior on returning home give her plenty of indication that something is wrong; but until actually forced by the daughter, she will not give up root-digging to return in time to encounter the physical evidence which (by convention of the myth) is the only way she can be told exactly what is wrong. (A situation of the general type [+—] also occurs with regard to the headsman at the end of the myth [Jacobs 1958:140–41], when he disastrously ignores his children's warning of the changing nature of the wife who has come to him.) In the Cock Robin myth Cock Robin perseveres in following his sister's instructions but without having understood what the particular instructions are and at the expense of the obvious consequences to be anticipated by so persevering. (The text makes clear that the misunderstanding of two similar words (more similar morphophonemically even than phonemically) is involved: *a-m-(a)-a-l-Ci-ya* 'you*(m)* will *(a . . . ya)* bake *(Ci)* it *([a])* for *(l)* her *(a)*': *a-m-(a)-u-Si-ya* 'you *(m)* will *(a . . . . ya)* bake *(Ci)* her *([a])*'.

In the myth of "Blue Jay and his older sister," there is no question of Blue Jay upholding social norms. Throughout Clackamas mythology he is variously cruel, thievish, stupid, a buffoon, and the like. Given that he also (as in all the episodes of the myth in question) responds incorrectly to what he is told to do at the expense of the obvious empirical consequences, the myth focused upon him as first-named character must be taken as being of type 4 (— —). (The situation is somewhat different as between this myth and the last. Cock Robin mistakes an actual word, and his sister explains to him what had actually been said; Blue Jay mistakes the import of words actually used [in the Clackamas version], as indicated by his sister's use of the introductory expression *"wiska pu"* and her admonishing use of *"dnuCi"* [not ever]; she explains to him how what was said should have been taken. In this respect Blue Jay violates a social norm as to speech.) "Skunk was a married man" (Jacobs 1958:179–80, no. 19) is a similar case. Skunk does not hunt as he should. When he does, he mistakes one homonym in his wife's complaint for another and brings back, not BREAST of deer, but his own pulled TEETH.

Other instances of type 4 (— —) are found in "She deceived herself with milt" (Jacobs 1959a:348–50, no. 39) and "KuSaydi" (Ibid.:350–65, no. 40). In the first a woman persists in insulting another woman whose (magically obtained) husband she has stolen, despite warning to desist, and in consequence she loses the husband. In the latter part of the second myth (Ibid.:365 *sq.*) the murderous hero KuSaydi insists upon eating something against which he has been warned by both his older brother and the woman preparing it; he dies in consequence, and his older brother pronounces that it shall be so for all killers. In both cases, thus, a person who has not observed social norms (mate-stealing, murder) fails to heed sufficient warning and suffers the consequences. (The case is the same with Fire's great-grandsons at the end of the myth of "Fire and his son's son" [Jacobs 1959a:129] and with Grizzly in the myth of "Grizzly Bear and Black Bear ran away with the two girls." The actors in question participate in murder, fail to heed warnings, and die in consequence.)

Type 1 (+ +) is not common in the Clackamas collection. I suspect that myths told aboriginally by males might have had more examples of male heroes to whom the type would apply. We find it here in "Coyote and his son's son and their wives" (Jacobs 1958:19–20, no. 2), wherein Coyote acts to maintain social propriety and heeds his grandson's information and advice (not without some intervening humor before the correct outcome for the cultural period is laid down). In "Black Bear and Grizzly Woman and their sons" (Jacobs 1958:143–56, no. 16) Black Bear's sons behave, especially the named hero Wasgúkmayli, responsibly, heed their mother's advice, and later Crane's, and succeed both in avenging her and outwitting Grizzly Woman. In "Greyback Louse" (Jacobs 1959a: 334–40, no. 36) the youngest Grizzly behaves well toward Meadow Lark, heeds her advice, and succeeds in outwitting and transforming Greyback Louse so that she shall not kill people, only bite them.

Type 3 (— +) is represented by the title character of "Crawfish and her older sister" (Ibid.:376–79, no. 43). While Crawfish misbehaves, she does respond properly to the consequent situation and her sister's instructions. The outcome is that the relation between the two is dissolved (at which Crawfish weeps), but without personal tragedy; each takes on its appropriate nature for the cultural period that is to come, and that of Crawfish is positively valued, as beneficial to mankind. (The second portion of the Cock Robin myth might invite the same interpretation, given its outcome with regard to him, which is quite parallel to that of Crawfish; but as he has both misbehaved [stealing fish and not sharing food with his siblings] and ignored opportunity to behave correctly, the outcome is rather a matter of "just desserts" [— —], modulated from incipient death by burning [cf. the fate of Grizzly] to transformation depriving him forever of what he had misappropriated.)

In "Seal took them to the ocean" the protagonist Seal Hunter has behaved meanly to his elder brother, but during the course of the adventures underwater consistently heeds Seal's advice, so that he and his fellows survive each test. They do not, however, return wealthy from their encounter with the supernatural, but poor (Jacobs 1958:226); later they become transformed. Notice that the otherwise puzzling outcome (Ibid.:290, no. 226) of the one brother, Seal Hunter, being poor, fits his place as protagonist in the semantic field being analysed (— +).

In other myths the people at the end of "Tongue" (Ibid.: 369–75, no. 52) and the wife (Sun) at the end of "The Basket Ogress took the child" (Ibid.:388–409, no. 46) fit the type. Misbehavior (insult in the one case, disobeying instructions in the other) is complemented by effort at correction ("Tongue") and positive deeds ("The Basket Ogress took the child"), with the result a mixed outcome in which actors are separated and transformed into the identities they will have in the cultural period.

A set of situations belonging to this type occurs when a series of girls come to obtain a husband (improper behavior) and are killed except for the fifth and last, who receives and follows the advice of Meadow Lark, and so saves herself ("Snake Tail and her son's sons" [Ibid.: 194–99, no. 24]; "Awl and her son's son" [Ibid.: 226–41, no. 27]). In each the youngest girl weeps at the fate of her older sisters, but also puts an end to the danger (pronouncing that snakes will not kill people in the cultural period to come in the one case, returning Awl from temporary identity as a dangerous being to status as an inanimate object again in the other).

The contrasting values of the four types can be rather clearly seen. When social norm is observed, and when advice and circumstances are properly heeded, events come out as they should for the actors concerned and for the future state of the world (the cultural period in which the people will have come) (Type 1, + +). When social norm is observed at the expense of heeding an empirical situation, the result is death and even tragedy (Type 2, + —). When social norm is violated, but advice and circumstances are properly responded to, the outcome is mixed (Type 3, — +). There is an ingredient of misfortune but it is not unrelieved. When social norm has not been observed, the consequences of not heeding advice and circumstances are effectively "just desserts" (Type 4, — —).

Second Interpretation (Resumed)

Significance of actors

The manifest action of the myth, and a view of the structural role of titles, led to the hypothesis that the myth expressed first of all the nature *(-k'ani)*, not of someone acting like the "wife," but of someone acting like Seal. Analysis of the place of the main actors in a larger series of myths and myth situations has confirmed the hypothesis. The leading theme of the myth is the conduct of Seal. The behavior of the girl is not a device to express the horror of an ambiguously sexed and hateful "female" in-law, but rather, an ambiguous "female" is a device to express the failure of a proper woman to relate to a danger threatening one she should protect. The myth uses a stock villain to dramatize a relationship subtler than villainy. The female figure whose nature is focused upon in the title and disclosed in the action is not one who is feared for her violation of social norms but one who is too fearful in her keeping of them.

The girl shares the stage with Seal, and as primary protagonist and most expressively characterized actor, ranks almost equal to her. (Her significance will be brought out further in the sections immediately following.) Although largely passive, the younger brother is important for the relationship identified in the title, and as object of the mourning of both Seal and the girl. He is the one whose fate exemplifies the nature of the actor the title first names. Notice, on this account, that he is presumably not homosexual. The trickster origin of the "wife" indicates that her female form is the result of transformation, not transvestitism or hermaphroditism, and that the urinating with the sound of a man is simply a clue to essential identity parallel to such clues in other

North Coast analogues. It is indeed a difficulty with the first interpretation that a horror reaction to homosexuals should implicate the younger brother and uncle who is the object of the women's great concern. On the second interpretation the difficulty disappears, together with any significance of the "wife" as a focus of homosexual fears. The horror of the second scene is not the copulation, nor the murder (which is committed off-stage and never stated as occurring), but its discovery, and the retrospective realization of what has preceded its discovery, the enormous disparity between the reality of danger and Seal's response. As observed, the "wife" is significant only as a means of dramatizing the relations among the other three via the husband, as is shown by the fact that the denouement is one, not of revenge toward "her," but of grief for him. In the myth as we have it, "she" is least important, a mechanical villain.

Dialectics of actors

A further richness of this short myth can be found by utilizing a second method demonstrated by Lévi-Strauss. It is that in which a myth is understood in terms of a progression from an initial proposition through a succession of mediating terms (Lévi-Strauss 1963b:224). I am not able to provide an analysis precisely comparable to those achieved by Lévi-Strauss, but if one asks, what in the present myth answers to the form of the method, further insight emerges.

An initial opposition is given in the title of the myth. It is Seal: younger brother. A development of the initial pair in the form of a triad is given in the introductory sentence of the myth, which presents Seal, her daughter, her younger brother, in that order.

Several aspects of the relationship suggest themselves. Seal and her younger brother are both adult, but the one is female, socially responsible (as elder sibling and mother), and sexually experienced, while the other is male, not yet socially responsible (as younger sibling and bachelor), and as yet sexually inexperienced, although eligible for such experience. The girl is female, like her mother, but sexually inexperienced, like her uncle. She is, I would suggest, attentive both to the claims of social responsibility, such as her mother should show toward her (the mother's) younger brother, and of sexual maturity, such as her uncle embarks upon. Hence she may be seen as an appropriate potential mediator between what Seal and Seal's younger brother respectively express.

As we know, the girl's efforts are to fail. The myth develops in two scenes which present now the girl and her mother as the opposing terms. Between them in each are posed middle terms which are not so much mediational as ambivalent, ambiguous, susceptible of interpretation in the light of either of two prior concerns. The first is the "wife," presented as a bundle of two features: a socially proper role, that of "your uncle's wife," and a behaviorally incongruous fact, that of urinating with a sound like that of a man. The second is the dripping from the uncle's bed. As a result of marital copulation, it is socially proper and not to be noticed. As a signal of danger, it is, as it proves to be, evidence of a murder. In each case the mother explains away in terms of social propriety what the girl has seized upon as experiential fact.

The final scene has also a triad, but perhaps only in narrative form. The girl remonstrates and mourns, then her mother mourns, then again the girl. Structurally there seems no middle term, unless it is the death to which each woman responds in character, but independently. Having remonstrated, the girl ends weeping alone; the mother ends repeating a formula.[16] The dialogue

---

[16]Notice that hitherto the speech acts of the two acts had been designated by the inherently transitive stem -lxam (rendered always 'told' in the revised translation). The mother's words in the denouement are introduced and concluded, and the last words of the girl are introduced, with the inherently intransitive verb stem -kim (always rendered 'said'). Choice of verb stem thus marks the final isolation of each speaker, speaking without addressee.

[Postscript, 9 July 1980]. While editing the manuscript for publication in this volume, I have been struck by the possibility that the syntactic contrast between -lxam and -kim, that of transitive versus intransitive, is not the whole story. True, -lxam requires a pronominal object as well as subject in the verb, and -kim can never have a pronominal object. This formal contrast, I now think, involves a subtler semantic contrast as well. Consider the name of the 'crier' or morning orator, i-ya-gi-xím-niL (see chap. 3). The root -xim- is an allomorph of -kim, the initial consonant being weakened between vowels, perhaps because preceding a stressed vowel (unlike ig-í-kim 'he said'). The stem consists of a nominalizing prefix with probably agentive implication, qi-; the root 'to say, speak'; and the repetitive suffix -niL. The prefix preceding the stem -ya- is the regular form of the third-person–masculine-singular possessive. The translation is literally something like 'his repeated saying' or 'the one who speaks regularly'.

Now it would be strange to impute irony to the name of an important traditional role, as if the Wishram and Wasco had intentionally named the morning orator as someone without audience: "the one who speaks regularly, to no one." The name of the morning orator makes sense if the speaking is understood as being not without audience but broadcast. The speaking is not targeted to a specific auditor or auditors; the speaker and auditor do not constitute a precise set.

This interpretation of -kim/-xim fits a semantic contrast that is pervasive in Chinookan, although often implicit. The contrast is explicit with the plural suffixes of nouns: -maX, like -kim, is appropriate in cases in which a plurality of things is distributed about, not constituting a definite, defined set; -kS is appropriate in cases in which a plurality is such a set. Cows (dispersed grazing) generally take -maX, and horses (carefully kept together) -kS.

On the new interpretation, the contrast between "intransitive" -kim/-xim and "transitive" -lxam is parallel to the contrast between distributive -maX and collective, set-like, -kS. 'To say' (-kim) is to speak broadcast, with or without auditors; 'to tell' (-lxam) is to speak to a specified addressee, speaker and addressee(s) forming a set. The distinction probably lies behind Philip Kahclamet's statement (chap. 3, p. 118): "I didn't just hear it. She told me the story."

In lamenting her younger brother, then, Seal is speaking broadcast without definite audience. The second occurrence of the root -kim, indeed, has the repetitive suffix -niL. The somewhat inceptive force of the final suffix -Ck adds a connotation of definitely beginning at that point. A literal translation of this second, and final, verb associated with Seal, na-gím-niL-Ck, might be something like 'she began to repeat saying', 'She started to repeat saying'. In remonstrating, Seal's daughter continues to address her mother as part of a dyad, with ga-ǵ-(a)-ú-lxam 'she (g-) told (-lxam) her ([a])'; but after the mother's lament, her second remonstrance is also without definite

is dissolved, and with it the possibility of resolution of the opposition of the underlying terms.

In outline form, we have:

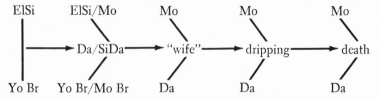

Given this formal development, what are we to make of it? In one sense, of course, it is another way of stating the place of the myth in the semantic field indicated above. In another sense, the dialectical form draws attention to implications of the myth that are matters not only of a place in a larger series, but also of individual qualities of imagery, tone, and expressive detail. In general, the structure and theme of the myth are as has been stated. In particular, they are something more.

Imagery

If the imagery of the myth had not been attended to before, the position of the dripping, correlative to that of the actors, would demand attention to it. In point of fact, three strands of imagery are interwoven in this brief narrative. The first is one of light: darkness in a relation like that of figure to ground. All the dramatized action takes place at night (they 'go out' at night to urinate; of the second scene the narrator remarks, before mentioning copulation: "I do not know what time of night it was. . . ."). Darkness is to be presumed. As the climax is realized, the visual setting changes correlatively: the girl rises, fixes the fire, and lights pitch. When she looks by that light into her uncle's bed to discover the dripping from it to be his blood, the moment is quite literally one of truth, and light the appropriate symbol of its acquisition.

The second strand of imagery sets off the two main actors in terms of experience of wetness, on the one hand, and of speech exclusively, on the other. Each major scene involves the girl in experience of something having a liquid aspect: the "wife's" urination; the uncle's blood; her own tears. These sensory experiences are specific to the girl. The mother hushes report of the first two and speaks, as against the girl's tears, in the last scene. Seal's relationship to speech is patently symbolic of social propriety. I suggest that the girl's

---

auditor, being introduced as *n(a)-a-gim-X* 'she *(a-)* said *(gim)* habitually *(-X)'*. If broadcast, then the effect is like saying "for anyone who might hear." Within the myth, there is no one. Within the setting of the performance of the myth, there would be an audience, now including ourselves, who even if unaddressed, could take the words to heart.

relationship to wetness expresses a different mode of experience, one in part at least sexual. (Compare, too, the concreteness of the girl's experience of urination, copulation, and ejaculation as against the euphemistic expression of each in ordinary Clackamas terms.)

The third strand of imagery focuses on the girl. She HEARS the urination. She then hears, but first FEELS, what drips down (on her face). At the climax she SEES blood. In the denouement she herself PRODUCES tears. I suggest that this sequence of modes of sensory experience (hearing, feeling, seeing, weeping) progresses from the more passive and remote to the more active and immediate (indeed, internally caused). Quite literally, in bringing light into the darkness, the girl has been brought to a knowledge of blood and death. The final weeping represents full assumption of the mode of experience symbolized.

Tone and expressive detail

The tone and expressive detail of the narration confirm the imagery in pointing to a special concern with the figure of the girl, contrasted to that of the mother. Her effort to prevent tragedy is heightened in the second scene by the detail that not only does she warn her mother verbally, but first shakes her. The intensification of the confrontation between the two is heightened on the mother's side by the fact that she does not immediately respond with *"ák'wáSka!"*, as in the first scene, but with *"mmmmm,"* as if hesitating or considering before deciding how to interpret the information as to dripping, and by the modulation of the hushing word, here occurring without exclamation mark.

The denouement, one of the finest in Clackamas literature is, within its terse conventions not only well prepared for, but also highly dramatized as a contrast between the girl and mother that reaches into the verbal particulars of the lament of each. Seal exclaims: "Younger brother! My younger brother! They [his house posts] are valuable standing there. My younger brother!" The myth adds: "She kept saying that." There is a touch of personal feeling in the directness of the first word, the uninflective vocative *(awi)* before the inflected term of reference (correspondingly used also by the girl). The statement as to the house posts may heighten the scene, showing the death to have been that of a rich and important man (as Jacobs observes[17]); it also suggests that concern for social position dominates. We know from another myth (Jacobs 1959a:408) that a formal lament was proper at the death of someone. With Seal we seem to have here almost exclusively that, although repeated and repeated, in an implicit state of shock.

---

[17] The verb in the reference indicates that long objects stand in a line. The noun is paralleled in Wishram by a form meaning 'a hardwood arrow forepiece, now also one of copper', or 'ornaments of tin, funnel-shaped, tied to belt, saddle'. Presumably the Clackamas expression characterizes the value of the house posts in terms of ornamentation by objects of some sort.

In its brevity and social reference Seal's lament sets in relief the extended laments of the girl that enclose it. Her first lament is the myth's longest speech, and an unusually long speech for any Clackamas myth. Its emotion is indicated in part by the adding of explicit reference to the urination like a man. (The precise words for "man-like" and "she urinated" are added here to the expression for "go out" with a sound like *tL'a* found in the first scene. Jacobs translates the two occurrences of the former addition "exactly [like]" and "just [like]" to convey that the use of the explicit term is forcefully expressive.)

The girl mingles remonstrance with remorse, throws back *"ák'waSka"* at her mother, and weeps. After Seal's lament, it is said: "But the girl herself wept." She repeats her remorse in heightened form, adding "in vain" *(kinwa)*, and ends with the kinship term preceded by a particle openly stating her emotion: *"áná* my uncle! *áná* my uncle!" (In Wishram the particle is glossed as expressing 'grief, pain, pity, remorse'.) Jacobs has observed that direct linguistic statement of grief is rare in Clackamas literature. Notice moreover that the use of the particle is modulated; first it is doubly stressed, then singly (Jacobs translates: "Oh! Oh!", then: "Oh!"), as if the words are descending into the tears that follow. It is only the girl who weeps, and it is with her weeping that the myth ends.

It is difficult to imagine a reading that does not find the denouement, like the scenes leading to the climax, a fabric woven about a character contrast between mother and girl, a contrast of which the girl is implicitly the heroine.

The role of women and the form of the myth

The myth, in short, has something more of significance as to feeling about women than its disclosure of Seal. To be sure, the girl is in part Cassandra in the first scene, part Greek chorus in the last. Her role fits the part of "youngest smartest," and represents as well the "immobilism," as Jacobs terms it (1959b:169–72) prescribed for Clackamas women—the expectation that women are not to take the lead and, although not passive, are to act through men if men in the correct social relationship are present. The girl can be seen to act properly by not going to the uncle herself, but by trying to act through the only proper intermediary available to her, her mother, the uncle's older sister. Her discovery of the murder, when all has failed, may still be assigned to the "youngest smartest" role. The ending of that climax, however, on her scream, and the expressive detail and tone of the denouement suggest something more, something which is equally pointed to by the way the strands of imagery are woven about her. Over against the structural significance of Seal, there emerges something of an individual quality in the role of the girl. She seems the voice of a concern for personal loyalty as against social propriety; sensory experience as against verbal convention; personal feeling as against formal experience of grief; of an existential situation.

Was this concern aboriginal? We cannot be sure. Two points, however, can be made. First, it would be foolish to assume that a uniform literary criticism and interpretation of myth prevailed among the Clackamas, or among any other "primitive" or "tribal" community. Indeed, the persistence of interpretative differences between men and women can be documented even today. I first heard a rather widespread plot as to how Coyote tricks a girl into intercourse, from a man who enjoyed telling it to me as a man's story at the expense of women. Later a woman mentioned it as a story her grand-mother had told her to warn her against men.

An aboriginal male audience may well have had a special interest in the myth in its original form, an interest perhaps including a horror reaction to homosexuals. The myth as we have it titled and told now is testimony to the special interests of women. I myself see no reason to think that as much of the myth as we have does not tell something about the aboriginal society's feelings about females; only it does so, not from a male, but from a female standpoint.

Second, as reinterpreted as a confrontation between women, from the standpoint of women, the present myth makes sense in terms both of its history and its form. It has reached us through a line of women. (Jacobs's informant, Mrs. Howard, had her knowledge of myths from her mother-in-law and her mother's mother ["Seal and her younger brother dwelt there" from the former].[18]) I find that transmission reflected in the detail of the handling of female actors, which is often more salient and moving than the handling of male actors; in the large proportion of myths that involve significant female actors; in the recurrent use of the rather matrilineal trio of Mo, MoDa, MoBr; and in the remembrance in some cases of only that portion of myths having to do with female actors. This last point applies to "Duck was a married woman" (Jacobs 1958b:184–85, no. 21) and "Robin and her younger sister" (Jacobs 1959a:380, no. 44); and I believe it applies to "Seal and her younger brother dwelt there."

The selective retention and phrasing of tradition under acculturation by a sequence of women is reflected in the form of the present myth, not only quantitatively (how much is retained), but also qualitatively.[19] The present form of the myth is not as such incomplete; rather, it has remarkable unity.

[18]Hymes (1965b:338) inadvertently substitutes mother's mother as the source.
[19]I have not succeeded in phrasing in English the exact effect the myth conveys to me. One component of that effect is that I feel there may somehow be something implicitly expressive of the acculturation situation in the contrast so thoroughly drawn between convention and experience—as if the mother accepts, or stands for the acceptance of, the strange newcomers, the whites (called *k'ani* for their marvelous customs, and *duxnipCk* 'they come up from the water', as ones with whom one can enter into conventional reciprocal relationships (i.e., trade), and as if the girl stands for a realization that the strange ways are not only different but dangerous and will destroy them (by destroying their men, who were the main casualty of the acculturation process). But all this is speculative.

In terms of the structural analysis of the title's focus upon Seal, and of the place of that focus in a larger semantic field, the text is a complete expression. In terms of the dialectics, imagery, and expressive detail woven about the girl, the text is not only a whole, but an expression whose unity is complex and effective.

The relation of the form of the myth to women, and a girl's personal experience, has been further supported by the work of Michael Silverstein with a Wishram speaker, Mrs. Ida White, at Yakima Reservation, Washington, in August 1968. Mrs. White volunteered a related story. The setting is different, involving a brother who disguises himself as a girl to revenge his twin sister against the husband who had beaten her to death, but the scene in which the murdered man's niece experiences dripping underneath his bed is the same. When Mrs. White reached this point, she lapsed into Wishram (having spoken hitherto in English), for the word 'blood' and the girl's encounter with it. The change suggests that this point of the myth was for her inseparable from its original verbal form, or at least that here the myth awoke most strongly her own experience of, and identification with, it.

I take the possibility of explaining the form of the myth as strong support for the interpretation offered here.[20]

Concluding Remark

The second interpretation gives the myth something of an Oedipal ring. It is perhaps ironic that the Oedipal theme, which the author of the first interpretation is quick to catch in his work with Clackamas literature, here is merely mentioned in passing (Jacobs 1960:239), whereas its pursuit might have led to a quite different understanding. Again, Seal Woman is discussed elsewhere in a tenor quite compatible with the second interpretation, indeed in a way that would seem almost to imply it. Discussing the occurrence of Seal in three myths, Jacobs finds no commonality, but comments on her role in the myth in question here as that of "a woman who followed etiquette in being so circumspect and uncomprehending about perils in an in-law relationship that she did not act in time to save the life of her younger brother, whose wife decapitated him. The delineation was of a well-mannered and weak or frightened woman" (Jacobs 1958:161).

In a similar context Seal is referred to as "a woman who was so cautious about in-laws' feelings that she failed to act in time to save her brother's life" (Ibid.:162).

I had worked through my reinterpretation in relation to the text before

[20]Cf. Burke (1950:162): "The ability to treat of form is always the major test of a critical method." Burke makes the point in reference to another case in which the conclusion of a work had been regarded as without motivation in relation to the rest.

coming to these passages. Obviously the statements apply brilliantly to the myth as reinterpreted here. Equally clearly, they were lost sight of in the interpretation of the myth as a whole when its turn came in the volume devoted to interpretation of the bulk of the myths one by one (Jacobs 1960: 238–42). Indeed, the statements and the specific interpretation seem contradictory.

The methodological point would seem to be this. Despite the richness a sociopsychological perspective provides, prior reliance upon its insights can override and even conceal the import of a myth. Focus first on what is essentially at best a latent content can lead interpretation far from actual dramatic poignancy and skill.

This is not to say that structural analysis is infallible. An a priori structural approach may be as mistaken as an a priori sociopsychological one. Both may mistake the relation between the underlying form ("deep structure") and the overt form ("surface structure") of a myth. In the present case a "typological" or "morphological" approach might readily find an instance of a relation INTERDICTION: INTERDICTION VIOLATED. Some such relation is indeed present in overt form, but, as has been shown, to infer that the violator of the interdiction is the culpable party, responsible for the consequences that follow, would be an error. It would be the very error made by the first interpretation.[21] Focus first on what is at best a part of overt form, and failure to distinguish it from underlying form, can also lead interpretation astray.

In sum, a structural analysis of the features and relationships of a myth must be made, and must be made in terms specific to the genre in the culture in question.

Postscript

I first discussed the myth, briefly, in a general review of Jacobs's Clackamas Chinook work (Hymes 1965b:327–32). The first version of this paper was read at the annual meeting of the American Folklore Society, Denver, Colorado, 21 November 1965, and I should like to thank Alan Dundes, John Fischer, Archie Green, William Hugh Jansen, David Mandelbaum, Warren Roberts, John Szwed, and Francis Lee Utley for their comments. Under the title "A Chinookan rule for interpreting Chinookan myth," the paper was also

[21]Here we can see justification for speaking of "surface" and "deep" structure. Just as in syntax the nouns occupying the roles of subject and object in surface structure may have the opposite roles in deep structure (as with a passive sentence in English), so in a myth actors occupying the roles of "admonisher," or "advisor," and "violator" in surface structure can be seen to have the opposite roles in deep structure. More precisely, perhaps, the girl appears as violator, her mother as admonisher, with respect to maintenance of social norms, but as advisor and violator, respectively, with regard to empirical situation. The same overt relation thus could be taken as serving two different underlying relations.

the basis for a presentation in a symposium on "Symbol and Society," organized and chaired by David W. Crabb, and held at the annual meeting of the American Anthropological Association, Washington, D.C., 1 December 1967; I appreciate the comments there of Victor Turner and Clifford Geertz. William Labov invited me to present my analysis at a meeting of the Columbia University Seminar on Language (which he founded and of which I was a member) sometime in 1967–68, and there used the English translation as something to which to apply methods of narrative analysis of his own.

The paper has been reprinted in Maranda and Maranda (1971:49–80) and in Kristeva, Rey-Debove, and Umiker (1971:296–326). The reprintings differ somewhat in amplification of the ending of the paper. The former version has been included also in Dolgin, Kemnitzer, and Schneider (eds.) (1971:221–42). A Hebrew translation has appeared in *Ha-sifrut/Literature* 20(V/4):28–43 (April, 1975), in an issue on "New theories in oral literature: Literary forms in social context," edited by Dan Ben-Amos.

Literary uses and related versions.   A verse analysis and translation of the text has been included by Jarold Ramsey in his anthology (1977:100–101). Karl Kroeber has modified the verse translation in a prose format in his "Deconstructionist criticism and American Indian literature" (1979), where the link of the story to a trickster-transformer figure is taken up.

The literary significance of the analysis of structure in this paper has been discussed by Frank Kermode in two articles, "The structures of fiction" (1969) and "Sensing endings" (1978), and by Jarold Ramsey (1977). Ramsey treats the relation of Mrs. Howard's text to a myth of the Coos Indians of the Oregon coast, pointing out that the two texts are part of a series of related myths of revenge. Ramsey notes versions recorded among the Tillamook (Boas 1898:136–38; Jacobs and Jacobs 1959:24–28) and Alsea (Frachtenberg 1920: 141–49) of the Oregon coast north of the Coos, and the Quileute (Andrade 1931:69–71) of northwestern Washington. There is a related text from the Nootka of Vancouver Island (Sapir and Swadesh 1939:77–81, dictated to Sapir in 1913). Lévi-Strauss (1971:515–17) discusses the series in terms of the Tillamook, Alsea, and Coos versions, and also a version recorded in the Takelma language of south central Oregon (Sapir 1909b:155–63). Lévi-Strauss does not mention the Clackamas text of Mrs. Howard, probably because it must appear to be simply an incident remembered from the longer sequence, and the transformation in point of view not the kind of transformation with which he is concerned.

See also an overlooked series in Washington and British Columbia, perhaps essentially Salishan in distribution. In it two brothers rescue the wife of the older. Among the Thompson of southeastern British Columbia, Fisher and Marten disguise themselves as female relatives of the Spring Salmon, who has taken Fisher's wife (Boas 1917:23), or Marten's wife (Teit 1898:64). Their identity is suspected by their gait and way of coming down a ladder, and they cut off the Salmon's head (Ibid.:64–66). The Upper Thompson version collected by Teit and published by Boas (1917:22–25) intersects the coastal Oregon myths in that the wife to be rescued is Red-Headed-Woodpecker (p. 23), corresponding to the red-headed-woodpecker father to be rescued in the Oregon texts.

Among the Okanagan neighbors of the Thompson in British Columbia (Maud 1978a:156–59) and north central Washington (Spier 1938:209–10), the two brothers kill two boys to don their clothing as disguise in the former, but two girls in the latter. The near-discovery of their identity, as they jump ashore from a canoe, occurs in the Oregon myths as well. The Southern Okanagan version (Spier 1938) is especially close to the Takelma version in that it involves a sea monster as the one who takes the older brother's wife (the monster is the big moose with enormous horns); and it is easy to understand that the Takelma heroes are Otter brothers, given that the Okanagan heroes are the brothers Fisher and Marten: Hiram Smith of Warm Springs refers to the fisher as "dry land otter" because of its appearance. Both fisher and otter are swift, playful carnivores. All these stories end with the Fish people diving to recover the Chief's head from under water (and, among the Southern Okanagan, with a flood that causes Fisher and Marten to remain permanently in the mountains).

Among the Cowlitz Salish and Cowlitz Sahaptin of south central Washington, the older brother's wife is stolen by a dangerous being from above, Cloud, and the older brother's head cut off when he goes to seek her. The younger brother and his nephew go, encounter two girls coming in a canoe for supplies, or roots, kill them, put on their clothes; are sensed as different but not discovered; and escape with the elder brother's head and wife, setting fire to the dangerous being's house. They then restore the older brother to life. Both Cowlitz stories end with a sequel, not concerning pursuit, but a unique daughter, born to the wife after her return. She is dangerous, taking out other children's eyes, and finally goes off as a cloud. (The Sahaptin version, probably borrowed from the Salish, substitutes Panther and Wildcat for Fisher and Marten.)

A Wasco version of the story of a man disguising himself as a woman to revenge the death of his twin sister upon her husband was explained in English to Michael Silverstein and myself in August 1968 by Ida White and George Forman of Toppenish, Washington.

The link of the story to a trickster (Raven) who deceives a Seal for food is amplified by a story from the Sechelt Salish of mainland British Columbia (somewhat north of present-day Vancouver), published by Hill-Tout (1904: 51), reprinted by Maud (1978b:117), and rerecorded from another speaker by Timmers (1974:10–16). For a similar story from the Squamish Salish (neighbors of the Sechelt just north of present-day Vancouver), see Boas (1895:57; 1916:706). On this theme, see also Boas (1916:702).

An image of the discovery of a loved one's decapitated head through the dripping of blood, then the raising of a light by a woman, figures in the Tsimshian myth of Gaúo: (Boas 1916:847ff), as does the waking of a child beneath the dripping of blood (see comparative references in Ibid.: 848).

In an unpublished paper, Frances Johnson's "The Otter brothers recover their father's heart," I analyze and retranslate the Takelma text. The verse analysis and certain corrections in translation permit a placement of the Takelma text as an intersection of this series and two others; clarify the place of the myth in the present revenge series in terms of sequences of speech events; show the Takelma myth to have a two-part structure that doubles a focus on achievement of maturity by young people against untrustworthy caretakers; and suggest a more adequate framework for comparative analysis of Native American narratives. (I want to thank Martin Steinmann for an invitation to the University of Minnesota, which stimulated preparation of the paper.)

Let me add some later observations on the interpretation presented in this paper regarding the symbolic role of speech meta-narrative expressions, wider implications of the myth, and the methodological perspective of the analysis.

Speech and Bernstein's codes.   The sensory sequence that begins with the hearing of unladylike urination is, in fact, intertwined with speech throughout. At the beginning of the story it may well be the case that the mother, Seal, is not responding solely to her daughter's words, but also to her own perception of the odd sound. The text states "they went out," presumably all together. We are to understand, then, either that the mother heard the urination and did not perceive that it was odd, or perceived that it was odd and repressed the recognition or the necessity for action on the recognition. In either case, the mother's failure to respond to the empirical situation is direct (not mediated by the daughter). The daughter's words are not a report, but a call for recognition of what both had the opportunity to hear.

At the end of the story "urination" is explicitly named in the girl's speech. The naming is part of a general culmination. The sequence of sensory experience ends in the production of tears, but its climax is speech. There is something of an internal contradiction in the nàrrative between norms of speech. That is, the two dimensions, social norm and empirical situation, each have expression in terms of speaking. The mother expresses a norm of polite speech, the girl a norm of adequate, or, warranted speech. In the dissolution of dialogue in the final scene, the girl's remonstrance can be taken as reflecting both cultural judgment and the narrator's identification. The remonstrance is indeed the only sustained discourse of the text. The shushed daughter speaks the wet, bitter truth, and in so doing shows a "breakthrough into performance" (cf. chapter 3) within the myth itself. In terms of the concepts of "elaborated" and "restricted" codes developed by Basil Bernstein (1971, 1972, 1975), the mother, the voice of established order and status, maintains a restricted code throughout. Her speech is entirely in the mode Bernstein calls "positional," focused on attributes of persons in terms of social position (as in-laws, as holders of wealth, as kin formally addressed in formulaic lament). The girl, the voice of subordinate position (in terms of both age and gender), breaks through into the only elaborated coding of the myth. Her final speech is "elaborated" in Bernstein's terms, both in being in the mode Bernstein calls "personal," focused on the discretion a person may have within a prescribed role and on personal needs and desires, and in being retrospectively analytical, in being "metalinguistic" in relation to the preceding speech. As Kroeber puts it (1979:76),

> the last third of the story is retrospective lamentation, primarily the girl retelling to Seal the tale we've just been told, and in virtually the same words. We are forced, futilely, back through the girl's inability to make her words force Seal's decorousness to respond to the brute reality of an impinging physical experience, though with the vents now given an interior distance by a telling within narration.

The speaking and the weeping now seem to me to go together, the tears giving sensory, the words cognitive, embodiment to the girl's assumption of maturity. In terms of the sensory dimension of wetness, she now is a "producer" rather than recipient. In terms of knowledge, she now is the one who knows and can tell.

Meta-narrative expressions.   What is one to make of the two expressions in the Seal story translated with "I do not know"? They appear to confess an ignorance on the part of the narrator. In point of fact the expressions do not contain a personal pronoun or a negative element. The Clackamas word is the particle *Luxwan* from the root of the verb-stem 'to think', *-Luxwa-it* (with stative *-it*). Recent speakers of Wasco readily translate the particle 'I don't know', but it is literally something like an impersonal 'think' with an ending that is apparently the continuative suffix *-n*. To be thinking as to the time (or place, as in other stories sometimes) is not to have completed the thought. The specific fact, therefore, is not certain.

Within the narrative, however, the effect is not ignorance or vagueness, but a very definite indefiniteness (to use the term proposed by Michael Silverstein). The expressions in the Seal story, *Luxwan qanCiXbEt* and *Luxwan qanCix wapul,* translated respectively as 'I do not know when it was' and 'I do not know what time of night it was' in Jacobs (1959a), heighten the moment in the action by stepping momentarily outside its frame. A myth would not normally specify exact time at either point. A sufficient context has already been established. The story could proceed normally without the expression. It is as if the narrator implies such a degree of accuracy that even such a superfluous detail would be provided if available.

Analogous devices may be widely recurrent in Native American narrative. In Takelma of southwestern Oregon (Sapir 1909b), when the narrator is detailing how Coyote rushed toward the sound of nubile girls singing at their puberty dance, one finds "He hurried, he ran, How long did he not run?" In Koyukon Athapaskan of Alaska one finds in a personal narrative, "Where would I have gotten tea? I just drank water" (Noholnigee 1979:12), and "I didn't even have a gun. How would I have gotten a gun?" (Ibid.:14). In different ways the Takelma and Koyukon devices also break the frame to entertain momentarily a possibility that is not realized (that Coyote ran forever, or exactly how long Coyote ran; having tea, having a gun), a possibility that presumably the audience would not themselves consider if the narrator did not bring it to attention. The device highlights the actual event by the contrast of the momentary possibility, only to withdraw it to proceed.

In any case, the Chinookan device is "definite indefinite" against the background of a deep-seated cultural pattern that contrasts what is complete, definite, certain, "perfective," with what is incomplete, indefinite, uncertain, "imperfective" (cf. discussion in Hymes 1966a, 1975d, 1979c). This pattern appears to inform the use of meta-narrative statements in direct discourse within myths. The "breakthrough into performance" by Seal's daughter is an instance of meta-narrative speech, speech that refers to, quotes, indeed provides a precis and explanation of the narrated action. And meta-narrative statements in direct discourse in myths appear always to be certain.

Certainty of discursive speech that states explicitly the nature and content of a relationship is restricted in the traditional culture to times when that nature and content has been validated and confirmed. Such at least is the case with the sets of speech events associated with three major institutions, those of guardian spirits, personal naming, and myth itself. With each there is a period when the nature of a relationship can be indicated through quotation or allusion but not made discursively explicit. That period alternates with a time when explicit disclosure is permitted or required: before death in the case of guardian spirit experience, within the naming ceremony, through the performance of myths in the winter sacred season (see Hymes 1966a).

Notice that Seal's daughter explains to, remonstrates with, her mother after the action of the story. Similarly, when Coyote constrains his two turd sisters to advise him as to how the news of his sucking himself has gotten about, it is after an event he cannot explain to himself (cf. chapter 3; Hymes 1975a:47). The two sisters retell what has happened. As they had predicted, he then says he had known all along.

Disclosure of something certain can occur beforehand, as when the successive wives of Gitskux's older brother (Jacobs 1959b) foretell that Grizzly Woman will return and what she will do and instruct their men how to respond. Disclosure beforehand fits the future tense of the language, which is inherently perfective. By itself it can only be used for events known to be going to happen. (Other words must be added in order to qualify the future as conditional.) The ability to foresee their own (temporary) death and the remedy is evidence of the unusual power of the women.

A related act in myths is that of "pronouncement." The Chinookan root is *-pGna,* used both in conferring a name and in pronouncing a judicial finding. A transformer, usually Coyote, pronounces the name, hence the identity, hence the characteristic acts, of a figure at the end of a myth. Here in verse form is an extended instance from *Wishram texts* (Sapir 1909a:6–7):

Now the two went to their house
Now he also went to them to their house.
He told them:
    "Now by what right could you two be ones to take care of fish?
    "You are birds;
    "Now I shall tell you two.
"Now the people will come to this land;
    "Listen!"
 Now the people are heard:
    "Dulululu."
"Now they will come to this land;
    "those will be their food.
"Whenever a fish shall be caught,
    "Then should you two come.
"Your name has become 'Swallows,' you two.
"Now this day I am done with you.
"Thus I pronounce you,
    'Swallows.'

"Whenever the people will come,
    "they will catch fish.
"Now then you two will come.
"It will be pronounced to you,
    "The swallows have come.
    "Coyote pronounced them."
"Thus should the people say:
    "From these two Coyote took their hoard of fish.
    "Now those two have come."
Thus now Coyote pronounced them.

There is a circle of validation in such pronouncements at the end of myths. (For other instances, cf. Hymes 1966a:146–47). The myth confirms practice, and practice confirms the myth. Why should people say certain things when the first salmon and swallows come? Because in the myth Coyote had said that they should. Why should one believe Coyote said such things? Believe the myth? Because what he, what the myth, said the swallows would do (come with the first salmon) and the people would do when they came, observably is the case. Within the circle of the traditional culture, before the coming of the whites, there is nothing promised that is not performed.

The performance of the myth itself, of course, is a repetition of words previously said by others, making the event formal and the words valid (cf. again Hymes 1966a). From the standpoint of the speech event of performance, all the meta-narrative statements are disclosed at a time after the event, a time when they are certain.

In general, meta-narrative statement, discursive speech, has to do with the ability or inability to make the future come out in a certain way. Meta-narrative statements before the event are expressions of ability, power to affect the future on the part of the speaker. The addressees are implicated as agents of that outcome. Gitskux's wives provide for their restoration after Grizzly Woman will have killed them by the men they address; Black Bear provides for the escape of her children after Grizzly Woman will have killed her; Coyote provides for the coming of the swallows with the salmon and for what the people will say (addressing the swallows in the myth and the people in the performance). Coyote's speech, of course, is accompanied by a direct display of power, transforming the two women into their permanent identity as swallows.

Meta-narrative statements after the event are indications of inability to prevent a certain outcome. Seal's daughter was unable to prevent the death of her uncle; the Sun in the Kathlamet myth could not prevent the fatal choice of gift on the part of her son-in-law, the chief; Coyote's turd sisters could not prevent his foolishness before he asked their advice. And the addressee is the one at fault: Seal, failing to heed the information offered by her daughter; the chief, refusing to accept the other gifts offered him; Coyote, one might say, just being Coyote.

There is no implication of fault on the part of the addressee in discursive meta-narrative speech before the event. Apparent exceptions are not meta-narrative statements but interdictions without discursive explanation of what will ensue. Actors may prove culpable by disobeying an interdiction or prove successful (if the interdiction was made with ill intent); but they never disobey a foresighted meta-narrative statement. As seen in the story of Seal and her daughter, the interdiction/interdiction violated sequence can be superficial, failing to capture the deep structure of the narrative. That deep structure appears in the daughter's speech of remonstrance, as a breakthrough into performance, as we have seen.

One and the same event can contain both retrospective and prospective elements. When Coyote pronounces about the Swallows, he begins with a remonstrance to them as being at fault for having hoarded the salmon, but proceeds to what will be the case in the future. Coyote's turd sisters may tell him not only what has happened, but what to do. The Sun remonstrates to the chief, but expresses also her enduring relation to mankind ("I tried to love you, and I do love you"). The breakthrough into performance and the sequence of sensory detail and imagery combine to imply that Seal's daughter has assumed the power of maturity.

A fourfold table may help to summarize these relationships:

	Before	After
Addressor	+Power to shape outcome	—Power to shape outcome
Addressee	Responsible agent	Responsible agent
	(will do)	(at fault)

Table 8–2. Meta-narrative types

Wider implications.   In the traditional culture, and in the culture as still observed by Chinookan descendants at Warm Springs Reservation, a woman does not put herself forward as a speaker of the language, as one who is a source of knowledge, in the presence of someone older, no matter how old one is oneself. But this is a myth of a time of the destruction of culture. The time requires transformation of the point of view, from the standpoint of conventional revenge to that of those who experience unmotivated killing. The time requires a girl to mature in sensory and verbal knowledge to be her own source, however prematurely.

In effect, the myth moves to the daughter's standpoint; sensory experience earns her verbal authority. Expressive detail and cognitive analysis are integrated at the end in her.

When Victoria Howard dictated for Melville Jacobs to record, this narrative was one of the later (notebook 17) and briefest of her performances of myths. Some of the others are longer and richer, yet the fineness of this fragment implies its meaningfulness to her. Its suggestiveness to those who discover it now reinforces the conviction that it is fully formed, analogous to a fine lyric or sonnet, or bagatelle or prelude, compressing much but lacking nothing of what it needs.

Some of the meaningfulness of the story is suggested by the theme of a book by Peckham (1965:xi). Having said that "the drive to order is also a drive to get stuck in the mud," he states:

> There must, it seems to me, be some human activity which serves to break up orientations, to weaken and frustrate the tyrannous drive to order, to prepare the individual to observe what the orientations tell him is irrelevant, but what may very well be highly relevant. That activity, I believe, is the activity of artistic perception.

Peckham's theme suggests that the myth incorporates a confrontation between "Dionysian" and "Apollonian" orientations. Hannah Arendt's analysis of the condition permitting persistent United States war in Vietnam also suggests something of the condition of Seal as against her daughter (1971, see esp. pp. 35, 37).

Finally, a comment on the *methodological perspective* of this paper. It has been denied that I, in fact, address the issue of structural ethnography, as against a priori universalizing. In a major review of Maranda and Maranda (1971), Hendricks (1973) states: "However, Hymes never really does deal with this issue in connection with his reanalysis of a Clackamas myth." Hendricks does not say just how the study does deal with the issue, if not *really*. For the sake of the record (since the editor of *Semiotica* was unable to accept a letter on this point), let me note: (1) the theoretical difference of position is stated (as shown by a quotation given by Hendricks [p. 259]); (2) the structural relations found to underlie the text (and other texts) are not derived from universalistic proposals of Lévi-Strauss, Greimas, or others; (3) the structural relations are derived inductively from evidence within Chinookan mythology, including the native name for the genre, the cultural setting for narration of myths, relations among titles, actors and outcomes specific to the myths, identification of constant features of small genres (such as speech of remonstrance); (4) the contrasting dimensions found within the myth might be translated, after the fact, into the well known Lévi-Straussian opposition of culture versus nature, but at some violence to their content, maintenance of social norms versus attentiveness to experience; (5) the principle of generalizing the logical possibilities of a semantic field is shared with Lévi-Strauss, but the resulting four possibilities may be specific to Chinookan, so far as is yet known; (6) the dialectical procedure of Lévi-Strauss is shown to lead here to an unanticipated dimension, to expressive detail, and to development of personal maturity; (7) an interpretation of the myth by another folklorist (who had collected it), based on a priori psychological assumptions, is shown to be incorrect in the light of structural relations internal to Chinookan myths; (8) the study begins, and ends, by stating this to be its point. That all this could be missed, or dismissed, with the ambiguous phrase "never really" may reflect the deep hold of an a priori universalizing perspective.

9

Discovering Oral Performance and Measured Verse in American Indian Narrative

I. Introduction

I should like to discuss a discovery which may have widespread relevance. The narratives of the Chinookan peoples of Oregon and Washington can be shown to be organized in terms of lines, verses, stanzas, scenes, and what one may call acts. A set of discourse features differentiates narratives into verses. Within these verses, lines are differentiated, commonly by distinct verbs. (Sometimes items in a catalog, expressions in a song, and the like serve to differentiate lines.) The verses themselves are grouped, commonly in threes and fives. These groupings constitute "stanzas" and, where elaboration of stanzas is such as to require a distinction, "scenes." In extended narratives, scenes themselves are organized in terms of a series of "acts."

A Wishram text, Louis Simpson's "The deserted boy," has been analyzed in a paper recently published, where the method of work is exhibited at length. The result of such analysis of a major Kathlamet text is given at the end of another paper (Hymes 1975c). Here I shall give a Clackamas example, because of its brevity, and because the narrative has been the focus of the paper in which a theory of the structure of relations between titles, actors, outcomes, and cultural meanings was presented (Hymes 1968a=chap. 8). When the Clackamas narrative was first analyzed, I did not recognize the kind of poetic and rhetorical form now seen in it. My paragraphing of the story did indeed correspond to the units recognized here as stanzas, but the verses and lines within them were not set out and the architecture of scenes not displayed. Nothing of the interpretation presented in the earlier paper need be changed here, but recognition of the presentational form of the particular performance recorded by Jacobs strengthens and completes it. Cultural meaning, personal expression, and patterns of performance are seen to work to one end.

This chapter is reprinted from the article of the same title in *New Literary History* 7(1977):431–57. I am grateful to Ralph Cohen for the opportunity to contribute it. Some additions are made in connection with footnotes 1, 4, 5, 6 (original notes 1, 13, 14, 24). Note 4 and the discussion of formal close in the text have been amplified to clarify concerns raised by Tedlock (1977) in his discussion of the original article and to include evidence from Takelma and Sahaptin (the one a reservation neighbor of the Clackamas, the other an aboriginal one). The table at the end of part IV of the paper has been revised in format and the lineation of the text added. The postscript to chap. 8 indicates reprintings and discussions of my work on this text and adds comments on its plot and meanings.

II. Translation and Text

Let me first give the translation and the text from which it is derived, then discuss the findings of the previous paper and present those of this. After the Clackamas example has been analyzed, I shall comment on the relevance of this sort of analysis to other approaches to oral literature.

The text is from Melville Jacobs (1959a:340–41). The conventions of presentation are these: lower-case italic numerals indicate scenes *(i, ii, iii);* capital roman letters indicate stanzas (A, B, C . . .); arabic numerals indicate verses. Lines begin flush left or with an indentation of three spaces. (An indentation of ten spaces or more shows continuation of a single line.) Expressions in single quotation marks are Clackamas euphemisms ('go out' = 'urinate', 'lie down' = (optionally) 'go to bed for intercourse', 'going' = 'copulating'). The transcription is explained in the orthographic note at the beginning of this book.

Seal and her younger brother lived there

[i. The "wife" comes]

(A) (1) They lived there, Seal, her daughter, her younger brother.   1
         After some time, now a woman got to Seal's younger brother.   2
(B) (2) They lived there.   3
         They would 'go out' outside in the evening.   4
     (3) The girl would say,   5
         she would tell her mother: 6
         "Mother! Something is different about my uncle's wife.   7
         "It sounds just like a man when she 'goes out.' "   8
     (4) "Shush! Your uncle's wife!"   9
(C) (5) A long long time they lived there like that.   10
         In the evening they would each 'go out.'   11
     (6) Now she would tell her: 12
         "Mother! Something is different about my uncle's wife.   13
         "When she 'goes out' it sounds just like a man."   14
     (7) "Shush!"   15

[ii. The uncle dies]

(D) (8) Her uncle, his wife, would 'lie down' up above on the bed.   16
         Pretty soon the other two would lie down close to the fire,   17
             they would lie down beside each other.   18
(E) (9) Some time during the night, something comes on to her face.   19
     (10) She shook her mother,   20
          she told her: 21
          "Mother! Something comes on to my face."   22

(11) "ṁmmmm. Shush. Your uncle, they are 'going.'"   23

(F) (12) Pretty soon now again, she heard something escaping.   24

   (13) She told her: 25

        "Mother! Something is going t'úq t'úq.   26

        "I hear something."   27

   (14) "Shush. Your uncle, they are 'going.'"   28

(G) (15) The girl got up,   29

       she fixed the fire,   30

         she lit pitch,   31

           she looked where the two were: 32

              Ah! Ah! Blood!   33

(H) (16) She raised her light to it, thus: 34

       her uncle is on his bed,   35

         his neck cut,   36

          he is dead.   37

           She screamed.   38

[iii. The women lament]

(I) (17) She told her mother: 39

     "I told you,   40

       'Something is dripping.'   41

     "You told me,   42

       'Shush, they are "going."'   43

     "I had told you,   44

       'Something is different about my uncle's wife. 45

       'She would "go out"   46

         with a sound just like a man she would urinate.' 47

     "You would tell me,   48

       'Shush!'"   49

   She wept.   50

(J) (18) Seal said: 51

       "Younger brother! My younger brother!   52

       "They are valuable standing there.   53

       "My younger brother!"   54

   She kept saying that.   55

(K) (19) As for that girl, she wept.   56

   She said: 57

     "In vain I tried to tell you,   58

       'Not like a woman,   59

       'With a sound just like a man she would urinate,

         my uncle's wife.'   60

     "You told me,   61

       'Shush!'   62

"Oh oh my uncle!   63
"Oh my uncle!"   64
She wept, that girl.   65

* * *

(20) "Now I remember only that far."

Wálxayu iCámxix gaLxílayt

[i. The "wife" comes]

(A) (1) GaLXílayt, Wálxayu, wagáxan, iCámxix.   1
         LHúxwan qánCíxbÉt, aGa iLGagílak galigúqam Wálxayu iCámxix.   2
(B) (2) GaLXílayt.   3
         ALúya tLáXnix xábixix.   4
    (3) Wak'áSkaS alagíma,   5
         agulxáma wákaq: 6
         "Áqu! Dángi iXlúwidix wíCLm ayágikal.   7
         "TL'á wiLÉkala-díwi alubáya."   8
    (4) "Ák'wáSka! IwímiLm ayágikal!"   9
(C) (5) Í::yatLqdix k'wátLqí gaLXílayt.   10
         Xábixix aLubáywa.   11
    (6) AGa agulxáma: 12
         "Áqu! Dáng(i) iXlúwida wíCLm ayágikal.   13
         "Alubáya tL'á wiLÉkala díwi."   14
    (7) "Ák'wáSka!"   15

[ii. The uncle dies]

(D) (8) WíCaLm ayágikal aSXugákwSida wilxÉmitba.   16
         Kwálá SdáX aSXúkSida q'wáp wátuL,   17
         aSXaSgmúkSida.   18
(E) (9) LHúxwan qánCiX wápul, dangi yáguwit wákxba.   19
    (10) GagulálalmCk wákaq,   20
         gagúlxam: 21
         "Áqu! Dángi ínguwit wákxba."   22
    (11) "ḿmmmm. Ák'wáSka. WímiLm SXlúyam."   23
(F) (12) Kwálá aGa wít'aX, dángi gagilCÉmaq síq'nukwtLpxix.   24
    (13) Gagúlxam: 25
         "Áqu! Dángi t'úq: t'úq:.   26
         "Dángi nilCÉmlit."   27
    (14) "Ák'wáSka. WímiLm SXlúym."   28
(G) (15) NaXÉlaCk wak'áSkaS,   29
         t'áya gagúXa wátuL,   30
         wáx gagÉLuX iLlásxwa,   31

gagíyukSdix qáXba Sdúktktba: 32
Á:dí::! ILGáwlkt! 33
(H) (16) Íwi gagÉLuq'wma: 34
íyalxmitba wíCaLm, 35
Lq'úp íyatuk, 36
yúmqt. 37
GaSaXÉlqiLX. 38

[iii. The women lament]

(I) (17) Gagúlxam wákaq: 39
"Íyamúlxam, 40
'Dángi t'úq t'uq.' 41
"Ímnúlxam, 42
'Ák'wáSka, SXlúym.' 43
"NiyamtLÉxam, 44
'Dángi Xlúwida wíCLm ayágikal. 45
'Alubáya 46
tL'á iLÉkala-díwi alaXunúda.' 47
"Amnulxáma, 48
'Ák'wáSka!' " 49
NagÉCaX. 50
(J) (18) Wálxayu nákim: 51
"Áwi! WiCúxix! 52
"ILk'áLmgwadi Líyaxinxat. 53
"WiCúxix!" 54
NagímniLCk. 55
(K) (19) Yáxa áX wak'áSkaS nagÉCaX. 56
NagímX: 57
"Kínwa iyamúlxam, 58
'NéSqi iLGagílak-díwi, 59
'TL'á wiLÉkala-díwi alaXunúda wíCLm ayágikal.' 60
"Imnúlxam, 61
'Ák'wáSka!' 62
"Áná wíCLm! 63
"Aná wíClm!" 64
NagÉCaX wak'áSkaS. 65
(20) AGa kwábt yáymayx inXÉlutkt. 66

III. Structural Analysis: Plot and Meanings

The point of the first paper about this myth was to show that the first
reading of the myth, by its recorder (Jacobs 1960:238–42), mistook the focus

and relative importance of the actors and misassigned responsibility for the outcome. The myth was read in the light of a general assumption as to the significance of such myths (in this case, psychosexual fears and in-law tensions), rather than in the light of a theory specific to the structure of narrative among Chinookans. The death was taken as precipitated by the young girl; the most important actor as the "wife"; the larger story of which this story presumably forms a part would show subsequent steps for revenge against the responsible relatives.[1] In point of fact, evidence from several sources converges to show that the primary reading of the myth is as a display of the consequences of acting as does Seal. The evidence includes the Chinookan word for "myth" itself, a structural covariation of myth titles and outcomes across the body of Clackamas myths (and, as is now known through work of Michael Silverstein, among Wasco as well), the invariant significance in the mythology of such conventional small genres as a speech of remonstrance and of such figures as "youngest smartest," and the placing of the myth in a semantic field of myth situations and outcomes. The myths in general are found to relate the conduct of actors named first in titles to outcomes in terms of two dimensions, *social norm* and *empirical situation*. (Morris Freilich has independently identified two such dimensions, which he calls "smart/proper," as fundamental to many myths and human life [1975, 1978].) The outcome of the present story is tragic because Seal, the principal actor (named first in the title), insists on maintaining a social norm (of propriety in speech) at the expense of attention to an empirical situation (reported by her daughter). (Other Clackamas myths involving the same consanguineal trio—mother, mother's younger brother, mother's daughter— are placed in terms of the table of possible outcomes generated by the two dimensions, and other examples cited, in the original paper.)

The tragic outcome, focused on Seal, can be seen as a cultural or pedagogical reading of the myth (recalling that the primary audience of myth narration consisted of children and that the telling of myths every year during the winter sacred season, with a certain formality and exchange of gifts, suggests an equivalent to a "world-renewal" rite).[2] Trial of a dialectic method proposed by Lévi-Strauss showed further pattern, not of cognitive categories, but of sensory imagery and expressive detail, focused on Seal's daughter. Two such complementary strands of structure and meaning have been found interwoven in other Chinookan myths as well.[3] Especially the second strand allows for,

---

[1] I am indebted to Michael Silverstein for discussion of performance tradition, of endings, and of linguistic details, during our research leave in Rhododendron, Oregon, in the second half of 1976; and to Virginia Hymes for assistance with the Sahaptin materials used in the revised discussion of endings. Some of the material is also used in a poem, "Fivefold fanfare for Coyote" (Portland, Oregon: Corvine Press, 1978).

[2] Cf. the discussion of the place of myth telling among major speech ways of the Wasco-Wishram Chinook in Hymes (1966a).

[3] Cf. the Kathlamet Chinook "The Sun's myth" (Hymes 1975c) and the Wishram Chinook "The deserted boy" (Hymes 1976 = chap. 4 of this book). The first published title of the latter,

and demonstrates, personal identification and expression. The joint presence of two strands of meaning is what I would myself expect, given that myths are verbal art and that an interdependence of cognitive and expressive functions is fundamental to the structure of language (cf. Hymes 1972, 1974b).

Since publication of the first paper on this myth, further evidence has confirmed its interpretation. It has become clear that the Clackamas narrative derives from a story of revenge, attested among the Nootka of Vancouver Island, the Coos of the central Oregon coast, and, indeed, the Wasco. In these stories the "wife" is disguised as a woman in order to revenge a relative whom the man to be killed has slain. The Coos in fact have the story in a full form in which there is precisely an incident in which a young child notices something strange about the "wife," reports it, is shushed, and later has the consequences of the slaying drip upon it (Ramsey 1977). The Nootka have a story in which the avenger is one of five brothers of a slain sister. And the late Ida White and George Forman, Wasco speakers of Yakima, Washington, told Michael Silverstein and myself a story in which "he came back to get back," that is, a murdered wife's twin brother disguised himself as her to revenge her death. Clearly the larger story of which Mrs. Howard told a part would not begin with her part, but end with it.[4]

"The deserted boy," was assigned by Sapir in keeping with the common designation for such stories among folklorists. No title is given in the Indian language, but the structure and the initial sentences of the story indicate that the Wishram title would parallel the title attested in Clackamas Chinook, "They deserted the mean boy" (Jacobs 1959a:409). That is, the cultural and pedagogical focus would be on the consequences of acting as did the people who deserted the boy and who are punished in the end. Clearly, the expressive and identificational focus is on the boy himself (as Mrs. Ruth Estabrook of Warm Springs Reservation made clear to me when I discussed the story with her some years ago in the summer of 1974).

[4]Mrs. Howard does say at the end, "Now I remember only that far," but, as will be shown below with regard to performance features, most of this remark is a stylistic convention, and the word that indicates something missing, "only-that," indicates a detail, the outcome with regard to the "wife," where she goes, what she says. As for Seal and her daughter, the dramatic realization of their expressive isolation from each other in the final scene is complete. That the Clackamas Chinook close is a stylistic convention is further shown by the analogous ending used by Mrs. Frances Johnson for myths in Takelma (Sapir 1909). A common formula includes "finished," followed by "Go gather your baap seeds and eat them." In addition, one sometimes finds equivalents of "that far":

"Now I have finished the myth [lit., put it off in front],
"Just going so far I, for my part, know it" (50);

and

"I, for my part, know indeed just that,
"There just so far, indeed, I know it" (64).

and,

"There just so far" (79, 94, 108).

Thus there is no question of the girl's remarks being responsible for the death of her uncle. The motive for the murder lies outside the drama of interaction between daughter and mother.[5]

Mrs. Johnson's Takelma endings generally fit the view of the place of myths in a myth-related world given later in this chapter in the discussion of formal closings. Cf.:

"Like that, just so, indeed I know it" (115);
"Like that I know it indeed" (167).

Particularly notable is the ending of Mrs. Johnson's version of the Takelma story cognate to the Clackamas text discussed in this chapter. The Takelma text ends:

Gana'nèx gìː'á yok'oyà'n,
    gwàla si'wàkdi,
      aldíː yukyàki' eíːte',
        malàxbi'n.
"Like that I, for my part, know it,
    there is much (more) perhaps,
      were all known to me,
        I should tell it to you."

The myth-world, not ignorance, seems implicit in the fact that the word for 'all', aldíː, is inherently animate, meaning "all" in the sense of "everybody," in contrast to the construction for "everything" (Sapir 1922:255). Since Mrs. Howard and Mrs. Johnson both lived at Grande Ronde Reservation, there could have been communication between them and other Takelma and Clackamas survivors. The myth finals of both do appear to be traditionally rooted. The parallel appeal at the end of a myth to imminent good weather, indeed, is widespread in the region. The use of a negative construction for emphasis is linguistically quite distinct and specific in the narratives of each, and far from unusual, so far as the semantic principle goes. There seems good reason to believe that in both cases we have authentic, if partial, indications of the patterns of aboriginal performance.

[5]No doubt the Clackamas story has been influenced also by stories reported to the north among the Salish, Tlingit, and Haida of British Columbia, stories in which a trickster (Raven) deceives Seal, sometimes disguised as a woman, in order to have Seal as food (cf. Hymes 1968:62–63). Such influence would explain the identification of the mother as Seal. In such a case, the motivation for the murder still lies outside the scenes presented in the text, having to do with the nature of the trickster. In the Salish versions and the more northerly Tlingit and Haida versions the full cast of characters of the Clackamas story is not found. The scant data suggest an aboriginal continuum from north to south. Farthest north, among the Tlingit there are just two characters, a chiefly seal (male) and a false "wife" (the trickster, Raven). There is also a child, but it is associated with the trickster, who brings it in disguise. There is no brother or child of Seal. Further south among the Sechelt just north of present-day Vancouver there are three characters, Seal (female), her daughters, and an uncle. There is no false "wife"; the trickster, Raven, is an undisguised male. But as collected by Hill-Tout (1904:51), and reprinted by Maud (1978b:117), the kinship trio is one found in the Clackamas story. Raven is brother to Seal and uncle to her daughter. (In a redictation of the text in recent fieldwork [Timmers 1974:10–16], Seal's daughters are identified still as nieces of Raven, but Seal is glossed in English as his cousin. Perhaps there has been a shift in kin term usage.)

These facts indicate that the Clackamas story is only akin to the northern stories about a trickster, not directly derived. If it owes identification of the mother as Seal to the trickster

In sum, comparative evidence and evidence from internal structure, from a theory of the "grammar" of Chinookan myths, coincide. The internal evidence remains fundamental. The revenge story might have been reshaped to a different point and moral. Comparative study of versions of such stories as "They deserted the mean boy" shows just such variation in focus and point. Indeed, the Clackamas story that we have has obviously *been* reshaped from an adventure told from the standpoint of the avenger to a domestic drama told from the standpoint of women left without a man by the revenge. The clustering of expressive detail and the sequencing of imagery have to do with sensory experience, especially of light and of liquid. These indicate that the consequences of acting like Seal are seen from the standpoint of an identification with her daughter. (This identification seems to have been important to Mrs. White as well. At the point at which something drips onto the girl, she went from English into Wasco [cf. chap. 3 on such shifts].) It seems not accidental that the story was told by a woman who had learned it from a woman (her mother-in-law), and in keeping with the impression that in Mrs. Howard's narratives it is commonly the women characters who are most fully realized.

IV. Structural Analysis: Presentational Form

I was led to reinterpret the story of Seal and her younger brother, and through it to a semantic field of general application to Chinookan myths, by the glaring discrepancy between the published interpretation of its meaning and the evident dramatic form of the story itself. It is not a pair engaged in sex and of uncertain sexual affinity who are on stage; it is a pair engaged in talk about them. The confrontation displayed in the story is between a daugh-

---

series, it equally owes its specific plot to a series of stories that are not about deception to satisfy a constant appetite for food, but about deception to accomplish revenge. That the uncle's head is cut off and the parts of the body left is indication enough that the point is not food.

With regard to transvestite deception for revenge, there is apparently a correlation between stories from north of the Columbia River, stories south of it, and plot. North of the Columbia, brothers seek to revenge a sister. South of the Columbia, sons seek to revenge and restore a father. In the latter stories, one point of the story is to recover the head (as in the Coos and Takelma myths). The leaving of the uncle's head and the absence of any other head to recover rather clearly indicates that the essential link in plot of the Clackamas story, as of a Wasco story recounted by Ida White and George Forman to Michael Silverstein and myself (see appendix to chap. 8), is to the stories of brotherly revenge for a sister from north of the Columbia.

An analogous story, intermediate in the role of the head, is found among the Okanagan (Maud 1978a:156–58). Two brothers, Fisher and Marten, kill two boys and disguise themselves in their clothing in order to recapture the older brother's (Fisher's) wife. They take the offending chief's head back with them but are forced to throw it into the water (where it belongs, being Salmon's head) to make good their escape. Here one has disguise as members of the enemy village, and decapitation, but without transvestitism, and without either a sister to avenge or a father to restore.

318 Titles, Names, and Natures

ter and her mother. The form in which the translation and text are presented brings out this confrontation and at the same time has independent justification. There is a theory and "grammar" of presentational form to be found in Chinookan narratives as well as one of semantic structure. Let me now discuss the principle of organization that underlies the form in which the Seal myth is presented, how the principle was arrived at, and how it applies in the Seal myth itself.

Discovery of Verse and Line. The principle of organization has to do with the initial elements of sentences. Certain initial elements frequently recur in structurally significant roles. In this respect, and some others, Chinookan narratives possess formulaic elements of the sort so important in the work on epic of Milman Parry, Albert Lord, and others. There is a fundamental difference, however, between the two. The formulaic elements of Slavic, Greek, and other oral poetries occur within, manifest and adapt to, verse that is regulated by another principle. In Chinookan and, I suspect, in American Indian oral narrative generally, the recurrent initial elements represent the regulatory principle itself. They are aspects of the measuring which makes the material verse.

I use the term *measure* because the material does not consistently exhibit either phonological regulation of lines (counting stress, syllable, or whatever) or grammatical regulation of lines (syntactic parallelism and framing). One or both of these properties is usually expected when one speaks of meter. To be sure, lines usually contain or consist of a verb, and a segmentation of narratives in accordance with the principle of one verb, one line, would go far toward approximating the true pattern. Not lines, but what are here called "verses," however, appear to be the pivotal unit. And verses are recognized, not by counting parts, but by recognizing repetition within a frame, the relation of putative units to each other within a whole. Covariation between form and meaning, between units and a recurrent Chinookan pattern of narrative organization, is the key.

In the narratives of Louis Simpson, such as that of "The deserted boy," recurrent initial linguistic elements make the task easy. The recurrent initial particles that have annoyed so many linguists, ethnographers, and readers by their monotony—"Now," "Then," "Now then," "Now again," and the like —turn out to be far from the tedious trivia of primitive minds. They are markers of measure. When a text by Louis Simpson is segmented according to the initial occurrence of the standard particle pair "Now then," the greater part of the poetic organization of the narrative becomes apparent at once. The initial particle pair defines a verse. The verses, so defined, are grouped in sets of three and five ("stanzas"). Within the verses, verbs signal lines. Sometimes other initial elements occur where the overall pattern leads one to expect indication of a verse. The overall pattern enables one to recognize a small set of substitutable initial elements which, once recognized, have clear expressive roles (e.g., "Now again" instead of "Now then" within a sequence of actions; "Indeed" to highlight a climactic point).

The use of initial particles is not limited to Chinookan narrative. The oldest layer of Alsea narrative to survive, as published by Leo J. Frachtenberg (1920), shows a similar use of initial particles, but there the grouping is in stanzas of four verses—quite to be expected, since the pattern number among the Chinookans is five, among the Alsea four. (Among American Indian peoples the number of repetitions of an incident in a story or an act in a rite, the number of brothers or sisters in a story, etc. is commonly in accordance with such a number, most often four.) Again, and perhaps ultimately of special significance for method and theory in the study of myth, the story of Asdiwal, made famous by Lévi-Strauss, shows such organization as well. The one version published in the native language, Tsimshian (Boas 1912:70ff.) shows recurrent patterning into verses and stanzas, commonly four verses to a stanza, marked by the initial particle *Ada(t)* and some other elements.

The discovery of such patterning was a surprise to me (and a delight). I had worked with the Chinookan materials for almost twenty years without appreciating its presence. That initial elements of certain kinds were significant markers of organization, yes (Hymes 1958), but not the pervasive structuring of narratives to the level of verses. Once discovered, the patterning does not seem surprising, in Chinookan or elsewhere. We know the languages to be marvels of intricate coordination of form and meaning. Why should the narrative use of the languages be less? And in a literature exclusively realized in oral performance, what better peg on which to hang signals of measure than initial elements?

Once such patterning has been discovered in cases with such markers, it can be discerned in cases without them. The Clackamas narratives of Mrs. Victoria Howard do not regularly make use of initial particle pairs, as do those in Wasco-Wishram of Louis Simpson. Mrs. Howard often makes use of "Now," "Soon now," and other such elements, but often does not. To determine the organization of her narratives, one has to recognize and abstract features that co-occur with the use of initial particle pairs in the narratives of Louis Simpson. Especially salient and important are statements of change in what Kenneth Burke calls the "scene-agent ratio"—indications of change of scene in either location or lapse of time, and indication of change among participants in the action. A series of three or five items, or actions of a single actor, always form a set and unit. Lexical recurrence is a criterion in two respects. A verb may recur at intervals and so show that there are units, marked and linked by it. A verb or noun may recur within a short span and so show that there is one unit containing it.

All of these criteria are valid in the Clackamas narratives of Mrs. Howard. Charles Bigelow and I have analyzed the complete Coyote cycle and a number of other myths as well as some legends and narratives of historical experiences. With patience a consistent pattern always emerges.

The discovery of such pattern is not mechanical, and it is not arbitrary. It is not mechanical because the pattern is a relation between linguistic elements and narrative form of the sort that linguists sometimes call "form-meaning covariation." While certain elements regularly serve to mark verses, this role is dependent upon the organization of the whole. The particle "now" may occur within lines in its purely lexical role. A mechanical segmentation of a text in terms of occurrences of "Now" would distort the narrative pattern. Conversely, elements not regularly used to mark verses may occur as the first element of a verse. Here, recognition of a verse is directly dependent upon the organization of the whole and the functional criteria of change of time, location, or participation.

The discovery of such pattern is not arbitrary, because it is governed by the coherence and articulation of the particular narrative, and in addition, by a rhetorical pattern that pervades Chinookan texts. (Whether this pattern extends beyond Chinookan, I do not know.) For the sake of a mnemonic device, I call this pattern by three words beginning with the same letter: *onset, ongoing, outcome.* More exactly, "onset" may involve a condition, preparation, or initiation of action; "ongoing" carries the action further—if the onset was a condition or preparation, the "ongoing" segment may set in motion the main action and otherwise continue or complicate it, even to the point of completion; "outcome" involves either completion of the main action or an outcome resulting from it.

My description must make the principle sound obvious, inevitable, and a little loose. I can only say that it is flexible in keeping with specific narrative situations, but inescapable. A favorite device of Chinookan narrators is to make a verse of three lines, whose three verbs exhibit the pattern; for example, to say of the trickster-transformer, Coyote, "he was going along, he was go—ing, he got there." Stanzas show this relation among their verses (cf. verses 2–3–4 in stanza B, 5–6–7 in C, and so forth); scenes show the relation among their stanzas (cf. stanzas A–B–C in scene *i,* D, E–F, G–H in scene *ii*); and whole myths show the relation among their scenes (cf. scenes *i, ii, iii*). It is this recurrence at all levels of organization that makes the pattern seemingly inescapable and convincing. Further, it is not a question of finding points within the narrative that can correspond to the three parts of the pattern, whatever else may intervene. At each level at which the pattern applies, it segments and organizes the material without discontinuity, without leftovers. Experience with the texts simply makes it seem the mold into which narration flows. Time and again, a point at which the organization was not clear has been clarified by viewing the material in terms of this pattern. And analyses that went forward without regard to the pattern have turned out to embody it.

Chinookan Presentational Form. Chinookan narratives, then, have an organization of *poetic* form, in terms of verses and lines; of *rhetorical* form, in terms of the organization of expectations, very much as enunciated by Kenneth Burke in his essay on "The psychology of the audience" (1931); and, one must not forget, a pattern of *vocal realization* as well. One might sum up these three aspects of oral performance in terms of "verses," "expectations," and "voices." When all three are fully realized in a performance, one would find the following. *Poetic form:* the organization in terms of verses, lines, stanzas, scenes discussed above, together with a disposition of markers of such organization. *Rhetorical form:* the organization in terms of sequences of onset, ongoing action, and outcome, discussed above. *Vocal realization:* direct quotation, rather than reported speech; the taking of the voices of those who speak, differentiating them; onomatopoetic precision, giving the words that define characteristic sounds (Chinookan has a rich taxonomy of kinds of sound); expressive interactional detail, through particles initial in a quoted statement (or statement from the point of view of the narrator) that define the attitude taken, for example, assent, pain, lament, pondering, expectation; recurrent audience response with such elements, ranging from *ã* at ordinary detail to *adí* and *aná* at moments of high drama; lengthening of vowels for emphasis; interchange of consonants (according to a regular pattern) to express augmentation and diminution.

These three aspects of performance are, of course, interwoven. Seal's 'Shush'! (verse 7) is to be performed in the voice of a reproving mother and is itself a word onomatopoetically apt *(Ak'wáSka);* as a change of voice and speaker, it marks a verse; as the third verse in a pattern already exemplified, it closes a stanza; in closing the stanza, it fits a patterned expectation of onset condition, ongoing of action, outcome; as third stanza of three, it is a candidate for outcome of a scene. (Its status as the last depends upon the change of actors and setting in the next line.)

These three aspects of performance vary together. As might be expected, not all the texts one hears or has are fully performed. Sometimes the speaker feels unable to take responsibility for a full performance. Then one often finds a telling about the story, rather than a doing of the story. (Cf. chap. 3 for analysis of the three Wasco-Wishram cases that bear on this.) Such tellings, reportings, rather than doings, are interspersed in our collections of Native American narrative with true performances. Sometimes a speaker capable of full performance does not feel comfortable in providing it, not knowing the hearer well enough, being tired, missing native conditions for such display, whatever. Jacobs observed that Mrs. Howard's first narrations to him lacked some stylistic features (such as formal close) that emerged later, and he had the luck to have her tell him toward the end of their work together a story she had told early on (texts 57 and 58 in Jacobs, 1959a). The later version has a full title (expanding the abbreviated title given for the first version), includes an appropriate onomatopoetic name for a sound, dramatizes the role of the leading actor—a village headman—in terms of a fivefold sequence of inner speech. (Inner speech, introduced by "he thought" or the like, functions like

322 Titles, Names, and Natures

quoted speech in these narratives.) There is a formal close. Both narrations manifest the aspects of performance identified above, but the first version rather partially, the late version rather fully. And the focus of the story in moral terms on the responsiveness and initiative of the village headman in caring for his starving people is more fully realized in the later story as well. One does not seem to find much display of performance for its own sake. The fuller the realization of performance, the sharper the etching of the moral point, which, amid all the enjoyment which the stories provided, remained their primary *raison d'être.*

Narrative performances varied on another dimension as well—that of explicitness and length. An admired narrator could spin out a story to any length desired by filling in detail, but could also convey the essence of a story in brief. Some people emphasize the latter ability in expressing admiration for narrators they have known—ability to tell everything yet keep it short. Any two performances might vary in any case in terms of the details made explicit. Those who already knew the stories would have them brought to mind by the details that were given. The assumption that a part stands adequately for the whole remains alive, and people who credit one with knowledge of the stories sometimes act surprised that one has to ask about a detail that had not been given. Michael Silverstein suggests that the title of a story represents one pole of the continuum of explicitness, sufficing to call to mind the whole for many adults. The other pole of the continuum is one that in native theory is not really ever reached. A story ends, as a story and as an event, but the body of narrative and the world of the stories is unending. Mrs. Howard's Clackamas narratives show this. Reading a single story, one may judge that the statement, "Now I know only (remember only) that far," expresses a lapse of memory. When one finds such an expression time after time, often at the end of stories of great length about which one could not think what more to expect, one realizes that one is in the presence of a convention. But this element of closings and closings in general require extended treatment, both in their own right and as a context for understanding the concluding words of "Seal and her younger brother."

Closings. A comparison of published Chinookan materials from three dialects (Kathlamet, Clackamas, Wishram-Wasco), of what Silverstein and I have gleaned from living speakers of Wasco, of Jacobs's Northwest Sahaptin materials, and of portions of Virginia Hymes's recordings from Sahaptin speakers at Warm Springs, indicates that a full close to a performance could have three major parts.

(1) First, there might be a summary conclusion of the action in progress. A story might proceed directly from action to the remaining parts of a close without a summary statement, but often enough there is one. Thus Joe Hunt's narrative of "Bear Woman kills Grizzly Woman's daughter" (Jacobs 1934:47) ends the action with "She ran in that direction now, but nothing! She became

completely confused, she never found her." Hunt then pauses for a summary: "Bear went far away, she was never found. She obliterated her own tracks as she went along. She did not find her, though she kept on looking for her."

(2) The second part of a full close would be an epilogue that states what becomes of the actors past the conclusion of the story—whether they just "stayed there," went their own ways separately, were transformed, were henceforth to have certain traits. The Hunt narrative just cited continues directly with such a second part:

> That is the Klikitat myth. Nowadays they are (just) bear and grizzly, they are no longer persons. That is as far as that myth goes. At the present time they never eat one another's food, wherever they have found one or the other's eating place. They never go to that place. And that is now they have been since that time.

In other words, the actors of the myth have been transformed from myth persons to their ordinary animal counterparts. (This distinction is morphologically marked in Sahaptin—thus Bear as myth person is Anahu:yái, but now in this part of the close, just Anahúi; Grizzly as myth person is Tuwit'áya, but now Túwit'aS [grizzly bears always receive the respectful suffix -S]). And they are as they are now in a certain respect because of what happened in the myth.

(3) The third part of a full close can be verbally distinguished in English as the *finis*. There is first a conventional formula that marks the end of the text. With Mrs. Howard, as with Charles Cultee in Kathlamet, and many Wascos, the finis is *K'ani k'ani* 'story story'. It is truly a finis. When Velma Smith at Warm Springs wanted her mother to end a story (in English in fact) because the meal she'd prepared was on the table, she came into the room, saying good-naturedly but loudly, *"k'ani k'ani,* dinner's ready." Louis Simpson, who narrated *Wishram texts* to Sapir, usually favored *Qédau iqánuCk* 'Thus the myth'. Joe Hunt, who narrated Klikitat texts to Melville Jacobs, favored *TLáXw-au* 'All now'. That is his finis to the story we have been quoting.

There are also conventional formulae that mark the end of the narrative event, performative words that bespeak the efficacy of the act of myth performance: "Tomorrow good weather" (Kathlamet); "Forever and ever the sun shone" (Hiram Smith in Wasco); "Hurry! Summer! Grouse hoot hoot hoot hoot!" (Mrs. Howard in one Clackamas myth [Jacobs 1958a:226]—I have matched the English to the Clackamas more closely); "May the weather tomorrow be as it was when the Thunder (brothers) and the East Wind came together" (Louis Simpson in one Wasco [Wishram] myth [Sapir 1909:131]); "In the sunshine, in the sunshine, all kinds of butterflies flying around, no flies!" (Susan Moses [Warm Springs Sahaptin]); and the conventional ending used by a Klikitat shaman, Susan Hollingworth (former wife of Joe Hunt), as recalled by Sam Eyley, Jr. (Jacobs 1934:174):

> Spring is starting,
> strawberries and salmonberries are starting to ripen,
> I eat them as I go by;
> hummingbirds are starting to fly about,
> they pass me by again and again,
> hm! hm! hm!

(I have slightly revised the published translation).

These formulae obviously reflect the fact that the myths were told in winter, when the people were surviving on food from the previous spring-summer-fall, and hoping for the quick return of another spring with its fresh roots, fruits, and fish.

The weather formulae occur less regularly in the published collections of this century, perhaps because the circumstance of dictating to a fieldworker (and in the summer) made them out of place. Mrs. Howard's only weather ending, a nicely framed, partly rhyming one, came late in her work with Jacobs and at the end of one of her longest, fullest dictations. Louis Simpson's only weather ending is specific to the story just told about the Thunder brothers. Among Chinookan narrators known to us, only Charles Cultee, working with Boas in the early 1890s, regularly supplied such endings. It also seems that these formulae may not be obligatory with each story, traditionally, but are with a storytelling session.

The weather formulae seem to go together with the story-ending formulae as a kind and aspect of *finis*. Mrs. Howard's only weather ending, indeed, is framed by "Story story!" at beginning and end (the whole thus having five parts; the pattern number five may account for the framing).

Each of the three major parts of a full close has a different status as an outcome: The summary conclusion has to do with the outcome of the agonistic action within the story; the epilogue has to do with the outcome of the story for the world—the nature and ways of its features and inhabitants; the finish has to do with the outcome of the story for those who participate in its performance—that the performance is over, at least, and that as a modest world-renewal rite, it calls for good weather. One might call the summary conclusion "pretransformational," the epilogue "transformational," the finis "posttransformational."

Some types of conventional statement may occur in either a summary conclusion or an epilogue—a speech of remonstrance, a statement of staying, a statement of parting. Louis Simpson ends the narrative of Coyote's freeing of the salmon first with a remonstrance by one sister to the other (summary conclusion), then, after a quick change of scene with the sisters and Coyote both going back to their house, a transformational speech by Coyote that is initially a remonstrance to them on behalf of the people who are to come (Sapir 1909a:7). An epilogue might be elaborate. Coyote's speech, just mentioned, Salmon's transformational speech to the Ravens who had rescued his wife for him (Ibid.:64), Panther's speech after burying his brother (Jacobs 1959a:365), are examples. A transformation may be just reported (as in Joe Hunt's account of Bear and Grizzly, cited above, or in Mrs. Howard's account of the end of "Seal took them to the ocean" [Jacobs 1958:226, the same story which has the weather ending]). When pronounced by an actor with the authority of a transformer, a threefold pattern is often found: the people who are coming are near now, your name (and nature) is now such-and-such, and further, you will do, the people will say, it always will happen that, such-and-such.

Mrs. Howard's frequent statements of limited knowledge in such a context fit the conventions. They are "definite indefinite" statements (cf. the discussion of *Luxwan* in part V below). An example is found at the end of her telling of the story of Mink and his elder brother (Panther) (Jacobs 1959a:365). Having disregarded his elder brother's advice once too often, Mink dies; Panther waits all day, all night (in case Mink might revive), it becomes day again, and Panther buries his younger brother. This passage concludes the agonistic action of the story, and perhaps has something of a summary conclusion in the account of waiting and burying. The text continues:

"Now he said,
 "Now the people are near.
 "A killer's badness does not matter,
   should he think,
     'I shall live so long a time.'
 "My younger brother just now did not go around the land.
 "Now he is dead.
 "Now that is the way it shall be."
"As for him, now he went somewhere.
 "I do not know what he became.
   "Now that is as far as I recall."
"Story story."

Notice that there is nothing more for Panther to do, be, or get to *in this story*. The story indeed is not his story but Mink's—Mrs. Howard's titling of it as "Mink and his elder brother" indicates as much. Mink's death completes the expectations elicited by focusing on his character, as exhibited in the action of the myth. There are, of course, other stories involving Panther. Mrs. Howard later told one fully (Jacobs 1958:52—this story is in Jacobs's field notebook 14, the one we have been discussing in notebooks 3 and 4). Mrs. Howard parallels Charles Cultee in his Kathlamet narrations, both in having two separate Panther and younger brother stories (cf. Boas 1901:90, 103) and in focusing on the younger brother in the story involving Mink (Cultee's title is "Mink's myth"). A minor difference is that the other younger brother in the Clackamas is Raccoon (-Sat'at, cf. Kathlamet -Latat, also translated 'Raccoon'), rather than Lynx (Kathlamet) or Wild Cat (Klikitat).

The difference in regard to fullness and organization is not in anything that follows where Mrs. Howard ends—nothing does in any known version—but in her integration of the story with a preceding one of Coyote and Panther, one attested uniquely from her. Again, notice that of three Chinookan narrators with published versions of the story, only Mrs. Howard gives a substantial close. Charles Cultee stops his Kathlamet narration rather abruptly at the end of an incident, giving no outcome, let alone transformation or disposition. The incident ends, and one has immediately, "Story story, tomorrow good weather" (Boas 1901:117). Louis Simpson does much the same. An incident is left hanging in the air, and rather abruptly one has "Thus did Eagle and Weasel; thus the myth." (Eagle and Weasel correspond to Panther and Mink in Wasco tradition, as attested also by Mr. Charley Jackson, the late Alfred Smith, and others.) (Sapir comments [1909a:120, n. 1] on the incompleteness of the story.)

It is striking that it is the Chinookan narrator who tells the story to a full close who also says "Now that is as far as I recall," while those who break off the story say nothing. This observation seems to me to point to the conventional status of the phrase. (The contrast between presence and absence of a referring pronoun in the phrase, analyzed below with regard to the Seal story, reinforces the conclusion that the phrase, when without pronoun, is conventional). We do not know whether or not the particular wording, especially the use of the first person, was unique to Mrs. Howard (or to the Clackamas). Apart from the first person, parallels, indeed, are not unknown; recall the expression "That is as far as that myth goes" in Joe Hunt's ending of a Klikitat myth, quoted above. Whether or not the particular wording is specific to Mrs. Howard, the meaning and function of the words seem not to be. Myths often end with statements of staying, or, as here with Mrs. Howard's Panther myth, of going, that permit linkage with another story. Such statements often indeed match statements that occur at the beginning of narratives. Sam Eyley, Jr.'s version of Cougar (=Panther) and Wild Cat (Jacobs 1934:113–21) is an apt example. Cougar told Wild Cat the two would part, Wild Cat wept, but Cougar left and Wild Cat went away. "I do not know how far away he had gone," continues Eyley, when he saw and killed a deer and then sought out Wild Cat to leave the food for him (implying, as some versions state, that he would always do so in the future). "Then Cougar left Wild Cat, Cougar went away. As he went along, he found a boy"—and the story of Cougar and Mink begins.

In sum, Mrs. Howard's conventionalized expression leaves open the linking of a story to another in the same world of myth, although in the case in hand we know of no other story to follow. The expression of openness, of potential linkage, seems in itself an expression of the nature of myth and its world. This conclusion is further supported by the fact that Mrs. Ida White and Mr. George Forman made similar statements to Silverstein with regard to Wasco narratives.

It is difficult to assign closings a place in the threefold division of aspects of performance. They are markers of the sequential organization of myths and at the same time an integral part of rhetorical expectations. The closings are also an integral part of the organization of plot and incident in relation to title and outcome, the dimension of narratives that might be set over against presentational form (poetic form, rhetorical form, vocal realization) as having to do with content. Perhaps it is only appropriate that closings seem to unite all aspects of the narratives.

Certainly all aspects of the narratives can be seen as united under the aegis of performance. One should imagine the narrator as holding together in mind both plot and incident, on the one hand, and presentational form on the other.[6] The aspects of presentational form serve effectiveness and enjoyment, of course—one must never forget that one reason such narratives were perpetuated is that they were enjoyed. In the unfolding of plot and incident in terms of presentational form, the specific role of the latter can be called that of "pacing" and "point." The placement of an element of narrative in terms of the formal patterns can give it point. Elaboration within a unit of formal pattern can give the emphasis of weight; absence of elaboration, steady succession of corresponding units, can give the emphasis of speed. In the story of Seal and her younger brother, the daughter's discovery has the latter, her concluding lament the former.

Presentational Form of "Seal and her younger brother."   Let me now indicate how the form of "Seal and her younger brother lived there" has been arrived at in the light of the considerations just given.

Scene i.   This scene is built up of three components. The first consists of a line containing "they lived there" and a line containing action involving the woman who comes. The second component consists of a statement by the girl to her mother. The third consists of the mother's response.

The first stanza, setting the stage for the scene and the whole story, has only the first component. The second and third stanzas have all three.

The first component provides the beginning of each stanza with double marking: "they lived there" (a marker often used by Mrs. Howard and also by Cultee) in the first line, a time reference in the second. (Verses 1, 2, 5 are, of course, simultaneously so marked.) The verses representing the other components are differentiated by specification of a speaker (3, 6) and change of speaker (4, 7).

---

[6]A case of momentary slippage between the two is analyzed in Hymes, "Louis Simpson's 'The deserted boy,' " now chap. 4 of this book. As was noted there, examination of Sapir's field notebooks in which Louis Simpson's "The deserted boy" was recorded makes possible a reconstruction of the performer at work at this point (Hymes 1976a).

Scene ii.   This scene is built up of three components that parallel those of *i,* together with a doubled action and discovery.

The first verse (and stanza D) is internally linked by repetition of a common verb stem ("to lie down [to sleep]"). The second line begins with a temporal marker, but it is the grouping of the lines, three in number, repeating the same verb, in an introductory role parallel to that of the preceding introductory verses (1, 2, 5) that differentiates the verse as a whole.

Stanzas E and F parallel stanzas B and C. Each begins with a temporal marker. The second and third verses of each are differentiated by specification of a speaker (10, 13) and change of speaker (11, 14). Notice the lexical parallelism between the corresponding verses of B, C: E, F (and the expressive variation as well). As in scene *i,* the first verse is shorter. Here it has three lines, while the rest of the stanzas in scene *ii* have uniformly five lines.

Stanza G (= verse 15) is differentiated by the completion of the preceding verse (four times established as conclusion of a verse), and by its own conclusion with *Adi.* In other narratives Mrs. Howard also builds a verse to such a conclusion, and there are generic parallels in other Chinookan narratives (cf. verses 8 and 9 of "The deserted boy" in Hymes, "Louis Simpson's 'The deserted boy,'" chap. 4 of this book). The common element is a sequence of actions by a single actor, leading to a perception of presence or absence. The statement of perception is treated as a separate line because it parallels quoted speech. It is as if the narrator spoke for the girl (and audience). In general, verbalized thoughts and recognitions in Chinookan narratives function in the same way as quoted statements. The verse as a whole thus has five lines.

Stanza H (= verse 16) is differentiated by the completion of the preceding verse and by the specification of a speaker in what follows. The last line ("She screamed") parallels and extends the last line of the preceding verse. There are three verbs in the verse, but five predications, those of the second and third lines being conveyed by apposition. (Literally, his-bed-at (is) her-uncle, cut (is) his-neck.)

In sum, five stanzas—the first a verse set off internally by lexical repetition and externally by parallel introductory role; the second and third parallel in form and function to the second and third of the preceding scene; the fourth and fifth bringing the action to a climax in sequences of five lines each.

Scene iii.   This scene is built of three turns of talk, and it is change of speaker that discriminates among the three verses and stanzas.

Stanza I (= verse 17) consists of ten lines of remonstrance by the girl, framed by two statements of communicative act (she told her mother, she wept). Single verses of this length are not common, but do occur. Stanza J (= verse 18) has three lines of the mother's lament, framed by two statements of communicative act (she said it, she kept on saying it). Stanza K (= verse 19) consists of seven lines of remonstrance by the girl, framed by three statements of communicative act (that she wept and that she said, that she wept). Thus the three verses appear to have respectively twelve, five, and ten lines.

One might think of verses 15 and 16 as completing stanza F, which would then have five verses in all (12–16). The strong parallelism between stanzas A–C and D–F and the recurrent definiteness of the end verse in each (4, 7, 11, 14) lead me to think that 15 cannot be considered as part of F. A fortiori, neither can 16. The resulting pattern for the narrative as a whole, a sort of arc among the three scenes with the central scene most elaborated in number of verses, matches a pattern found in other narratives as well (cf. Simpson's "The deserted boy").

One might think of verses 17, 18, 19 as belonging together to a single stanza. Turns of speech by the girl and her mother have been verses within a single stanza in the preceding scenes. This scene seems different. It is far more elaborated in length and internal complexity (notably in the case of the girl). Most important of all, the two are not to be understood to be engaged in verbal interaction, the mother responding to the girl, as in the preceding scenes. At the outset the girl seeks to tell her mother (the verb stem *-lxam* is inherently transitive and both addressor and addressee are morphologically marked before it) but ends weeping. The mother speaks without an addressee (*-kim* is inherently intransitive, and only a speaker is marked) and ends continuing to do so (the suffix *-niL* is repetitive, *-Ck* perfective). The girl now speaks also without addressee (the forms of the stem *-kim/-gím* are regular alternants depending on the place of stress), and this turn at speaking is enclosed both before and after by "she wept." Indeed, each of the three turns of speech is not simply introduced (as in the preceding scenes) but enclosed.

The elaboration of turns of speech as interaction is not between the two parties to the scene, but within the remonstrance of the one speaker, the girl. Here one has what amounts to a *tour de force* in elaboration of a quintessential feature of Chinookan verbal performance, the saying, rather than reporting, of speech. The girl is said to speak by the narrator, then says she spoke, quotes what she said, says the mother spoke, quotes what the mother said; again says she spoke, quotes, says the mother spoke, quotes; and is said to weep. Ten acts of speech, stated and quoted, in the twelve lines. (It is perhaps in this respect that the verse observes the Chinookan pattern of multiples of five.)

The mother's lament is perhaps addressed to the dead younger brother, but not to her daughter. It is a formal lament, using both the vocative form for the kin relationship *(a-wi)* and the honorific possessed referential form *(Wi-C-uxix)*. Notice that the girl's concluding apostrophe of her uncle does not follow the prescribed form. She does not use the vocative form for 'uncle', but only the honorific possessed referential form *(Wi-C-Lm)*. In form her last two utterances are not addressed even to the dead, but are outbursts of grief.

The elaboration, framing, and expressive weight of these three verses leads me to think that each has the status of a stanza.

Clearly such an analysis finds the recognition of structure to be as much a matter of proportion as of overt punctuation.

What of Mrs. Howard's last sentence, translated by Jacobs as 'Now I remember only that far'? Three of the four words, *AGa kwapt inXÉlutkt*, occur frequently as part of the closing of narratives in the Clackamas texts; they are part of the conventional closing discussed above. A study of their occurrence by Silverstein indicates that they may refer to the possibility of something more to be said, but not in the sense of further scenes of a story. The implication seems rather to be that more detail might be given as to the specific outcome for individual actors. Thus at the end of the myth of Mink and his Elder Brother (Jacobs 1959a:365), a very long and complete narrative, Mrs. Howard recounts the end of Mink, the pronouncement over him of his elder brother (Panther), and then says of Panther that he went somewhere, perhaps he became something. *"AGa kwábt inXÉlutkt,"* and the formal closing, *"k'áni k'áni."* Pretty clearly she is saying only that something more might be said about Panther perhaps, not that the story is unfinished. One gets a sense that the closing is like bringing the actors before the curtain for a bow. More exactly in terms of Chinookan culture, it is to indicate the disposition of each actor in the world that is to be when the people, who are nearby, have arrived. (In keeping with the infinite openness of the world of the myths, the people are always only near; they never, in the myths, have come. Given a language and a world view that emphasized the distinction between perfectivity—completion of action—and imperfectivity, it is suggestive of an eternal presence for the myth world that the passage over into the Indian world is always approached, never completed, in myths themselves.) It is this disposition of Panther in the world of the people who are near that is left unspecified and to which the conventional phrase appears to refer.

The case appears different with the six occurrences of the conventional phrase together with the pronominal word *y-ayma-yx* (literally, 'it' [third-person masculine singular]—only—with regard to location). In these six cases (the narratives numbered 8, 18, 35, 37, 38, 39 by Jacobs) there seems a suggestion that there is a bit more to tell, that the outcome left unresolved for an actor is more a completion of the story itself. This interpretation is strongly indicated by the successive endings of the myth of "Flint and his son's son" (Jacobs 1958:166–79, no. 18). First Mrs. Howard says, "I do not know where he went, And so she remained there, Now I recall only that far, no more," using the pronominal word *yaymayx*. A day or so later she added: "There she was. A little later then she saw smoke far away there. She thought, 'Where shall I stay overnight? I shall go, I shall stay there overnight.' So she went, she got there, to be sure her husband was there! She had found him. Now then they continued to live at that place with their son. That is as far now as I recall."

This second close has precisely the same words as the preceding close, apart from the absence of the pronominal word. The first is *"Kwába aGa yáymayx inXÉlutkt,*" the second *"Kwábt aGa inXÉlutkt."* It is hard to escape the conclusion that the referent in the discourse of the pronoun in the first close is the added incident (in Chinookan the third-person–masculine-singular pronoun is generally used as the unmarked form) and that its absence in the second close reflects full closure—one might add detail, one might go on, the actors may go on, but this story is now complete.

It seems likely that the occurrence of the pronominal word in the last sentence of Mrs. Howard's performance of the Seal story refers to an additional incident, presumably connected with the return whence "she" had come of the "wife" (cf. the Coos narrative studied by Ramsey, "The wife who goes out like a man"). I confess, however, to finding the story as we have it expressively complete.[7]

Let me now sum up the results of the analysis of the presentational form of Mrs. Howard's "Seal and her younger brother lived there." In the monograph in which the story was published, the text occupies thirty-seven lines. It is presented in nine numbered sections, grouped in five paragraphs of prose. Here I have argued that the text contains some sixty-five lines, organized in nineteen verses, themselves apportioned among eleven stanzas and three scenes. The scene/stanza ratio is 3 : 5 : 3, showing an arc found in some other Chinookan narratives. Three other numerical relations of interest are the elaboration of verses within the stanzas in which the daughter and mother speak to each other (B, C, E, F); the elaboration of lines within the verses (stanzas) in which each laments (I, J, K); and the general elaboration of lines within verses in which the daughter speaks (3, 6, 10, 13, 17, 19). These relations can be seen from the following general table. Parentheses show tabulations of the units identified; brackets show internal structure.

The threefold rhetorical pattern of expectations (onset, ongoing, outcome) can be recognized at each level of this organization. Within verses in which the girl tries to inform her mother, one has the onset (indicating the speech act), the ongoing part (the address and initial statement), the outcome (the critical statement that the "wife" sounds just like a man). Within each of the two verses of action on the part of the girl (G, H), there is an onset involving upward action (of the girl, of the light), an ongoing activity and its

---

[7]Cf. the remarks in the appendix to chap. 7 on the unity of the text. In consequence, I have given the final remark a number as a putative verse and line, but I have not included it in the analysis of the narrative into stanzas and scenes. Closings in general stand apart in this way. Therefore, the formal close of Louis Simpson's "The deserted boy," "Thus the ways," while counted in my analysis as verse 56, does not enter into the patterning of verses into stanzas and scenes and acts. Cf. my "Louis Simpson's 'The deserted boy,'" pp. 164–70 (where there is nothing to be said with regard to pattern of stanzas), and pp. 170–75 (where there is nothing to be said with regard to scenes). (See chap. 4.)

Titles also stand apart. A performance would begin with the first line, not the title. The title would be used to mention or ask for the story. (Hence Silverstein's view of the title as minimal performance, a view in keeping with Kenneth Burke's notion of entitlement.)

Scenes	Stanzas		Verses		Lines		
i	A	1			1–2	(2)	
	B	2–4	(3)		3–9	(7)	[2–4–1]
	C	5–7	(3)		10–15	(6)	[2–3–1]
ii	D	8			16–18	(3)	
	E	9–11	(3)		19–23	(5)	[1–3–1]
	F	12–14	(3)		24–28	(5)	[1–3–1]
	G	15	(1)		29–33	(5)	
	H	16	(1)		34–38	(5)	
iii	I	17	(1)		39–50	(12)	[1–10[2–2;4–2]–1]
	J	18	(1)		51–55	(5)	[1–3–1]
	K	19	(1)		56–65	(10)	[2–7[3–2–2]–1]

Table 9–1. Profile of "Seal and her younger brother lived there"

outcome (G), a discovery and its outcome (H). In each of the verses of lament there is again the onset (indicating the speech act), the ongoing body of the verse (the words of lament), the only outcome (the continued weeping and saying, respectively, of daughter and mother).

Within stanzas, one has the threefold relationship among verses 2–3–4 of stanza B, 5–6–7 of C, 9–10–11 of E, 12–13–14 of F, that is, in each case in which there are three verses within a stanza to make the relationship possible.

Within scenes one has the relationship among stanzas. In scene *i* it obtains among the three stanzas (A–B–C). In scene *ii* it obtains among the five stanzas in the pattern of D–E, F–G, H. In scene *iii* it can be seen to obtain among the three stanzas (I, J, K) if one takes the girl's initial attempt to speak to her mother as defining an onset, the ceaseless saying of the other as an ongoing continuation, the girl's weeping and saying as the outcome, defining the separateness of each in her own form of grief.

The three scenes, given here the headings of "The 'wife' comes," "The uncle dies," "The women lament," have clearly the threefold relationship.

The "outer" and "inner" aspects of presentational form, so to speak, mutually condition and reinforce each other.

V. Implications and Other Approaches

The discovery of such organization in Native American narratives seems to me of fundamental importance. It makes it possible, indeed essential, to regard such texts as works of literary art. From the point of view of translation, interpretation, appreciation, the analysis gives a degree of control over matters of emphasis, tone, foregrounding, and the like. One can provide the rudiments, at least, of a theory of the structure of literary discourse in the language and culture in question.

Structuralism.   The development of such theories would go beyond the two main approaches to Native American texts today. The first, associated with Lévi-Strauss, seeks dialectical structures of content and a universal model of such structuring. It neglects, even ignores, the ways in which narratives are organizations of linguistic means and diverts attention from the basic task of finding theories adequate to specific literatures. In its leap to universals, the approach seems to resemble the confident general linguistics of the turn of the century, before the "analytic" approach of Boas showed the confidence unfounded. There is need in this respect for a Boasian stance again, perhaps even for works analogous to those he and his students provided for languages, a "Handbook of American Indian narratives," to set forth representative types in detail, together with integrating and generalizing chapters of the sort Sapir provided in his book on language of 1921. But these chapters should be "Form in narrative: Structural processes," "Form in narrative: Structural categories," "Types of narrative structure."

The approach of the present paper is undoubtedly structuralist in a fundamental sense, the sense of the Prague School of Trubetzkoy and Jakobson and of the American tradition of Sapir, that of seeking form-meaning covariation and patterning based upon it. It is also structuralist in its insistence on language, a requirement that anthropologists so often conveniently forget. Interpretation of myth must be grounded in philology. Let me select one or two points of a revised translation of "Seal and her younger brother lived there" to show this.[8]

A translation may allow one to recognize the presence of many elements and actions, but not necessarily all of them. The very direction of an action, its physical character, its timing relative to other acts, the parties present to it or responsible for it, may be signaled in Chinookan in elements that an unannotated translation does not convey or even misrepresents. For example, the recurrent translation 'I do not know' for phrases involving the word *Luxwan* is true to the English idiom of Chinookan speakers, but misses the tone of voice and intent. The original word has no 'I' or 'don't' in it. Its root is the stem 'to think', its meaning when used alone 'perhaps', its negative force

---

[8]We lack a grammar and dictionary in published form of Clackamas, but the dialect is close enough to Wasco (Wishram) for knowledge of its structure and lexicon to be consistently helpful. The continuum of grammatical and semantic change from Shoalwater at the ocean to Wasco (Wishram) two hundred miles upriver has been clarified in a recent monograph by Silverstein ("Dialectal developments in Chinookan tense-aspect systems: An areal-historical analysis," *International Journal of American Linguistics*, Memoir 29; issued together with Memoir 28, "On aspect theory and Homeric aspect," by Paul Friedrich [Chicago, 1974]). The work in progress by Silverstein and me on a dictionary of Wasco has deepened our understanding of *kiksht* (of which Clackamas is a part). In interpreting forms in a text or for a dictionary, we regularly bring to bear what is known of the other dialects; the whole frequently illuminates a part.

of 'not know' a development in conjunction with other particles in conventional phrases. It is indeed in keeping with Chinookan concern with definiteness and perfectivity that such a word shifts from 'think' to 'perhaps' to 'not know'. But the rest of the phrases in which it occurs show by their makeup that what is being asserted is what may be called (in Silverstein's phrase) "definite unspecific": a definite time that is not specified, say, or a definite place or act. When it occurs in relation to time, it does not replace a more exact statement that might have been supplied. One finds "a long time ago," "a long time," "morning," "evening," "night," "yesterday," "the next day," "five days," and so forth. In the context of the opening of the Seal narrative, Seal and her kin have been indefinitely there, so that it would make no sense to say "five days later." And myths simply do not say "in April" or "on the first day of the week." One might say "in winter" or "in summer" if germane, but nothing in this story depends on season (though the implicit season is indeed winter).

The phrase (verse 9), in fact, occurs again where no definite hour could be given in a myth, only a substitute such as "later" or "soon." There is a three-step progression here, from the unstated time that the husband and wife go to bed, through the time (pretty soon, presently) when the mother and daughter lie down, to the time when the girl first perceives something. The phrase with *Luxwan* seems the marked, emphasizing form. It seems significant that the two occurrences of phrases with *Luxwan* are at two crucial onsets of the action, the first coming of the "wife" and the first discovery of the evidence of the murder. Within the development of a narrative, then, such phrases seem to have a rhetorical role. One simply has to attend to the language of texts to avoid being misled by initial translation. In the case in question, one should not look for what is missing, but for the significance of what is being emphasized.

Again, the particle *tL'á* is apparently a pun. Jacobs translates it with strict accuracy in its syntactic role. When preceding a noun that is followed by *diwi*, it means precisely 'just. . . . .like'. (There is a parallel construction in Kathlamet.) But the particle is also a word that stands for the sound made by water coming out of a hose or, in the present case, a human orifice that would be the height of a man's penis above the ground. (Women, squatting, would make a different sound.) Seal's daughter is made to say both "that" and "what" the "wife" sounds like in the one word.

Again, the verb in verse 12 that indicates what the girl hears in bed is a complex verb that does not in fact precisely mean "something dripping"; the published translation is not wrong, but inexact. The verbal construction actually states, as a subordinate clause of perception, that something is "missing" (in the sense in which a bullet or arrow misses a target), going out of the intended line; so far, the stem. It also says that it is doing so 'out of a small enclosed space' in the indirect object—postposition sequence, *i-q'n* (where *q'n* is diminutive of *-q'l*). And it says that it is doing so in relation to a body, since the diminutive dual prefix *s-* is always (and frequently) used in verbal constructions that refer to activities involving dual parts of the body. ("To jump" thus involves specification of the feet, one verb "to look" thus involves reference to the eyes, and so on.) The final suffix *-ix* designates a location. In sum, the word indicates to the audience something the girl does not yet know, namely, that what she hears is a place where something inherently part of a body is escaping. Blood as such is not implied, since the prefix of concord with the noun for blood would be *L*. Probably the channels of blood in the already severed neck are implied.

For visualization of the drama, the precise translation of verse 8 is most important. My own understanding of the translation of this verse, as of the words just mentioned, has grown with further work with Clackamas texts and with Wasco lexicography. In the original paper (n. 6) I took the *-ga-* of the verb in the first line of verse 8 to be a verbal intensifier, derived from the root *-ga*, 'to fly'. Such an intensifier exists, parallel to the root *-da*, both having the force of 'fast motion', the one in the air, the other on the ground. Still, *-ga* is not otherwise attested with the stem 'to lie down'. It is plausible enough, since the stem itself can be used as a euphemism for having sex, and *-ga-* would add an ingredient of 'flying at each other' (an ingredient attested in a stem meaning 'to fight'). But Silverstein has discovered a series of verb themes in Wasco in which the motion of doing something 'up on' makes use of a *-ga-* preceding the verb stem. This *-ga* is a postposition of local relation, and the *-u-* preceding it is the required indirect object marker, specifically, a marker of third person. The use of *u-ga-* in such constructions is well attested, although the sequence itself is a fossilized one without literal meaning so far as *u-* itself is concerned. It occurs with verbs of putting things, and oneself, up, especially (with people) on a horse, or by extension, a car, and with the alighting of birds.[9]

The translation of the verb as 'to lie down above' fits perfectly the setting and disposition of actors sketched in the verse. In an aboriginal Chinookan house the honored bed associated with a fire was a platform bed, extending between posts. (There might be several such beds and associated fires in a large house.) The valued, decorated posts of which Seal speaks in her lament presumably are the posts of this bed. Again, in an aboriginal Chinookan house it would be customary for an older person and a younger person of the same sex to sleep together below by the fire. Thus the three verbs of verse 8 describe for us, not one, but two pairs of people. That is why the second occurrence of the verb stem 'to lie down' is preceded by the independent pronoun *SdáX*. The pronoun is not needed if there is no change of actors (or contrastive

[9]The combination would usually occur as *-u-gwa*, the *-w-* being induced by the preceding *-u-* (a common habit of pronunciation in all the Chinookan dialects), but Mrs. Howard, like other speakers, varies in this regard. In the text of the volume in question (Jacobs, 1959a), the word *nuXwilayt* ('they lived there') occurs as the first word, while in line 2 from the bottom of the next page, it occurs as *nuXilayt*.

emphasis). The verb itself is inflected by pronominal prefix for actor, the dual prefix *S-* (followed by reflexive *X*). If only the verb occurred, indeed, the obvious translation would be that in the published monograph, and unfortunately followed unreflectingly by me in my first paper. The "two" of all three verbs in the verse would be taken as the same two. But the independent pronoun has force. (Cf. *áX* ['she'] at the beginning of verse 19.) It is contrastive.

The third line of this verse, it should be noted, does several things at once. It completes the three-part pattern for the setting of the scene, and indeed, the repetition of the stem 'to lie down', might be thought to be merely an easy way to fulfill the pattern before going on—a pause for narrator and audience, as it were (Finley 1965:23). Each occurrence of the stem, however, is differently inflected and complemented. As we have seen, the first occurrence identifies the younger brother and his "wife" with local relational prefix *-ga-* 'up on' and complement *wilxmit-ba* 'at the bed', while the second identifies Seal and her daughter with the separate pronoun for 'those two' and the phrase 'near (the) fire' *(q'wap wátuL).* The third line has no complement, being solely the verb, but the verb has a different local relational prefix, *-gm-* 'beside'. Its contrast to *-ga-* 'up on' anchors the reference to Seal and her daughter in two ways. Of course, there would not be an unannounced shift of actors as between the second and third lines, and the reference continues to be to Seal and her daughter in any case. The use of *-gm-* clarifies the contrast between the two pairs by specifying 'beside' rather than 'upon', but also by implying, as it were, 'beside' rather than 'inside'. Used without such prefix, the stem 'to lie down' with dual, reflexive subject, is an idiom for mutual copulation (cf. Jacobs 1958:35, line 11 of the text). That is why the translation is put in quotes in the first line, and the subsequent action of the very next verse shows that sexual position as well as location is meant. Seal and her daughter are shown in this third line of the first verse of the scene to be, retrospectively, merely "beside" each other, and, prospectively, to be beside each other for what immediately follows. What comes onto the girl's face must barely miss the face of the mother and be equally well heard. In sum, the one-verb line simultaneously completes structure, clarifies idiomatic implication, and highlights subsequent drama.

In short, interpretation of a verbal prefix and a pronominal word in the light of other knowledge of the language helps to etch more accurately the image projected in the story. It is as if the action were projected onto an Elizabethan stage. Let me imagine the three scenes in this way.

After a prologue, one sees as if in an inner stage a platform bed on ornate posts. It is evening and the bed is barely lit by a fire below and in front of it. The bed on its posts seems to loom above an old woman and her daughter, who enter to the front, toward the audience. They exchange words about two others not yet seen, part, return, exchange words again in the same way and to the same effect.

Now the figures of a man and woman enter to the rear and climb up on the bed. Their figures are indistinct. Shortly, the old woman and young girl lie down together below and in front of the bed, beside the fire. Twice again the girl speaks and is shushed by the older woman. The girl rises, goes to the fire, prepares a torch, goes toward the inner stage, raises the torch above it: the decapitated body of a man is revealed.

Now the girl and the older woman come each to one side of the front of the stage. The girl speaks toward her mother and weeps. The mother speaks, either toward the platform bed, or out over the heads of the audience. The girl speaks now, as if to herself, and weeps.

I submit that such a drama is worthy of our attention, and that it bespeaks, not the imperturbable self-transmogrification of myth, but lived experience and a voice.

Ethnopoetics.   One of the most important contributions to our understanding of Native American narratives as performances has come from the work of Dennis Tedlock with Zuni. In what follows I criticize certain observations by Tedlock, because of what I believe to be unfortunate implications that might mislead and limit what can be done in the field as a whole, but yield to no one in my admiration for what he himself has accomplished with Zuni and is now doing with Quiché Maya.

Tedlock believes all oral narrative to be inherently poetic in the sense of being organized in lines. He writes (1972b:221):

> The outward appearance of a printed collection of oral narratives immediately gives away a basic feature of our attitude toward such narratives: we regard them as a sort of primitive or nonliterate counterpart to our own written prose fiction and thus set them forth in gray masses of words broken only by paragraphing. . . .
>
> My own consideration of the paralinguistic features of Zuni narratives, including voice quality, loudness, and pausing, has led me to treat these narratives not only as drama but as poetry, with each pause indicated by a line change as in written poetry and other oral features noted in parentheses at the left-hand margin as in a play.

This method, that of identifying pauses in spoken performance, is unavailable for narratives in Shoalwater, Kathlamet, and Clackamas Chinook, such as that of "Seal and her younger brother," and for the narratives in Wasco (Wishram) told by Louis Simpson. If poetics is to depend on paralinguistics, any line-organized poetic nature of such texts could not be known, nor could they in turn contribute to general poetics in this regard. If one must use only tape-recorded material, most of what is recorded in Native North American tradition must be forgotten. Tedlock comes close to saying this: "Moreover, nearly all of the published narratives were collected by the dictation method, which distorts narrative flow and results in the total loss of paralinguistic features. Our most valuable resource, far more valuable than the phonetically transcribed texts so cherished in the past, will be our tape recordings of actual performances" (1972b:238).

Let me comment on the phrases "total loss" and "most valuable." First, as to "total loss." The best dictated texts are not in fact wholly without indication of the features in question. In the transcription of Louis Simpson's "The deserted boy," Sapir noted departure from normal pitch for expressive particles and regularly indicated extra length for emphasis. His marking of stress enables one to detect expressive departures from normal stress and to recognize stress rhythms. His field notebooks show that Sapir used abbreviatory formulas for recurrent words and phrases; occasional insertions suggest that he was writing in phrases and short sentences. He did not interrupt for translation at the time of dictation.

Jacobs, like Sapir a student of Boas, worked in a similar way. His comments in the notes to the two volumes of Clackamas texts indicate that he recorded straight through a text, seeking translation later, and include such observations as the following (1958:4–5):

> Where I note lengthened vowels or consonants the lengthening is in nearly all instances rhetorical. . . .
>
> As valuable as current emphasis upon phonemic texts may be, we should not permit a high standard for phonemic precision to function so as to exorcise indicators which ticket sundry features of communication which are primarily emotional or rhetorical. I have therefore been lavish in use of lengthenings and other sound indicators wherever I judged that they reported something significant about the speech style of the informant. For example, although phonemic tone is no more a characteristic of Chinook than are long phonemes, I have resorted to tonal symbols from time to time in order to provide some record of tone as a facet of rhetorical behavior. . . .
>
> Raised dots after a phoneme indicate lengthening for rhetorical purposes, as in *adi· ´. . .*, 'oh dear me'.

Tedlock probably has in mind, as did Jacobs, the view that developed among many linguists in the 1930s and 1940s that transcription should be solely phonemic. Such a view is understandable inasmuch as the phoneme was a badge of the new, descriptivist generation; its members often enough dismiss "prephonemic" records. That view is instructive in another way as well: it highlights the unquestioned assumption that linguistic structure should be built up on the basis of referential function alone, to the exclusion of features serving stylistic function. Transcription grosser than the purely phonemic, of course, reflected this second elementary diacritic function of linguistic structure (Dyk and Hymes 1956). The assumption of so many descriptivists remains with us in transformational generative grammar and is a major cost accompanying the benefits from the successive waves of Bloomfieldian and Chomskian dominance. The contrary view of Boas, Sapir, and Jacobs that one should record and present conventional phonetic habits, expressive as well as referential, comes to seem in the context of ethnopoetics, not old hat, but a cause for gratitude. Their texts preserve some of the information one seeks and that others lose.

Now, as to "most valuable." Texts dictated without benefit of tape recorder, though deficient for some purposes, are often the only monument of their kind to a heritage. That the texts exist at all in usable form may make them the only avenue to a tradition for descendants of those who dictated them. When one assesses the value of Native American materials, one must consider the situation of Native Americans themselves.

The older, dictated texts, moreover, may still be grist for the ethnopoetic mill. I hope to have shown this with regard to "Seal and her younger brother lived there." Let me now take up the issue in general, methodological terms.

To identify poetic lines and to do so by means of pauses are not necessarily the same thing. The method of identifying pauses raises questions that need to be addressed. Would other performances, repetitions, disclose the same placing of pause? If not, is there a pattern to which the variation is to be referred? If there is a pattern, if the verse nature of the narrative is not wholly ad hoc, how is this pattern established? What is it like? Is it the same for all narratives, texts, speech? The taking of breath, after all, introduces pauses into all extended speech. Can sheer division by pauses suffice to determine specifically poetic organization? Some may happily accept the implication that all speech is inherently poetry, that poetry is essentially paused speech. In his introduction to Tedlock's book, Jerome Rothenberg focuses on interplay of sound and silence, on listening to breath pauses (Rothenberg 1972:xii–xiii), and Tedlock himself is convinced by his Zuni experiment that "prose has no real existence outside the written page" (Tedlock 1972b:xix). Yet even if pause is basic to poetry, there remains the problem of differentiating pause that is motivated, that heightens the organization of lines, from pause that is inherent in the spoken medium. There remains the problem of detecting the invariants of cultural genres and the characteristics of personal styles. Exciting as is the possibility of initial demarcation through pause, it is only a step toward poetics.[10]

[10]Cf. the following passage from Jakobson (1960:364–65):

Far from being an abstract, theoretical scheme, meter—or in more explicit terms, *verse design*—underlies the structure of any single line—or, in logical terminology, any single *verse instance*. Design and instance are correlative concepts. The verse design determines the invariant features of the verse instances and sets up the limits of variations. A Serbian peasant reciter of epic poetry memorizes, performs, and, to a high extent, improvises thousands, sometimes tens of thousands of lines, and their meter is alive in his mind. Unable

When Tedlock discusses actual lines, in fact, he begins to mention features other than pause. He observes that some sequences of lines are marked by stress on final syllable, and others by chanting, accompanied by a characteristic distribution of pitch (pp. xxi–xxiii). Perhaps it is not accidental that the passages cited to illustrate such points also show parallelism of structure, enclosing an apposition, in the first case (p. xxi); full clauses (p. xxii) in the second; and also threefold repetition (pp. xxii–xxiii). Not only is pause not the only phonic marker of lines; one begins to suspect that lines have a grammatical aspect as well. Perhaps a study of the narratives in terms of the repetition of features other than pause would show an organization into lines, and not necessarily the same organization. Perhaps pause does not so much define lines, as provide a counterpoint to them, analogous to the ways in which variation and effect are gained in European verse by caesurae within lines, enjambment and end-stopping between them, all the ways in which variations and effect may be gained by playing off sources of periodicity and rhythm against a regulated base.

Should this be so, then to lack tape recordings would be to miss something valuable, the realization in performance to which Tedlock so rightly and creatively calls attention; but it would not be to lose everything. Poetic structure could still be found. The indispensable tool would not be a tape recorder, but a hypothesis.

In short, one can accept a minimal definition of poetry as discourse organized in lines. Such a view indeed was arrived at on other grounds by the late A. W. de Groot (1946, 1964; cf. Stutterheim 1948) and later, without awareness of de Groot's work, by me (1960). (Tedlock has indicated that this note was brought to his attention at Tulane by J. F. Fischer.) But one cannot be content with a purely definitional victory for the claim of the pervasiveness of poetry as lines, a definition that identifies poetry with a physical necessity of spoken discourse. Pausing may itself be culturally shaped, but if it is, one

---

to abstract its rules, he nonetheless notices and repudiates even the slightest infringement of these rules. Any line of Serbian epics contains precisely ten syllables and is followed by a syntactic pause. There is furthermore a compulsory absence of word boundary before the fifth syllable and a compulsory absence of word boundary before the fourth and tenth syllable. . . .

This Serbian epic break, along with many similar examples presented by comparative metrics, is a persuasive warning against the erroneous identification of a break with a syntactic pause. The obligatory word boundary must not be combined with pause and is not even meant to be /365/ perceptible by the ear. The analysis of Serbian epic songs phonographically recorded proves that there are no compulsory audible clues to the break, and yet any attempt to abolish the word boundary before the fifth syllable by a mere insignificant change in word order is immediately condemned by the narrator. The grammatical fact that the fourth and fifth syllables pertain to two different word units is sufficient for the appraisal of the break. Thus verse design goes far beyond the questions of sheer sound shape; it is a much wider linguistic phenomenon, and it yields to no isolating phonetic treatment.

needs evidence beyond the fact of its occurrence. In Kenneth Burke's terms, one must get from the realm of motion to that of action. One does not fully face the issue posed by the claim that a body of oral narrative is poetic, in the sense of organization into lines, until one goes beyond the existence of lines to principles governing lines and relates such principles to the organization of texts in other respects as well.

Older texts make us face the issue directly. If they are manifestations of a tradition of organization into lines, that organization can be discovered only in the lines themselves, and in their relations to one another, for that is the evidence available. I do not expect that all Native American traditions will be found to parallel the Chinookan, but I do think that the starting point of the analysis of Chinookan texts, the identification of verses and lines in terms of initial elements and associated discourse features, will likely prove general. The task is the development of theories adequate and specific to each tradition.

VI. Conclusion

The situation for the discovery of poetic structure and the lineaments of performance in Native American texts is one that has been recurrent in the history of insight into poetries not our own. It is a situation almost hallowed by association with discovery of parallelistic verse in the transmitted text of the Old Testament and of alliterative Anglo-Saxon lines in the run-on transcriptions of such poems as "The Wanderer" in the *Exeter book*. Austerlitz has made such a discovery in Ob-Ugric poetry (Hymes 1960); Edmonson has begun for the Popol Vuh of the Quiché Maya. Native North American texts have many such contributions to make, both human and scholarly. In each case, the uncovering of poetic sculpture within stony, facing-page prose will have meaning to descendants of the original artists; simply in terms of accessibility, versions of texts organized in terms of verses are found more attractive. There is much to be done in the development of necessary typefaces and fonts, and typographic layouts, if the texts are to be presented in their original language as well as in translation. But ultimately perhaps the literary traditions native to our land may be given something approaching the degree of sustained attention given Anglo-Saxon. There is greatness to be found in both. And there may be an essential contribution to general poetics and literary theory. The contribution to a truly comparative, general literature, in which the verbal art of mankind as a whole has a place, might be analogous to the effect once had by grammars of Native American languages on general linguistics, expanding and deepening our understanding of what it can mean to be possessed of language.

10

Reading Clackamas Texts

I want to show that close attention to a detail of language can illuminate the meaning that Native American myths must have had for their narrators and can have for us today.

An odd beginning, you may say. Do we not know that literature exists in the medium of words? Do we not live amidst a smorgasbord of efforts to deal with verbal form? Not, sad to say, in the study of Native American narratives. The reviver of serious attention among scholars to the riches of Native American collections, discoverer of the principle of transformational inversion in the creation of myths, Lévi-Strauss, has set aside control of linguistic detail as both impractical for the work he intended and of little importance to structure. Melville Jacobs, the man who made possible this study by seeking out and preserving the texts on which it is based, disparaged focus on the linguistics as a route to meaning and style. This is not the place to speculate on the reasons for such views, but I believe that a basic element is that those who take an interest in Native American materials do not find

This chapter is a revised version of an essay first published in Karl Kroeber (ed.) *Traditional literatures of the American Indian* (Lincoln: University of Nebraska Press, 1981), pp. 117–59. There are changes in references and forms of citation to accord with the present book, and also changes in translation and analysis, particularly of passages from the myth of "Gitskux and his older brother." The entire myth had not yet been analyzed at the time that portions of it were drawn upon for the essay. No essential findings are affected but refinement of the analysis has changed specific details and brought to light additional points. There are also some differences of wording and conclusion, due to different editing of the two versions.

The essay in Karl Kroeber's book itself draws upon chapters in the first draft of a book dealing with the figure of the Grizzly Woman, tentatively entitled *Bears that save and destroy* (Hymes ms. d).

For the spelling of Clackamas words, see the orthographic note.

Single citations of passages in Clackamas texts refer to the two original collections. Thus, 1958:97:5 refers to Clackamas Chinook Texts Part I, page 97, line 5. A subsequent citation of 98:11 refers simply to page 98, line 11 in that volume. The two volumes are paginated consecutively, so that any single page number is uniquely found in one or the other volume. Volume Part I (1958) has page numbers 1–299; Part II (1959) has page numbers 301 onward. Where the citation has two parts, the first part refers to the verse analysis indicating structural units of the narrative; the second part is a page citation to the Jacobs volumes. Thus, (One I ii Bc; 316:10) refers first to part One, act I, scene ii, stanza B, verse c, and then to p. 316, line 10. Sometimes references are given to the lineation of the analyzed text itself. Some references are given to the as yet unpublished verse analysis of the myth of "Gitskux and his older brother."

in place an adequate philology on which to build and lack the patience, or at least the opportunity, to bring such philology about. Again and again, we are reduced to dealing with literature in translation, unable to control what lies behind the translation.

The problems of understanding what Native American narrators have intended and expressed is difficult enough. It is far more difficult if, in a certain sense, we do not know what they said. Such a circumstance would not be tolerated in serious study of classical Greek and Latin literature, of the Bible, of Old English poetry, of the Russian novel, and the like. It should not be tolerated in the serious study of Native American literature. A tacit double standard and the shameful neglect of institutional support for scholarship in the subject permit it to continue.

Even if one agrees in principle with the position just stated, it is not easy to point to an example of the difference that adequate philology would make. It is hard to point to an example of *reading* a Native American text in the Native American language for interpretation dependent on features of the language. I hope that this paper will provide an example of the kind required. So far as I know, it is the first instance of developing an interpretation of the meaning of a set of Native American texts on the basis of a linguistic variable, a stylistic device that cannot be represented in English translation.

The device—I did not know it to be one to begin with—consists of variation in the prefix to noun stems in Clackamas Chinook. In all the Chinookan languages a noun is not a complete word unless its stem is preceded by a prefix. There are exceptions to this, in that speakers are able to cite the stem of the word, especially, it seems, the name of a creature, if they wish. The speech of the youngest generation to learn something of the language has sometimes been criticized by older speakers for dropping these prefixes, and it indeed seems that the prefixes are the last layer of structure to be fixed in the noun. The contemporary situation may be influenced by the rise in the nineteenth century of Chinook Jargon, a trade language based in important part on Chinookan vocabulary that dropped Chinookan grammatical machinery, as is normally the case with pidgin lingua francas. In the middle and late nineteenth century, surviving Chinookan speakers usually knew this prefixless code alongside their other languages.

The prefixes have both a lexical and grammatical role. On the one hand, change of prefix can change the meaning of a word. All the prefixes of concern to us can be characterized as expressing third-person meanings (and are clearly derived from third-person pronoun elements), distinguishing between singular, dual, and plural in number, and between "masculine," "feminine," and "neuter" in the singular itself. Lexical gender matches biological gender with words for human beings and creatures of a certain size: *a-dúiha* 'cow', *i-dúiha* 'steer'; *a-k'aSk'as* 'girl', *i-k'aSk'as* 'boy'. Some nouns are inherently dual, never occurring with a singular prefix (e.g., words for "eyes," "testicles," "double-barreled shotgun"). There are a variety of interesting specifics of this sort, more than need be considered for our purpose.

The point about the prefixes on which this study focuses is that they do not differ as to number or gender. At first glance, the difference appears arbitrary. *a-* is third-person-singular feminine, and so is *wa-*. *i-* is third-person-singular masculine, and so is *wi-*.

The great linguists Franz Boas and Edward Sapir once suggested that the occurrence of *wa-* or *a-*, *wi-* or *i-*, depended on the length of the following noun stem. The forms with *w-* occurred with monosyllabic stems, preserved or elaborated to balance their brevity. One might also suspect that the variation reflects a change in progress in the language, a change not yet brought to completion. That idea would fit better the fact that one and the same noun stem can sometimes be found with both alternatives, as is the case with the names of interest here. One might suspect dialect difference or dialect mixture in the materials collected by Jacobs, since Victoria Howard reported hearing some of her narratives from her mother's mother, some from her mother-in-law, who came from a somewhat more easterly community along the Columbia. For reasons tedious to expound here, none of these explanations holds. A reading of the texts points to the use of *wa-* or *a-* as motivated by expressive intent, by point of view. Recognition of this device deepens understanding of the texts. Specifically, a reading of the texts shows that the significance of the naming of Grizzly Women depends upon placement as well as shape of prefix.

Placement has to do with where the Grizzly Woman is named, whether in the title or in the text, and at what point in the text.

Prefix has to do with two levels of choice. One is choice of a singular or nonsingular prefix from the regular paradigmatic set of noun-initial prefixes. The dual and plural prefixes seem to go together with a view of Grizzly Women as a *type* encountered in adventures, although some such Grizzly Women are indeed named with a singular prefix. The second level of choice is that of *wa-* or *a-* or Ø (zero). It is this choice that appears to be most frequent, subtle, and revealing of point of view.

In this essay I am especially concerned with the significance of distinctions between *wa-* and *a-*. Some twelve texts in Jacobs's two collections are relevant to the naming of Grizzly Bears as a whole.[1] Here we will deal only

[1]The texts are listed in the order of publication, together with the numbers assigned them by Jacobs, and the source he reports Mrs. Howard as having given. A question mark indicates that he was not able to report information as to source. Texts through #30 are in Jacobs (1958), the others in (1959a).

#3. Coon and Coyote went and stole. (Mother's Mother)
#9. Coyote went around the land. (?)
#16. Black Bear and Grizzly Woman and their sons. (MoMo)
#17. Grizzly Woman killed people. (?)
#30. Thunder and his Mother. (MoMo, Mother-in-law)
#31. Cock-Robin, his older sister, and his sister's daughter. (Mo, Mo-in-law)

with those involving Grizzly Woman (Grizzly Ogress) herself. They form four sets, distinguished in terms of pattern of naming:

(1)	a- (wa- in title)	(Text 134)
(2)	wa-, a- (wa- in title when so named [16])	(Texts 9, 16, 34)
(3a)	a-, Ø (wa- in title)	(Text 17)
(b)	a-, Ø	(Text 31)

Table 10–1. Four types of prefix alternation

The first two sets (1–2) can be treated together as involving both *wa-* and *a-* but not Ø (zero); the third and fourth sets (3a, b) can be treated together as both involving alternation with Ø. Within the first pair, the second set especially indicates the significance of naming and of the distinction among prefix-alternants. The second pair confirm such significance and open up a more general perspective and interpretation. Within the second pair (3a) is a favorable opportunity to present and explore an entire myth.

Variable Prefix and Point of View: wa-/a-   (1) *a-* (*wa-* in title). In "Grizzly Woman pursued him" (Jacobs 1959a:557–59, text 134), the title has *wa-*, while the text names the Ogress once with *a-* (558:7). She is named at the peripety of the action. Old Watcheeno's father has fled from her to a tree and shot at her vainly while she has been digging up the tree. Out of arrows, he thinks of starting a fire. When he throws down burning dry limbs and moss, Grizzly Woman sees them, throws herself on the bundle, puts it out. It is at this point that the action of the story reverses direction. It changes from her pursuit and digging to her being diverted and drawn away by fire. To name her at this turning point seems to heighten the confrontation, identifying just whom the man is escaping and besting. That the naming is with *a-*, not *wa-*, suggests that Grizzly Woman occurs here in the role of a dangerous creature of the forest, not any role of kinship and personal identity. Indeed, there is nothing of the latter in the adventure.

(2) *Wa-, a-*. Three texts alternate *wa-* and *a-* (9, 16, 34). In "Coyote went around the land" (9), Coyote meets women who are gathering grass. They tell him that Grizzly Woman covers them with it, then bakes them (as food for her husband). Here (Jacobs 1958:97:5) she is named with *wa-*. Coyote succeeds in pushing Grizzly Woman into the fire (rather like Gretel saving Hansel), where she will be left for her returning unsuspecting husband to eat.

#34. Gitskux and his older brother. (MoMo) (Gitskux=-Gickux [Jacobs])
#40. KuSaydi and his older brother. (Mo-in-law)
#134. Grizzly Woman pursued him. (Mo-in-law)
#143. The Grizzly Women. (MoMo)
#144. Spear fishing near Grande Ronde. (Mrs. Howard, quoting MoMo)

The grateful women take Coyote to their houses, telling people, "This man saved our hearts; we have killed Grizzly Woman." Here (98:11), she is named with *a-*.

On the assumption that the difference is significant, not accidental, the contrast in connotation is clear. With *wa-*, Grizzly Woman is a living, controlling, threatening being. With *a-*, she is dead.

In "Black Bear and Grizzly Woman and their sons" (16), both women are named with *wa-* in the title and a number of times in the text. Black Bear herself is named always with *a-* (*skintwa*). Her name occurs once with *wa-* in reference to her children (146:12), signaling a shift in generation (from Black Bear to her children) and a reversal in power (from Grizzly Woman's side to Black Bear's side). Grizzly has returned from finally killing Black Bear while out berrying. The three-line sequence goes: she went, she went homeward, she arrived. It is followed by a sequence which begins: "Black Bear's children were going about by the river. / They did not see their mother. / Now he (her eldest son, the hero of the rest of the story with name-title of his own Wasgúkmayli) thought, / 'Now she has killed her'. He said nothing to her." From now on the action centers on the revenge and escape effected by Black Bear's children under the leadership of Wasgúkmayli. The placement seems at a turning point, as in the case of the naming in "Grizzly Woman pursued him."

The Ogress herself is consistently named with *wa-* in the first part of the myth. The contrast to the *a-* with which Black Bear is named is consistent with the difference between the two in power and control. *Wa-* is retained for Grizzly Woman's name in reference to her children at the point of their being killed by Black Bear's son (147:8), after she has gone off again. Perhaps this heightens the identification; it would seem to retain the threat of her own revenge in full force. A change to *a-* with her name comes when Wasgúkmayli halloos to Crane to take him and the rest of Black Bear's children across the river, because Grizzly Woman (here *a-*) is following them (150:16). By now the story has shown her deceived as to the stew she eats on her return (it has her child in it); deceived by the dog left behind as to the direction in which Black Bear's children have escaped; deceived by a trick in which excrements fall on her from a tree. She has indeed "died" (become unconscious) as a result of the last deception, and is in that state, so far as the text goes, at the time she is named in the halloo to Crane.

The Ogress is *wa-* again as she revives and takes up the pursuit (151:5). She is not named again until the end—not in her drowning, after Crane tips her into the river, or when her vagina is picked at by Crows, or when she smears its blood on her face, or when she journeys through the woods to ask each tree its opinion of her looks, rewarding those who flatter by endowing them as useful to the people who will come. At long last she reaches a house where people are saying: "When Wasgúkmayli and his younger brothers went, it was really long long ago." Then, the text says, Grizzly Woman *(wa-)* ate them up. She repeats as if in a dazed stupor what the people had said, and that Grizzly Woman *(wa-)* ate them up (156:3, 5). In sum, she has *wa-* when she is in control, pursuing, eating people, but *a-* once when temporarily she is "dead."

It may be significant that Grizzly Woman is not named in the long epilog to the main story. It is in the main story, widely known in native North America, that she is the Grizzly Ogress who kills kin, pursues people; and it is when the main story is recalled in the coda and she eats people that her name (with *wa-*) returns. In the interval—an interval not unique to the Clackamas, but shared with the Kathlamet version of the story—Grizzly Woman is variously a victim, crazed or absurd, and caught up in a long sequence of looking ahead to what the world should be like when the Indian people come. When she interrogates trees and rewards or punishes them for their answers by making them useful or useless to the people who will come, she is enacting the fundamental premise of Indian world view that Robert Redfield called "participant maintenance." People and nature are joined in a relationship of mutual benevolence, and it is a punishment to trees to be excluded. The same role with trees is taken by Skunk in a long story I had the privilege of hearing once from Mrs. Blanche Tohet, a Sahaptin speaker. There the role balances Skunk's part otherwise as comic victim, while here in the Clackamas story it balances Grizzly Woman's part as monstrous aggressor. Perhaps we have here an indication that dramatic balance could be a factor in the transformation of myths, the ordaining of the usefulness of trees being thought suitable for such balance.

In "Gitskux[2] and his older brother" (34), the name of the Grizzly Ogress begins with the prefix *a-* four, perhaps five, times. Each fits easily into the semantic distinction that has emerged. When named with *a-*, Grizzly Woman is passive and inactive. When Gitskux and his older brother are out hunting, their bows break, they return to find Grizzly Woman simply there in their home: *(a) úxt Akitsimani* '(she) is there Akitsimani' (316:10). In the next scene, the two brothers have brought back a little raccoon, which Grizzly Woman takes as a pet, although the elder brother's two children cry for it. While Grizzly Woman is absent, the elder brother's first wife kills the coon.

---

[2]The name is invariably *igitskux* in the Clackamas text. Thus the Clackamas title is Igitskux *wi-ya-lxt* (literally, Gitskux third-person-singular masculine respectful *wi-*, plus *ya-* 'his', plus *-lxt* 'older brother'). Jacobs's regular use in the English translation of the part of the word after the *i-* indicates that *i-* is the masculine-singular–number-gender prefix. That is what one would expect from the usual form of noun stems in Chinookan. I infer that *I-gitskux* was the name of an animal, whose identity has been forgotten, as in the case of *kusaydi* 'mink' and a few other cases in the Clackamas collection. I have not been able to identify the animal from materials in other dialects, but it was almost certainly the fisher, given its hair color, habitat after the myth age in the mountains, and the attestation of Fisher and Marten as brothers in myths among the Cowlitz Sahaptins and Cowlitz Salish on the Washington side of the Columbia not far from the Clackamas. The older brother is Panther, the common older brother in Chinookan, and killer of deer *par excellence*. (Ability to kill deer points also to Fisher as younger brother.)

Grizzly Woman is named as absent with *a-* (137:7). She becomes angry because her husband's younger brother has brought back a raccoon for the children, while she has none, and, left alone, kills the raccoon. She and the first wife fight, she kills the other wife, and dons her skin. The wife had foreseen this and warned the children, and Grizzly Woman in disguise makes certain mistakes. Gitskux feeds her heavily, as his elder brother's late wife had advised, and she torpidly falls asleep. He is then able to take off her sister-in-law's skin: "Oh dear? Akitsimani is the one lying here!" (139:15).

This section of the story ends with Grizzly Woman being killed, but not successfully, since her bones were not mashed up and blown away. Eventually she returns, kills the wife and people, and takes Gitskux captive away with her. The older brother has another, good wife come to him, and then two sons, who become big. At that point the new wife inquires and is told that her husband had not come there alone, but had had a younger brother: "Grizzly Woman took him, maybe she ate him" (324:11). The Ogress is named without prefix, *kitsimani,* but I suspect that the form is *a-kitsimani.* The preceding word, *gagigitga* 'she took him', ends with /-a/, and it is a regular rule of Wasco that /a + a/ will coalesce into a single vowel, if not separated by pause. Since *gagitga kitsimani* is a single phrase, it is likely that the /a/ that is printed at the end of the first word stands as well for an /a/ that began the second. The point in the story is analogous to that in the story of Grizzly Bear and Black Bear at which Black Bear's escaping children halloo to Crane. In the latter story, Grizzly Bear was temporarily "dead." In this story, she is indeed remote. Attention has turned to the elder brother and the steps by which he is united with his new, supernaturally powerful wife; as said, two boys have been born to them and have become big. Throughout this long section (322:2 to 326:10), Grizzly Woman has not been mentioned, even by a pronominal prefix. She has been offstage in a state of silent "hold."

The elder brother and his new wife rescue the younger brother, Gitskux, and kill Grizzly Woman but, as before, fail to kill her completely. She again returns, kills, and skins the wife, dons the skin as disguise; she makes some mistakes in accustomed conduct, falls asleep, and is killed, this time for good, and the new wife restored. At the point at which Gitskux is removing the wife's skin from Grizzly Woman, she is named: "Grizzly Woman *(a-)* sleeps" (330:13). Nothing could be more appropriate than to underline her passivity by a prefix here, as the rhetorical lengthening in the verb 'she sleeps' also shows *(ú:::::qiw),* as may also the "historical present" tense.

The questions with "Gitskux and his older brother" arise with the use of *wa-.* Most of the occurrences of *wa-,* to be sure, fit the sense of purposive activity that other texts have shown. The Grizzly Ogress is named when she comes to the two brothers (316:5), when she goes and lies down with the elder brother as his unasked-for second wife (316:11), when she claims the little raccoon for herself (317:2), and when she plays with it, while her husband's two children cry (317:4). Again, she is named when anger acts on her about the second raccoon (317:12); when she takes Gitskux away after she has killed the elder brother's wife (321:18); and when Gitskux's bow breaks and he knows from the sign that "Grizzly Woman has come now" (329:15). At that point in the story, she is not dead or remote. She has just returned for the last time, killed the elder brother's wife, skinned her, put on her skin, dragged her to the rear of the house, laid her down, covered her. (This rapid sequence of six actions is in lines 7–9 of p. 329).

Two occurrences of wa- with the naming of the Grizzly Ogress do *not* seem to fit. The associated verbs appear to show Grizzly Woman as inactive. The first instance comes a little after she has gotten angry about the second pet raccoon. Here is a translation with verse analysis (One II iv):

> Now they lived there,
>> all day long the boys played with it;
> on a certain day they went to the water,
>> they went for a swim;
> only she, Grizzly Woman, is there.

The Clackamas text has *Ayma Wakitsimani (a)uXt* (Jacobs 1959a:316, line 10). The verb *(a)uXt* '(she) is there' is indeed the same verb used at the outset of the story to say 'she is there'. There are, however, differences in context between the two.

In the earlier scene (One I ii), Grizzly Woman is clearly inactive when named with *a-* in co-occurrence with *uXt*. She is named three times in the scene. (Such threefold occurrence of a key word in a scene is common.) She is named with *wa-* at the outset when she comes to the family, entering the myth for the first time, and she is named with *wa-* at the end of the scene when she intrudes herself into the elder brother's marriage bed. It is in the middle of the scene that she is named with *a-*. There she is clearly an object of perception, what the two brothers see when they hurry home and enter their house:

> As for those two,
>> Gitskux got his two nephews,
>>> they went,
>>>> they went inside:
>
>>> there is Grizzly Woman.

This occurrence at the end of a verse, and indeed of a stanza, is clearly a local close. The next line introduces a shift in time ("It became night") and of actor ("he [the older brother] went and lay down"). Only then is Grizzly Woman mentioned again ("right away Grizzly Woman herself also went and lay down").

In the later scene, involving the pet raccoon, Grizzly is again named as being there, with *uXt*, in the last line of a verse, but the verse is the first of a scene and stanza. The additional, initial word "only" frames her as the only actor present. Since no one else is there, she, of course, is not now an object of perception. The next three lines, the middle verse of the stanza, continue without a shift in time or actor to state her own actions:

> Now she herself also cleaned,
>> she clubbed the raccoon,
>>> she killed it.

The use of the pronoun translated "herself also" puts the earlier and later scenes into dramatic contrast. In both it occurs in a line indicating aggressive action on Grizzly Woman's part: when she goes and lies down in the older brother's bed, when she cleans, and clubs, and kills the raccoon. In the earlier case the setting has changed ("It became night"), while in the later case the emphasis comes immediately upon specifying Grizzly Woman as there. This pronoun picks up and continues the force of the the pronoun translated "only she." Both pronouns are indeed optional and emphatic, since in each case the verb itself indicates a feminine subject.

In the earlier scene, in short, other actors in the stanza in question come and find Grizzly Woman there. In the later scene, other actors leave, so that Grizzly Woman is there as the only actor on stage. In the earlier scene she "herself also" acts after a change of setting and actor. In the later scene she acts immediately. The use of *wa-* in naming her in the later scene is appropriate as a signal of her incipient potency and purpose already in mind. The initial "she-only" of the line in which Grizzly Woman is named is pregnant with opportunity.

The second apparent exception to the rule that associates alternation of *wa-* and *a-* with active/passive state also yields to close reading, aided by more literal translation and analysis of the discourse structure as verse.

The sentence containing the naming of Grizzly Woman with *wa-* appears to put her in a subordinated, perhaps inactive, state: "She (the first wife) sat on Grizzly Woman who was underneath" (Jacobs 1959a:320, English line 12). The context is the return of Grizzly Woman from the first attempt to overcome her, and the immediate outbreak of a fight between the two wives. The Clackamas words are literally "Under*neath* someone-sat-on-her Grizzly Woman." The word translated 'who was underneath' *(gagi:::glx)* is not an appended relative clause, but an adverb prominent as the first word of the line. It is emphasized by rhetorical lengthening of its main vowel, 'under*neath*', so to speak, as if to convey something contrary to expectation. Most important, the verb *ga-q-a-gé-Layt* mentions no agent, neither the first wife nor any specific person. There is no "she" who has sat on Grizzly Woman. The place for the marking of transitive actor is filled by an impersonal prefix, *q-*. Agency is displaced by a construction that focuses on the grammatical object, Grizzly Woman (identified by the -a- that follows q-). The construction can be translated 'Someone-sat-on-her', but equally well as 'She was sat on'. In this context there can be no question of an uncertain or indefinite person. The exclusion of the known antagonist, the first wife, gives the impersonal construction the force of a passive with deletion of the agent.

The force of this line is better appreciated in the context of an analysis of the passage into lines and verses. There are five verses in the stanza. More literal translation helps here, enabling us to distinguish lines that enter into the verse pattern, where the English translation has obscured their presence. Thus, "They came to watch them fight" (Ibid.: lines 11–12) is accurate enough, but where there are two predicates in Clackamas, there are generally two lines of verse. The first line, in fact, states the onset of a verse, "They came to watch the two." The second line continues the situation (in the historical present): "They are fighting on." The two lines are completed by the third and last of the verse, that just discussed, "Grizzly Woman was sat on underneath."

Here is how these lines appear in the context of the stanza as a whole (Two i; 320: 5–12):

> Now they lived there;
>> I do not know just when,
>>> now again she reached them.
> The two (wives) fought,
>> they fought on;
>>> the children were crying and screaming;
>>>> the people said,
>>>>> "Dear oh dear*rrr!* Our chief's wives are fighting."
> They came to watch the two;
>> they are fighting on;
>>> Grizzly Woman *(wa-)* was sat on under*neath.*
> *Soon* she would raise herself up,
>> now again she (the first wife) would throw her down;
>>> the people kept calling out;
>>>> anger,
>>>>> now that acted on Grizzly Woman *(wa-).*
> She thought,
>> "Now she injured me";
>>> now she became a dangerous being,
>>>> she swallowed her;
>>>>> now she ate up *allll* the people.

The first naming of Grizzly Woman in this passage is the first naming of her on her return. It occurs in a line which ends the third, pivotal verse of the stanza, the verse which shows the outcome of the action initiated and carried on in the preceding two verses, and which initiates the action to be carried on and completed in the next two verses. Grizzly Woman may be down, but she is not inactive; she is in the midst of a fight, and the line describes the outcome of round one.

There is a grammatical parallel between the last line of this third verse and the last line of the next verse, indeed, that reinforces a sense that the naming of Grizzly Woman in both is motivated, and is interdependent with the arrangement of lines into verses that has been shown. Both lines name her with *wa-* yet treat her name grammatically as object. Let me explain the second instance, which again involves a more literal translation that shows the presence of two lines instead of one, before discussing the significance of both. The published translation of the line is a single sentence "Now Grizzly Woman became angry" (Jacobs 1959a: 320, line 16). Comparison to a similar, but not identical, passage will show the import of the wording here.

Grizzly Woman had been described as angry earlier in the myth (One II iii Ca; 317:12): "As for Grizzly Woman, now she became angry." The second line in Clackamas is: *aGa i-kalálgwli gac(a)úXa*, literally, 'now *i-*anger past-he-(her)-act upon'. The idiom is paralleled elsewhere in the language. The common instance is "hunger," which is always expressed as a noun that acts upon one. "I am hungry," which Coyote often says, is literally, 'Hunger she-me-acts upon-present' *(Wa-lu g-n-ú-X-t)*. In the passage in question here, the stem for 'anger' is not inflected as a noun; there is no *i-*. It would have been possible to have *Kalálgwli gal-a-X-uX* 'angry she-became', I think; the "act upon" construction seems a choice. (The verb has the third-person-singular masculine prefix *C-*, even without *i-* on the word for 'anger', since that prefix is the unmarked one for crossreference.) And the placing of "anger" and "now" in relation to each other clearly is a choice, reversing the placing of the earlier passage. AGa 'now' normally introduces a line, and the recurrence of three- and five-line verses in this scene indicates that it does so here. (Otherwise we would have only four lines in this verse.) The result is to place "anger," unusually and almost awkwardly, as a single, apostrophized line itself. The rhetorical exposition highlights Grizzly Woman as again acted upon at the end of this intermediate verse and stage of the final three.

The effect of the final three verses can be suggested by abstracting the last lines:

> Grizzly Woman was sat on under*neath.*
> now that (anger) acted on Grizzly Woman.
> now she ate up a*llll* the people.

Each of the first two final lines names Grizzly Woman with *wa-*, yet as grammatically acted upon. The effect seems to me to be to elaborate and intensify the state of incipient potency for Grizzly Woman. The states in which she is acted upon are not outcomes, but steps toward an outcome. In both she is indeed the antagonist who will prevail. The use of *wa-* expresses her potency and incipient victory.

In the scene as a whole, the third verse is pivotal, constituting an outcome for the series of the first three verses, and an onset for the series of the last three. One can observe such a pivotal role of the middle verse in many sets of five; it seems to be a principle that can be invoked at all levels of organization, from five lines of verse to five acts of an entire narrative (cf. chap. 6). Here its use seems especially revealing and dramatic, a true peripety.

Incipient potency fits the use of *wa-* in both cases. In the first case, discussed above, the naming is followed by her action. Here the effect is elaborated. The present case is paralleled by the highlighted confrontation between Grizzly Woman and Water Bug in the myth of "Grizzly Woman killed them," discussed below. Water Bug is named with *wa-* as object of address and perception by Grizzly Woman in just those scenes of confrontation in which Water Bug is going to prevail.

Prefix choice and rhetorical-poetic form: The alternation of wa-/a-.

In sum, the choice of *wa-* or *a-* is not random, nor is it to be explained within the immediate sentence. The choice involves an active or passive state of the named actor, but the active or passive, transitive or intransitive, causative or stative character of the accompanying verb construction or verb stem is not a criterion in itself. The state of the named actor depends upon the use of the sentence in the action of the story, an action that is shaped and expressed through the rhetorical-poetic organization of the discourse. That organization employs modes of ordering experience recurrent in Chinookan narrative, and, indeed, conversation to this day: the threefold sequence with its logic of onset, ongoing, outcome; the placement of something perceived or something said as a local outcome; the framing of action through an introduction, first, of key actors, and then of a morally emblematic activity characteristic of one or more; recurrent use of local parallelism and of change in "scene/agent ratio" (to use Kenneth Burke's term), such changes in place, time, or leading actor often being accompanied by particles such as "now," "soon, a little later" in Clackamas.

In the Clackamas texts that enter into this essay, as in Chinookan texts generally, there is constant recurrence of formal means, together with individuality of overall shape. No single formal criterion serves to identify rhetorical-poetic form, nor does any set. One learns to expect the principles stated in the preceding paragraph not to be violated. It becomes easy to block out the rhetorical-poetic form of a passage. Yet blocking out is not the same as final version. The parallelisms, repetitions, contours specific to a passage have to become vivid to the mind. One has to reconstitute a version of narrative intention, of intended narrative effect. To do so is not to be arbitrary. One is forced to enter more deeply into a presumably intended narrative effect by the loose ends that blocking out may leave. Entering more deeply means attention to the place of a passage in overall narrative design and sensitivity to the formal options that make formal sense of the passage in hand. Sometimes, most notably, action moves threefold with three verbs, clippety, clippety, clop; sometimes it moves pairwise with two verbs, this this, that that, thus thus. One may have blocked out this this that, that thus thus, but be forced to reconsider by failure of fit. Confidence comes from experience of fit being there to find and of coming to experience pattern without conscious analysis.

Inquiry into a minor, almost neglectable, variation in grammar has turned out to implicate the major modes of organization of discourse. In larger context the choice of shape of a prefix with apparently constant meaning, feminine singular, has turned out to imply an additional dimension of meaning. *Wa-* has to do with an active, *a-* with a passive state, in those texts in which the two alternate. In those texts, shape of prefix varies with point of view.

This finding opens up need for investigation of use of both *wa-* and *wi-* throughout the Clackamas texts and other Chinookan materials. It poses a question for the history of the language as well: is there a source within Chinookan, perhaps within Penutian, for such an element? A **w-* "active"? Could the Takelma prefix *wa-*, of demonstrative pronoun origin but used in an instrumental meaning before noun stems, be distantly connected? Or has the active/passive contrast in the discourse use of *w-* emerged within recent times in Chinookan itself? The association of "active" with *w-* could reflect an old, otherwise submerged, state of affairs, or the recent dynamics of narration, the existence of a variation attracting intentional use.[3]

[3]The discovery of an active connotation for *wa-* as opposed to *a-*, and presumably for *wi-* as opposed to *i-*, makes sense of what would otherwise be an exception to a pattern discovered by Walter Dyk, and amplified by Michael Silverstein, with regard to the order of person-marking prefixes in nouns and in verbs. The constructions for 'my father' and 'my mother', *wi-na-m-S* and *wa-na-q-S*, would violate the general pattern. These constructions are unique in having the honorific suffix *-S* (presumably borrowed from Sahaptin), and are unique as well in being the only kinship terms in which the first person "possessor" is expressed with *n-*. This uniqueness goes together with the uniqueness of having initial *w-*. To *wi-na-m-S* 'my father', compare *i-C-xan* 'my son'; to *wa-na-q-S* 'my mother,' compare *a-k-xan* 'my daughter', where *-C* and *-k-* are allomorphs after *i-* and *a-* respectively. When *w-* is recognized as having an "active," or "animate," force, these two exceptional kinship terms are no longer exceptions to the general pattern for the order of occurrence of person markers. *wi-na-m-S* is parallel to *m-n-wlx* 'my nephew', literally, 'you *(m-)* uncle *(-wlx)* me *(na-)*'. In both cases the pronoun occurring in the position before *n(a)-* has animate force.

This significance for *w-* also indicates that it is significant that in the title to "Seal and her younger brother lived there," Seal is named with *wa-*, but the younger brother only with *i-*. He is referred to with *w-*, when referred to as the uncle of the girl, but not as the younger brother of Seal. The daughter, on the other hand, is referred to with *wa-* throughout, whether as 'daughter' or as 'girl'. This parallelism with *wa-* recalls the parallelism between Grizzly Woman and Water Bug. Notice further that the person who comes is prefixed with indefinite *iL-*, as a

Whichever is the case, there remain two Clackamas texts in which there is variation of prefix, but without *wa-*. The first of these, "Grizzly Woman begins to kill people," especially shows understanding to depend on the overall shaping of the narrative. After examining the alternations in themselves, we can venture a more general view of the role of *wa-* and all prefixes in such alternations.

Variable Prefix and Point of View: a-/∅-:   (3a). In "Grizzly Woman killed people" (17), the Grizzly Woman is identified with *wa-* only in the title of the myth: *"Wakitsimáni gaqdudínanmCk idÉlxam."*[4] Within the text, the alternation is between *a-* and *∅-*. The norm of the text is *∅-*. Out of thirteen namings of the Grizzly Woman, eleven are with *∅-*, only two with *a-*. This matter of proportion must be taken up, but let us first attend to the contexts of the text in question. Here is the full text of the myth in a revised translation based on the principles explained in chapters 4, 5, and 9.

Grizzly Woman Began to Kill People

Part One. Grizzly Woman deceives and kills women.

Preface.
Act I.   Grizzly Woman becomes a headman's wife.
II.   Grizzly Woman takes women for camas (1).
III.   Grizzly Woman takes women for camas (2).
IV.   Grizzly Woman takes women for camas (3).
V.   Grizzly Woman takes women for camas (4).

Part Two. Waterbug overcomes Grizzly Woman.

Act VI.   Grizzly Woman discovered.
VII.   Grizzly Woman disclosed.
VIII.   Grizzly Woman overcome.
IX.   Grizzly Woman escaped.
X.   Grizzly Woman destroyed.

woman who comes, and *a-*, as 'wife', but with *wi-* by the daughter when she identifies it as 'going out' like a man *(wi-kala -diwi)*. The active potency is again conveyed in the choice of prefix.

[4] The published title, "Grizzly Woman killed people," has been changed here to "Grizzly Woman began to kill people," because the final suffix of the verb, *-Ck*, has an inceptive force. Cf. its translation by Hiram Smith with 'start to' in chap. 5 in reference to the fire caused by At'unaqa. The preceding suffixes of the verb, *-nan-m-*, have a continuative force. The stem itself, *-dina-*, is used only with plural objects. Thus the verb itself grammatically indicates the beginning, the continuing, and the plurality of the killing. But Water Bug prevents its completion.

Part One. Grizzly Woman deceives and kills women

Preface   They lived on and on in their village;
             their headman's house was in the center.

I. [*Grizzly Woman becomes a headman's wife*]

A   Soon now,
              a woman reached him;   5
                     they said,
                            "Some woman has reached our headman";
                            now they lived on there.
B   In spring,
              she went I don't know where,   10
                     she came back at evening:
                            Oh dear! she brought back camas;
                            now she began to share it about.
C   They told her,
              "Where did you gather them?"
       She told them,   15
              "Well, I reached a burned-over place,
                     "It's just camas there,
                            "The camas stand thick."
D   They told her,
              "Goodness, whenever you go again,   20
                     "We'll follow you."
       "Very well,"
              she told them,
                     "Perhaps tomorrow."
E   "Indeed. We will follow you too."   25
       "All right,"
              she told them.

II. [*Grizzly Woman takes women for camas (1).*]

A   In the morning,
              now they go,
                     I don't know how many canoes went,   30
                            they arrived,
                                   they went ashore,
                                          they dug.
B   It became evening,
              now they camped;   35

they said,
    "Later tomorrow, then . . ."
    They were caused to sleep the night.
C   At daybreak,
    she took her arrow-spear,   40
      she went among them,
        she pierced their hearts,
          she killed them *all.*
D   Now it was day,
    now she carried them off;   45
      she laid them down,
        she hid their paddles;
      she thought,
        "Now I will go,
        "I will go home."   50
E   She brought those very camas, the people's;
She arrived at the village,
    she told them,
      "They sent these to you."
She went to another house,   55
    she told them,
      "Later tomorrow,
        "Then I will go fetch them."
They told her,
    "We will follow you too."   60
"To be sure,"
    she told them.

III. [Grizzly Woman takes women for camas (2)]

A   In the morning,
    now they get ready,
Now they go, three canoes;   65
    they went,
      they arrived;
Their (predecessors') canoes are tied,
    they tied their canoes too,
      they went ashore.   70
She told them,
    "Oh *dear,* perhaps they are over yonder.
    "*There* there are even lots more camas.
    "Stay here first.
    "Later tomorrow,   75
      "Then we'll go in that direction."

"Indeed,"
    they told her;
      they dug.

B It became evening,   80
    they (the camas) were brought up,
      they started fires.
Soon,
    now Grizzly Woman arrived on the run,
      she told them,   85
        "Oh dear . . . , now they have lots of camas;
        "They tell me,
           'Perhaps we will cook them right here.'"
"Indeed,"
    they told her.   90

C Now they began to eat,
    they ceased:
      no Grizzly Woman.
Soon they heard singing;
    they said,   95
      "Oh dear! they are singing!
        "Listen to them!"
          They listened.
Soon she arrived on the run,
    she told them,   100
      "Why are you silent?"
      "Yonder those folks are singing."
"To be sure!"
    they told her,
      "We hear them";   105
        they said,
          "Let us sing too."
Now they began to sing.
    They ceased.
      They lay down to sleep.   110

D At daybreak,
    now again she went among them,
      she numbed them (with her spirit-power).
Now again she took her arrow-spear,
    she pierced their hearts,   115
      she killed them all.
In the morning,
    now again she carried them off,
      she laid them all
        where she had put away the first ones.   120

E   She gathered up their camas,
      she put it in (her bag);
  Now she went home,
      she arrived;
  Now again she informed them the same way: 125
      "They won't come (today),
         "After a while,
            "Then they will come,"
               she told them.
  "Indeed,"   130
      they told her.
  Now others said,
      "We will go too."

IV. [Grizzly Woman takes women for camas (3)]

i A   In the morning,
      now they got ready,   135
         they went;
            again she took them,
               they arrived,
                  they went ashore.
  B   They became somehow (disturbed).   140
     She told them,
         "Right here they kept working.
         "Perhaps they moved off a little yonder,
            "There are even lots more camas."
      "Indeed,"   145
         they told her;
         they dug.
  C   One said,
         "What do you think?
         "Seems a long long time since these (were) digging places."   150
      "Surely,"
         they told her,
            "We noticed (that about) them."
     They ceased.
ii A   In the evening,   155
      they camped there;
         they said,
            "It's not as it should be,
               "Something somehow (is wrong)."

B   Soon,   160
          now Grizzly arrived on the run,
              she told them,
                  "Why are you so silent?
                  "Those yonder,
                          they are singing,   165
                              they are giggling,
                                  they are laughing—
                                      those who came first—
                      "Now they have baked their camas there."
    "Indeed,"   170
          they told her,
                  "It's just (that) we became somehow (disturbed)."
    "Goodness!"
          she told them,
                  "What for?   175
                  "Soon,
                      again they will begin dancing.
                  "Suppose I run,
                      I go to see them again."
                          She ran.   180
C   Soon,
              as they stayed there,
                  they heard singing.
          They said,
                  "Truly it is so;   185
                  "Now they sing,
                  "Listen."
          "Surely,"
              they said;
                  they stayed there.   190
iii   Now again she got back to them,
              she told them,
                  "You start to sing too!"
          "To be sure,"
              they told her;   195
                  they started to sing in vain,
                      no,
                          they ceased.
          They lay down to sleep;
              Grizzly also lay down;   200
                  they slept.
iv   Now Grizzly Woman arose,
              she numbed them (with her spirit-power),
                  she got her arrow-spear.

Now again she went among them,   205
    she pierced their hearts,
        she killed them all.
In the morning,
    now again she carried them
        where she had put down those first ones;   210
      all done;
        she ceased.

v   A   Now she put their camas in (her bag);
Now she went back,
    she arrived;   215
Now again she told them the same way,
    "They sent these to you."
    B   "Indeed,"
    they told her;
"The first ones who went,   220
    "now they are baking them."
    C   "Oh dear! Let us go tomorrow too!"
"Yes,"
    she told them.

V. [*Grizzly Woman takes women for camas (4)*]

i   A   In the morning,   225
    now they get ready,
        they go;
    they arrived,
        they went ashore;
    they arrived   230
        where their (predecessors') fire was.
    B   One burst out crying.
She was told,
    "Why are you making a bad omen for yourself?"
She told them,   235
    "No.
    "Somehow something (is wrong).
    "It happens to our people
        where you are looking."
"No::::::!   240
"A long long time (since) their fire,
    now it is gone there,"
        they told her.
"Never mind! She keeps saying nothing at all!" (said Grizzly).
    C   They went to dig,   245
    they dug;

that one tries in vain,
    she will become silent,
        now again she will cry.

ii A   They ceased at evening,   250
     they went to their camp,
        they sat;
           they said,
               "We will not build a fire."

   B   Soon,   255
     now again Grizzly arrived on the run,
        she told them,
           "Why have you become this (way)?"
    They told her,
         "This one has become ill."   260
    "Indeed. Soon she will cease (to be)."

   C   Now again they lay down to sleep.
    She arrived on the run,
        she told them,
           "Oh *dear!* Have you laid down to sleep there?"   265
    They told her,
         "Yes . . . Later tomorrow morning,
           "we will dig."
    "Indeed,"
        she told them,   270
           "I will go inform them."
    They pay no attention to her.
    She ran.
    Soon,
        they heard: 275
           "Oh *dear!* they are singing."
    They said,
         "Listen! they are singing."
    One said,
        she said,   280
           "Do you really think it is true?"
    They became silent.

iii   Now again she hurried to them,
        she told them,
           "They were going to come;   285
           "I told them,
              '*Long* ago they lay down to sleep.
              'Nevermind.'
           "Now I will lie down too."
    Now she lay down.   290
    They slept.

iv   Now again she numbed them (with her spirit-power).

    Now she arose,

      she got her arrow-spear;

    Now again she went among them,   295

      she pierced their hearts.

    In the morning,

      now again she carried them.

    All done . . .

      she ceased.   300

v A She put their camas in (her bag),

    a very few.

    Now she went back,

      she arrived,

        she shared their camas around.   305

  B She told them,

    "They became lazy,

      "They dug a few,

        "They said,

          " 'Later tomorrow morning, then.' "   310

    "Indeed,"

      they told her.

  C Now some again said,

    "We too will go in the morning."

    Her sister-in-law also said,   315

      "I also will go in the morning."

    Right away her little younger sister said,

      "I also will go, older sister!"

  D She (Grizzly) said,

    "Already you also!   320

    "Why should you go along?"

    She (Waterbug) said,

      "I will just go along with my older sister."

  E *"No!"*,

      she told her,   325

        "You will not go."

    She said,

      "I will go!"

    She told her,

      "No."   330

    "I will go."

    Her older sister told her (Grizzly),

      "She is just saying that to you.

        "We two (you and I) will go in the morning."

Part Two. Waterbug overcomes Grizzly Woman

VI. [*Grizzly Woman discovered*]

A   In the morning,   335
            now they got ready,
                     the very first is Water Bug;
                           she went,
                                  she hid in the canoe.

They went to the river,   340
            they got in their canoe,
                     they went.

Grizzly turned and looked,
            she saw her,
                     she said,   345
                               "Dear oh dear! I told you not to come."

She pays *no* attention to her there.

They went,
            they arrived,
                     they went ashore.   350

B   Grizzly Woman forgot (about her);
            she forgot,
                     she did not take her older sister's paddles.

Water Bug took them,
            she went,   355
                     she hid them;

She ran about,
            she got *all* those paddles (previously hidden by Grizzly),
                     she moved them away.

C   Now she went ashore,   360
            she reached her older sister,
                     she told her,
                               "Those here are *all* dead.
                                   "Let us go."

Now the two went,   365
            they reached them,
                     Dear oh dear . . . . there are corpses.

The two sat,
            they wept;
                     she told her older sister,   370
                               "Wash your face;
                               "She will become suspicious."

VII. [*Grizzly Woman disclosed*]

A   The two arrived,
      they informed them;
         they wept;   375
            they ceased,
               they washed their faces.
    Water Bug told them,
      "Say nothing at all.
      "When she will tell us,   380
        " 'You should sing,'
      "You should do that.
          "Be very careful!"
    Soon,
      now she hurried to them;   385
    she nudged her older sister,
      she nudged her;
    she said,
      "Now she will tell us!"

B   She told them,   390
      "Why are you so *still?*
      "You are lying to the people about something, Water Bug!"
    She pays *no* attention to her.
    She told them,
      "Oh *dear!* Now they are drying their cooked camas."   395
    She nudged her older sister.
    She (Grizzly) ceased,
      now she left them.

C   Again now the two informed them, Water Bug (and her sister).
      She said,   400
        "Be careful!"
    "Yes indeed,"
      they told her.
    "You are not to be first,
      "Her plan is to kill me first";   405
        she informed them of everything,
        she told them,
          "When she falls asleep,
          "Now we will leave here."
    "Indeed,"   410
      they told her.
    She ran to the river,
      she picked up shells,
        she brought them to her older sister.

VIII. [*Grizzly Woman foiled*]

i   Now it *became* night,   415
        they had lain down to sleep;
            she got to them.
     "Surely,"
        she said,
            "Now you lied about something to them."   420
     She paid no attention,
        she said nothing whatever;
            they had lain down to sleep.

ii A   Grizzly Woman said,
        "Now I too,   425
        "Now I lie down."
     Water Bug picked up a lot of wood.

  B   She (Grizzly) told her,
        "Why will you make a fire all night?
            "So that is why you came—(to be a nuisance)—   430
        "You're thinking,
            "Maybe some young man will get to your sister!"
     She paid no attention.

  C   "Sleep acts on them,
        "In the morning they will get up,   435
            "They will dig."
     She paid no attention,
        she lay down to sleep,
            she put those shells on her eyes.

iii A   Soon,   440
        the fire went down a little;
            Grizzly Woman arose slowly, silently.
     She saw her,
        she nudged her older sister,
            the two see her.   445
     She went up to them,
        she looked at Water Bug:
            she is watching her.

  B   "Oh, goodness!"
        she told her,   450
            "Aren't you going to go to sleep?"
               "Youths are going about."
     "Oooo,"
        she went,
            Water Bug went
               (feigning sudden fright at being awakened).   455

C   She got up,
             she fixed the fire,
                   she put large pieces of wood on the fire.
     "Ahh,"
             she told her,   460
                   "Why indeed are you going to make a fire all night?"
     She told her nothing whatever,
             she lay down again.

iv A   Soon,
             the fire went down.   465
     Now again Grizzly Woman got up,
             she approached slowly, silently;
     She (Water Bug) heard,
             "*T'áLmu t'áLmu.*"

     B   "Ooooo!"   470
             went Water Bug.
     "Oh *dear!* Aren't you going to go to sleep?"
     "Oooo I was dreaming,
             "I saw a bloody arrow-spear."
     "Goodness! Now she will lie to them;   475
             "Leave them alone,
                   "They are sleeping."
     Now again she lay down to sleep.

     C   Water Bug got up,
             again she put more wood on the fire.   480
     She told her,
             "So that is why you came!
                   "You might wake people all night."
     Waterbug lay down to sleep.

v   Now it was close to dawn,   485
             now Grizzly Woman became sleepy,
                   she would nod off to sleep.
     She would wake up,
             she would get up slowly, silently,
                   she would look at Water Bug: 490
                   she is watching her;
                         now again she lay down.
     Soon now it is dawn;
     Now Grizzly Woman fell asleep,
             Water Bug arose;   495
     Now she cast *t'áLmu t'áLmu* on her, (she numbed her)
             She slept.

IX. [*Grizzly Woman escaped*]

A She told them,
      "Quickly! Get up!"
   They got up,   500
      they hurried;
   They went down to their canoes,
      they got on them.
B She ran,
      she fetched their paddles,   505
         she put *all* of them in—
            her older sister's paddles had holes—
               now they went.
C They are going,
      they turned to look,   510
         now she is pursuing them there.
   She curses Water Bug:
      "So that is why you came!
      "You tell the people lies."
   She gets close to them,   515
      she took her snot,
         she threw it at them:
            their paddles broke.
D She pursued them;
      she will get close to them;   520
         she will blow her nose,
            she will throw her snot at them;
               their paddles will break;
                  all the paddles they brought,
                     all became broken.   525
E Now they have gotten close (to their village);
      now she took out her (older sister's) paddles;
         in vain she threw her snot at them;
            there it will go right through them;
               they go.   530

X. [*Grizzly Woman destroyed*]

A The people said,
      "Something (is wrong).
      "A canoe is coming,
         hurrying this way."

They went out,   535
    they said,
        "Seems like our chief's wife pursues them."
They got their bows,
    their arrows,
        they arrived.   540
Water Bug ran,
    she told their older brother (the chief):
        "She consumes people.
        "She has taken along a certain number,
        "She kills them all.   545
        "She pursues us."
Now they waited for her.

B   Soon,
    she came ashore,
        now they shot at her.   550
She would tell them,
    "Goodness! Why does Water Bug just lie and lie to you?"
She is *going,*
    They shoot at her.

C   Her husband sat on top of the house,   555
    he shot at her;
She is close to him there,
    now he has only one arrow.
He thought,
    "Never mind!"   560
He threw it at her (shot it despairingly),
    he wounded her little finger,
        it split,
            there she fell,
                he had killed her.   565
In truth there she put her heart,
    in her little finger.

D   Now they burned her;
    he got all of her,
        they ground up her bones;   570
        they blew them (ashes) away.

E   Now they went,
    they went to gather up the corpses,
        they arrived.
There they went ashore,   575
    they took Water Bug along,
        she showed them the whole place there;

they arrived,
      where the first ones (were),
            now black,   580
                  rotting;
they took them *all* to the canoes.
Now they were taken to their graveyard,
      they buried them *all*,
            they ceased.   585
                  All done.
                        Story story.

The Grizzly Woman is named with *a-* for the first time in the midst of the third of the five times that she persuades women of a village to go to gather camas roots with her.

An overview of the naming of Grizzly Woman in this text seems to show two culminating arcs. One ends in the naming of her with *a-* in the third trip, the other in the interaction with Water Bug in the fifth, where she is named seven times, one of them again with *a-*.

The first series has to do with her deception and killing of her women victims. When she comes to the village headman to be his wife at the outset of the story, she is not named. Neither is she named in the course of the first trip, when she lures women away from the village in hopes of camas, then kills them. She is named for the first time, and twice, in the course of the second trip. After all have arrived, she tells the second group that their predecessors must have gone to a place where there are even more camas. She advises them to stay where they are for the night. Having gone off as if to visit the first group of women (actually slain), Grizzly Woman (157:18) is named for the first time in the story when she returns to say that the others have lots of camas and that they said they would eat where they were. After the second group eat and finish their meal, she is named again (158:1): "Grizzly Woman is not there." Then they hear singing, and soon she returns, saying, "Why are you silent? They are singing yonder." The women reply that they had heard, and begin to sing, too.

In the course of the third trip, Grizzly Woman is named a third time at the same point of deception. She comes to the women and says, "Why are you silent?" (159:2). Then, she is named twice more, once when she lies down to sleep with the others, and once when she arises to kill them.

There is something grimly grotesque in finding Grizzly Woman in the role of community organizer and sing-along leader, as it were. To go gathering roots or berries was one of the most enjoyable activities of women, a social occasion as well as practical necessity. In pursuit of her deception, the one who is using an activity of group enjoyment as cover for mass murder exerts herself to maintain the appearance of group enjoyment.

Through the sequence of trips there emerges a current of increasing suspicion and uneasiness, calling for greater exertion on Grizzly Woman's part, both as mistress of ceremonies and as user of spirit-power. From the first to third trips there is a development, both in the steps she takes to deceive the women before nightfall, and in the expression of her exertion of the special spirit-power by which she makes them sleep, dead to the world, so that she can kill them all without detection during the night.

On the first trip, the text is terse. There is no need to deceive the first group about predecessors, and the use of spirit-power is not named, but expressed through a sentence fragment and a causative suffix *t-xit in n-u-gwa-Giwit-xit* 'they were caused to sleep', II B; 157:3):

It became evening,

now they camped,
they said,
"Later tomorrow, then . . ."
They were caused to sleep the night.

After Grizzly Woman is named in regard to her reporting on the preceding group, and with regard to going off to deceive the new group by pretending to be the first group singing, the account of the second trip introduces the word for her special spirit-power for inducing sleep (158:7–10).

The line translated "she numbed them (with her spirit-power)" contains the verb phrase *t'áLmu gagÉLuX*, literally, *t'áLmu past (ga-)* she *(g-)* them *(L)* do *(-u-X)*, she did *t'áLmu* to them.[5]

On the third trip, after Grizzly Woman falsely reported about predecessors, the women stop digging and think "It's not as it should be. Something somehow (is wrong)" (158:20–159:1). Shortly Grizzly (named) gets there and asks, as with the second group, "Why are you so silent?" She adds that the women yonder (actually slain) are singing, giggling, laughing, and have baked their camas where they are. The women say they are just beginning to feel queer. Grizzly replies, "Oh dear, why? Soon they will be dancing again. Suppose I go see them again." Soon they hear

[5]This spell was known among the Wasco, and probably the story as well. The lexical files of Walter Dyk, recorded at the beginning of the 1930s, have "t'aLmo; 'used by a character in a story to put her victim to sleep'." Notice "her" victim. Dyk noted the connection of this word to a word that must be its augmentative counterpart. Given *t'* as diminutive, and *d-* as augmentative, it is easy to see the connection with "daLamo: 'to have died, of a population, and by lying spread about'." Grizzly Bear enacts the small death of loss of consciousness with a word that implies extinction.

(The last vowel of the word is indeed /o/. Usually in Wasco this sound is an allophone of the phoneme usually written /u/. A few highly charged words, all of them particles, invariably have a mid- or low-back rounded vowel [written with omega by Dyk] that is not conditioned such by environment and cannot be properly pronounced with high back [u], low central [a], or anything else. Expressivity has become lexically intrinsic.)

singing, and when she returns, she tells them to sing, too. They agree, and attempt to sing, but no, they quit (as shown in the presentation of this passage earlier).

It is in this third trip that it is mentioned for the first time that Grizzly Woman lies down to sleep with the others. She may have lain down in the first two trips as well; mention now has to do, not with description, but dramatic tension. She has deceived the second and third groups by false reports and singing, but in the face of the first explicit uneasiness, and the failure of the attempt to sing, must add a third explicit step. She lies down to sleep as $\emptyset$- and gets up as *a-kitsimani* (159:10–14).

The contrast between the passive state—lying down to sleep—and the active state—arising to kill them all—is parallel to the contrast found with alternation of *a-* and *wa-*. The parallel suggests that in a text in which the terms of alternation are *a-* : $\emptyset$-, the overt element *a-* stands in the same relation to $\emptyset$- as does *wa-* to *a-*. In summary form, there appears to be a proportion:

$$wa\text{-} : a\text{-} :: a\text{-} : \emptyset\text{-}.$$

It is natural to Chinookan rhetoric to have a culmination in a third scene of a series, and that is what seems to be the case here. Along with the introduction of *a-* in the contrast between Grizzly Woman as deceptive partner in sleep and as user of sleep to kill, there is doubling of the word for the power she uses. In the Clackamas the eighth line in the passage just quoted is *"t'áLmu t'áLmu gagáLuX."*

The fourth trip seems in tone both a development and a preparation. It continues the growth of suspicion and uneasiness. As soon as the fourth group of women arrive, one begins crying. Asked why she is making a bad omen for herself, she replies, "No, something is wrong, something happened to our people at the place you see." Others dismiss her fear, but when she tries to dig, she cries again. In the evening the women say they will not build a fire (because of their worry). It is then that Grizzly Woman comes, presumably from having pretended to visit the groups that had come already. This is the one point in the scene in which she is named (with $\emptyset$-prefix) (160:7). She asks what is the matter, is told that one is ill, and says she will soon stop being sick.

Surprised that the women are already lying down for sleep, Grizzly Woman is told that they will dig the next day, and says she will go to tell the others (actually already slain). The women do not attend, but soon hear singing. One says, "Do you suppose it is really so?" There is no mention of attempt on their own part to sing. Returning, Grizzly Woman says the supposedly-still-alive others had planned to come, but she had told them the fourth group was already asleep. Extending the mention of her lying down herself in the third trip, she says, "Now I will lie down too," and, the text continues, now she lay down.

At this point the wording is almost the same as in the third trip:

Now again she numbed them (with her spirit-power),
Now she arose,
    she got her arrow-spear;
Now again she went among them,
    she pierced their hearts.

There is diminution in the expressive weight of the passage in that Grizzly Woman is not named at all; moreover, the fact that she kills them all is left unstated. She had been named twice in the corresponding passage of the third trip. The impact of naming Grizzly Woman explicitly is shown in the use of the device in the second and third trips with regard to her deception of the women about their predecessors. Naming her in the context of the deception and death of sleep is reserved for two climaxes: the intermediate climax of the third trip and the major climax and reversal of the whole story on the fifth.

(Enter Water Bug). The growing uneasiness was collective in the third trip and individuated as well, but anonymously, in the fourth. It was crystallized in a decisive heroine in the fifth, a trip that became the whole of a second part. (Such extraposition of a culminating fifth step in a series is a major feature of Louis Simpson's "The deserted boy" [chap. 4], and here, as there, serves structurally to highlight the narrator's theme.) When the others at the village say they will with Grizzly Woman in the morning, a young girl, Water Bug, insists on going along. Grizzly Woman does not want her to. In point of fact, "When a little girl was especially intelligent and perceptive, older people might refer to her, during the years when she was still very small, as *amaLk'wilkwiq.* This is the name of a flat water bug which although very quiet sometimes bites" (284, n. 168). Grizzly Woman was presumably aware of this potentiality, and there is a sustained spoken exchange over the issue between her, Water Bug, and Water Bug's older sister. In the next scene, Grizzly Woman is named, once with Ø- and once with *a-*.

The significance of the second naming of Grizzly Woman, the naming with *a-*, is its connection with the turning point of the action. Heretofore Grizzly Woman has been successful in the pretense that everything is all right, that the women who had preceded (after the first) are farther away, rolling in camas, as it were, and singing before they sleep. After magically causing them to sleep, and killing them, she has hidden their bodies and their paddles, all in the same place. The hiding of the paddles had followed the killing. In this fifth, and culminating trip, she has intended to take the paddles in advance, apparently to preclude escape and flight by canoe, before she can kill the women. Which is just what will happen. In the event, Grizzly Woman in pursuit succeeds in breaking most of the paddles by hurling her nasal mucus at them. Close to home, Water Bug takes out the only paddles remaining— her older sister's—and they reach home, because these paddles have holes, and the nasal mucus goes right through.

That Grizzly Woman forgets Water Bug and forgets the paddles, then, is the turning point that leads to her downfall. The Clackamas verb, translated here "forget," has the same stem as the word (appearing earlier) for the fact that Water Bug pays no attention, but in a different construction. The verbal contrast highlights, perhaps humorously, the contrast between little girl and murderous ogress.

The naming of Grizzly Woman at the turning point that leads to the success of her antagonist is analogous to the naming of her at the turning point in the adventure of Old Watcheeno's father (134). In both stories the explicit naming seems to underscore the identity of the ogress and to heighten the ensuing success of escape. In both stories, indeed, the title identifies the Grizzly Ogress with *wa-*, but *wa-* does not occur in the text. In "Grizzly Woman pursued him," the creature is referred to only by pronominal prefix until the proper name is introduced with *a-* at the turning point. In this story of "Grizzly Woman killed people," she is named a number of times, but only with zero noun prefix, except for the description of the central action in the third trip (discussed above) and here at the turning point in the fifth.

These parallels between the two texts seem striking to me. The parallelism is reinforced by attention to the location of the explicit naming of Grizzly Women. Although the sums are disproportionate (thirteen namings in this text, one in that of Old Watcheeno's father), the locations are not. Of the thirteen namings in "Grizzly Woman killed people," seven are in the account of the fifth and last trip, and five of the seven are in the crucial scene involving sleep. It is the counterpart of the scene involving sleep from the third trip presented above but with opposite outcome. Water Bug has discovered the corpses of the women Grizzly Woman killed and shared the knowledge, first with her older sister, then with the other women. Each time those who are told weep, and wash their faces to avoid suspicion. Grizzly Woman does accuse Water Bug of lying to the people about something, while proceeding herself to say that the other women (now known to be dead) are drying their cooked camas. When she leaves them, Water Bug instructs the people again to watch carefully, that she (Water Bug) is the one Grizzly Woman intends to kill first, that they will leave her when she has fallen asleep. She then gets shells from the river (presumably to protect her eyes against Grizzly Woman's magic). The story proceeds in an act in which namings of Grizzly Woman are concentrated and concluded (VIII).

The concentration of namings of Grizzly Woman in this passage is hardly accidental, nor, I think, is the fact that the sum of namings is the pattern number, five. It is the great reversal scene. As we have seen on the first trip, it is briefly, if effectively, presented that the women are caused to sleep. On the second, the spirit power *t'aLmu* is named once, and in the third, reduplicated. It is reduplicated in the fourth trip as well. In the fifth trip it is reduplicated twice, once when used (to no avail) and heard by Water Bug, a second time when used by Water Bug herself! The sequence of the five namings of Grizzly Woman tell the story in themselves:

Grizzly Woman said, "Now I too, now I lie down in bed."
Grizzly Woman arose slowly, silently.
Now again Grizzly Woman got up.
Now Grizzly Woman became sleepy.
Now Grizzly Woman fell asleep.

It may be significant that Grizzly Woman is not named again beyond this point.

A consideration of the reversal in this scene goes together with consideration of the other concentration of namings that it shows, namings of young Water Bug. She is named sixteen times in this last part of the myth, eleven times in the section just discussed. (The remaining five occur in the successful flight back to the village and the killing of Grizzly Woman by her headman-husband, Water Bug's older brother.) The concentration in itself shows the emergence into the text of a new motivation, focused on the young girl. Four of the sixteen namings are with wa-, rather than a-, and these are revealing as well.

The first naming of Water Bug is in Act VI, which we have seen to be the beginning of the end for Grizzly Woman, when she forgets Water Bug and forgets the paddles. Water Bug is named when she comes onstage, as it were, with a- (161:12), but is named with wa- when she takes the paddles (161:17). It is at that same point that Grizzly Woman is named for the second time in the long story with a-. This conjunction of the two stronger prefixes for the two actors at the peripety of the story seems no accident.

The other three times Water Bug is named with wa- each involve her as the crucial opponent of Grizzly Woman. When she speaks to the people about what to do, after she has disclosed the murder of their companions, she is named with a-. When Grizzly Woman then comes, asks "What are you being quiet about? You have lied to the people about something or other, Water Bug!", she names her with wa-. This naming introduces a recurrent theme, for Grizzly Woman will several times try to convince others that the trouble is all lies spread by Water Bug, even when she addresses her headman-husband in the village, having pursued the escaping women there. The next naming of Water Bug with wa- is in the night. When the fire has gone down a little, and Grizzly Woman arises stealthily, she goes first to Water Bug and her sister, and looks at Water Bug (wa-) (163:10), as shown in the long passage presented above. Finally, Water Bug is named with wa- when the women escape and Grizzly Woman begins to follow them. The text states: "She curses Water Bug. 'So that is why you came! You tell the people lies.' " (164:15).

Notice that Water Bug is not named at all at the end of Part One, and is named with wa- just once in each of the next four acts (Two VI, VII, VIII, IX). These are the acts of direct confrontation with Grizzly Woman at the place where the other woman had been killed.

Each of the four namings of Water Bug with wa- introduces and expresses a crucial element in the struggle between them: (1) the hiding of the paddles, forgotten by Grizzly Woman, which will later permit escape; (2) the telling of the people the truth about the deaths of their companions, which Grizzly Woman senses and tries to stamp as lies; (3) invulnerability to Grizzly Woman's power of causing sleep; (4) escape afterward back to their own village. The demise of Grizzly Woman is accomplished, no doubt appropriately in Chinookan terms, by a man, Water Bug's closest older male relative. That any women are saved at all, and that Grizzly Woman can be killed, is the culmination of Water Bug's overcoming of her in each of the four respects just listed.

The hiding of the paddles involves Water Bug alone; but in each of the succeeding three namings of her with *wa-*, Grizzly Woman is also involved, and *involved as the actor.* Water Bug is named as addressee, as object of perception, and again as addressee. One might have expected naming of Water Bug with *wa-*, when Water Bug herself acts powerfully; but, after the hiding of the paddles, not so. I take the pattern of naming Water Bug with *wa-* as object of address or perception, by Grizzly Woman, as an expression of what Grizzly Woman is now up against, in regard to her own lies, her sleep-causing power, her pursuit of the escaping women. This interpretation is parallel to the interpretation of the naming of Grizzly Woman herself with *wa-*, when grammatically the object of action, in a scene of "Gitskux and his older brother," discussed above. The two cases are indeed parallel as wholes. Here Water Bug is named with *wa-*, first acting alone, then against Grizzly Woman, named with *wa-* in confrontations that will result in her victory. There Grizzly Woman is named with *wa-*, the first time she acts (alone) against the family of Gitskux and his older brother, then named with *wa-* in a confrontation that results in her victory over them all. Perhaps the parallel discloses a convention, or point of style.

This connection between naming with *wa-* and confrontation reinforces the interpretation of the point of naming Grizzly Woman in "Grizzly Woman pursued him" (134) (page 345 above), and of the concentration of Grizzly Bear naming in this same, fifth section of the present myth.

Before taking up further generalizations, let us consider the one remaining text involving Grizzly Woman, the second text in which there is an alternation of *a-* : *Ø-* in naming Grizzly Woman.

3(b). In "Cock Robin, his older sister, and his sister's daughter" (31), a Grizzly Woman does not enter until very late in the story. The cast of characters named in the title has been succeeded by another. Cock Robin's older sister has left him, ordaining that he will live in the mountains and not find fish for food, and has had two sons by another husband. The two boys then travel by themselves. A woman holding a baby tells them several times that it is their child. After a long time, the older brother says, "Let us go to the woman." The younger one laughs, "What are you going to say to her?" The older replies, "I shall say, Yes, it is my own child." The younger responds:

"Why no,"
> he told him,
>> "she will kill us:
>>> "that one is Akitsimani;
>>>> "Let us be going!"

Here a Grizzly Woman is referred to by name and demonstrative pronoun as a statement of her nature as a fatal danger.

The two boys transform themselves into Snake and Feather, respectively, and go to her, Snake getting the infant. She drops rocks over them, and after a long time thinks (Kitsimani) (with ∅-) they must be dead. When she raises the rock, Feather wafts up, and Snake crawls between the rocks; both escape. The point at which she is named the second time is a point at which there is a turn toward escape. Her nature as a fatal danger is not in question, and confrontation with Snake and Feather may not be thought to call for heightening. Certainly nothing is done in this tag-end of the story to build up either fear of her or identification with them. They meet and this is the outcome, nothing more.

Naming and Prefix-Alternation as Foregrounding. The stories involving Grizzly Woman suggest a hierarchy of expressive alternatives. It is possible to relate a story in Chinookan without naming an actor at all. If the identity can be taken for granted, the person-marking prefixes of the verb will suffice for the roles of the actor in narrative action. Should an actor be named, it is theoretically possible to have the stem without prefix; to have one of the common third-person-singular prefixes; or to have prefix preceded by *w-*.

The order in which the alternatives have been listed would seem to be the order of increasing characterization and dramatization. That *w-* is at the top of the hierarchy seems indicated by its exclusive use when Grizzly Woman is named in titles and by the role it has been seen to play, both with Grizzly Woman and with Water Bug. A full study of Clackamas usage for all myth actors is needed, but I think these conclusions from the story of Grizzly Woman texts will be borne out by the rest of what we have of Clackamas from Mrs. Howard. The weighting and dramatic point of the narratives will be found to involve the stylistic choice of whether and where to name, and if to name, then how. Concentration of naming and choice of prefix provide foregrounding in the text and express underlying conceptions of identity as well.

An attentive reader may ask: if these relations of alternation *within* texts are correct, what about the alternation *among* texts? What about the alternation between kinds of alternation? Why *wa* ː - *a* in some stories, and *a-* ː ∅- in others?

The use of a zero prefix in the myth that ends with Grizzly Woman's encounter with Water Bug might seem to fit the fact that she attempts to deceive others throughout the myth. Perhaps zero prefix goes with concealment of identity. But there is no disguise of identity in the other myth with zero prefix for her. Furthermore, when Grizzly Woman attempts to disguise herself drastically in another identity, even donning another woman's skin, in the myth of Gitskux and his older brother, she is never named with a zero prefix.

Eating versus only killing.   There is an explanation of the occurrence of zero prefix in the corpus we have, if a statement of Mrs. Howard's grandmother can be taken as metaphorical, rather than literal. In the course of the story of Gitskux, it may be recalled, Mrs. Howard reported that her grandmother would intervene to say that the Grizzly Woman in question was the only one who eats people (320:14). That seemed a reason for connecting her particularly with the girl *(Lagiq' aq' inwapS)* who becomes a grizzly woman in another story told by the grandmother, "Grizzly Bear and Black Bear ran away with the two girls." The connection indeed seems valid, because of the many similarities, including the eating of people. But careful attention to other stories shows the Grizzly Woman actors to be associated with humans as food in almost every one!

There is no such association in "Coon and Coyote went and stole" (3), which, as has been said, is a recent extension of the Grizzly Woman identity to the two sisters who hoard fish. And they are never individually identified but always treated as dual *(is-)*. In "Coyote went around the land" (9), Coyote saves women from becoming the food prepared by Grizzly Woman for her husband. "Grizzly Bear and Black Bear ran away with the two girls" (14) has just been mentioned. In "Thunder and his mother" (30), the Grizzly Women encountered prepare "earth stew" containing human bones. "Gitskux and his older brother" (34) has just been mentioned. In "KuSaydi and his older brother" (40), the Grizzly Women again prepare "earth stew."

Beside the two short explanatory texts (143, 144), there remain just three. In none of these does a Grizzly Woman eat humans or her own kind, and in none of these texts is she named with the prefix *wa-*.

In "Grizzly Woman killed people" (17), she is said only to kill the successive groups of women. In "Cock Robin . . ." (31), the danger is only said to be that she will kill the two brothers. In "Grizzly Woman pursued him" (134), the indicated danger is presumably death.

This correlation suggests that the full Grizzly Woman character did include the eating of humans or her own kin; that *wa-* is associated with the full character of Grizzly Woman; and that the absence of *wa-* in texts in which the eating of humans or kin is not in question is not accident, but appropriateness. (And in text [14] the figure is not explicitly named as *kitsimani*, but only referred to, first by her own personal name, and then as having become a 'dangerous being', *a-qSXiLau.*)

The statement by Mrs. Howard's grandmother makes still a certain sense. Only in the myth in which she makes the statement (Gitskux [34]), and the myth with which we have connected it (14), does a Grizzly Woman enter into a kinship, indeed, nuclear family relationship with human beings, only to eat them later. The other stories have the obtaining of human food anonymous or offstage.

Frequency of alternation and personal concern. The dramatistic rightness of the grandmother's statement goes together with an interesting statistic. Prefix alternation is not all that common in the texts in which it occurs. If the five texts are tallied, excluding titles, the result is as follows:

	wa-	a-	Ø
(9)	1	1	
(16)	9	1	
(34)	9	5	
(17)		2	11
(31)		1	1

Table 10-2. Frequency of prefix alternation

We should note in passing that the tally shows that *a-* is always the marked case. In (9) there is a simple before-and-after difference in the state of Grizzly Woman, danger : no danger, to which perhaps (31) can be seen as analogous. In (16), *a-* is used at the one point at which Grizzly Woman has become inactive. Conversely, in keeping with the scale suggested earlier, *a-* is used in (17) at two culminating points of her identity, as against the common use of Ø-.

The story of Gitskux (34) fits the semantic pattern established for *wa-* : *a-*, but it stands out as the only story in which alternation is at all common. As the tally shows, only one other story has as many as two uses of the marked alternative, and the concluding encounter with Water Bug becomes a full narrative in itself there (17).

The appropriateness of alternation in the story of Gitskux is understandable in comparison with the two other stories in which *wa-*, expressing the full characterization of Grizzly Woman, alternates with *a-*. The story involving Coyote (9) has Coyote come, Lone Ranger-like, to the rescue of a group of women. The Grizzly Ogress is hardly on stage and not named when she is. The story of "Black Bear and Grizzly Bear" (16) is a gripping drama, sister killing sister, and cousins killing cousins in revenge, but it is set among bears, and much of the attention is focused on the successful escape of Black Bear's children. Once the action is set in motion, the mother anticipating her death and advising the sons, the success of the sons under the leadership of Wasgukmayli can be anticipated.

The story of "Gitskux and his older brother" is the one story of the three that has a periodic character. The plot is extended, not by escape and journey, but by the repeated return of the Ogress thought safely dead. The drama, perhaps nightmare, of the monstrous figure who comes uninvited, kills the proper wife and dons her skin, comes back and comes back. And where the children of Black Bear conduct a heroic and humorous escape, the children of Gitskux's older brother are shushed, stay away from their father in fright, have their pet taken, have a pet killed, see their mother killed in fighting begun for their sake, and finally are killed and eaten with the rest of their village. To be sure, the corresponding pair of nephews in the later marriage of the elder brother survive, but the children of the first marriage are a continuing witness, and eventual casualty, of the first two comings of Wakitsimani.

The unique frequency of alternation between active and passive prefixes for the Grizzly Ogress in this story reinforces the inference that the Ogress was of special concern to Mrs. Howard's grandmother. It is as if sensitivity to the expressive possibility of the alternation reflected a sensitivity to instability latent within personality within the home. The story is in effect a dramatization of the difference between a would-be wife (Grizzly Woman) and true wives, the first and second wives of Gitskux. More than that, it is a dramatization of the contrast between failure and success in integrating the "masculine" components (aggression, strength) and "feminine" components of personality. The first wife is strong, bringing in deer that her husband kills with one hand; the second wife is a paragon of both strength and spiritual power. Grizzly Woman tries to emulate each and fails each time.

The other story with more than one alternation is that of "Grizzly Woman killed people," and if we extend consideration to the use of naming itself, together with prefix-alternation, it is rich, too, as we have seen. Moreover, it also suggests concern with the integration of "masculine" and "feminine" components of personality. It does so especially in imagery.

Imagery. In the story of Seal, the daughter emerges from the darkness of the scenes to light, herself building the fire and raising the torch that discovers her uncle's murder. (Whereas Water Bug is able to build a fire in advance to prevent murder [and arises and builds it in the same words as Seal's daughter].) Seal's daughter is associated with symbolic wetness: she first hears that the uncle's wife must be a disguised man because of the sound made when all go outside at night to urinate. She then feels something wet dripping onto her at night underneath the bed of her uncle and his "wife." Her mother sets it aside as the result of intercourse; it turns out to be her uncle's blood. At the end she weeps three times, framing her remonstrance to her mother and lament for her uncle. This imagery seems to me to express emergence into sexual awareness and maturity as an individual: from darkness to light, from hearing one product of a phallus at a distance, to feeling what is taken to be another such product in bed (but is blood), to herself producing tears, while assuming the right to remonstrate.

The imagery associated with Grizzly Woman and Water Bug is of quite a different kind. Grizzly Woman inveigles the women into going off to use their digging sticks to get camas bulbs. While they are away from the village, she kills them at night with an arrow-spear. When Water Bug does not sleep, she accuses her of being concerned about young men who might come to her older sister. Water Bug herself says that she has dreamed of a bloody arrow-spear. Grizzly Woman is killed by the last arrow of Water Bug's older brother. Danger and death are rather closely associated with long pointed things. Safety, on the other hand, is mediated by things that are long but not so pointed, paddles. The safest paddles of all are those that are not intact, but have holes (presumably from use), those of an elder sister. All this strongly suggests an opposition in terms of phallic symbolism. The opposition seems to express a contrast between the danger of sex outside, away, as against the safety of sex that is more domestic, more muted. Arrow-spears versus paddles, as it were.

Let us look more closely at the scene of flight and escape. The nasal mucus that Grizzly Woman casts can perhaps be associated with the body's other secretion from a longitudinal part with opening, semen. That fits the consistent character of the other images associated with her, just noted. The elder sister's paddles seem a dual image. The fact that they have holes might imply an association with the female organ. Grizzly Woman casts an obnoxious surrogate of semen, but the escaping women, having implements that contain a surrogate of the female organ, are invulnerable. The unity, or integration, of attributes of the two genders is the means of safety. The presence of the holes does not seem to exclude the phallic symbolism. Not only are the paddles long, but the women insert them as steadily and rapidly as they can into the water. It may be the unity, or integration, of attributes of the two genders that expresses the means of safety.

The third story in which naming is frequent, that of Black Bear and Grizzly Woman and their children, is a direct confrontation between Grizzly Woman and a mother with her children, which fits with the fact that it is a child, a young girl, Water Bug, who overcomes Grizzly Woman in the story discussed here, and fits the significant witnessing by children in the story of Gitskux.

Altogether, these myths indicate a special concern with home as haven, in the phrase of Christopher Lasch, with the Grizzly Woman figure as an expression of failure of integration of "masculine" with "feminine" qualities in a woman, and the response of children to situations that result.

It is particularly in myths from Mrs. Howard's grandmother that there is a focus on the Grizzly Woman figure as more than a well-known ogress and danger. So concentration of naming and choice of prefix do indeed provide foregrounding in texts and express underlying conceptions of identity. The use of an alternation almost unnoticeable, and easy enough to dismiss, is thus found to say something of fundamental concern about women, and about girls growing up to be women, in both traditional and acculturationally shattered societies.

Epilog

The reader who has come this far may have had the pleasure in the intermittent texts somewhat smothered by detail and scaffolding. It would be worthwhile to go back, turning just to the pages with the final versions. (To aid in this, an index of the twenty final translations and analyses follows this epilog.) If one finds a degree of genuine imaginative life, then the rest, the laying of foundations, erecting of scaffolding, sifting and sorting of detail, will have the justification I most desire.

To be sure, there are other justifications. The chapters can stand as contributions to linguistics, folklore, and ethnology. Through them something is added to what is known about the role of elements in the languages; something new is shown about old texts; something is gained in understanding of the traditional cultures and peoples. Such knowledge, however interesting to the scholar and to the descendant, might lack interest for others. However accurate, it might lack power. Do these texts, restored to something like their true form, have power to move us, as part of the first literature of our land? They do for myself, and I hope for others.

The hope must be qualified by the reflection that my own delight comes partly from the work of discovery itself. To have read the texts as prose, the eye moving margin to margin along lines of an arbitrary equivalence, and then to discover lines of another kind; to have scanned block paragraphs, and then discover shapes concealed within them; to feel oneself the first to see the true form of the original, its actual proportions, ingredients and relations; that is something like finding an original that had been painted over, or a Schubert manuscript that had lain unknown and unplayed. To adapt Yeats's lines from "A woman young and old," one has a sense of looking for the face texts had before a later world was made. But whether or not·what is found is indeed a treasure, as well as an addition to truth, must be judged by an audience that comes to the discovery without a share in the performance.

The enjoyment of the texts as literature does require the analysis that accompanies it here. Philology is needed to establish and justify the form of the text. Here the analysis and presentation in terms of lines is fundamental. Native speakers themselves find such presentations easier to read and use. For most of us, the essential contribution of the presentation in lines is to slow down attention so as to be able to attend to shape and meaning as they unfold. These texts, after all, are somewhat analogous to *haiku*, not only in stating or implying a seasonal reference and relying on direct expression, but also in asking much of the reader, by leaving much understated or unsaid. There must be time in the reading for the mind of the reader to do its work, reading not only for information but also for form, visualizing the picture so briefly sketched. In this regard, Americanist philology converges with the conception stated once by Nietzsche (Preface to *Daybreak* [2d ed., 1886], quoted in Nietzsche 1977:17):

> perhaps one is a philologist still, that is to say, a teacher of slow reading:
> . . . For philology is that venerable art which demands of its votaries one thing above all: to go aside, to take time, to become still, to become slow—. . . it is more necessary than ever today . . . in the midst of an age of "work," that is to say, of hurry . . . this art does not so easily get anything done, it teaches to read *well*, that is to say, to read slowly, deeply, looking cautiously before and aft, with reservations, with doors left open . . . .

It is, of course, right to speak of reservations, of doors left open. Once the form of the text has been established as well as possible, other interpretations than that of the philologist may be given. To use a musical analogy, this book provides in each case an edited score and one "reading" of the score. Other knowledge, other perspectives, may provide other readings. If these texts are literature, as I believe, that is to be expected, and, indeed, to be hoped. The life of a literary text begets imaginative life. Contemporary audiences, Indian and non-Indian, like traditional audiences, will individually visualize settings, identify with actors, interpret moral weight. It is probably not accidental that my own discoveries so frequently occur in texts that have to do with children, constrained by propriety, achieving sometimes against it and monstrous odds.

I hope that what is shown in this volume will help to bring imaginative life to other texts as well as these. The devices and designs considered in these chapters are indeed like the actors in myths. The text has a stop, but not its world. The ingredients may go on to other adventures in other texts. We have discovered makings, not a single mold; a bed that is Protean, not Procrustean. What has been shown in these chapters is barely a beginning.

From the point of view of Chinookan alone, although the texts preserved to us are a scant portion of what was once performed, the texts analyzed here are but a fraction of those that are preserved. For each narrator from whom we have a considerable number, the individual set of texts should be consistently analyzed and presented in order to discover personal style. From the point of view of North America, the Chinookan peoples, although prominent in their own world and in the world of scholarship, are but one people among many. The principles of verse analysis should be explored among other groups, so that we may begin to understand what is general to American Indian literature in this regard, what is specific to a language and group, what personal. Where verse analysis strikes a vein of special focus, as with the figure of Grizzly Woman in the Clackamas texts from Victoria Howard, all that comparative linguistics, folklore, and ethnology can provide by way of context and ground for interpretation should be brought to bear.

I shall try to accomplish some of these things in succeeding volumes. Some are largely complete. One, tentatively titled "Myth as speech," extends the principles of verse analysis to two languages, Takelma of southwestern Oregon and Tonkawa of Texas, in which lines and verses are indeed found to be present, but to be organized in accord with a different rhetorical pattern, a different "narrative logic." Another book culminates with a Kathlamet Chinook text, the "Sun's myth," which offers an opportunity to probe active personal poesis. An earlier presentation of the myth in terms of verses (Hymes 1975c) is changed; the wording of translation revised and deepened; new elements of pattern and symbolism found. Another volume, "Bears that save and destroy," is built around the figure of Grizzly Woman. Chinookan texts from Cultee, Hiram Smith, and, particularly, Victoria Howard, allow one to discern the twin names and complementary conceptions of an ancient concern with the female grizzly as an ambivalent figure of destructive aggression and saving power. Beyond these, volumes devoted to the individual texts of Louis Simpson or Charles Cultee are not to be despaired of, although they can be only an aspiration now. A selection of texts from Victoria Howard, presented in a format and typography designed by the printer-poet Charles Bigelow is also to be hoped. Eventually all the old collections must be redone in such a way. Their recorders preserved more than they knew: authentic monuments, to be sure, but something more. We must work to make visible and audible again that something more—the literary form in which the native words had their being—so that they can move again at a pace that is surer, more open to the voice, more nearly their own.

Index to Analyzed Translations and English-Language Texts

Bibliography

Abrahams, R. D. 1972. The training of the man of words in talking sweet. *Language in Society* 1:15–30.

Adamson, Thelma. 1934. *Folk-tales of the Coast Salish.* American Folklore Society, Memoirs, 27. New York: G. E. Stechert.

Andrade, Manuel. 1931. *Quileute texts.* Columbia University Contributions to Anthropology, 12. New York: Columbia University Press.

Aoki, H. 1979. *Nez Perce texts.* University of California Publications, Linguistics, 90. Berkeley and Los Angeles: University of California Press.

Arendt, Hannah. 1971. Lying in politics: Reflections on the Pentagon papers. *New York Review of Books,* 18 November, pp. 30–41.

Astrov, Margot. 1946. *The winged serpent. An anthology of American Indian prose and poetry.* New York: John Day.

Banaji, Jairus. 1970. The crisis of British anthropology. *New Left Review* 64: 71–85.

Barbeau, Marius. 1951. Tsimshian songs. In *The Tsimshian: Their arts and music,* by Viola E. Garfield, Paul S. Wingert, and Marius Barbeau. Publications of the American Ethnological Society, 18, ed. Marian W. Smith. New York: J. J. Augustin.

Barker, R. G. and H. F. Wright. 1954. *Midwest and its children.* Evanston, Ill.: Row, Peterson.

Barnett, D. 1972. *The performance of music.* New York: Universe Books.

Bauman, Richard and Joel Sherzer, eds. 1974. *Explorations in the ethnography of speaking.* London and New York: Cambridge University Press.

Beals, Ralph and Harry Hoijer. 1953. *An introduction to cultural anthropology.* New York: Macmillan.

Beckham, Stephen Dow. 1971. *Requiem for a people: The Rogue Indians and the frontiersman.* Norman: University of Oklahoma Press.

———. 1977. *The Indians of western Oregon. This land was theirs.* Coos Bay, Ore.: Arago Books.

Bernstein, Basil. 1971. *Class, codes and control. Vol. I: Theoretical studies towards a sociology of language.* London: Routledge, Kegan Paul (2d rev. ed. 1973).

———. ed. 1972. *Class, codes and control. Vol. II: Applied studies towards a sociology of language.* London: Routledge, Kegan Paul.

———. 1975. *Class, codes and control. Vol. III: Towards a theory of educational transmissions.* London: Routledge, Kegan Paul.

Boas, Franz. 1891. Dissemination of tales among the natives of North America. *Journal of American Folklore* 4: 13–20.

———. 1894. *Chinook texts.* Bureau of American Ethnology, Bulletin 20. Washington, D.C.

———. 1895. *Indianische Sagen von der Nord-Pacifischen Küste Amerikas.* Berlin: A. Asher. (An English translation by Dietrich Bertz for the British Columbia Indian Language Project, *Indian myths and legends from the North Pacific Coast of America,* was in typescript in 1977.)

———. 1896. Songs of the Kwakiutl Indians. *Internationales Archiv für Ethnographie,* 9, Supplement, pp. 1–9. Leiden.

———. 1897. The social organization and the secret societies of the Kwakiutl Indians. *Report of the U.S. National Museum for 1895,* pp. 311–737. Washington, D.C.: Government Printing Office.

———. 1898a. The mythology of the Bella Coola Indians. *The Jesup North Pacific Expedition,* Part 2. American Museum of Natural History, Memoirs, II; Anthropology, I. Pp. 25–127. New York and Leiden.

———. 1898b. Notes on the traditions of the Tillamook Indians. *Journal of American Folklore* 11: 23–38, 133–50.

———. 1901. *Kathlamet texts.* Bureau of American Ethnology, Bulletin 26. Washington, D.C.

———. 1902. *Tsimshian texts.* Bureau of American Ethnology, Bulletin 27. Washington, D.C.

———. 1911. Chinook. In *Handbook of American Indian languages,* ed. F. Boas, pp. 559–677. Bureau of American Ethnology, Bulletin 40, Part I. Washington, D.C.

———. 1912. *Tsimshian texts: New series.* American Ethnological Society Publications, III. Leyden: E. J. Brill.

———. 1916. *Tsimshian mythology.* Based on texts recorded by Henry W. Tate. Bureau of American Ethnology, Annual Report 31. Washington, D.C. Pp. 29–979.

———. ed. 1917. *Folk-tales of Salishan and Sahaptin tribes.* Collected by James A. Teit, Marian K. Gould, Livingston Farrand, Herbert J. Spinden. The American Folk-Lore Society, Memoirs, II. Lancaster, Pa. and New York: G. E. Stechert.

———. 1921. *Ethnology of the Kwakiutl.* Bureau of American Ethnology, Annual Report 35 (1913–1914), pt. 2, pp. 795–1481. Washington, D.C.: U.S. Government Printing Office.

———. 1925. Stylistic aspects of primitive literature. *Journal of American Folklore* 38: 329–39. (Reprinted in Boas, *Race, language, and culture.* New York: Macmillan, 1940, pp. 491–502.)

———. 1932. *Bella Bella tales.* American Folklore Society, Memoirs, 25. New York: G. E. Stechert.

———. 1935. *Kwakiutl culture as reflected in mythology.* American Folklore Society, Memoirs, 28. New York: G. E. Stechert.

———. ed. 1938. *General anthropology.* New York: D. C. Heath.

Bouchard, Randy and Dorothy I. D. Kennedy. 1977. *Lillooet stories.* Sound Heritage VI (1). Victoria B.C.: B. C. Indian Language Project.

Brooks, Cleanth and Robert Penn Warren. 1949. *Modern rhetoric.* New York: Harcourt, Brace.

Burke, Kenneth. 1931. *Counter-Statement.* New York: Harcourt, Brace. (2d ed. Chicago: University of Chicago Press [Phoenix Books], 1957.)

————. 1945. *A grammar of motives*. Englewood Cliffs, N. J.: Prentice-Hall. (Reissued by University of California Press.)

————. 1950. *A rhetoric of motives*. Englewood Cliffs, N. J.: Prentice-Hall. (Reissued by University of California Press.)

————. 1957. The philosophy of literary form. In *Philosophy of literary form*. New York: Vintage Books. (First published, Baton Rouge, La.: Louisiana State University Press, 1941; reissued by University of California Press.)

Burling, Robbins. 1966. The metrics of children's verse. A cross-cultural linguistic study. *American Anthropologist* 66(6):1418–41.

Bursill-Hall, G. L. 1964. Linguistic analysis of North American Indian songs. *Canadian Linguistic Journal* 10:15–36.

Cassirer, Ernst. 1961. *The logic of the humanities*. New Haven: Yale University Press. (Translated by Clarence Smith Howe from *Zur Logik des Kulturwissenschaften* [Göteborg, 1942].)

Chomsky, N. 1964. The logical basis of linguistic theory. In *Proceedings of the ninth international congress of linguistics*, ed. H. Lunt, pp. 914–78. The Hague: Mouton.

————. 1965. *Aspects of the theory of syntax*. Cambridge: M.I.T. Press.

Clark, Ella E. 1953. *Indian legends of the Pacific Northwest*. Berkeley and Los Angeles: University of California Press.

Collingwood, R. G. 1938. *The principles of art*. London: Oxford University Press.

Conklin, H. C. 1964. Ethnogenealogical methods. In *Explorations in cultural anthropology*, ed. W. H. Goodenough, pp. 25–56. New York: McGraw-Hill.

Corman, Cid. 1976. Seymour Chatman's A theory of meter. *The act of poetry and two other essays*. (Sparrow 44). Santa Barbara, Calif.: Black Sparrow Press.

Crystal, David. ms. Intonation and metrical theory. Mimeographed. Presented at a meeting of the Philological Society, 7 May 1971, under the title "Competence in performance: Phonological variables in literary effect." (Now in Crystal, *The English tone of voice. Essays in intonation, prosody and paralanguage* [London: Edwin Arnold, 1975].)

Curtin, J. 1909. Wasco tales and myths. In *Wishram texts*, ed. Edward Sapir, pp. 239–314. American Ethnological Society, Publications 2. Leyden: E. J. Brill. (Collected in 1885.)

Curtis, Edward S. 1911. *The North American Indian, VIII*. Seattle and Cambridge, Mass.

Day, A. G. 1951. *The sky clears. Poetry of the American Indians*. New York: Macmillan.

DeGroot, A. W. 1946. *Algemene Versleer*. The Hague.

————. 1964. The description of a poem. In *Proceedings of the Ninth International Congress of Linguistics*, ed. H. G. Lunt, pp. 294–301. The Hague: Mouton.

Dolgin, Janet, David Kemnitzer, and David Schneider, eds. 1971. *Symbolic anthropology*. New York: Columbia University Press.

Drucker, Philip. 1965. *Cultures of the North Pacific Coast*. New York: Harper and Row.

Dundes, A. 1963. Structural typology of North American Indian folktales. *Southwest Journal of Anthropology* 19: 121–30.

———. 1964. *The morphology of North American Indian folktales.* Folklore Fellows Communications, no. 195, vol. 81. Helsinki: Suomalainen Tiedeakatemia.

Dyk, W. and D. H. Hymes. 1956. Stress accent in Wishram Chinook. *International Journal of American Linguistics* 22: 238–41.

Edmonson, Munro S. 1971. *The book of counsel: The Popol Vuh of the Quiché Maya of Guatemala.* New Orleans: Middle American Research Institute, Tulane University.

Elmendorf, W. W. 1961. Skokomish and other Coast Salish tales. *Research Studies* 29(1):1–37; 29(2):84–117; 29(3):119–50. Pullman: Washington State University.

Finley, M. I. 1965. *The world of Odysseus.* rev. ed. New York: The Viking Press.

Foster, John L. 1980. Sinuhe: The ancient Egyptian genre of narrative verse. *Journal of Near Eastern Studies* 39(2):89–117.

Foster, M. 1971. Speaking in the longhouse at Six Nations Reserve. In *Linguistic diversity in Canadian society,* ed. Regna Darnell, pp. 142–48. Edmonton and Champaign: Linguistic Research.

Frachtenberg, Leo J. 1920. *Alsea texts and myths.* Bureau of American Ethnology, Bulletin 65. Washington, D.C.

———. 1913. *Coos texts.* Columbia University Contributions to Anthropology, 1. New York: Columbia University Press; Leyden: E. J. Brill.

———. 1914. *Lower Umpqua texts and notes on the Kusan dialects.* Columbia University Contributions to Anthropology, 4. New York: Columbia University Press; Leyden: E. J. Brill.

———. 1920. *Alsea texts and myths.* Bureau of American Ethnology, Bulletin 67. Washington, D.C.

Frake, C. O. 1962. The ethnographic study of cognitive systems. In *Anthropology and human behavior,* ed. T. Gladwin and W. C. Sturtevant, pp. 72–85. Washington, D.C.: Anthropological Society of Washington.

Francis, W. N. 1961. Review of T. A. Sebeok, ed., *Style in language. Language Learning* 11: 183–87.

Freilich, M. 1975. Myth, method and madness. *Current Anthropology* 16(2): 207–26.

———. 1978. The meaning of "sociocultural." In *The concept and dynamics of culture,* ed. Bernado Bernadi, pp. 89–101. The Hague: Mouton.

French, David. 1958. Cultural matrices of Chinookan non-casual language. *International Journal of American Linguistics* 24: 258–63.

———. 1961. Wasco-Wishram. In *Perspectives in Amerindian cultural change,* ed. Edward H. Spicer, pp. 337–430. Chicago: University of Chicago Press.

Friedrich, Paul. 1966. Structural implications of Russian pronominal usage. In *Sociolinguistics,* ed. William Bright, pp. 214–53. The Hague: Mouton.

Frisbie, C. J. 1980. Vocables in Navajo ceremonial music. *Ethnomusicology* 24(3): 347–92.

Georges, R. 1969. Toward an understanding of story-telling events. *Journal of American Folklore* 82: 314–28.

Gifford, E. W. 1917. *Miwok myths.* University of California Publications in American Archaeology and Ethnology 12(8):283–338. Berkeley.

Goddard, P. E., ed. 1907. Myths, prayers and songs of the Navajo. *University of California Publications in American Archaeology and Ethnology* 5(2):21–63.

Goffman, E. 1959. *The presentation of self in everyday life.* Garden City, N.Y.: Doubleday Anchor Books.

———. 1963. *Behavior in public places.* New York: Free Press.

———. 1967. *Interaction ritual: Essays in face-to-face behavior.* Chicago: Aldine.

Goodenough, W. H. 1956. Residence rules. *Southwestern Journal of Anthropology* 12: 22–37.

———. 1957. Cultural anthropology and linguistics. In *Report of the Seventh Annual Round Table Meeting on Linguistics and Language Study,* ed. P. L. Garvin, pp. 167–73. Washington, D.C.: Georgetown University Press.

———. 1970. *Description and comparison in cultural anthropology.* Chicago: Aldine.

Greenway, John. 1964. *Literature among the primitives.* Hatboro, Pa.

Gunther, Erna. 1949. The Shaker religion of the Northwest. In *Indians of the urban northwest,* ed. Marian W. Smith. New York: Columbia University Press.

Halliday, M. A. K. 1978. *Language as social semiotic. The social interpretation of language and meaning.* London: Edward Arnold.

Haring, Lee. 1972. Performing for the interviewers: A study of the structure of context. *Southern Folklore Quarterly* 36:383–98.

Harris, Marvin. 1964. *The nature of cultural things.* New York: Random House.

Henderson, H. G. 1958. *An introduction to haiku. An anthology of poems and poets from Basho to Shiki.* Garden City, N.Y.: Doubleday Anchor Books.

Hendricks, W. 1973. Review of P. and E. K. Maranda, eds., *Structural analysis of oral tradition. Semiotica* 8(3):239–62.

Hill-Tout, C. 1904. Report on the ethnology of the Siciatl of British Columbia, a Coast division of the Salish stock. *Journal of the Royal Anthropological Institute of Great Britain and Ireland* 34:20–91. (Reprinted in Maud 1978.)

Hinton, Leanne. 1980. Vocables in Havasupai music. In *Southwestern Indian ritual drama,* ed. C. J. Frisbie, pp. 275–305. Albuquerque: University of New Mexico Press.

Hymes, D. 1953. Two Wasco motifs. *Journal of American Folklore* 66:69–70.

———. 1954. The dog-husband tale. Bloomington, Ind.: Indiana University, manuscript.

———. 1955. The language of the Kathlamet Chinook. Ph.D. dissertation. Indiana University.

———. 1956. Review of *Papers from the symposium on American Indian linguistics. Language* 32:585–602.

———. 1958. Linguistic features peculiar to Chinookan myths. *International Journal of American Linguistics* 24:253–57.

———. 1959. Myth and tale titles of the Lower Chinook. *Journal of American Folklore* 72:139–45 (=chap. 7 of this volume).

———. 1960. Ob-Ugric metrics. *Anthropos* 55:574–76. (A review article, concerning Robert Austerlitz, *Ob-Ugric metrics: The metrical structure of Ostyak and Vogul folk-poetry* [Helsinki, 1958].)

———. 1962. Review of T. P. Coffin, ed. *Indian tales of North America. American Anthropologist* 64:676–79.

———. 1964a. Directions in (ethno-) linguistic theory. *American Anthropologist* 66(6):Part II, 6–56.

———. 1964b. A perspective for linguistic anthropology. In *Horizons of Anthropology*, ed. S. Tax, pp. 92–107. Chicago; Aldine.

———. 1965a. Introduction. In *The ethnography of communication*, ed. J. Gumperz and D. Hymes, *American Anthropologist*, 66(6), Part II, 1–34.

———. 1965b. The methods and tasks of anthropological philology (illustrated with Clackamas Chinook). *Romance Philology* 19: 325–40.

———. 1965c. Some North Pacific Coast poems: A problem in anthropological philology. *American Anthropologist* 67: 316–41 (= chap. 1 of this volume).

———. 1966a. Two types of linguistic relativity. In *Sociolinguistics*, ed. W. Bright, pp. 131–56. The Hague: Mouton.

———. 1966b. Some points of Siuslaw phonology. *International Journal of American Linguistics* 32: 328–42.

———. 1967. Why linguistics needs the sociologist. *Social Research* 34(4):632–47 (=Hymes 1974a, chap. 3).

———. 1968a. The "wife" who "goes out" like a man: Reinterpretation of a Clackamas Chinook myth. *Social Science Information* (Studies in Semiotics) 7(3): 173–99. (Reprinted in Pierre and Elli Kongas Maranda eds., *Structural analysis of oral tradition*. Philadelphia: University of Pennsylvania Press, 1971, pp. 49–80) [=chap. 8 of this volume].)

———. 1968b. Review of Kenneth Burke, *Language as symbolic action*. *Language* 44: 664–69 (=Hymes 1974a, chap. 7).

———. 1970. Linguistic method in ethnography. In *Method and theory in linguistics*, ed. Paul Garvin, pp. 249–311. The Hague: Mouton.

———. 1971a. The contribution of folklore to sociolinguistics. *Journal of American Folklore* 84: 42–50 (=Hymes 1974a, chap. 6).

———. 1971b. (=1968a, slightly revised). In *Essays in semiotics*, ed. Julia Kristeva, Josette Rey-Debove, and Donna J. Umiker, pp. 296–326. Approaches to Semiotics, 4. The Hague: Mouton (=chap. 8 of this volume).

———. 1972. Introduction. In *Functions of language in the classroom*, ed. Courtney Cazden, Vera John-Steiner, Dell Hymes, pp. xi–lvii. New York: Teachers College Press.

———. 1974a. *Foundations in sociolinguistics*. Philadelphia: University of Pennsylvania Press.

———. 1974b. Ways of speaking. In *Explorations in the ethnography of speaking*, ed. Richard Bauman and Joel Sherzer, pp. 433–51. London and New York: Cambridge University Press.

———. 1975a. Breakthrough into performance. In *Folklore: Performance and communication*, ed. Dan Ben-Amos and Kenneth S. Goldstein, pp. 11–74. The Hague: Mouton (=chap. 3 of this volume).

———. 1975b. For Philip. *Alcheringa* n.s. 1(2): 99–101.

———. 1975c. Folklore's nature and the sun's myth. *Journal of American Folklore* 88: 345–69.

———. 1975d. From space to time in tenses in Kiksht. *International Journal of American Linguistics* 41:313–29.

———. 1976a. Louis Simpson's "The deserted boy." *Poetics* 5(2): 119–55 (=chap. 4 of this volume).

————. 1976b. The Americanist tradition. In *American Indian languages and American linguistics,* ed. Wallace L. Chafe, pp. 11–33. Lisse: The Peter de Ridder Press.

————. 1977. Discovering oral performance and measured verse in American Indian narrative. *New Literary History* 8:431–57 (=chap. 9 of this volume).

————. 1979a. How to talk like a bear in Takelma. *International Journal of American Linguistics* 45(2): 101–6 (=chap. 2 of this volume).

————. 1979b. Foreword. In *Portraits of "The Whiteman,"* by Keith Basso. New York: Cambridge University Press.

————. 1979c. The religious aspect of language in Native American humanities. In *Essays in humanistic anthropology,* ed. Bruce T. Grindel and Dennis M. Warren. Washington, D.C.: University Press of America.

————. 1980a. Verse analysis of a Wasco text. *International Journal of American Linguistics* 46:65–77 (=chap. 5 of this volume).

————. 1980b. Reading Clackamas texts. In *Traditional literatures of the American Indian,* ed. Karl Kroeber, pp. 117–59. Lincoln: University of Nebraska Press (=chap. 10 of this volume).

————. 1981. The news concerning Coyote (first published in this volume as chap. 6).

————. ms. a. Frances Johnson's "The Otter brothers recover their father's heart." Read at University of Minnesota, 3 May 1978. Intended for *New Literary History.*

————. ms. b. *Myth as speech* (Studies in Native American Literature 2).

————. ms. c. *The Sun's myth* (Studies in Native American Literature 3).

————. ms. d. *Bears that save and destroy* (Studies in Native American Literature 4).

————. ms. e. Poetic structure of a Chinook text. In *Essays in honor of Charles F. Hockett,* ed. A. Makkai and V. B. Makkai. Hamburg, N.Y.: The Press at Twin Willows.

Irvine, Albert. 1921. How the Makah obtained possession of Cape Flattery. trans. Luke Markistan. *Indian Notes and Monographs,* pp. 5–11. New York: Heye Foundation, Museum of the American Indian.

Irving, Washington. 1836. *Astoria.* 2 vols. Philadelphia.

Jacobs, E. D. and M. Jacobs. 1959. *Nehalem Tillamook tales.* University of Oregon Monographs, Studies in Anthropology, No. 5. Eugene: University of Oregon Books.

Jacobs, Melville. 1929. *Northwest Sahaptin texts.* 1. University of Washington Publications in Anthropology 2(6): 175–244. Seattle.

————. 1934. *Northwest Sahaptin texts,* Part I (English). Columbia University Contributions to Anthropology, 19 (1). New York: Columbia University Press.

————. 1937. *Northwest Sahaptin texts,* Part II (Sahaptin). Columbia University Contributions to Anthropology, 19(2). New York: Columbia University Press.

————. 1939. *Coos narrative and ethnologic texts.* University of Washington Publications in Anthropology 8(1):1–126. Seattle.

————. 1940. *Coos myth texts.* University of Washington Publications in Anthropology, 8(1):127–260. Seattle: University of Washington Press.

————. 1945. *Kalapuya texts.* University of Washington Publications in Anthropology, 11. Seattle.

————. 1957. Titles in an oral literature. *Journal of American Folklore* 70:157–72.

———. 1958. *Clackamas Chinook texts, Part I.* Research Center in Anthropology, Folklore and Linguistics, Publications 8: *International Journal of American Linguistics* 24(1), pt.2. Bloomington: Indiana University.

———. 1959a. *Clackamas Chinook texts, Part II.* Research Center in Anthropology, Folklore and Linguistics, Publication 11, *International Journal of American Linguistics* 25(2), pt. 2. Bloomington: Indiana University.

———. 1959b. *The content and style of an oral literature. Clackamas Chinook myths and tales.* Chicago: University of Chicago Press (also Viking Fund Publication in Anthropology, 26. New York: Wenner-Gren Foundation for Anthropological Research).

———. 1960. *The people are coming soon. Analyses of Clackamas Chinook myths and tales.* Seattle: University of Washington Press.

———. 1972. Areal spread of Indian oral genre features in the northwest states. *Journal of the Folklore Institute* 9(1):10–17.

Jackson, Lillian Reeves. 1929. The tale of the Dog Husband. M.A. thesis, Indiana University.

Jakobson, Roman. 1960. Closing statement: Linguistics and poetics. In *Style in language,* ed. Thomas A. Sebeok, pp. 350–77. Cambridge: The Technology Press; New York: John Wiley.

Jansen, W. H. 1957. Classifying performance in the study of verbal folklore. In *Studies in folklore in honor of Distinguished Service Professor Stith Thompson,* ed. W. Edson Richmond, pp. 110–18. Indiana University Publications, Folklore Series, 9. Bloomington, Indiana. (Reprinted Westport, Conn.: Greenwood Press, 1972.)

Kahclamet, P. and D. Hymes. 1977. Iyagiximnilh [=IyagixmniL]. *Alcheringa* 3(2): 8–9.

Kermode, F. 1969. The structures of fiction. *Modern Language Notes* 84(6): 891–915.

———. 1978. Sensing endings. *Nineteenth-Century Fiction* 33(1): 144–58 (Special issue: Narrative Endings).

Kirshenblatt-Gimblett, Barbara. Culture shock and narrative creativity: Code-switching in immigrant humor. In *Ashkenaz: Essays on Jewish folklore and culture.* Philadelphia: University of Pennsylvania Press, forthcoming. (See in original version of 1972, distributed under the title "Multilingualism and immigrant narrative: Code-switching as a communicative strategy in artistic verbal performance.")

Kristeva, Julia, Julia Rey-Debove, and Donna J. Umiker, eds. 1971. *Essays in semiotics.* Approaches to Semiotics, 4. The Hague: Mouton.

Kroeber, K. 1979. Deconstructionist criticisms and American Indian literature. *Boundary* 27(3):73–89.

———, ed. 1980. *Traditional literatures of the American Indian.* Lincoln: University of Nebraska Press.

Labov, W. 1966. *The social stratification of English in New York City.* Washington, D.C.: Center for Applied Linguistics.

Leach, M. E. 1963. What shall we do with "Little Matty Groves?" *Journal of American Folklore* 76:189–94.

Lévi-Strauss, C. 1952. Recherches de mythologies américaines, compte rendu. *Annuaire, 1952–1953*, École pratique des hautes etudes, section des sciences, réligieuses, 19–21. Paris.

———. 1955. The structural study of myth. *Journal of American Folklore* 78:428–44. (Reprinted in Lévi-Strauss [1958a:227–56, 1963a:206–31].)

———. 1956. Structure et dialectique. In *For Roman Jakobson, essays on the occasion of his sixtieth birthday*, ed. Morris Halle et al., pp. 289–94. The Hague: Mouton. (Reprinted in Lévi-Strauss [1958a:257–66, 1963a:232–41].)

———. 1958a. *Anthropologie structurale*. Paris: Plon.

———. 1958b. La geste d'Asdiwal. *Annuaire, 1958–59*, École pratique des hautes études, section des sciences religieuses, 2–43. Paris.

———. 1960. Four Winnebago myths. A structural sketch. In *Culture in history: Essays in honor of Paul Radin*, ed. Stanley Diamond, pp. 351–62. New York: Columbia University Press.

———. 1963a. *Structural anthropology*. New York: Basic Books. (Translation of Lévi-Strauss [1958a].)

———. 1963b. The structural study of myth. In *Structural Anthropology*, pp. 206–31. New York: Basic Books. (First published, *Journal of American Folklore* 78: 428–44.)

———. 1963c. *Totemism*. Boston: Beacon Press. (First published, Paris, 1962.)

———. 1964–1971. *Mythologies*, vols. *I–IV*. Paris: Plon.

———. 1964. *Le cru et le cuit* (Mythologiques, 1). Paris: Plon. (Translated by John and Doreen Weightman as *The raw and the cooked*. New York: Harper and Row, 1969.)

———. 1971. *L'Homme nu* (Mythologiques, 4). Paris: Plon.

Lord, Albert. 1960. *The singer of tales*. Cambridge: Harvard University Press.

Lowie, R. H. 1908. Catch-words for mythological motives. *Journal of American Folklore* 21:24–27.

Lyman, H. S. 1900. Reminiscences of Louis Labonte. *Oregon Historical Quarterly* 1:167–88.

McAllester, D. P. 1980. The first snake song. In *Theory and practice: Essays presented to Gene Weltfish*, ed. S. Diamond, pp. 1–27. The Hague: Mouton.

McAllester, D. P. and S. W. McAllester. 1980. *Hogans. Navajo houses and house songs*. Middletown, Conn.: Wesleyan University Press.

Malkiel, Y. 1962. Review of T. A. Sebeok, *Style in language*. *International Journal of American Linguistics* 28:268–86.

Mandelbaum, D. G., ed. 1949. *Selected writings of Edward Sapir*. Berkeley and Los Angeles: University of California Press.

Maranda, P. and E. K. Maranda, eds. 1971. *Structural analysis of oral tradition*. Philadelphia: University of Pennsylvania Press.

Maud, R., ed. 1978a. *The Salish people. The local contribution of Charles Hill-Tout. Vol. I: The Thompson and the Okanagan*. Vancouver, B.C.: Talon Books.

———. 1978b. *The Salish people: The local contribution of Charles Hill-Tout. Vol. IV: The Sechelt and the Southeastern tribes of Vancouver Island*. Vancouver: Talon Books.

Meacham, A. B. 1875. *Wigwam and warpath, or, The royal chief in chains*. Boston: John P. Dale.

Messing, G. M. 1961. Review of T. A. Sebeok, *Style in language*. *Language* 37: 256–66.

Naroll, R. 1962. *Data quality control—a new research technique*. New York: Free Press.

Newman, S. 1962. Review of T. A. Sebeok, *Style in language*. *Journal of American Folklore* 75: 84–85.

[Nietzsche, Friedrich]. 1977. *A Nietzsche reader*. Selected and translated with an introduction by R. J. Hollingdale. Harmondsworth, Middlesex, England: Penguin Books.

Noholnigee, Chief Henry Yugh. 1979. *The stories that Chief Henry told*. Transcr. and ed. Eliza Jones. Fairbanks, Alaska: Alaska Native Language Center, University of Alaska.

Paredes, A. and R. Bauman, eds. 1972. *Toward new perspectives in folklore*. American Folklore Society Publications, Bibliographical and Special Series, 23. Austin: University of Texas Press.

Peckham, M. 1965. *Man's rage for chaos. Biology, behavior and the arts*. Philadelphia and New York: Chilton Books.

Pike, K. L. 1954. *Language in relation to a unified theory of human behavior, Part I*. Glendale, Calif.: Summer Institute of Linguistics. (See now Parts I–III revised under the same general title [The Hague: Mouton, 1965].)

Powers, W. 1960. American Indian music: An introduction. *American Indian Hobbyist* 7(1): 5–9.

———. 1961. American Indian music. Part II: The language. *American Indian Hobbyist* 7(2): 41–45.

Ramsey, J. 1977. The wife who goes out like a man, comes back as a hero: The art of two Oregon Indian narratives. *Publications Modern Language Association* 92(1): 9–18.

———, ed. 1977. *Coyote was going there: Indian literature of the Oregon country*. Seattle: University of Washington Press.

Ray, V. 1938. *Lower Chinook ethnographic notes*. University of Washington Publications in Anthropology 7(2). Seattle.

Reagan, Albert B. 1929. Traditions of Hoh and Quillayute Indians. *Washington Historical Quarterly* 20: 178–89.

Reichard, G. 1947. *An analysis of Coeur d'Alene Indian myths*. American Folklore Society, Memoirs, 41. (With comparative notes by Adele Froelich.)

Rexroth, K. 1961a. The poet as translator. *Assays*, 19–40. Norfolk Conn.: New Directions.

Rexroth, K. 1961b. American Indian songs. *Assays*, 52–68. Norfolk, Conn.: New Directions. (Reprinted from Perspectives USA, No. 16.)

Riffaterre, M. 1961. Review of T. A. Sebeok, *Style in language*. *Word* 17: 318–44.

Robins, R. H. and N. McLeod. 1956. Five Yurok songs: A musical and textual analysis. *Bulletin of the School for Oriental and African Studies* 18(3): 592–609.

———. 1957. A Yurok song without words. *Bulletin of the School for Oriental and African Studies* 20: 501–6.

Rolls of certain Indian tribes in Washington and Oregon. 1969. Fairfield, Wash.: Ye

Galleon Press. (Introduction by the publisher, Glen Adams, summer 1970; rolls recorded by McChesney; reprints of related material and photographs.)

Rothenberg, J. 1962. From a shaman's notebook. *Poems from the floating world* 4: 1–6. Hawk's Well Press.

———. 1972. Appreciation. In *Finding the center: Narrative poetry of the Zuni Indians,* ed. Dennis Tedlock, pp. xi–xiv. New York: Dial.

Ruby, Robert H. and John A. Brown. 1976. *The Chinook Indians. Traders of the Lower Columbia River.* Norman: University of Oklahoma Press.

St. Clair, H. H. and L. J. Frachtenberg. 1909. Traditions of the Coos Indians of Oregon. *Journal of American Folklore* 22:25–41.

Sapir, E. 1909a. *Wishram texts.* Together with *Wasco tales and myths,* coll. by Jeremiah Curtin and ed. by Edward Sapir. American Ethnological Society, Publications 2. Leyden: E. J. Brill.

———. 1909b. *Takelma texts.* University of Pennsylvania, The Museum, Anthropological Publications, 2(1). Philadelphia: The University Museum.

———. 1910. Song recitative in Paiute mythology. *Journal of American Folklore* 23: 455–72.

———. 1915. *Abnormal types of speech in Nootka.* Canada Geological Survey, Memoir 62, Anthropological Series no. 5. Ottawa: Government Printing Bureau.

———. 1917. The twilight of rhyme. *The Dial* 63: 98–100.

———. 1922. The Takelma language of southwestern Oregon. In *Handbook of American Indian Languages* 2, ed. Franz Boas, pp. 3–296. Bureau of American Ethnology, Bulletin 40. Washington, D.C.: Government Printing Office. (The volume was submitted for publication on 20 February 1911.)

———. 1934. The emergence of the concept of personality in a study of cultures. *Journal of Social Psychology* 5:408–15.

———. 1938. Why cultural anthropology needs the psychiatrist. *Psychiatry* 1:7–15.

Sapir, E. and M. Swadesh. 1939. *Nootka texts. Tales and ethnological narratives, with grammatical notes and lexical materials.* William Dwight Whitney Linguistic Series. Philadelphia: Linguistic Society of America, University of Pennsylvania.

Scharbach, A. 1962. Aspects of existentialism in Clackamas Chinook myths. *Journal of American Folklore* 75:15–22.

Sebeok, T. A., ed. 1960. *Style in language.* New York: John Wiley; Cambridge: The Technology Press of M.I.T.

Segal, D. 1976. Folklore text and social context. *PTL: A Journal of Descriptive Poetics and Theory of Literature* 1(2):367–82.

Silverstein, M. 1974. *Dialectal developments in Chinookan tense-aspect-systems: An areal-historical analysis.* International Journal of American Linguistics, Memoir 29. Chicago: University of Chicago Press. (Issued with Memoir 28, on aspect theory and Homeric aspect, by Paul Friedrich, as Part 2 of *International Journal of American Linguistics* 40[4].)

Singer, M., ed. 1966. *Krishna: Myths, rites and attitudes.* Honolulu: East-West Center Press, Phoenix Book P329, 1968.

Skeels, Dell. 1949. Style in the unwritten literature of the Nez Perce Indians. Ph.D. dissertation. University of Washington.

Skinner, Q. 1971. On performing and explaining linguistic actions. *The Philosophical Quarterly* 21: 1–21.

Sklute, Barbro. 1966. Folkstories about supernatural beings and occurrences in Swedish-American life. *The Swedish Pioneer* 17(1):22–35.

Snyder, G. 1960. *Myths and texts.* New York: Totem-Corinth paperbacks. (Reviewed in *Journal of American Folklore* 74: 184 [1961].)

Spier, Leslie. 1931. Historical interrelation of culture traits: Franz Boas' study of Tsimshian mythology. In *Methods in social science: A case book,* ed. Stuart A. Rice, pp. 449–57. (Compiled under the direction of the Committee on Scientific Method in the Social Sciences of the Social Science Research Council.)

——. 1936. *Tribal distribution in Washington.* General Series in Anthropology, 3. Menasha, Wisc.: George Banta.

Spier, Leslie, ed. 1938. *The Sinkiaetk or Southern Okanagon of Washington.* General Studies in Anthropology, 6; Contributions from the Laboratory of Anthropology, 2. Menasha, Wisc.: George Banta.

Spier, Leslie and Edward Sapir. 1930. *Wishram ethnography.* University of Washington Publications in Anthropology 3(3):151–300. Seattle: University of Washington Press.

Spitzer, L. 1948. *Linguistics and literary history: Essays in stylistics.* Princeton, N.J.: Princeton University Press.

Strong, Thomas Duncan. 1905. *Cathlamet on the Columbia.* Portland: Binfords and Mort.

Stross, B. 1972. Serial order in Nez Perce myths. In *Toward new perspectives in folklore,* ed. Americo Paredes and R. Bauman, pp. 104–13. American Folklore Society, Bibliographical and Special Series, 23. Austin: University of Texas Press.

Stutterheim, C. F. P. 1948. Review of de Groot 1946. *Lingua* 1: 104–117.

Swanton, J. R. 1911. Haida. In *Handbook of American Indian languages,* ed. Franz Boas, pp. 205–82. Bureau of American Ethnology, Bulletin 40, part I. Washington, D.C.: Government Printing Office.

——. 1912. *Haida songs.* Publications of the American Ethnological Society, 3. Leiden: E. J. Brill.

Tedlock, D. 1970. Notes to "Finding the middle of the earth." *Alcheringa* 1: 6.

——. 1972a. *Finding the center: Narrative poetry of the Zuni Indians.* New York: Dial. Reissued with new preface, Lincoln: University of Nebraska Press, 1978 (Bison Books 676).

——. 1972b. Pueblo literature: Style and verisimilitude. In *New perspectives on the Pueblos,* ed. Alfonso Ortiz, pp. 219–42. Albuquerque: University of New Mexico Press.

——. 1977. Toward an oral poetics. *New Literary History* 8(3): 507–19.

Teit, James. 1898. *Traditions of the Thompson River Indians of British Columbia.* The American Folk-Lore Society, Memoirs, 6. Boston and New York: Houghton, Mifflin.

Thompson, Stith. 1929. *Tales of the North American Indians.* Cambridge: Harvard University Press. (LXVII "The deserted children" [s300]). (Reprinted, Bloomington: Indiana University Press, 1966.)

——. 1946. *The folktale.* New York: Dryden.

Timmers, J. 1974. A Sechelt text. Dutch Contributions to the Ninth International Conference on Salish Languages, held at Vancouver, B.C., 12–14 August 1974, pp. 11–16. Leiden.

Toelken, B. 1969. The "pretty language(s)" of Yellowman: Genre, mode and texture in Navaho Coyote narratives. *Genre* 2(3):211–35. (Reprinted in *Folklore genres*, ed. Dan Ben-Amos. Publications of the American Folklore Society, Bibliographical and Special Series, 26. Austin: University of Texas Press, 1976. Pp. 145–70.)

Uitti, K. D. 1961–1962. Review of T. A. Sebeok, *Style in language. Romance Philology* 15:424–38.

Van Doren, M. 1928. *Anthology of world poetry.* New York: Reynal and Hitchcock.

Voloshinov, V. N. 1973. *Marxism and the philosophy of language.* Trans. L. Matejka and I. R. Titunik. New York and London: Seminar Press.

Von Sydow, C. W. 1948. On the spread of tradition. In *Selected papers on folklore: Published on the occasion of his seventieth birthday,* ed. Laurits Bødker, pp. 11–18. Copenhagen: Rosenkilde and Bagger.

Weinreich, U., W. Labov, and M. Herzog. 1968. Empirical foundations for a theory of language change. In *Directions for historical linguistics: A symposium,* ed. W. P. Lehman and Yakov Malkiel, pp. 97–195. Austin: University of Texas Press.

Wycoco, R. S. 1951. The types of North American Indian tales. Ph.D. dissertation, Indiana University.

Wyman, Leland C. 1970. *Blessingway.* With three versions of the myth recorded and translated from the Navajo, by Father Berard Haile, O.F.M. Tucson: The University of Arizona Press.

Index

University of Pennsylvania Publications in
Conduct and Communication

Erving Goffman and Dell Hymes, General Editors

Erving Goffman, *Strategic Interaction*
Ray L. Birdwhistell, *Kinesics and Context: Essays on Body Motion Communication*
William Labov, *Language in the Inner City: Studies in the Black English Vernacular*
William Labov, *Sociolinguistic Patterns*
Dell Hymes, *Foundations in Sociolinguistics: An Ethnographic Approach*
Barbara Kirshenblatt-Gimblett, editor. *Speech Play: Research and Resources for the Study of Linguistic Creativity*
Gillian Sankoff, *The Social Life of Language*
Erving Goffman, *Forms of Talk*
Sol Worth, *Studying Visual Communication*, edited by Larry Gross
Dell Hymes, *"In Vain I Tried to Tell You"*